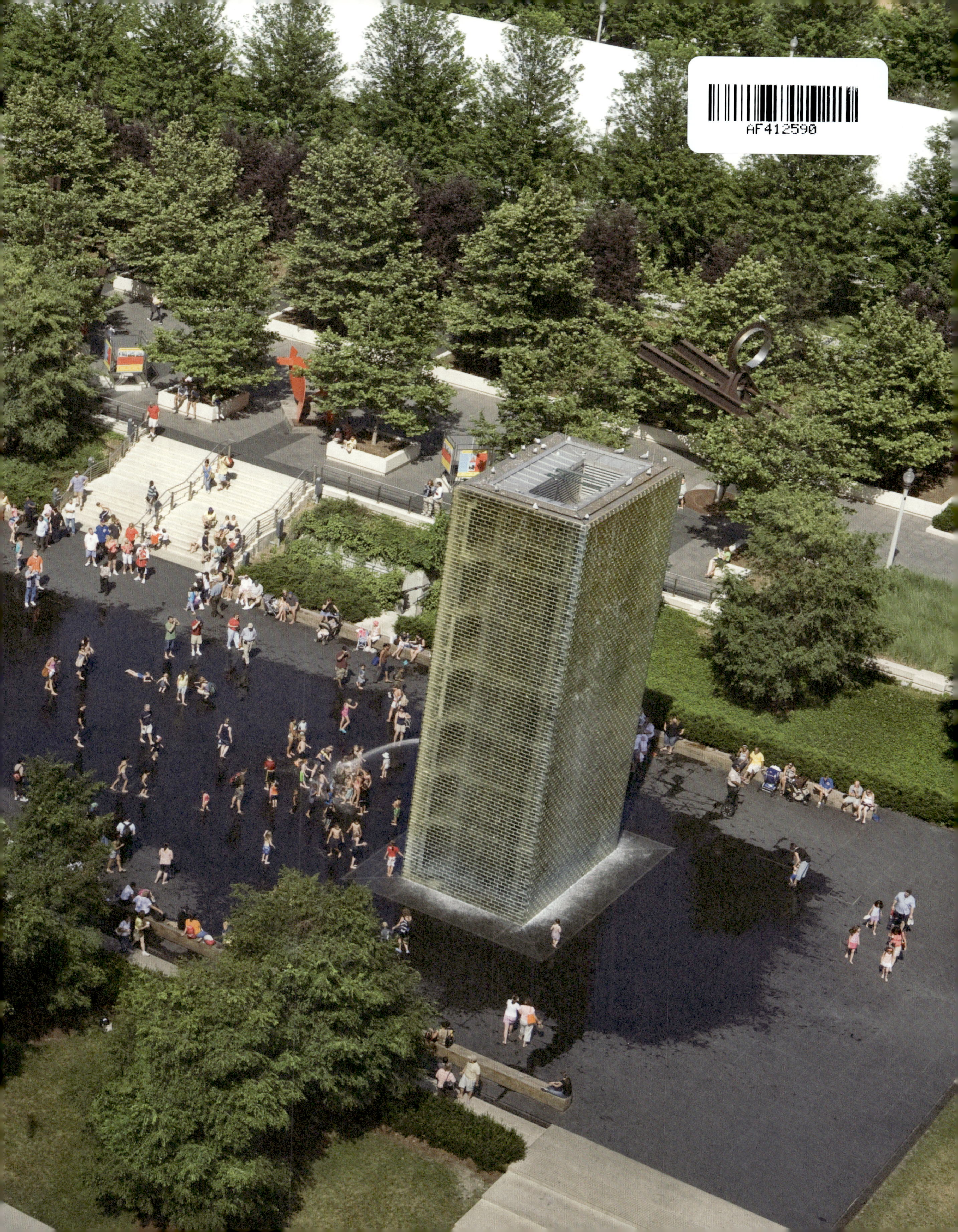

AF412590

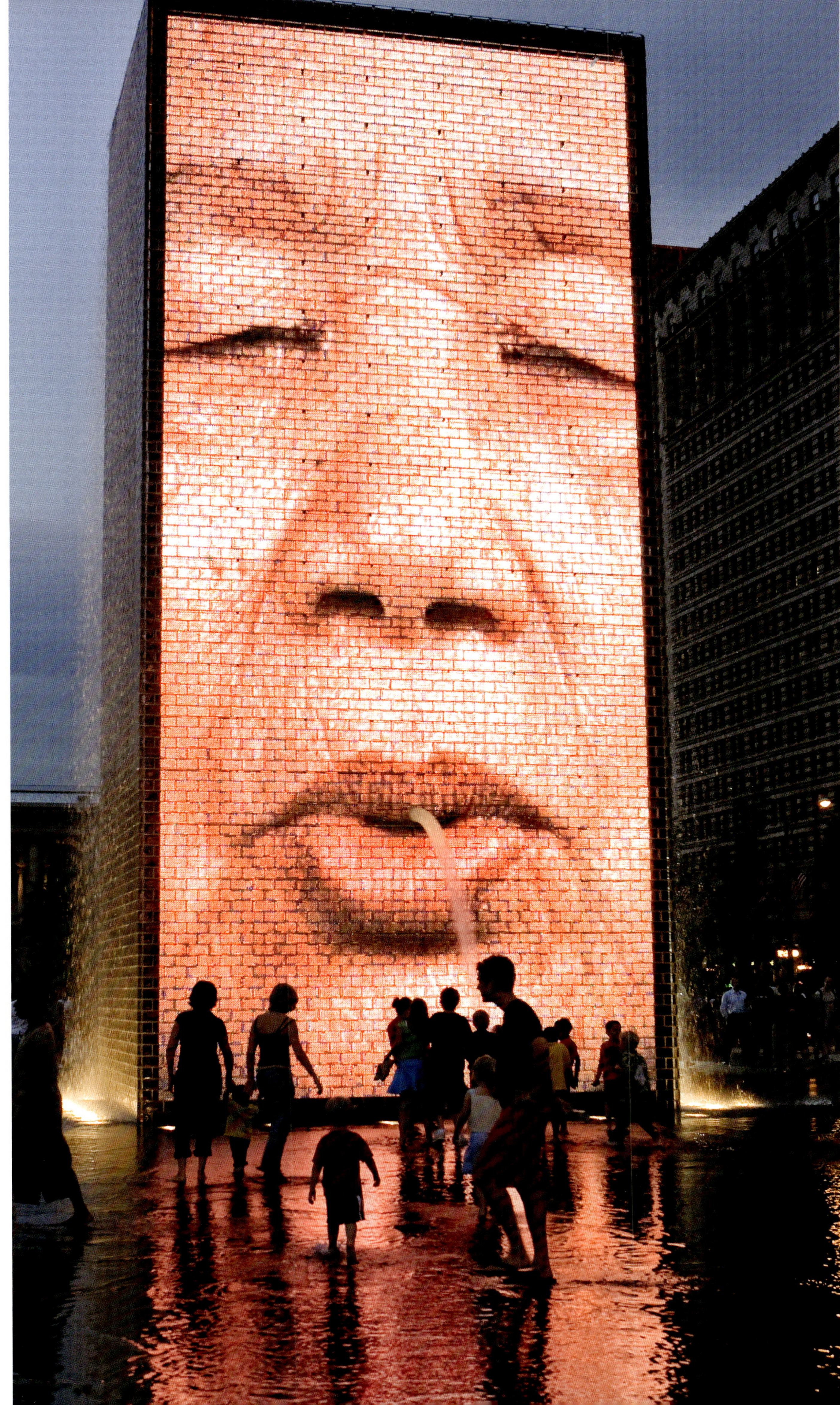

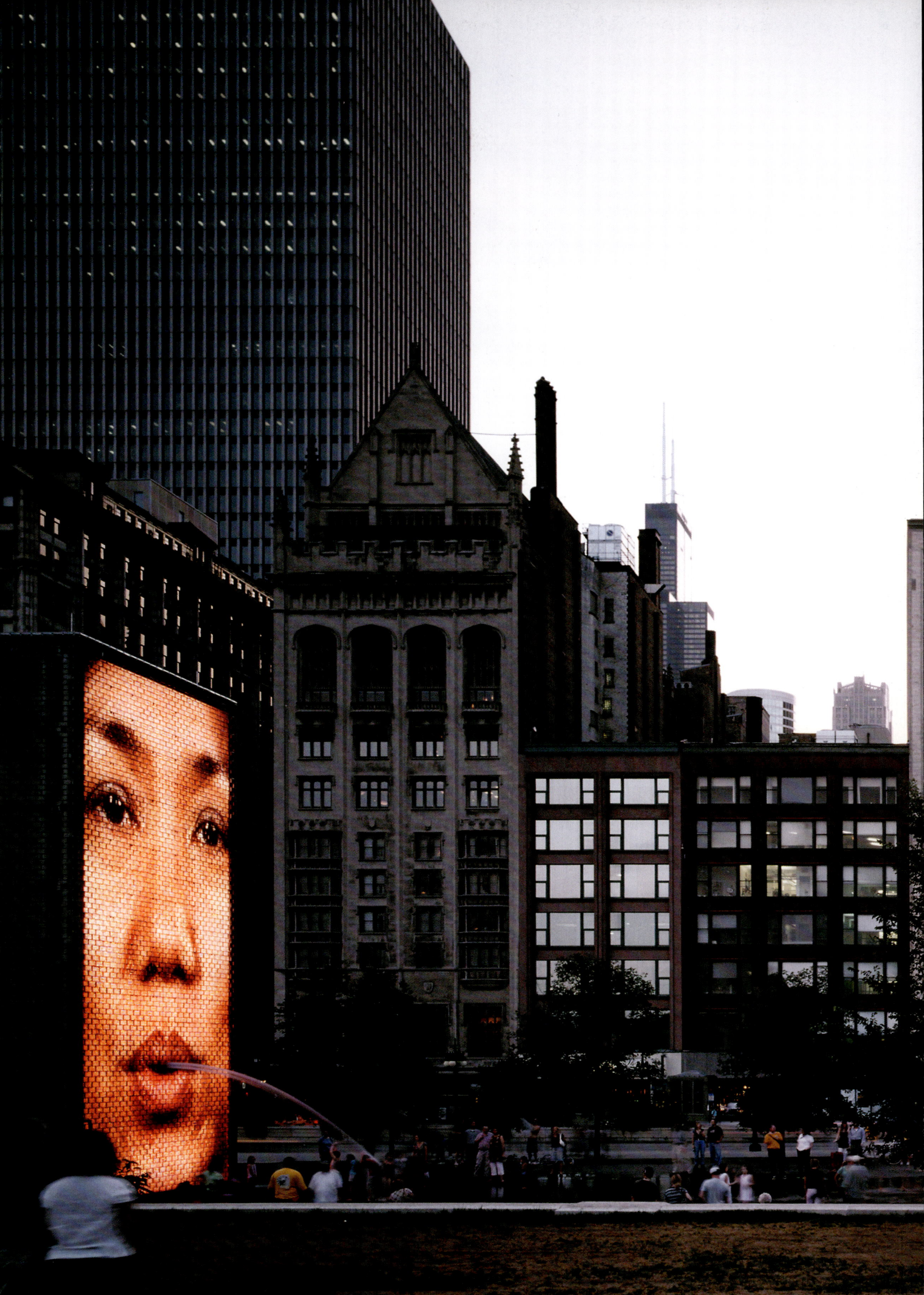

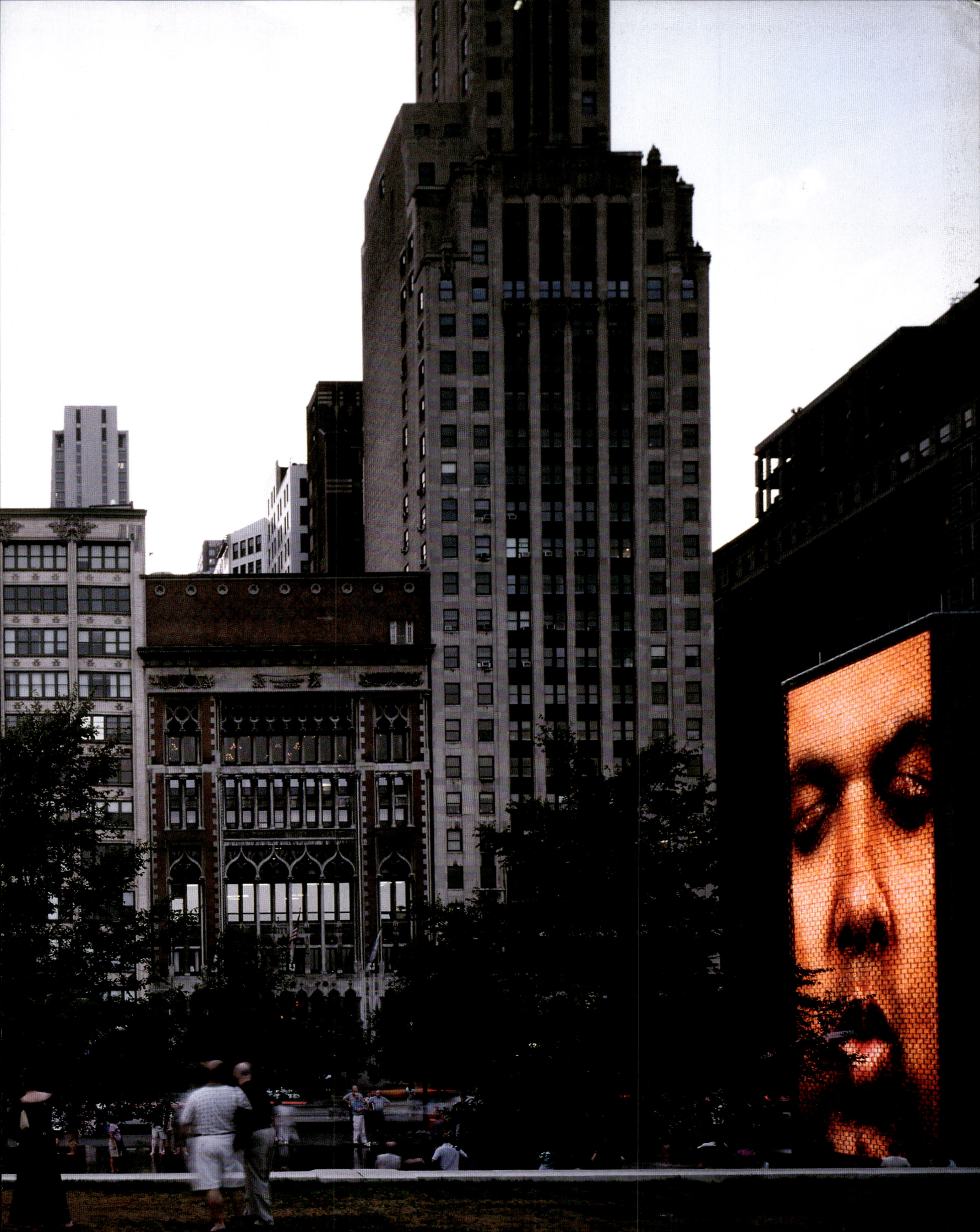

Jaume Plensa
The Crown Fountain

Text by Keith Patrick

Principal photography by Kenneth Tanaka

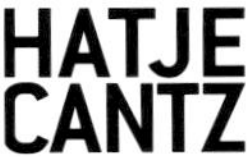

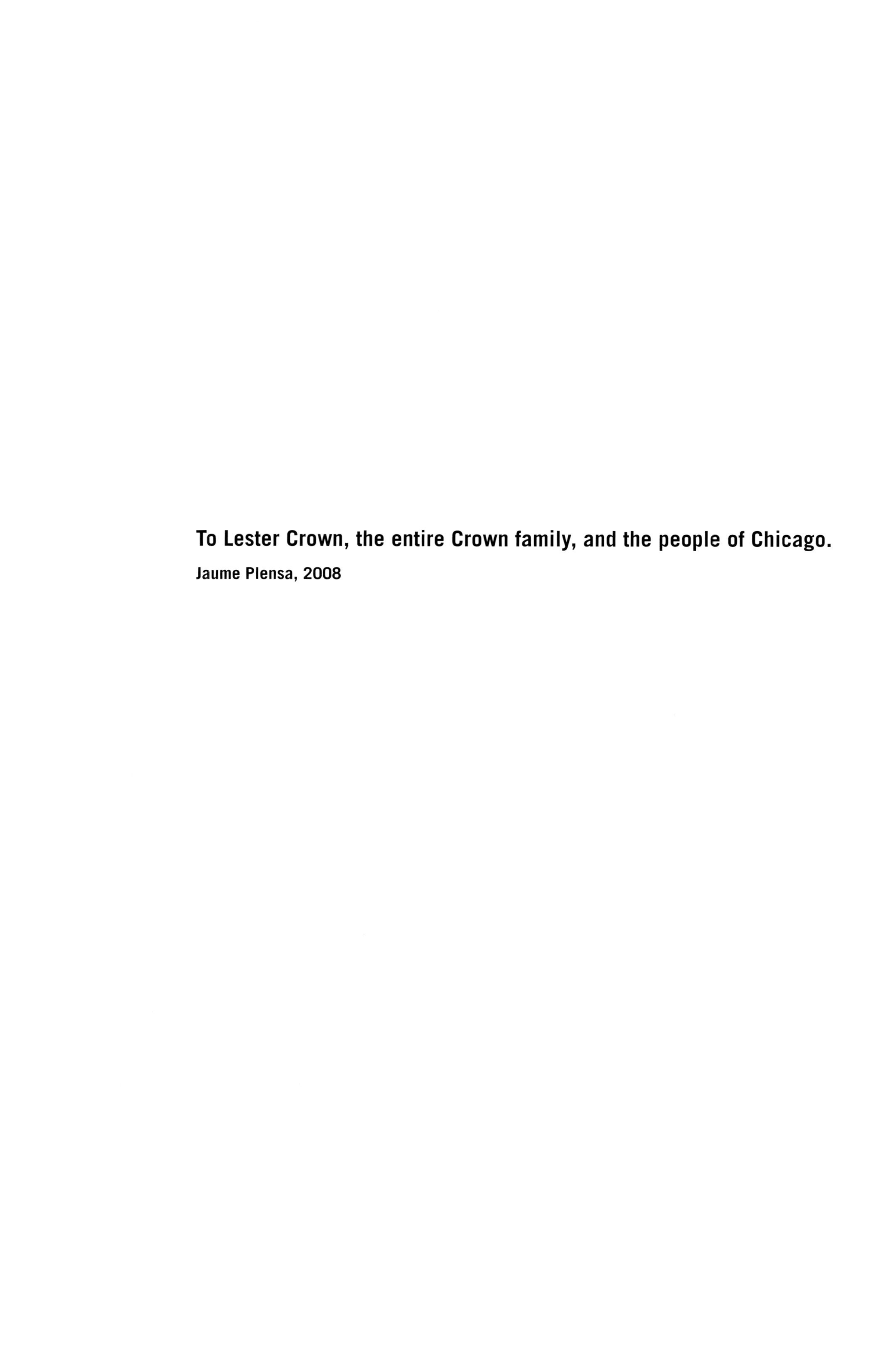

To Lester Crown, the entire Crown family, and the people of Chicago.

Jaume Plensa, 2008

Contents

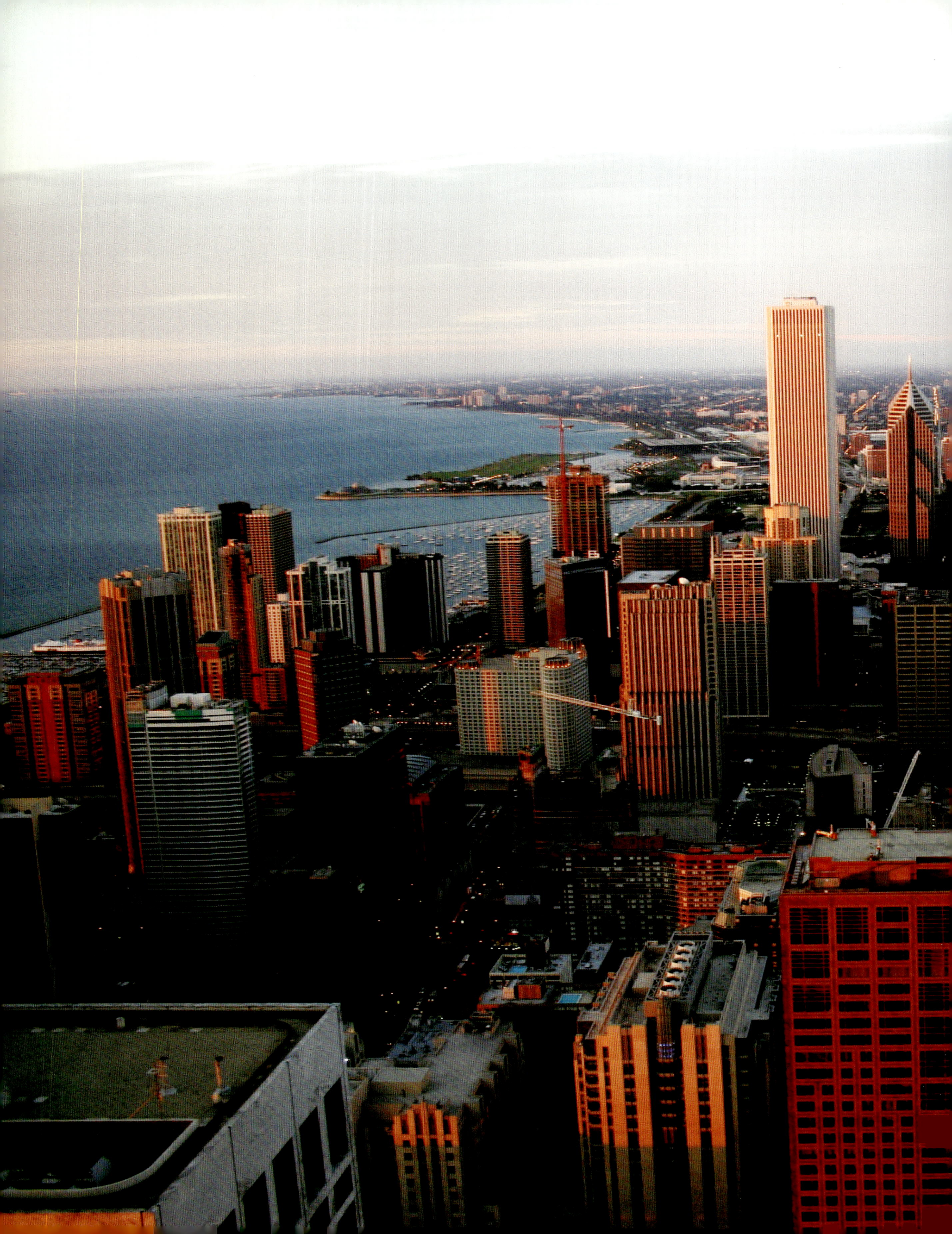

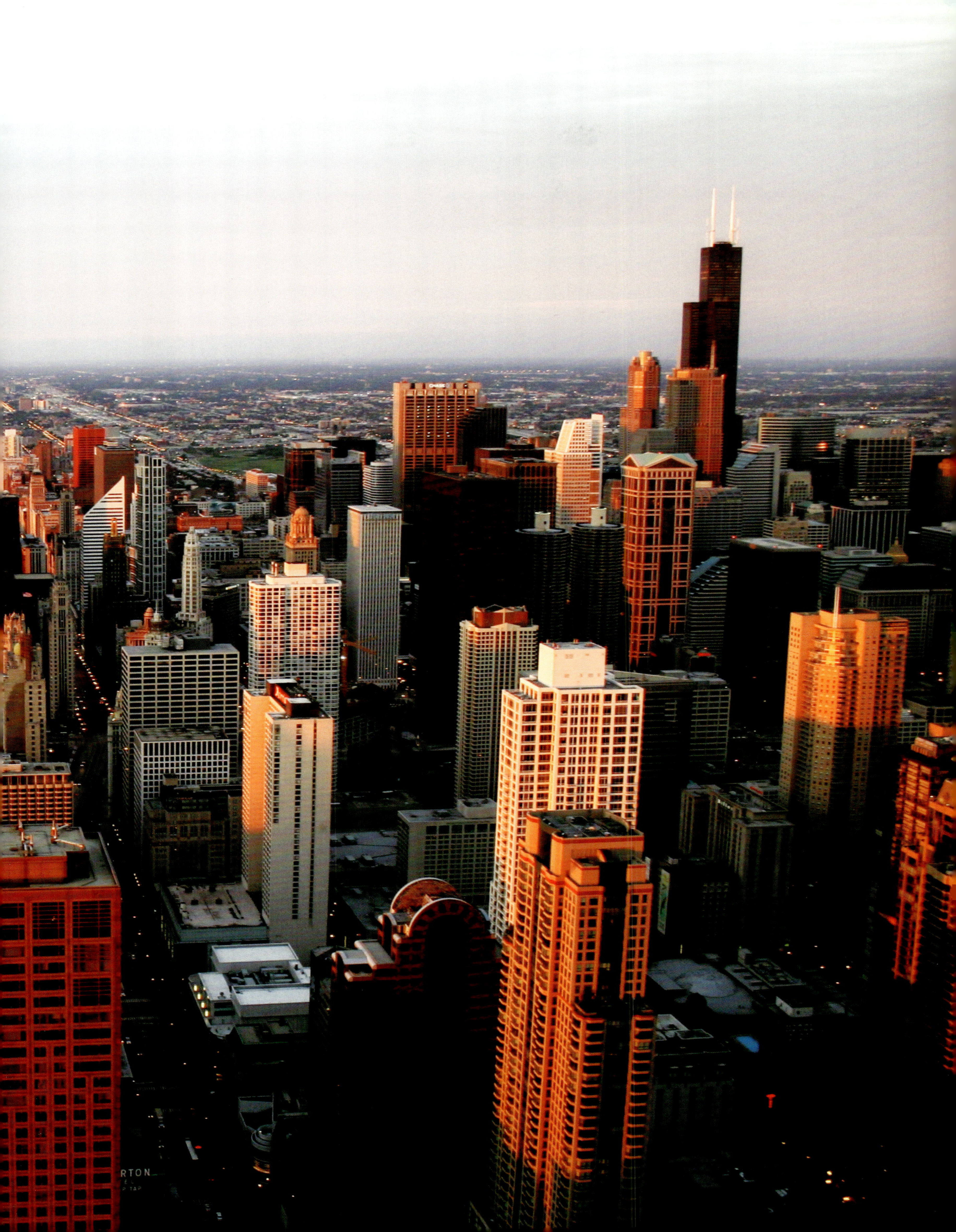

Foreword

All great ideas start out with a vision, an idea, or maybe just a dream. Such was the genesis of the *Crown Fountain*. When our family was given the opportunity to contribute to Millennium Park by designing and building a fountain, we were extremely honored. We invited artists from around the world to submit their ideas, and from this esteemed group we unanimously selected a brilliant and talented artist from Barcelona, Jaume Plensa, to be the creative genius behind this fountain for future generations.

What appealed to us from the start was Jaume's clarity of vision and complete conviction of what he felt this fountain should be—"a fountain for the people." Jaume envisioned this structure as a meeting place, a place for people from all walks of life to come and interact, to reflect, to think, or just to rest while pondering the cool waters. The towers with their images, comical water spouts, and colored lights reflecting on a black granite surface covered with a thin layer of water is exactly what Jaume Plensa presented to our family from the outset. Today, his dream is Chicago's reality.

Many individuals helped make this fountain come to life. Mark Sexton and his firm, Krueck & Sexton, were the technical quarterbacks. Roark Frankel and Alan Schachtman of U.S. Equities served as our owner reps. W.E. O'Neil, Crystal Fountains, ESD, Halvorson & Kaye, Schuler & Shook, Shen Milson & Wilke, Barco, Circle Redmont, and many more all came together to form a unique team that worked tirelessly to integrate a variety of materials and technologies while still holding true to the artist's design.

After numerous trials and errors we were able to build the structure you see today, but still something was missing. Jaume wanted the faces of the City of Chicago displayed on each of the towers. We enlisted the help of Alan Labb and John Manning of the School of the Art Institute to provide this feature. Chicagoans from all backgrounds, ages, and ethnicities were photographed and displayed on the towers, giving the fountain its life and personality. These gargoyles, as Jaume calls them, are the soul of the fountain. Their images, when flooded by the lights and cascading water, make this fountain a true blend of the fountains of old and those of the future.

The opportunity to leave a lasting legacy for the citizens of Chicago was an important part of our family's motivation, and particularly one of my father's wishes. Chicago has been home to our family for four generations, and we have witnessed its growth and prosperity. This great city has provided us with many opportunities, and this fountain is just one way for us to give something back. We could not be more pleased with what Jaume Plensa has created.

On behalf of our entire family, I would like to take the opportunity to thank John Bryan and his team for their tremendous leadership and tireless efforts to make this park a reality. But most of all, I would like to applaud our Mayor, Richard Daley, who had the vision and the conviction to "make no small plans" and has provided Chicago and its citizens with this magnificent park for the new millennium.

From Steve Crown's inaugural speech,
Millennium Park, July 24, 2004

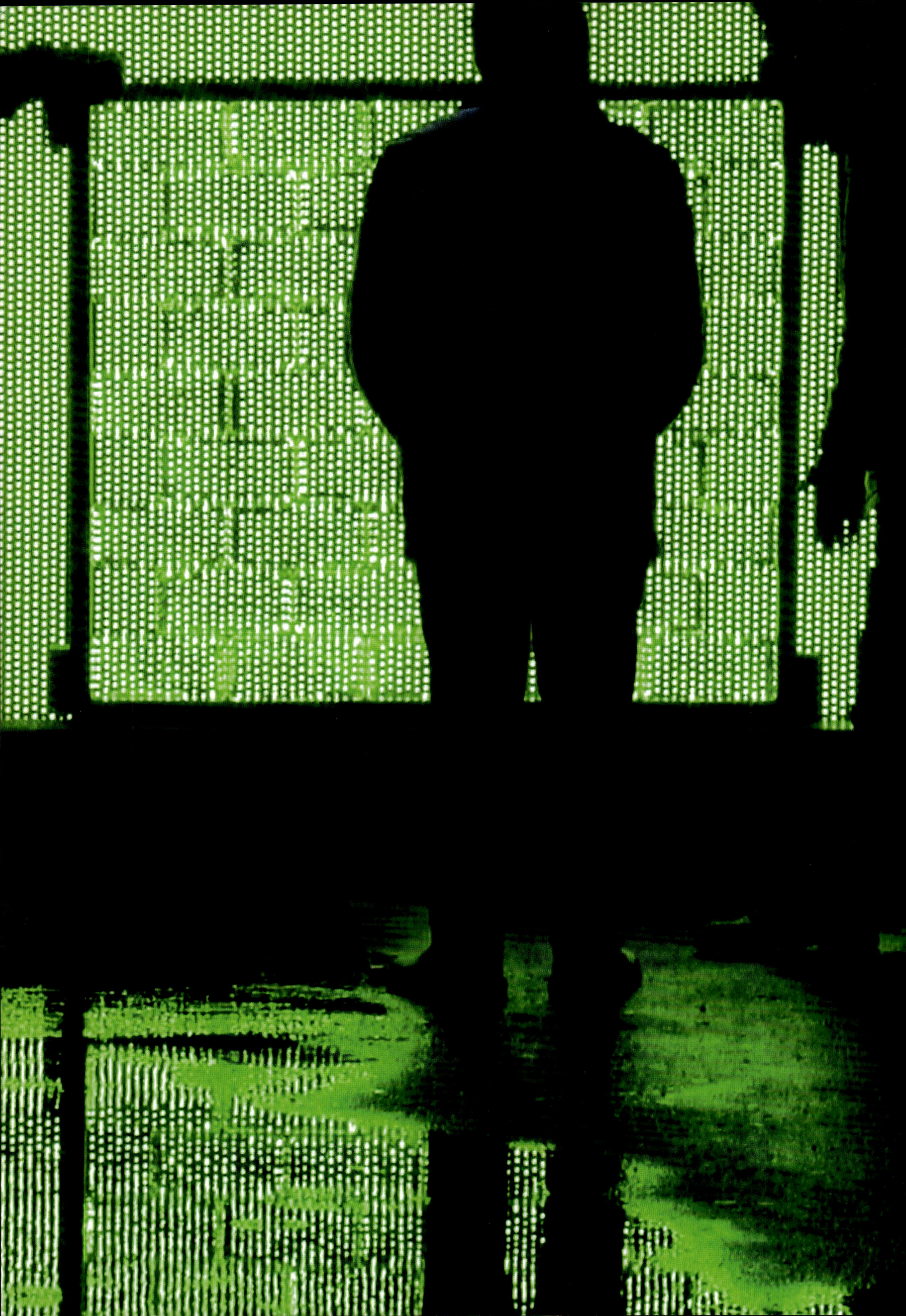

Introduction

Jaume Plensa

One of my first meetings with the Crown family was in Millennium Park at the site of the future fountain. The family's enthusiasm, together with the visual impact of the city of Chicago, was overwhelming. mmediately ideas for the project began to germinate, although I also recognized the magnitude of the challenge that lay before me.

I was already familiar with the city, having visited on many previous occasions. Chicago is one of only a handful of cities to truly embrace change and weave a love of the unknown, of flux, and of evolution into the very fabric of its society. It has been able to integrate into its identity all of the human challenges— cultural and technological—that it has faced.

To walk the streets of Chicago is to wander through one of the great examples of American culture. It is emblematic in terms of its architecture, urban plan- ning, art, music, and theater. It is a city with innovative social, technological, and environmental programs; a city with a long history of embracing exciting, cutting-edge projects in the arts. As a result, it has become a stimulating urban mosaic, one which set the stage for a project such as Millennium Park.

For over twenty-five years I have exhibited in both galleries and museums, and designed opera sets and public sculpture, and so it was exhilarating to face the new challenge of creating a concept for a fountain in a city such as Chicago, bearing in mind that the *Crown Fountain* was to be my first major public project in the United States.

I am fortunate enough to have been invited to install my works in places as diverse as England, Japan, Korea, Germany, France, Italy, Spain, and Israel. These experiences have contributed to my ever-growing interest in, and great respect for, the concept that we call "the public space," whether it is to be found in an urban context or in a more natural environment.

I have learned to value intangible characteristics, subtle sensations, and "time"—that most ephemeral of elements—which invisibly envelop the physical and architectural aspects of spaces. These are the traits that confer upon the work its true personality.

I have experienced the energy of the people who live with my works. I have grown by learning from their reactions to beauty, from their endeavors to understand and appreciate the unknown, and from their determination to participate fully in the development of the works.

It was as a result of all this that my immediate reaction in Chicago was to create a project that would be inspired by and created for the city's residents amidst the vibrancy and energy of both the park and the city.

My aim was to emphasize and expand upon the poetic, sensorial, and social aspects of my own experience of the public space. I wanted to generate an interactive and multidisciplinary relationship with the city and to expose the souls of its inhabitants by creating an archive of its people, as well as to provide a link connecting Chicago with the rest of the world.

I wanted to produce a project for the twenty-first century based on the concept of the fountain in the great classical tradition, but one that would create a bridge to the future at the same time. I wanted to put the city's inhabitants once more at center stage, a position I felt they had lost in recent years. I wanted to bring them out of anonymity by incorporating them fully into the process of the work.

I wanted to build a space for silent reflection amidst the natural sound of falling water, a place where people, whether young or old, could be themselves; a place to be enjoyed. I wanted to create a living work, which, like the city, would perpetually transform itself.

Millennium Park is an extraordinary place, conceived as a series of individual spaces where visitors experience a wide range of activities and stimuli. Thanks to its integrating design, the park manages to unify seemingly diverse traits, and thus becomes an ideal meeting place in the heart of the city.

The *Crown Fountain* is located in the southwest corner of the park, at the junction of Michigan Avenue and Monroe Street. Following the same carefully planned design the space assigned for the fountain is surrounded on all sides by trees and defines a visually pure rectangle.

In general, however, the public space is not delineated solely by architectural elements, but also by visual, acoustic, social, and environmental features, among others, which help to define its unique personality and which have had a decisive influence on the form and scale of the fountain. These considerations were especially important in the working space of Millennium Park and its urban surroundings.

On its east side the space is delineated by a slope planted with trees and shrubs, above which the first terrace of the park opens out. This raised platform provides a vantage point that reveals a perfect profile view of the fountain silhouetted against the backdrop of the city.

The north side, bordered by a tree-lined path that separates the ice rink from the fountain, is the site's main link with the park and its numerous attractions.

I designed the fountain's north-south orientation to emphasize its relationship to its immediate surroundings, which include the prestigious Art Institute to the south. Along the west side the site opens onto Michigan Avenue, and the corner with Monroe Street forms a natural entrance to the park for visitors arriving from the south or from the El subway stop on Monroe Street. As a result, the project is conceived as an open door that beckons passersby to enter.

Restoring the concepts of water and the fountain to the public space, and turning them into a new experience for all the senses, took me back to the origins of the tradition: to the small springs in the mountains, to the great rivers in the plains, to the dark oceans. From the damp silence of Japanese fountains to the sunlit fountains in the Mediterranean. From the murmuring of medieval gargoyles to the Italian fountains of the Renaissance. From the Iguaçu Falls to the fountains by Luis Barragán. From Niagara Falls to the Trocadero and Antoni Gaudí.

History, which is full of such marvelous examples, belongs to us all. It is part of our collective memory.

"If there is heaven on earth, it is here, it is here."
Mughal Gardens, Red Fort, New Delhi

The surface area of the project is covered with matte, black granite, a vast, dark, and empty surface that creates a space of peace and tranquillity. In the center is a film of water upon which people can walk. Thus, the ancient dream of being able to walk on water becomes a reality. All cultures refer to water as a symbol of life and transformation. Sixty percent of our body is water, as is three-quarters of the Earth's surface.

I wanted the towers to be like transparent houses that embody the true notion of community. I wanted them to embody the idea of communication and the social aspect of our lives as individuals. They suggest the opening of our homes: a place where we can shelter and protect the souls of others as if they were our own. I wanted them to shatter the barriers that separate us, to help us share our experiences through light and transparency.

The glass bricks, like transparent stones, call to mind the great tradition of the Sefer Yetzira, or the Book of Creation, that tells of how Yahweh created the world: "Yahweh engraved, modeled, weighed, and combined the twenty-two basic letters on a wheel, as if they were walls…. How did he combine and arrange them? Aleph with all the Alephs, Beth with all the Beths … and he found that every creature and everything said comes from a single name…. Two stones build two houses. Three stones build six houses. Four stones build twenty-four houses. Five stones build one hundred and twenty-two houses. Six stones build seven hundred and twenty houses. Seven stones build five thousand and forty houses. Thereafter, go away and think about everything that the mouth cannot say and the ear cannot hear."

> "The eyes of fire, the nostrils of air, the mouth of water, the
> beard of earth."
> William Blake

One of the most important aspects of the project is the incorporation of real people, the inhabitants of the city, as an integral element of the work. One of the great traditions in fountains throughout history, gargoyles were the faces of mythological beings sculpted in stone or bronze, and through their open mouths flowed the water of life. The *Crown Fountain* draws on this tradition, using the faces of the people of Chicago as modern adaptations of the gargoyle. Water flows through their mouths as a symbol of life. These faces, made sacred and majestic through their grand scale and prominence, offer a mythical significance to our daily lives and pay tribute to the people who, through their anonymity, give their energy as a gift to the community.

At the same time, however, fountains have been used in all cultures as a reference to nature in our everyday domestic and urban settings. The fountain is an ever-present reminder of our roots in nature.

> "There is a moment between waking and sleeping when dream
> and reality are indistinguishable."
> Robert Hopper

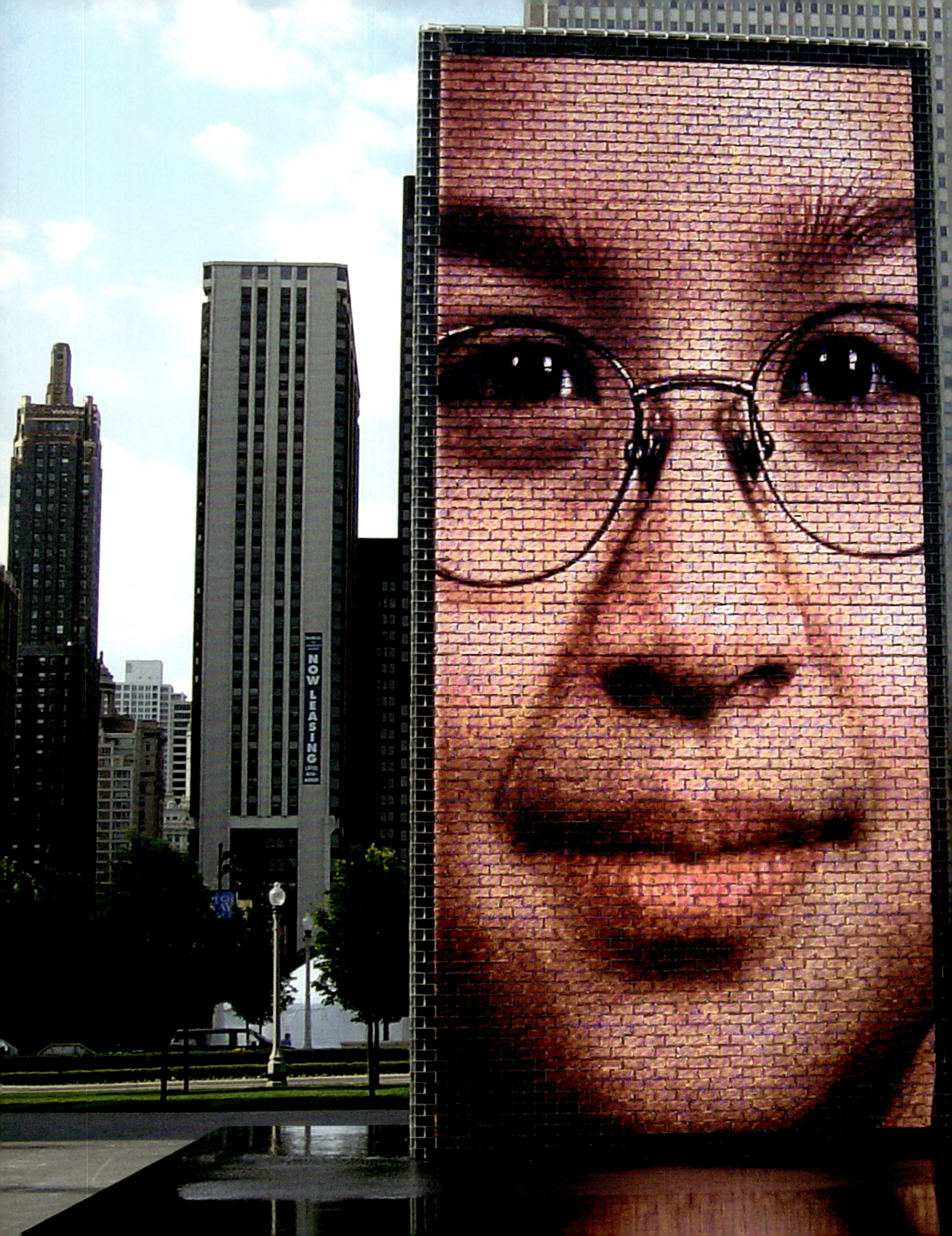

NOW LEASING

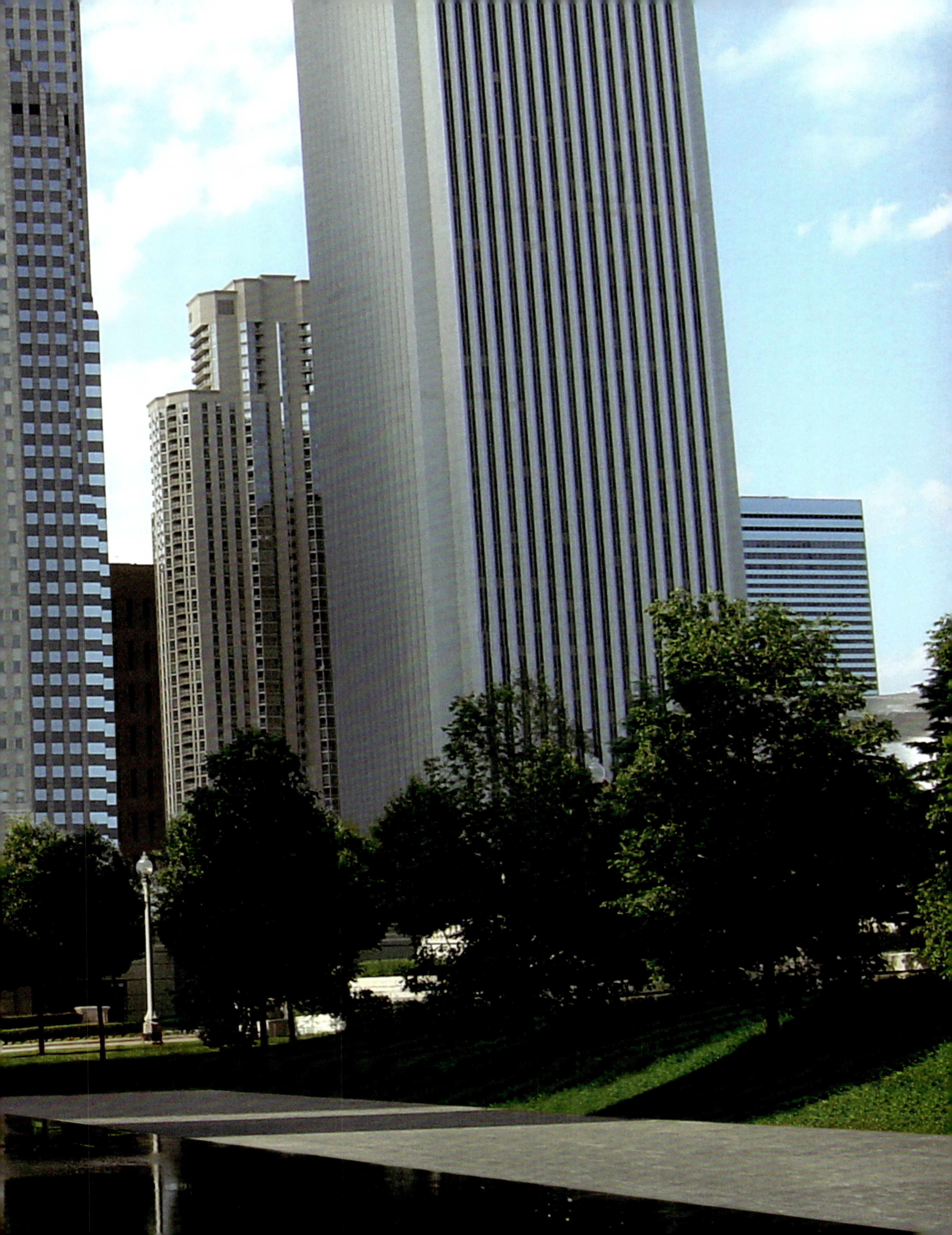

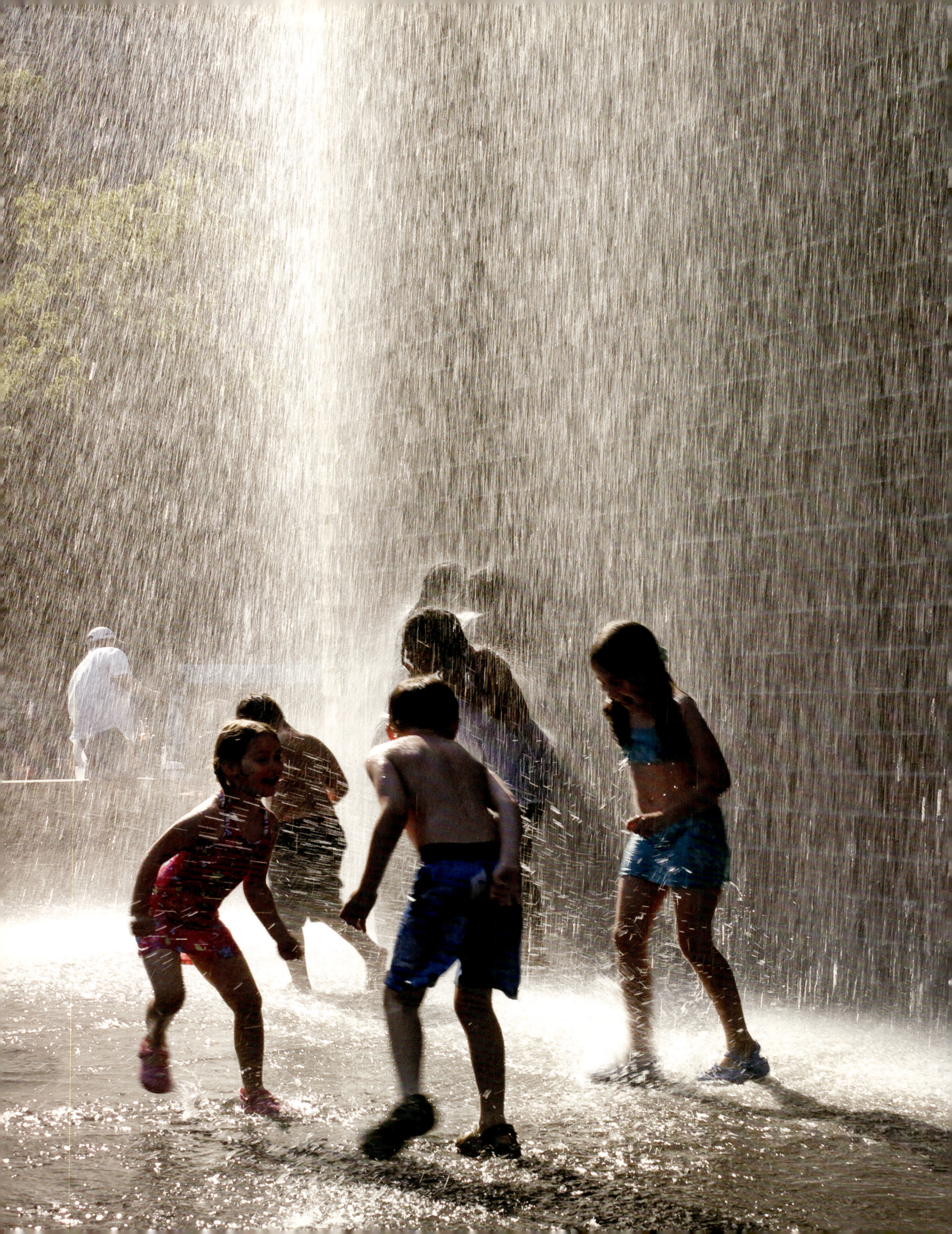

1

Niagara Falls on Michigan Avenue

Narrated by Keith Patrick

A Time and Place

There are moments when it seems I have spent a lifetime getting to the *Crown Fountain*. It's true there are quicker routes: by plane, by subway, or by taxi, you can arrive there in a matter of hours or minutes. But this is not that kind of journey. In an age when you can be on the other side of the world within twenty-four hours, places have to be savored, to be approached slowly. Like a novel, no one wants to discover how the story ends on the first page. But if you like, I'll tell you. Or rather, I'll let T. S. Elliot do the telling: "And the end of all our searching shall be to return to the place where we started and know it for the first time."

A Story with No Beginning

The story of the *Crown Fountain* has no beginning, or perhaps it has too many, for there was no definitive moment when the project began. Its origins

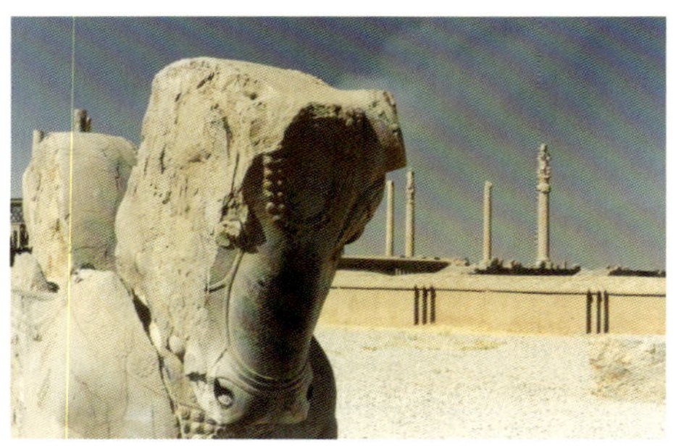

The squares and open spaces of Persepolis, capital of the Persian Empire, were among the most important meeting places of the ancient world.

lie in the city of Chicago itself, its people, its long involvement with art in the public space, and the evolving infrastructure of a city that is changing to meet the demands of a new millennium. They also lie in the evolution of an artist's work that stretches back twenty-five years. And beyond that, even, to the ancient meeting places, the agoras and public squares of Rome and Athens and of those forgotten cities that now lie under the desert sands of Assyria and Mesopotamia. They lie in the psyche and our need as human beings to collect together, to socialize. And so the story of the *Crown Fountain* is really a journey, both in time and space, a road movie that ends on the corner of a park in the Windy City.

> "The *Crown Fountain* is an important slice of the history of the Crown family and the history of Chicago."
> Mark Sexton, architect

Don't rush there. Don't be anxious to stand under its towers, to walk on its waters, or to watch the images change as one watches a movie before dining in a favorite restaurant. For the *Crown Fountain* reveals itself slowly, as I was to find out.

The Long Road to Chicago

Wim Wenders, the movie director who himself is no stranger to road movies, tells a story about a day spent with Ry Cooder. The musician was uncharacteristically quiet and distracted all morning and, when asked why, explained he was preoccupied with the music he'd just been recording with some guys in Cuba. Wim asked to hear it and was bowled over by the sound these "kids" were making. "Oh, they're not kids," the musician replied. And that's how the movie of the Buena Vista Social Club came about.

Back in the fall of 2001, the artist Jaume Plensa and I were working on his exhibition in Ljubljana, Slovenia. Ljubljana is a medieval city presided over by a magnificent castle and meandering streets redolent of Kafka's frustrated efforts to ascend another hill in another town, never quite making it to the

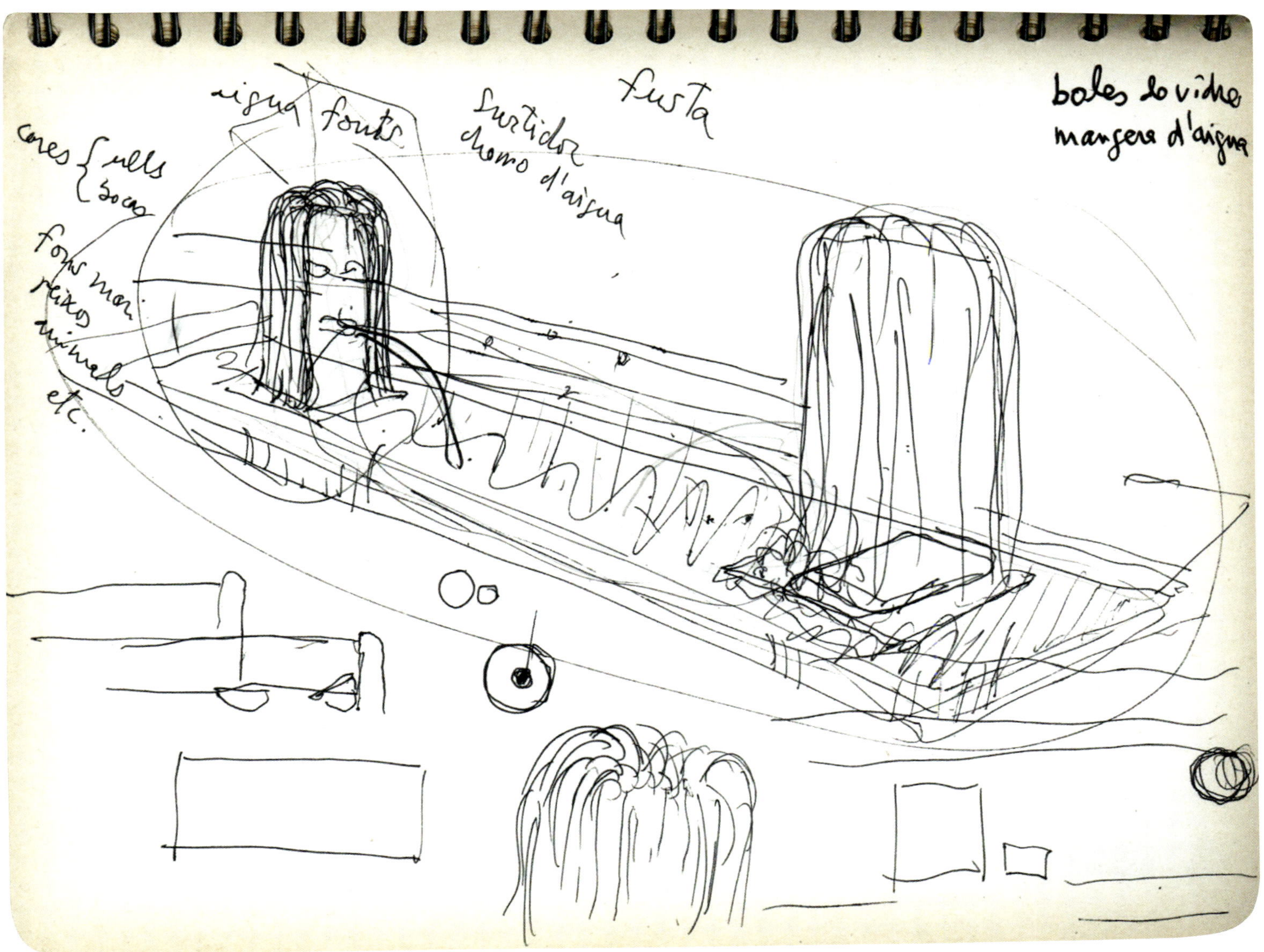

eponymous castle before night descended and K was forced back to his lodgings. We fared better, installing Jaume's work in both the castle and the city museum in the old town below. The show was looking good, yet the artist seemed unusually preoccupied, as if the night had always fallen too quickly for his liking.

One afternoon we were cutting through the modern city when the artist's face lit up. We were passing a hoarding, a vast LED screen advertising the latest Western products to a consumer society that, until so recently, had

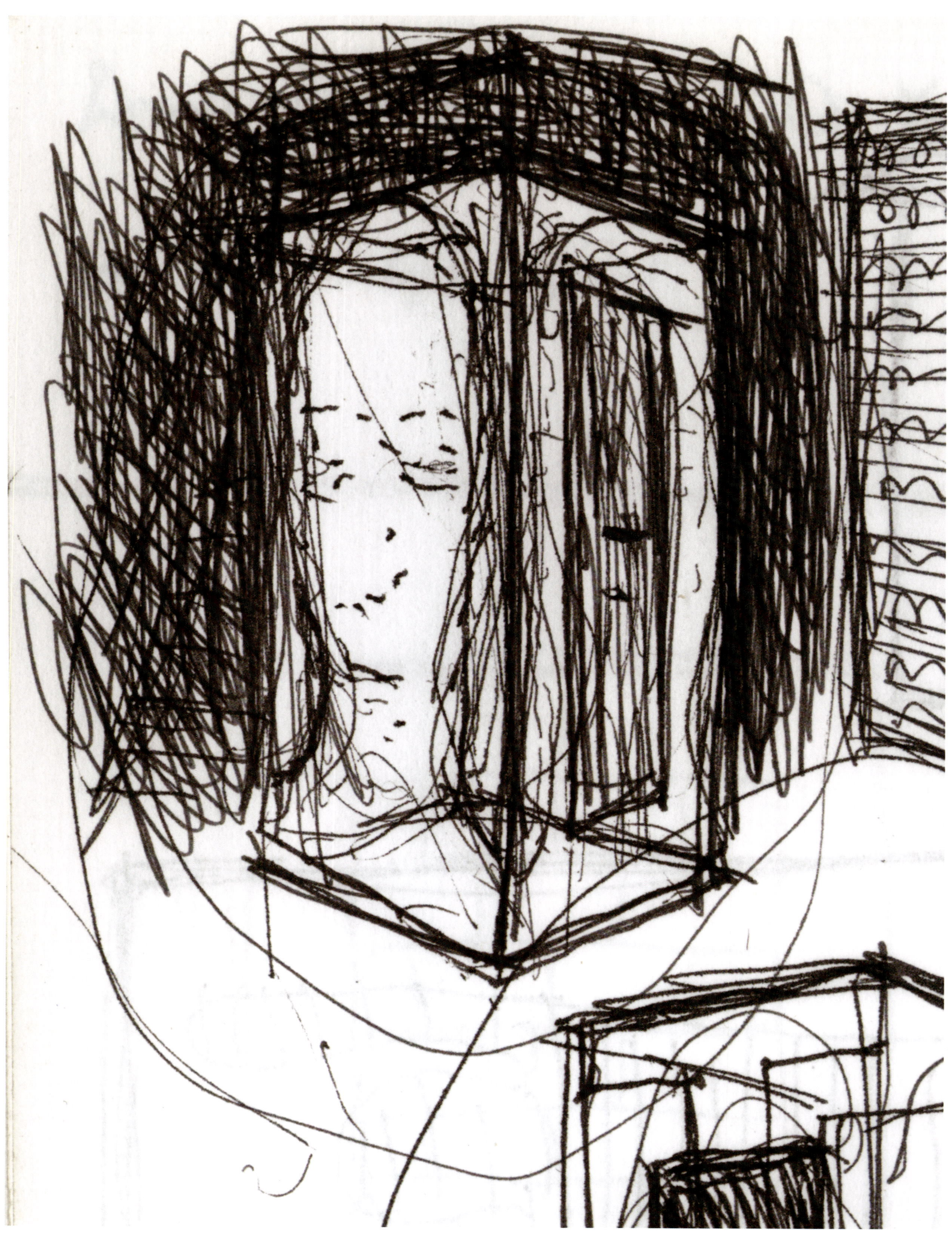

been starved of such luxuries. "That's my next project," he remarked. And that, for me, was how the *Crown Fountain* began.

Nomadic Lives

I saw Plensa only occasionally over the intervening years. He was always traveling and, even after I moved to Barcelona, it seemed we were more likely to cross paths in London or Tokyo than in his hometown. But, of course, besides a constant stream of exhibitions, what was continuing to occupy him was the *Crown Fountain*. It was the project that was to draw together all the strings of his career to date and become what many regard as the most significant public space of the early twenty-first century: a model against which all future fountains would be measured.

But I'm getting ahead of myself. This isn't principally the story of one work or even of one space, but of a journey that began many years before.

A Miraculous Fountain

We traveled by train, a journey northwards through the bare countryside of England in winter. It was Elliot's midwinter spring, "sempiternal though sodden towards sundown." The gray skies lay heavy on the empty fields, which eventually gave way to the rolling moors of Yorkshire. Leeds is a uniquely English town, built by the burghers of a bygone era, grown wealthy on the cotton mills and the spoils of the slave trade. Even today it retains the somnambulism of the middle classes, a university town that was once home to Henry Moore.

Back in 1994, it was also one of the principal centers for sculpture in Britain, thanks to the Henry Moore Institute and its then director, Robert Hopper. And one of the Institute's more enlightened contributions was the Henry Moore Sculpture Studio. Located in a rambling former carpet mill in nearby Dean Clough, Halifax, the likes of James Turrell and Jannis Kounellis had been invited to work and exhibit in its cavernous spaces.

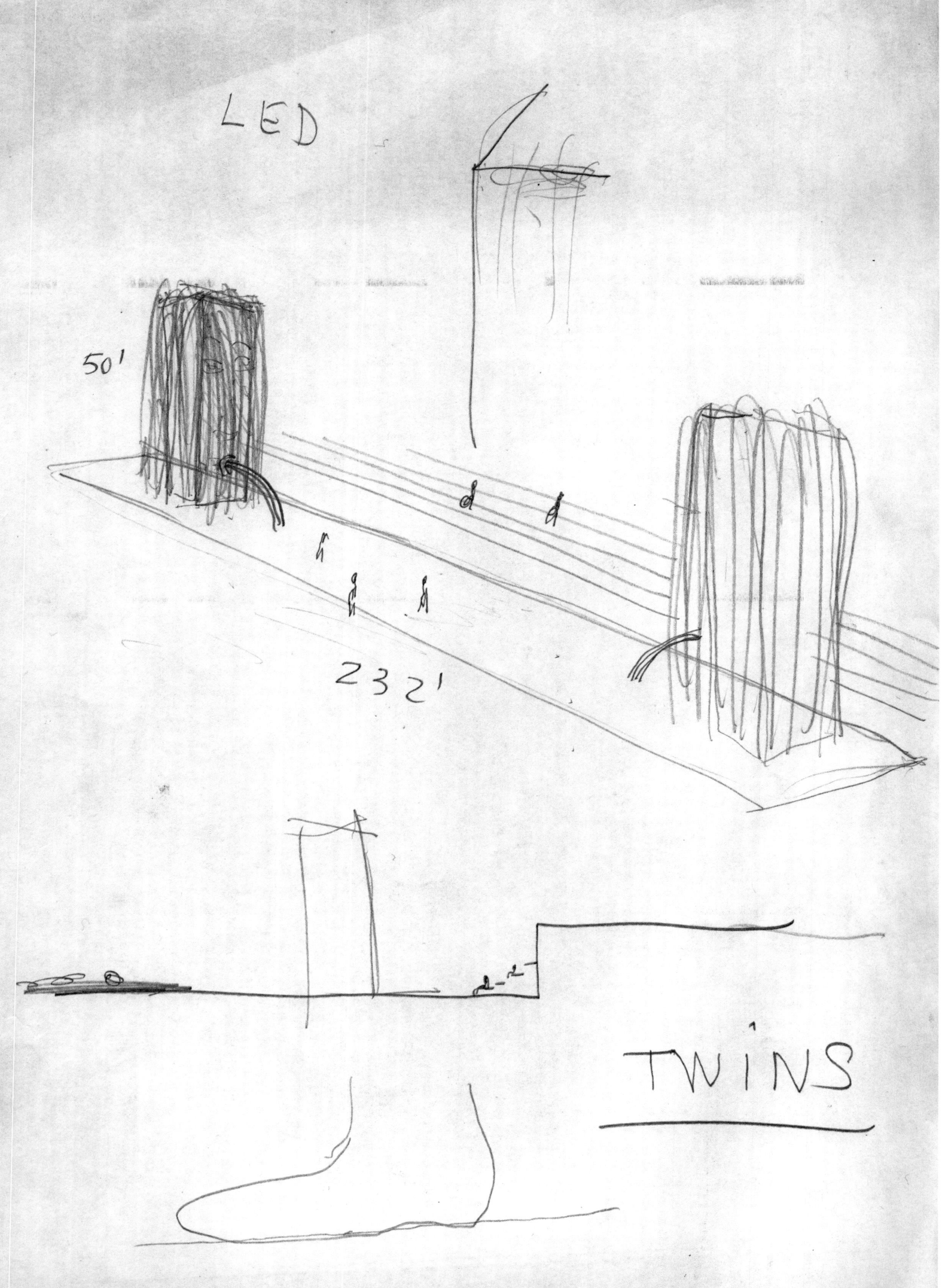

LED
50'
232'
TWINS

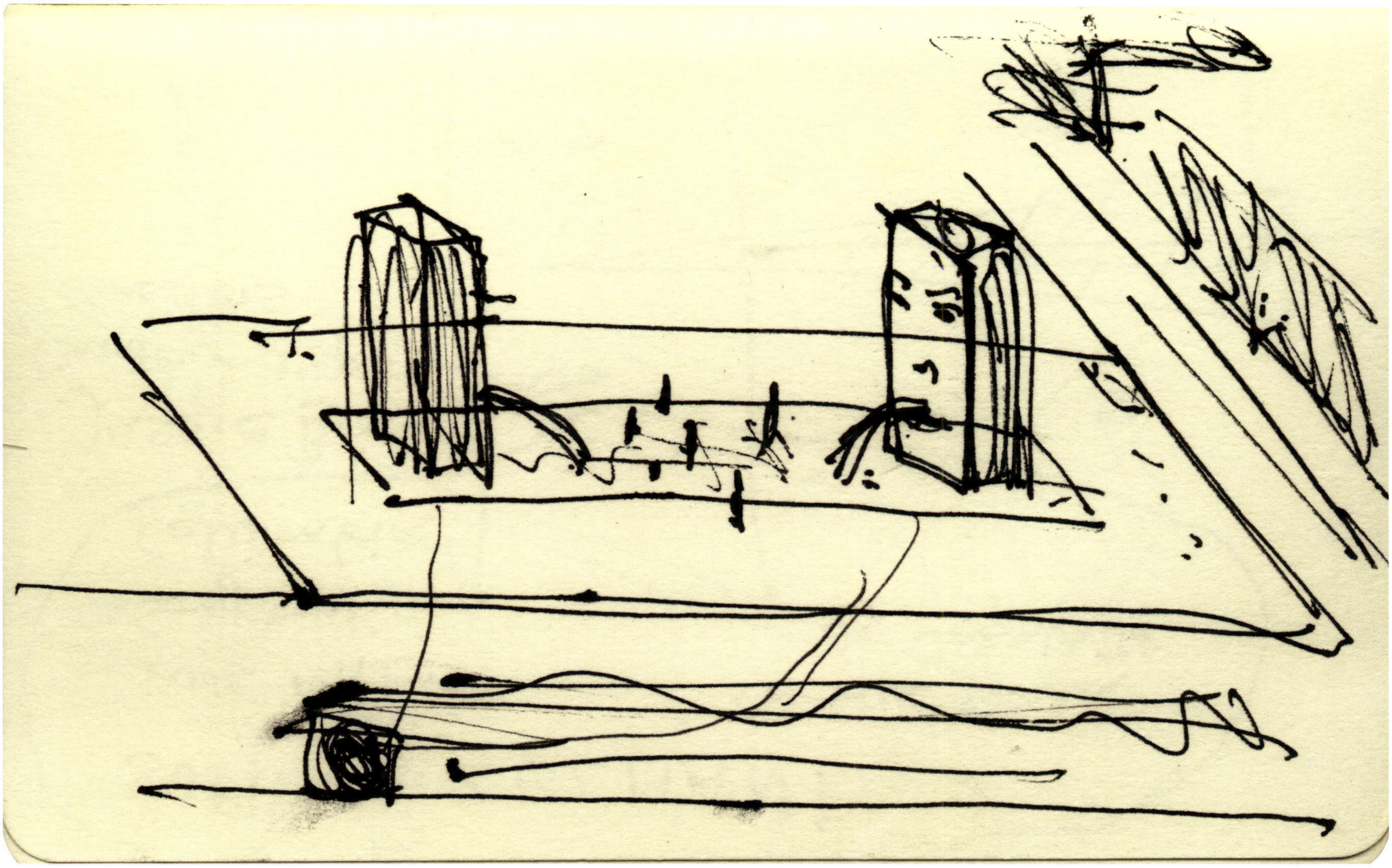

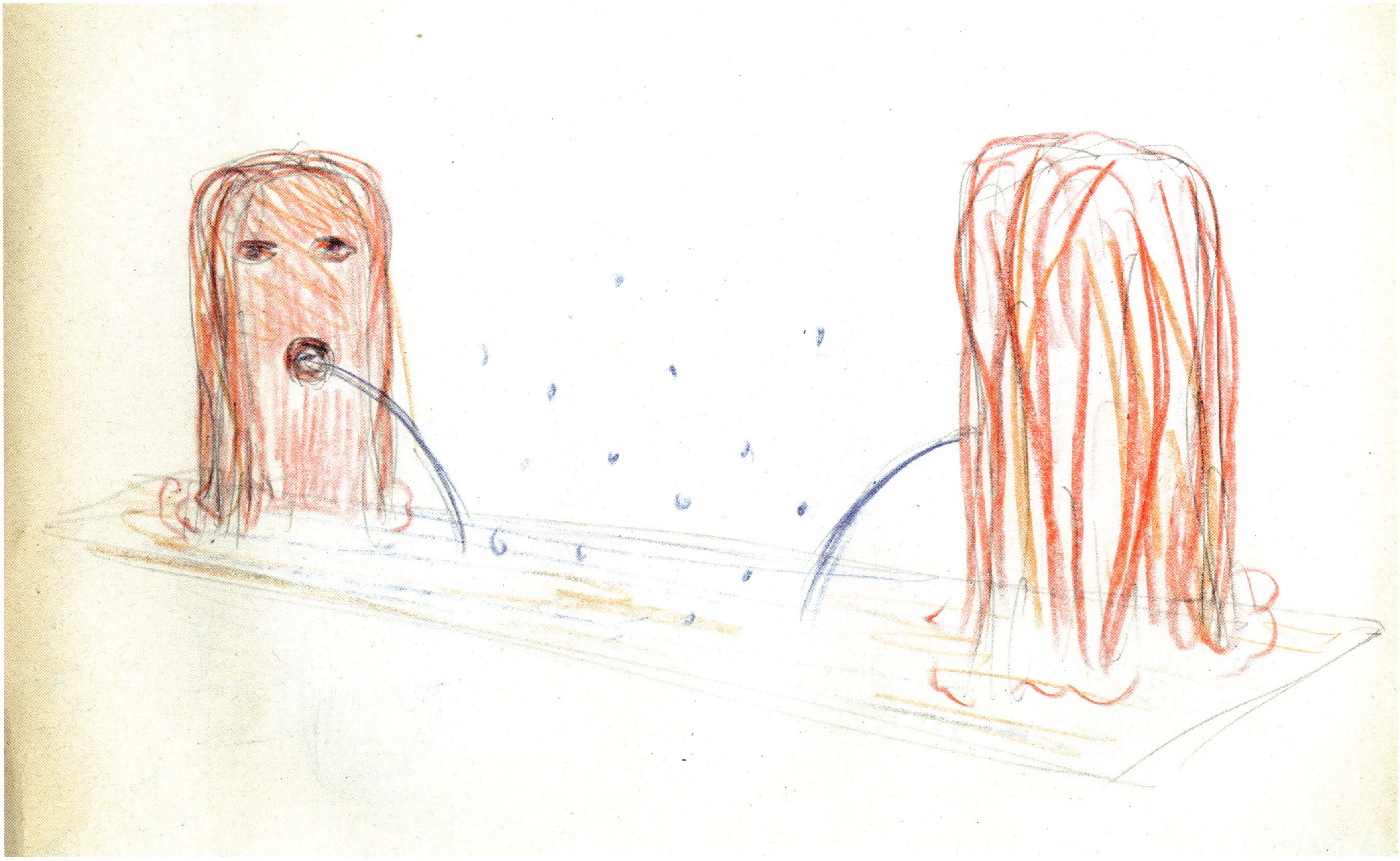

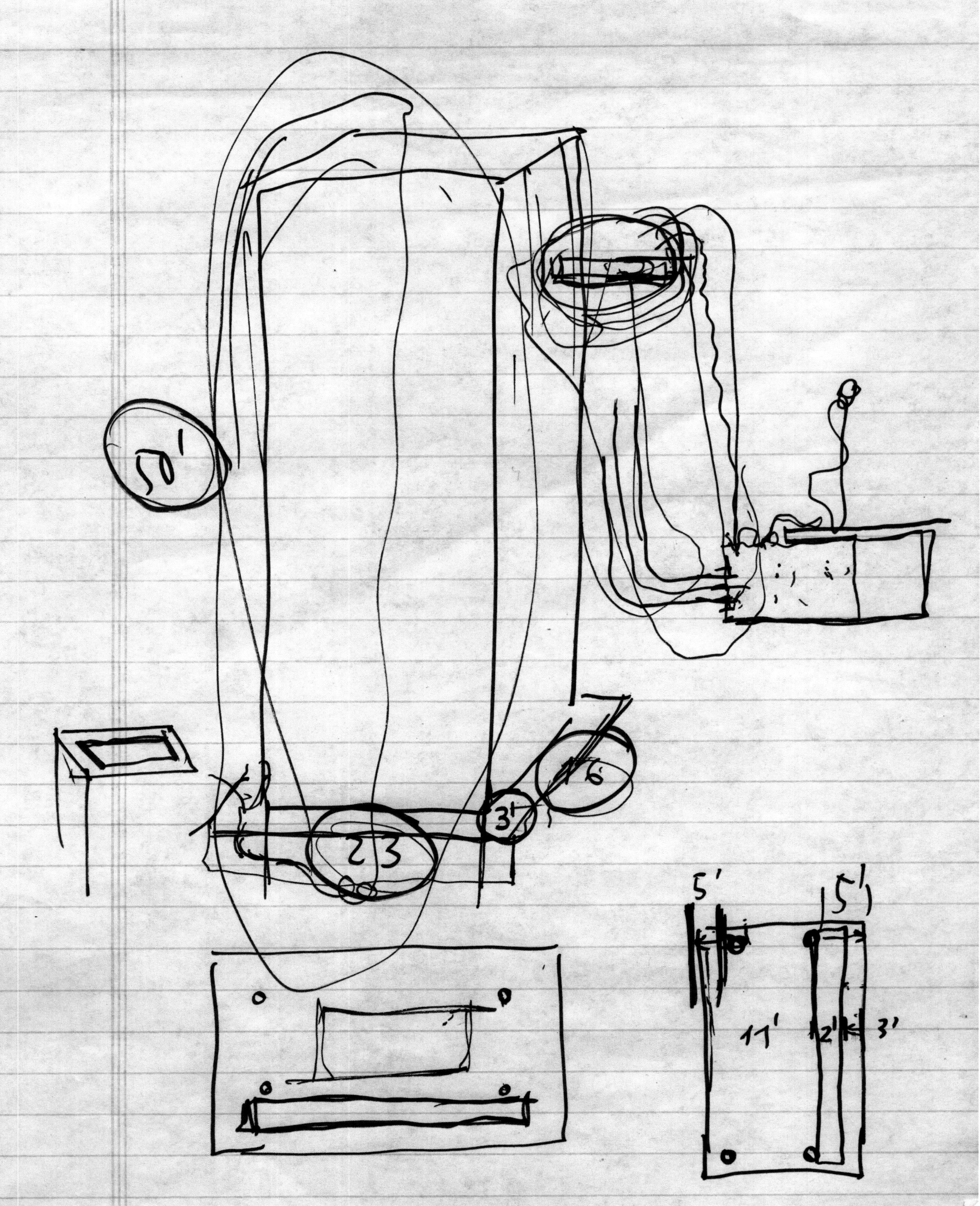

10'
23
3'
6
5'
5'
1'
2'
3'

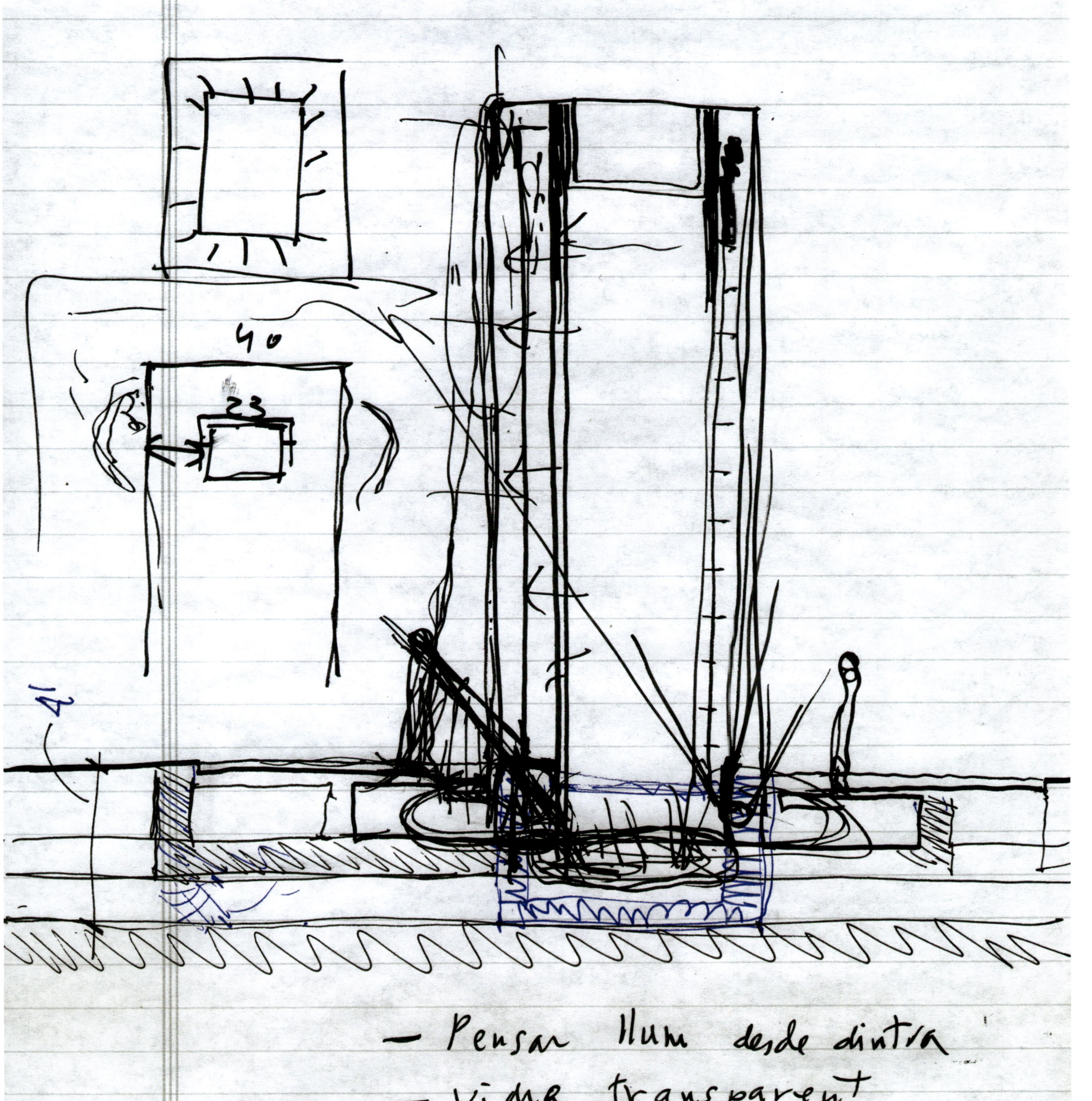

- Pensar llum desde dintra
- vidre transparent
- Produir silenci
- Treballar l'interior

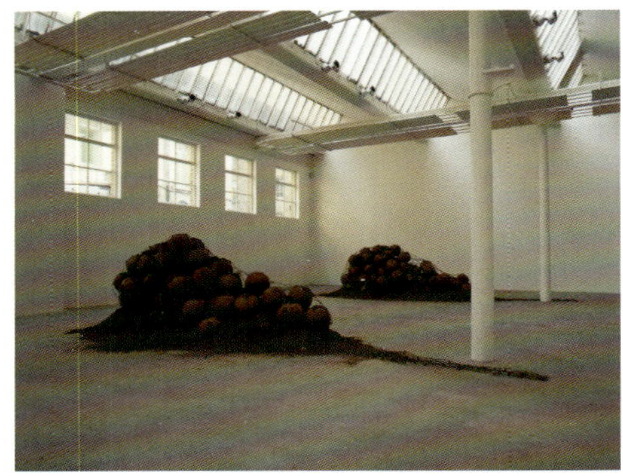

Jaume Plensa's *Twins* at the Henry Moore
Sculpture Studio, Halifax, 1994.

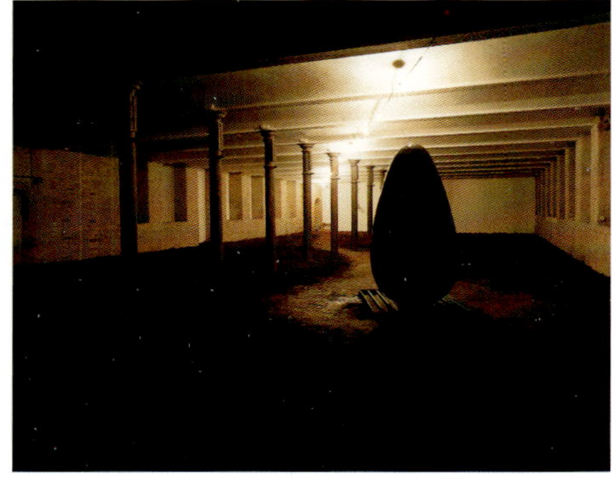

The Personal Miraculous Fountain at the Henry
Moore Sculpture Studio, Halifax, 1994.

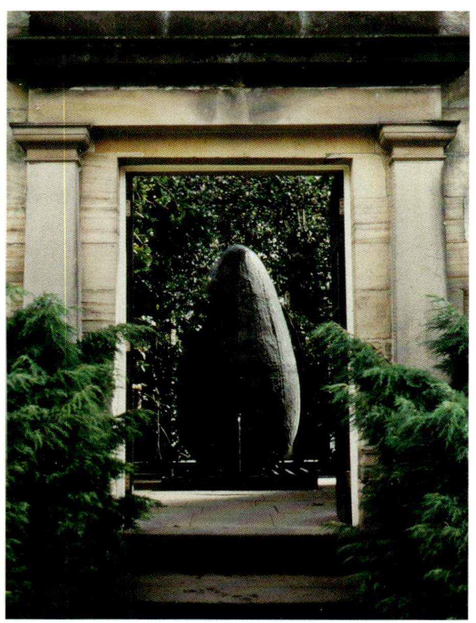

The Personal Miraculous Fountain at the
Yorkshire Sculpture Park, 1995.

The show we were to visit that morning was Plensa's, a Catalan sculptor whose work I had only infrequently seen before. And what I'd seen hadn't prepared me for what awaited.

The first space of the Henry Moore Studio was a vast hangar, where some of the largest carpets in Europe were once woven, and Plensa's installation was a tribute to the men, women, and children who had toiled there in the early nineteenth century. The air was cold, the winter light raking in at a low angle over the two mountains of cast-iron balls. *Twins* was an extraordinary sculpture: somber and massive, yet weighted down by vast steel meshes as if, left to their own devices, the balls would take flight. Each carried either a name culled from the local churchyards or that of some disease prevalent among the working classes in those far-off days.

But the best was yet to come. A small doorway opened onto a gloomy corridor that in turn led to a second space. With eyes adjusting to what little light was shed by a dozen naked bulbs, the visitor was overpowered by a humidity that filled the lungs: the rank dampness of decay, of autumn woods and rain forest floors. Rivulets of water ran down the blacked-out windows. The ground beneath felt soft and when your eyes became accustomed to the penumbral light you realized it was strewn with soil: one hundred tons of damp garden compost. And standing in the center was Plensa's *Personal Miraculous Fountain,* a giant egg-like form that issued water. Miraculous water.

The Umbrian Hills

Years later the artist told me a story. The scene shifts to an Italian village and it's the summer before Dean Clough. We'll have to imagine this village, a small, typical Umbrian hamlet, surrounded by farmland and vineyards, and famed for its waters. For centuries people have used its fountains and springs, but this particular year a foreigner has come to bottle its water and sell it as a miracle cure. An old woman approaches the stranger, knowing the fountain of old. "Is this really miraculous water?" she asks. But before the stranger can reply, she answers her own question. "Well, I suppose you never know," and she buys a bottle.

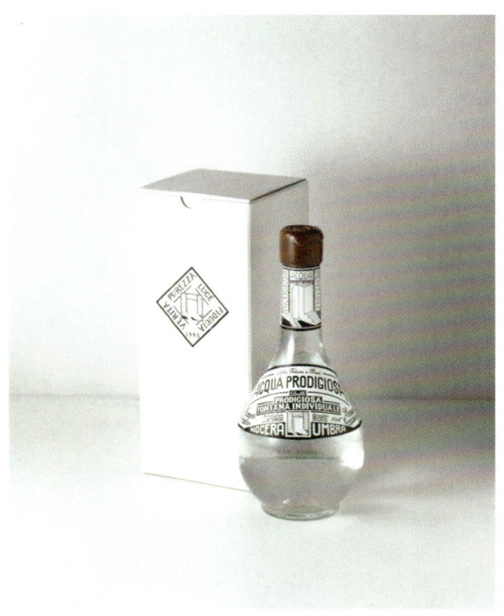

Jaume Plensa's *Acqua prodigiosa*, Nocera Umbra, Italy, 1993.

The stranger, of course, was Plensa, and despite the success of this one-day performance, it's doubtful that the water ever cured anybody. But if art is about anything, it is about the suspension of disbelief. At the heart of the Christian faith lies the belief in transubstantiation, that wine can become blood and bread flesh. At the heart of art lies the belief that inanimate matter can become a vehicle for the expression of our profoundest aspirations. After all, even Masaccio's sublime creations for the Brancacci Chapel in Florence are just plaster and pigment.

So, was Plensa's water miraculous or not? In reply to the old woman's question, I would like to stand her in front of Masaccio, transport her to Dean Clough, and now take her to the *Crown Fountain* and let her answer her own question. But perhaps she has already visited the Brancacci Chapel. Well, she did buy the water.

A Night on the Road

Plensa talks of building Niagara Falls on Michigan Avenue. It was part of the original dream and he gets animated when he talks about the dream. It's like he's seeing something the rest of us mortals can't yet make out: a mirage just forming out of the desert heat. Maybe it's water, or maybe just refracted light. Plensa, however, knows it is water and is already talking about the taste.

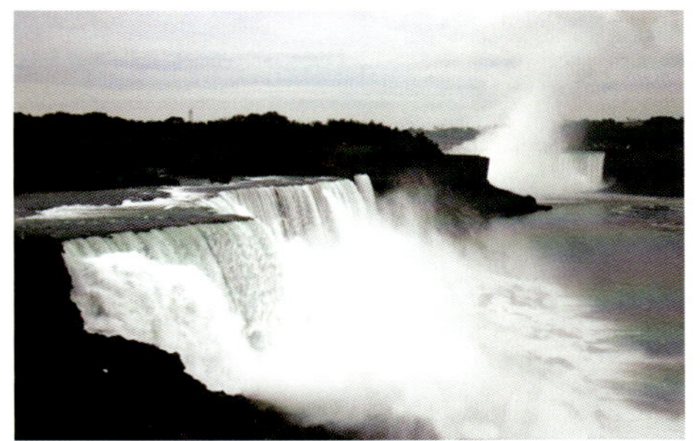

Niagara Falls.

I've only been there once: Niagara, that is. It would have been the summer of seventy-one and I'd gotten together with some other kids in a beat-up sedan. We crossed the border and somehow we were just there: Niagara, that is. There must have been all the water in Canada emptying over the Falls that night. Nearly full moon: white light and white noise, deafening.

I know what Plensa means. It's not Niagara he wants to build on Michigan Avenue; it's the *idea* of Niagara. The idea of all that water—falling water. It's an abstract idea but made up of the real stuff; the liquid we take for granted but that is really the key to life.

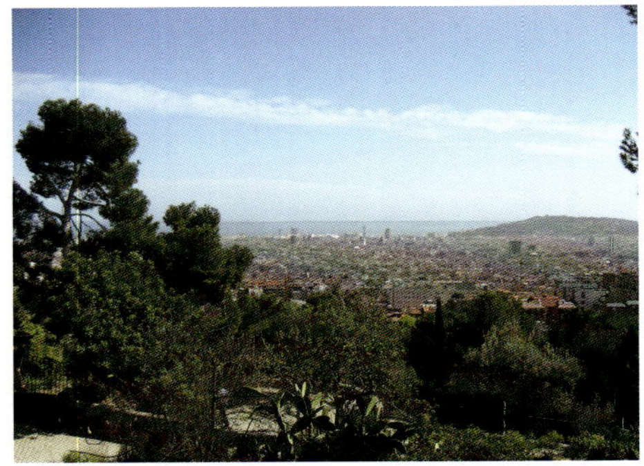

Barcelona: sea and mountains.

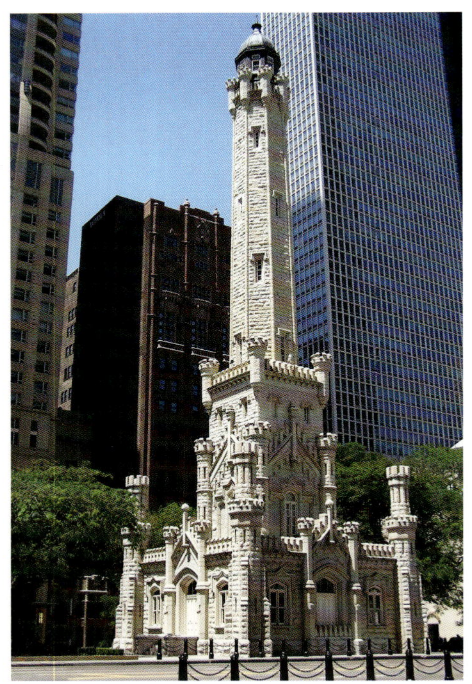

The Water Tower, Chicago.

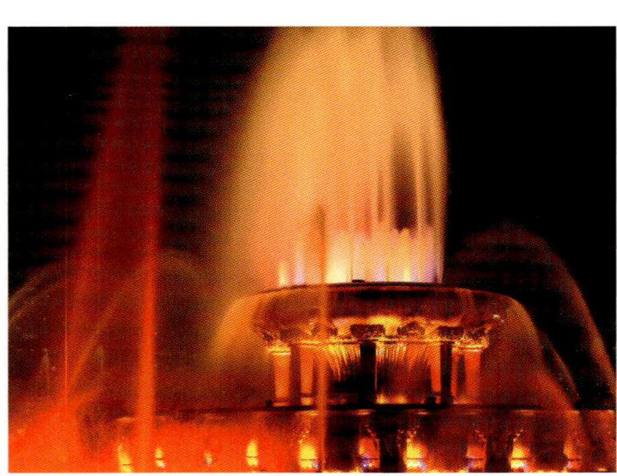

Buckingham Fountain, Chicago.

Sea or Mountains

It threw me for weeks. I'd be meeting with friends and they'd say they would see me "seaside" or "mountainside." Then I realized that "sea" and "mountain" were coordinates, far more natural in a city like Barcelona than the abstractions of north and south. The city is shoveled in, cramped, between the Mediterranean and the first diminutive mountain they call the Tibidabo.

People brought up by water—whether the sea or a lake like Michigan—develop a singular attitude to it. Not only respect or dependency, but as if that vast body of water becomes one of the coordinates of the psyche, as tangible as north and south, or in Chicago's case east.

Chicago is blessed by the presence of its freshwater lake and shrines to it are found all over the city. There's what Oscar Wilde unkindly called the "naïve Gothic" of the Water Tower, which from 1866 helped provide the city with its first alternative to the rank and muddy water drawn from the shore and which miraculously survived the Great Fire of 1871. There's Lorado Taft's *Fountain of the Great Lakes* (1914), linking those five great expanses of water with the Greek myths. In common with the *Buckingham Fountain* (1927), Taft's original title honored his patron, Benjamin Ferguson, as witnessed by a plaque, now obscured on the rear. But most of all there are countless fountains on anonymous street corners and squares that bear witness to the city's awareness of water.

"The *Crown Fountain* is the equivalent of going to the ocean and watching waves. There's a cycle, a structure, a rhythm: yet every time it's different because it's organic. I truly think it is one of the great urban spaces of this city, and possibly of the world. It is certainly one of the icons of Chicago."
Mark Sexton, architect

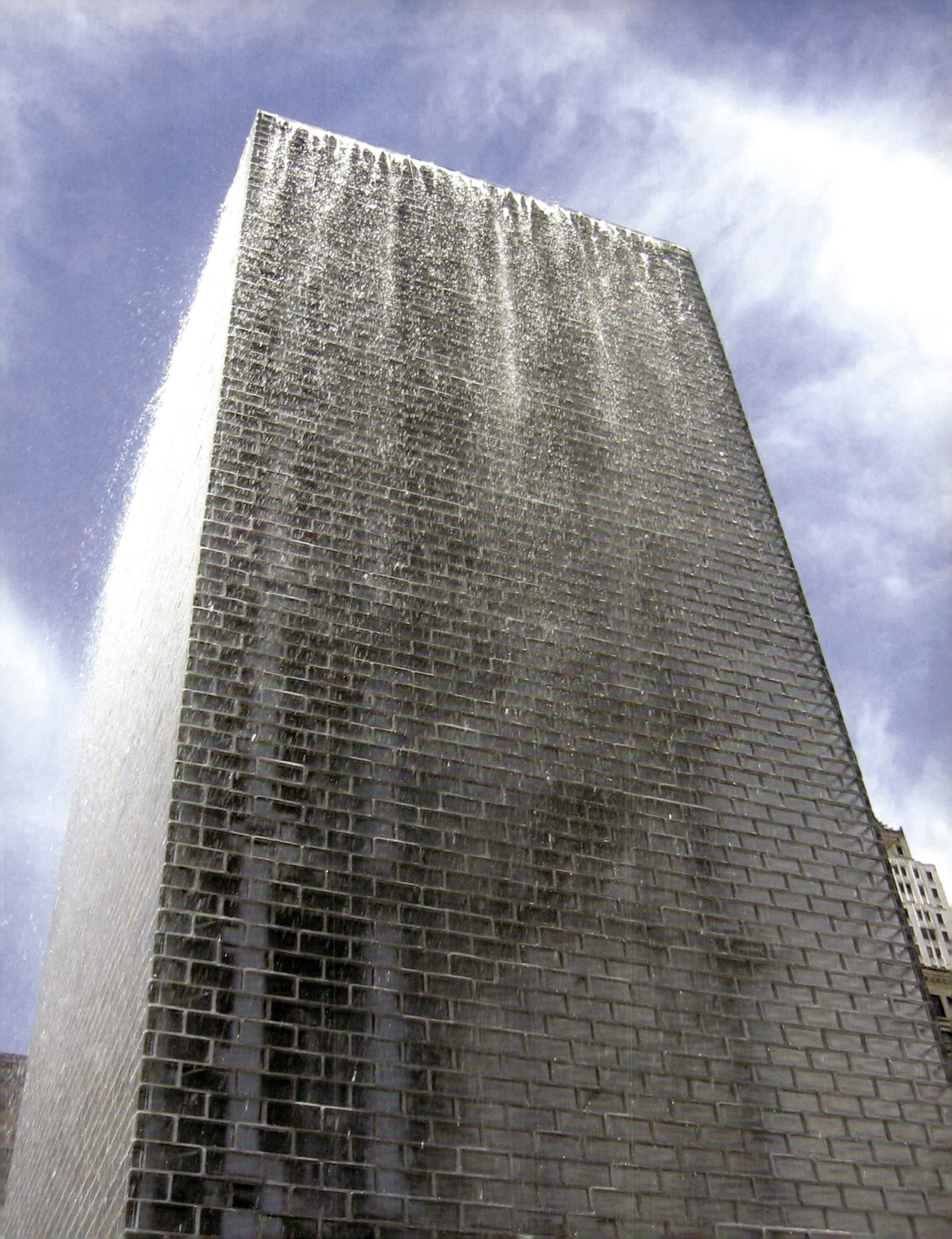

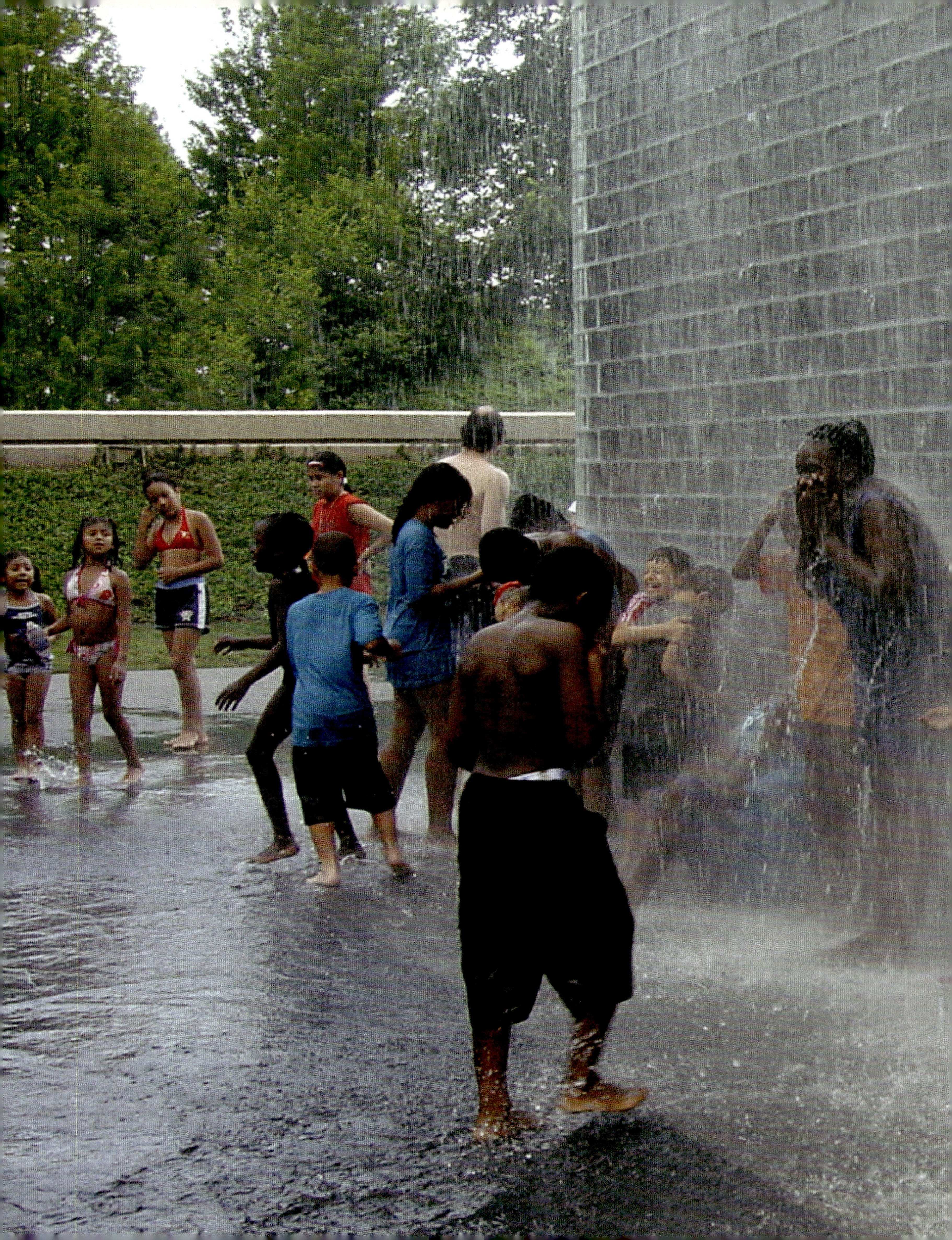

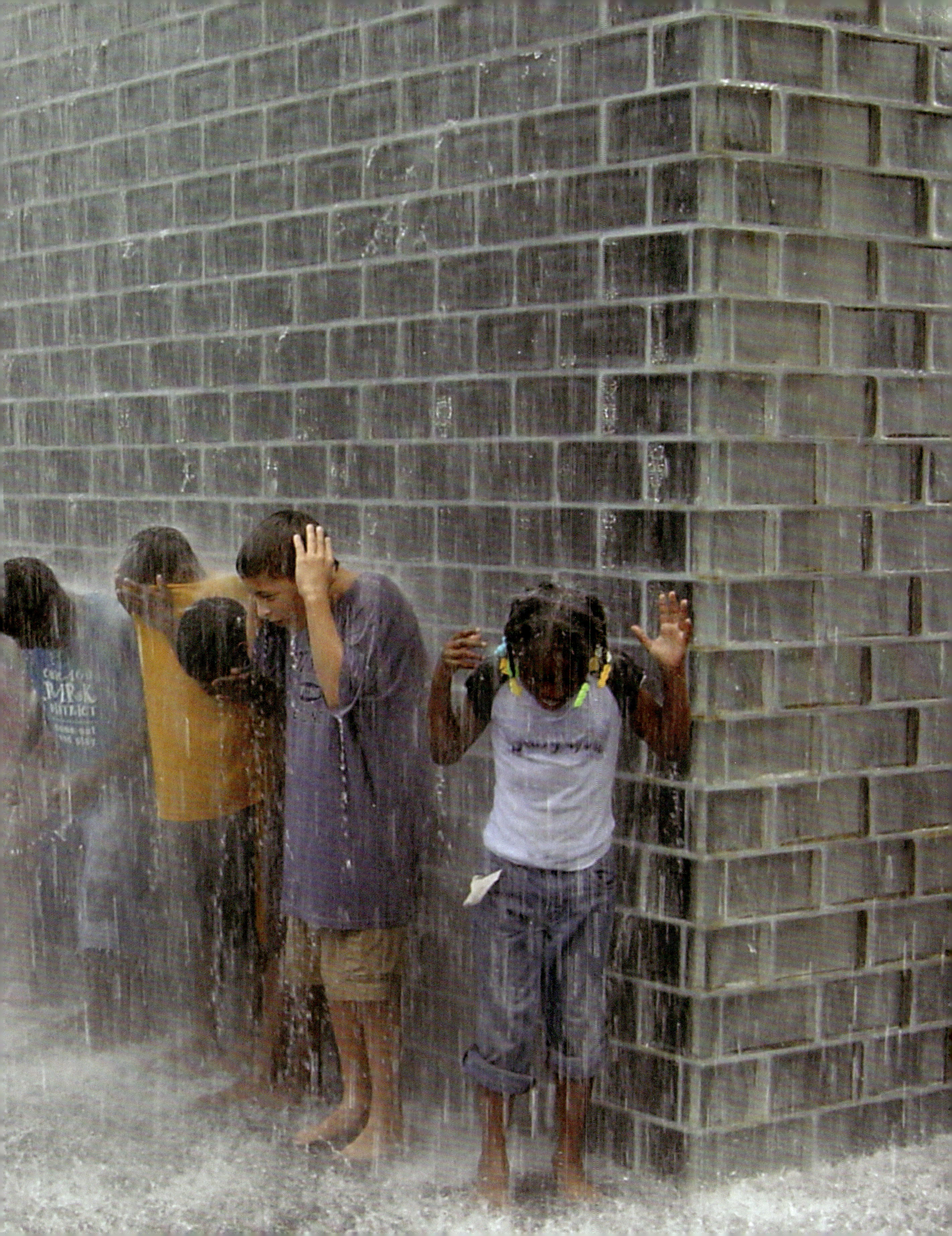

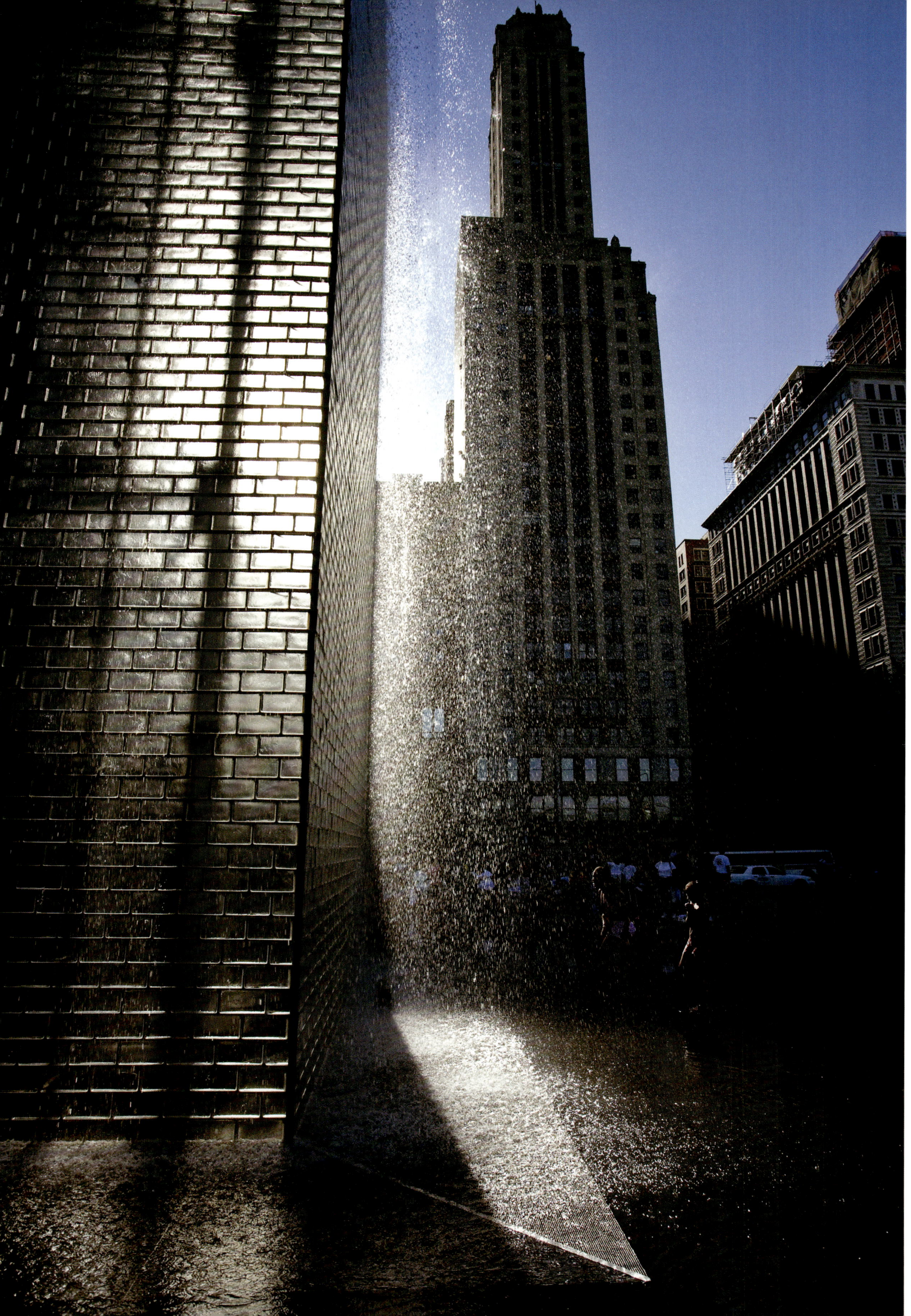

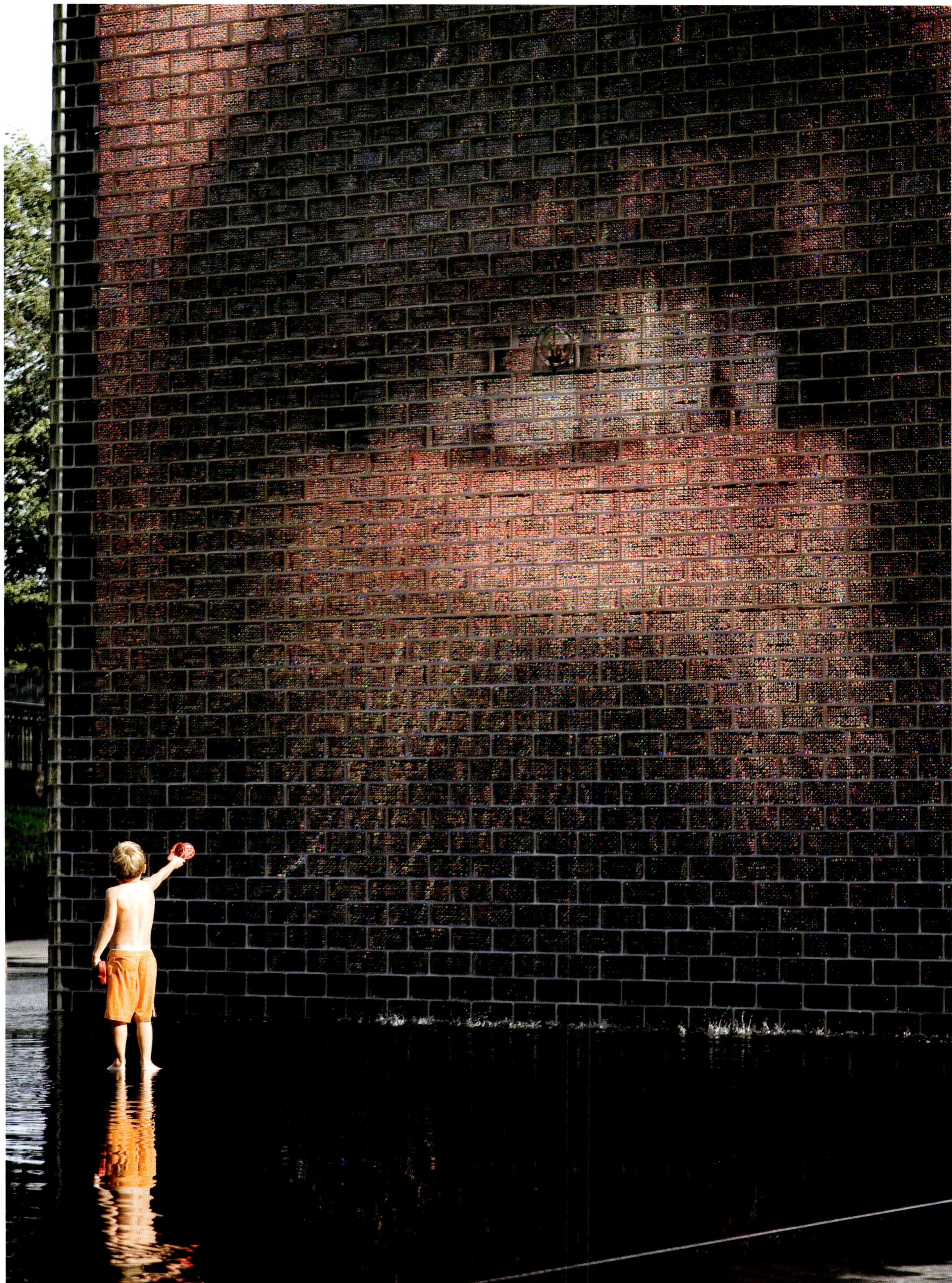

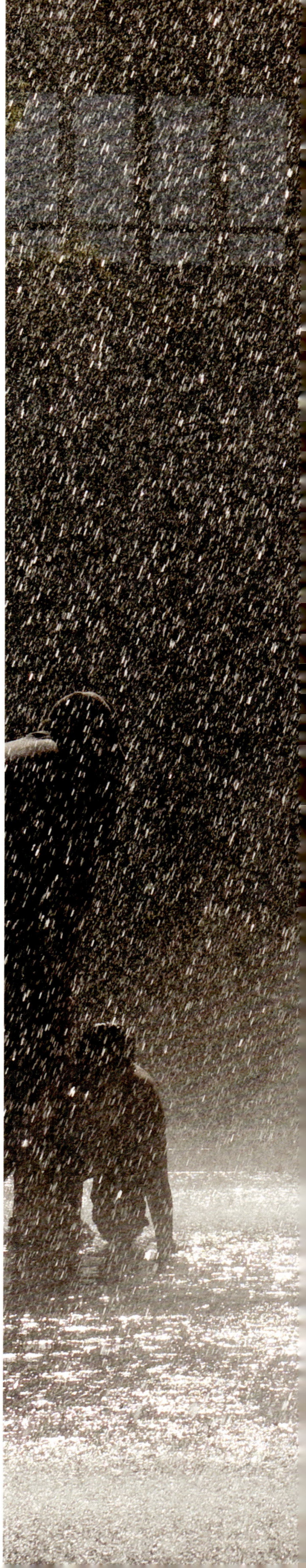

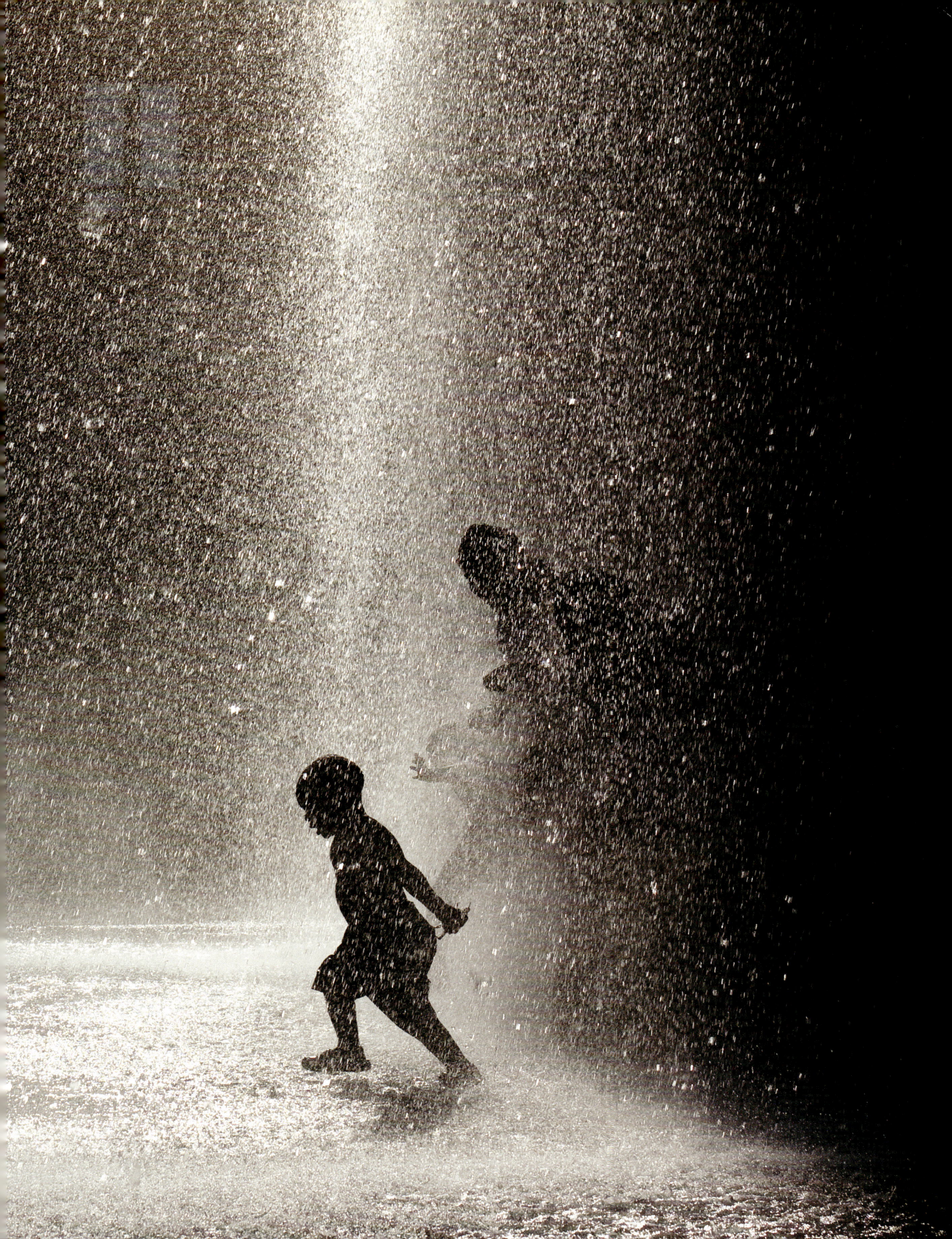

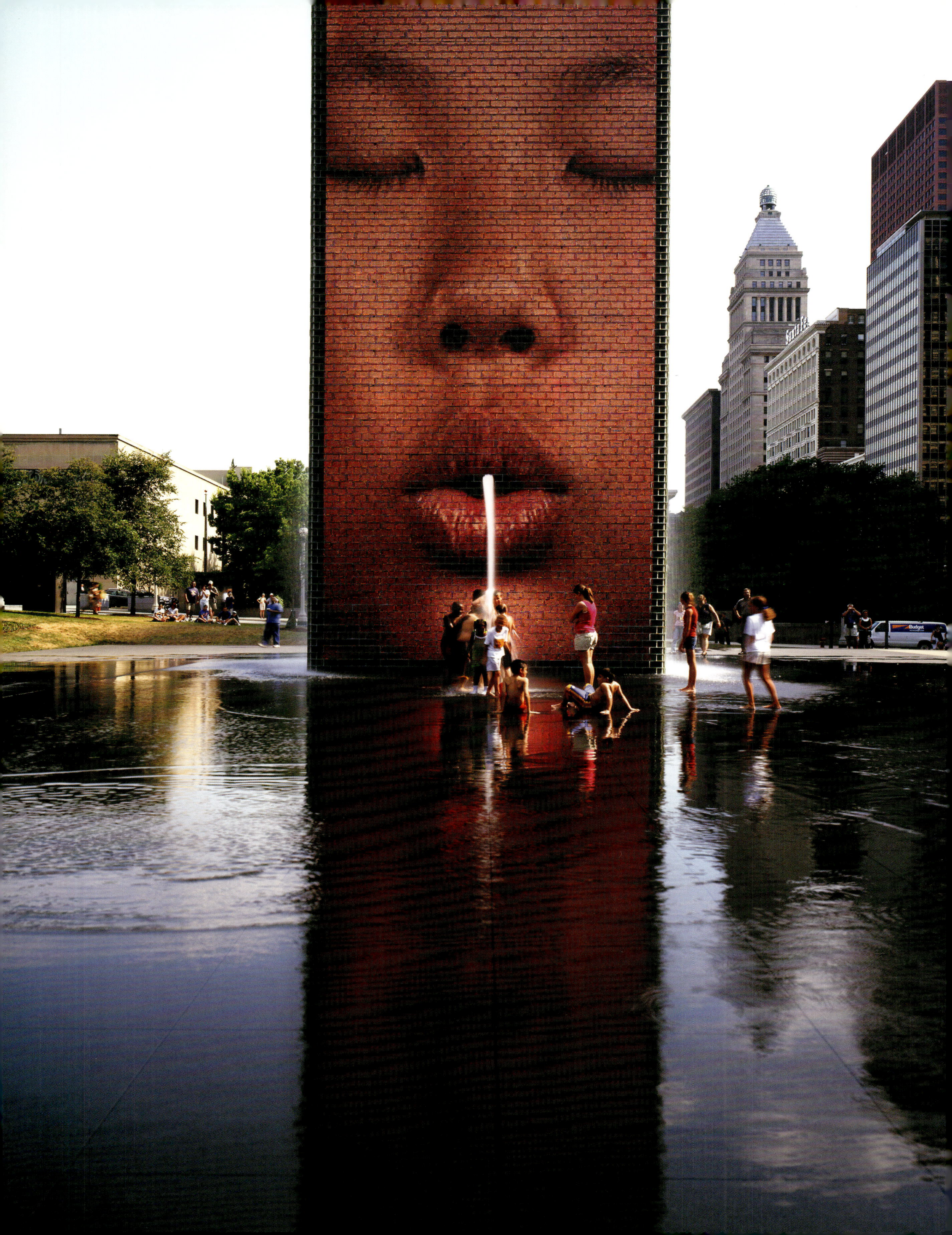

2

The Park That Almost Never Was

The story of the site that became Millennium Park is labyrinthine, but
here's the simplified version that I first encountered over a beer one night.
It's a particularly Chicagoan tale with a late-capitalist twist and, of course,
a happy ending.

Until well into the nineteenth century the area to the east of what was yet to
become Michigan Avenue, between Randolph and Monroe, was marshland,
with a sand spit that gave onto the shores of the lake. Pine Street, now
renamed Michigan Avenue, was extended southwards from the Chicago River
in the mid 1830s. By 1836, concerned that further development would
compromise their lakefront status, local property owners petitioned to have
the remaining area designated a park: "A common to remain forever open,
clear and free of any buildings."

By all accounts, it wasn't much of a park. Still largely marshland, Lake Front
Park was prone to inundation during the winter storms and put at risk
property along Michigan Avenue itself. All of this was bad news for what was
fast becoming one of the city's most fashionable streets. So in 1852 the city
struck a deal. The Illinois Central Railway would construct a breakwater out
beyond the spit in return for the right to run trains along it, and in so doing
would create a recreational lake bordering Michigan Avenue. Then came the
Great Fire of 1871, which pretty much destroyed everything in central Chicago,
including the fine buildings bordering Lake Front Park and the Great Central

Railway Station that lay just to the north. Undaunted, its citizens immediately set about rebuilding themselves a modern city: in fact the population almost doubled within a decade. And nothing grew faster than the railroads, with Chicago becoming the country's natural hub through which almost all east-west traffic passed. But for a token strip bordering Michigan Avenue, within just a few years of the original agreement the remaining park area was overrun by tracks and remained that way for more than a century.

And then something rather remarkable happened. In 1996, while checking the small print on the original agreement, an attorney by the name of Randall Mehrberg discovered that the railroad company was in default. Moreover, Mehrberg just happened to be a director for the Chicago Park District with responsibility for the Lake Front areas. And the Park District had long regarded the rail yard as an eyesore and as a constant problem to its planning strategies. Given that few of the tracks were currently in use and that much of the space was given over to staff parking, Mehrberg was able to demonstrate—although not without an initial lawsuit—that it was in the company's own interests to relinquish the land.

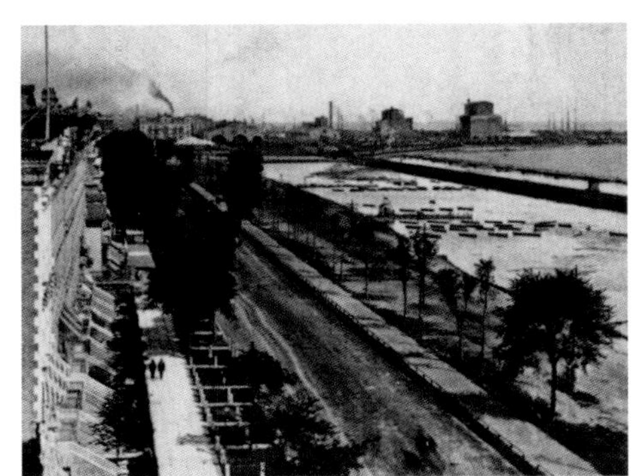

Chicago's Lake Front Park, 1868–69.
Courtesy of Chicago History Museum.

This is where Mayor Richard M. Daley enters the story. For some time Mayor Daley had been aware of the wasted land monopolizing a key slice of down-town Chicago. On the one hand the rail yards were a dead zone between the commercial center and the lake, and on the other between the river and Grant Park. Conclusion: the main axis of the city was cut in two. But like everyone else, he'd assumed the land actually belonged to the railroad company. When Mehrberg concluded that this wasn't so, wheels began to turn. With the millennium looming, the mayor was keen to improve the downtown infrastructure and, for the first time in many years, bring visitors into the area. In particular, he had his eyes set on the potential for turning the rail yards into… an underground parking lot.

As unromantic as it may sound, the genesis of Millennium Park lies two stories down. In a grand scheme that is reminiscent of the original deal struck with the Illinois Central Railway, Daley sees both the potential to provide much needed parking space and to create the hub of a new integrated public

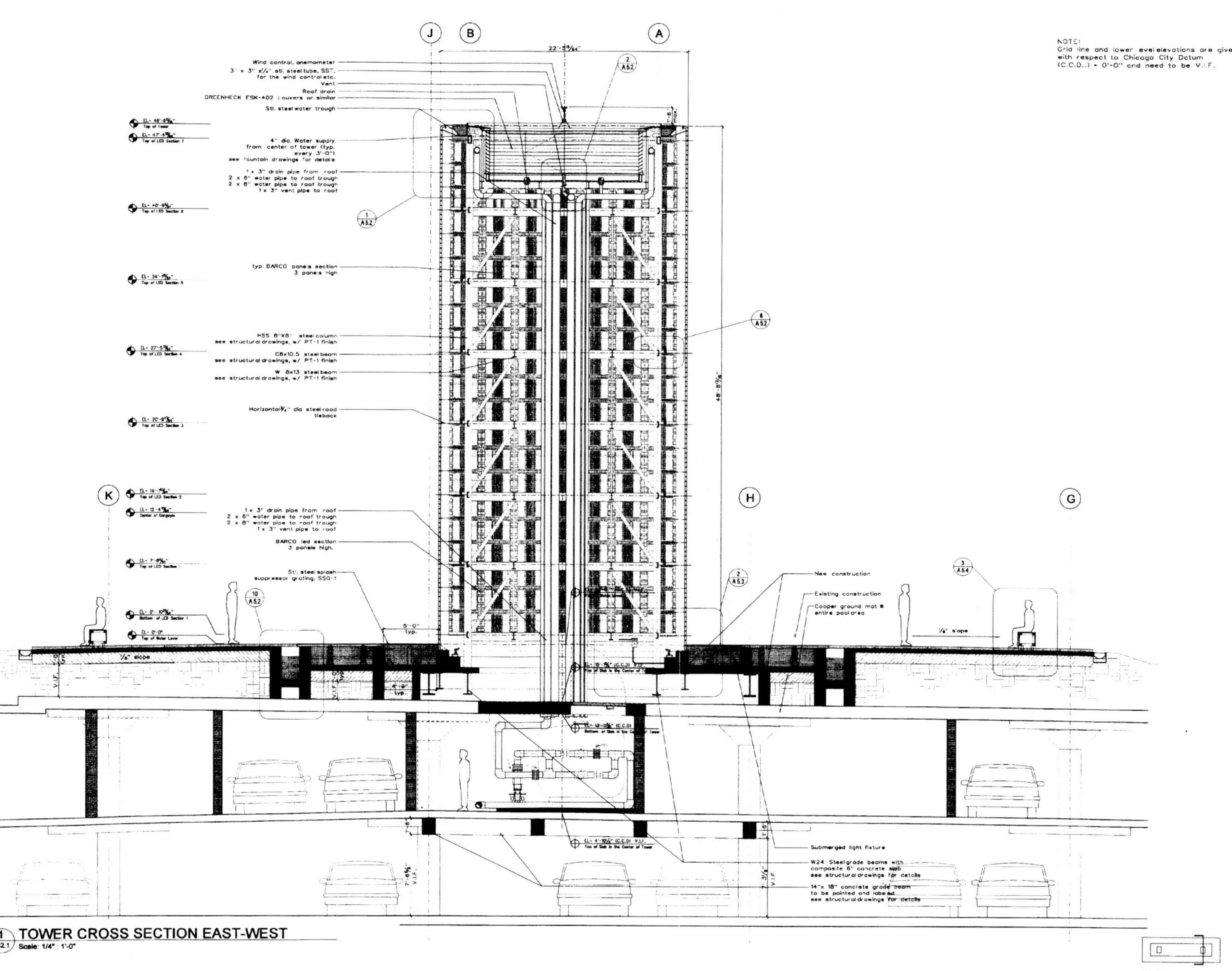

NOTE:
Grid line and lower level elevations are given with respect to Chicago City Datum (C.C.D.) = 0'-0" and need to be V.I.F.
Wind control, anemometer
3" x 3" x 1/4" stl. steel tube, SST, for the wind control etc.
Vent
Roof drain
GREENHECK ESK-402 Louvers or similar
Stl. steel water trough
4" dia. Water supply from center of tower (typ. every 3'-0") see fountain drawings for details
1 x 3" drain pipe from roof
2 x 6" water pipe to roof trough
2 x 8" water pipe to roof trough
1 x 3" vent pipe to roof
typ. BARCO panels section 3 panels high
HSS 8"X8" steel column see structural drawings, w/ PT-1 finish
C6x10.5 steel beam see structural drawings, w/ PT-1 finish
W 8x13 steel beam see structural drawings, w/ PT-1 finish
Horizontal 3/4" dia steel rod tieback
1 x 3" drain pipe from roof
2 x 6" water pipe to roof trough
2 x 8" water pipe to roof trough
1 x 3" vent pipe to roof
BARCO led section 3 panels high.
Stl. steel splash suppressor grating, SSG-1
New construction
Existing construction
Copper ground mat @ entire pool area
1/8" slope
Submerged light fixture
W24 Steel grade beams with composite 6" concrete slab see structural drawings for details
14"x 18" concrete grade beam to be painted and labeled see structural drawings for details
TOWER CROSS SECTION EAST-WEST
Scale: 1/4" : 1'-0"
Key Plan

transport system. Both are income generating, and the monies would go towards the upkeep of a park at ground level: almost literally the icing on the cake. In 1998 Ed Uhlir is appointed as director, responsible for the overall design, architecture, and landscape of the site. And so, give or take a few additions and innovations, after some 130 years the people of Chicago were set to get their park back.

The Project Manager's Tale

Roark Frankel is Senior Vice President of U.S. Equities Realty, the company appointed to project-manage specific aspects of the new park. He was in on the project from early on, even before the Crown family or Jaume Plensa, and stayed with it until the end. By the time the Crowns had reached their decision, Roark was already engaged with organizing the engineering teams that would realize two other major contributions on the Millennium Park site. Nevertheless, Plensa's approach of involving himself personally with every

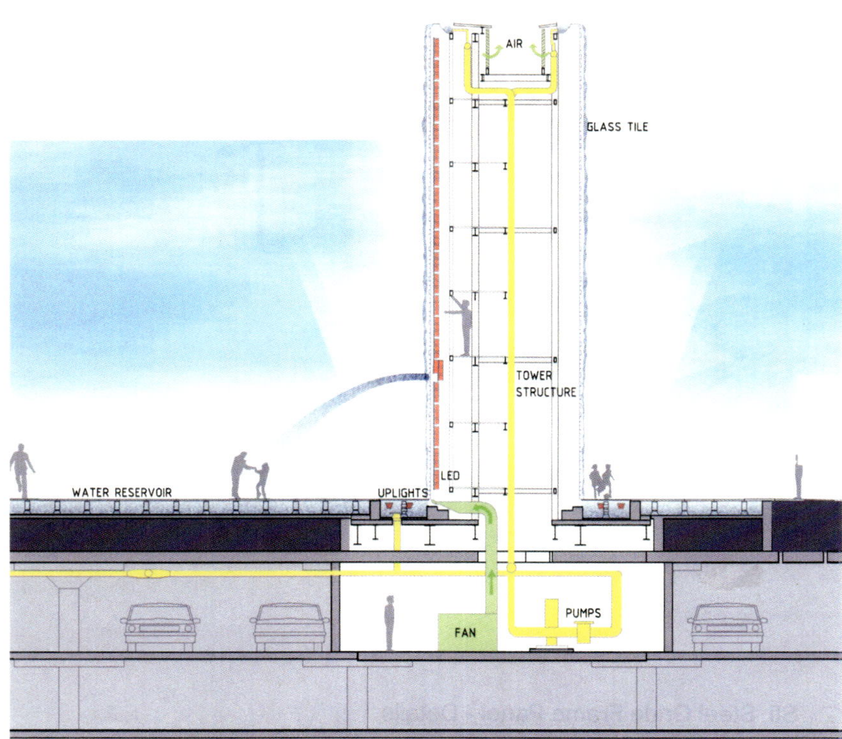

Ⓑ **Tower Section Shallow**

aspect of the fountain quickly led to an intense working relationship, which Roark describes as "one of the most rewarding of my professional career."

The initial challenge is one of marrying Plensa with a core team sympathetic to the idea of applying the latest technology to the artist's vision. Other projects on site are creating headaches for U.S. Equities, but this is only to be expected. However, the *Crown Fountain* proves to be far more technically complex and diverse than any other single project. Moreover, it gradually becomes apparent that Plensa's all-important philosophical inquiry into fountains, public spaces, and the origins of life itself is simply not understood by the engineers.

Therein lies the real challenge that Roark faces and it will lead to near insurmountable problems in the months to come. The saving grace is what he calls the "insight and patience" of the Crowns themselves, and their acceptance that blind alleys and false starts are an inevitable consequence of such an ambitious project. "It's been the project of a lifetime," he concludes. "The experience of working with Jaume has changed the way I think and work."

A Park for the New Millennium

We haven't quite finished with Dean Clough and the *Personal Miraculous Fountain,* but let's spend a few minutes more with the park. Or rather the bare earth that covers the still incomplete underground parking lot, for it's now 1999 and decisions are being made about what form the new park will take. The initial schedules for completing the parking lot and "grassing it over" in time for the millennium have gone by the board. But in the interim a far more ambitious scheme has been developed: something that will not only look to the future, but also celebrate what the area had once been and what it has striven to be at various points in its long and tortuous history.

Back in the 1860s, Lake Front Park had its own recreational lake, though more by default than design. I know because there are photographs and where the *Crown Fountain* will sit there's a broad stretch of water. Small sailing boats are flitting on the breeze, and close to where the breakwater draws a hard line between the boating lake and the vast expanse of water that lies

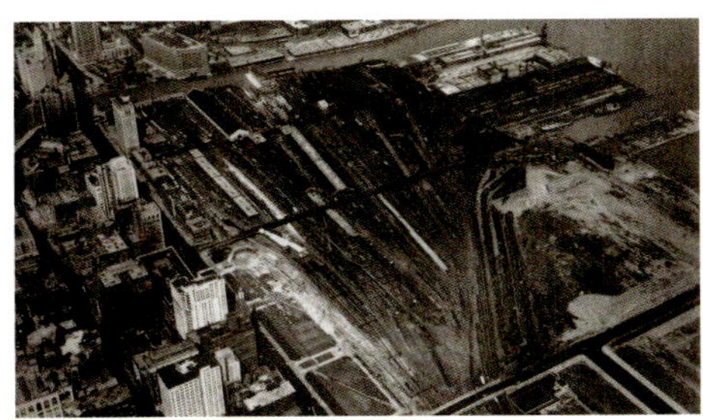

The rail yards, 1929. Courtesy of Chicago History Museum.

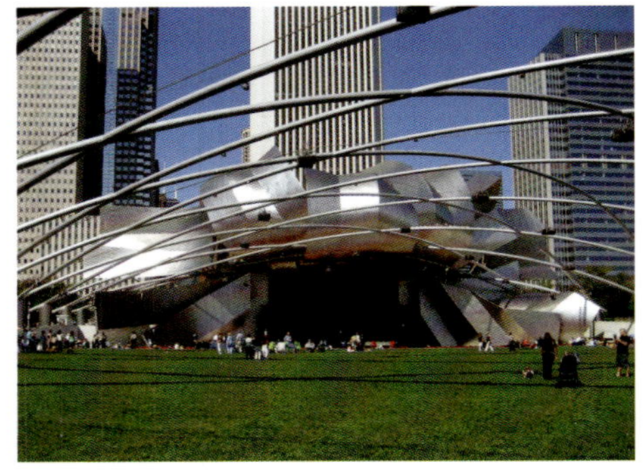

Frank Gehry's Music Pavilion.

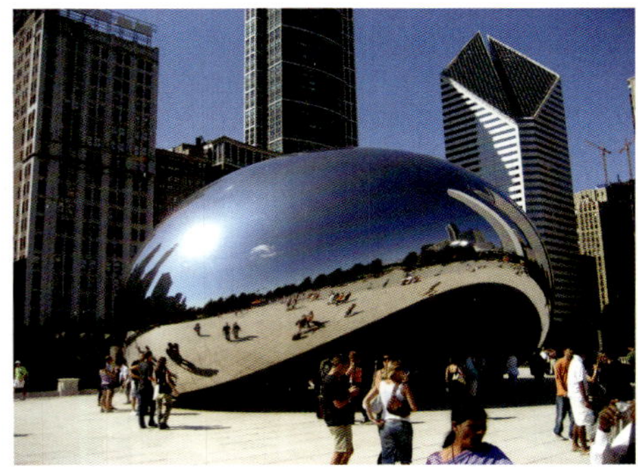

Anish Kapoor's *Cloud Gate*.

beyond, there's a locomotive billowing smoke. There are few signs of the vast expansion of tracks that would shortly follow. The accounts are contradictory, some narrators dating the expansion of the rail yards to the 1860s. Or perhaps it came in two stages, with the railroad's big land grab coming just a few years later, when the recreational lake was filled in with the masonry and still-smoldering timbers of the Great Fire.

What can we learn from these photos? That at this time Michigan Avenue was a prosperous-looking boulevard that occupied but one side of the road, just as today. That the eastern approach was lined with elm trees, but otherwise bare. That the lakeshore reached to within a couple of hundred yards of the front steps of these houses. But also that Lake Front Park was already destined as a place of recreation—a place to promenade, to socialize, and to reflect upon the "city by the lake" and its people. In fact, coincidence or not, one hundred and fifty years ago, on the corner of Monroe and Michigan, there was already a shallow pool of water, a wooden boardwalk and seats, and a parade of people silhouetted against the backdrop of two twin monolithic buildings on the northern horizon. I cannot identify them, but they are eerily reminiscent of the towers of the *Crown Fountain*.

But we were talking of 1999, the very eve of the new millennium. The park has already been divided up, and decisions reached about some of the principal players. Award-winning architect Frank Gehry will design the music pavilion, a project that incidentally has dogged the planners for generations, as the legacy of 1836 and its prohibition on buildings in Lake Front Park continues. London-based artist Anish Kapoor has been selected to construct "The Bean," an appellation chosen by the people of Chicago because the artist is so long in coming up with its official title of *Cloud Gate*. And a partnership led by Kathryn Gustafson has been assigned the task of designing the *Lurie Garden*.

Naturally, money is the key issue, but the people of Chicago are not being asked to pay. Rather, sponsors are courted on a project by project basis and the thankless task has fallen to John Bryan.

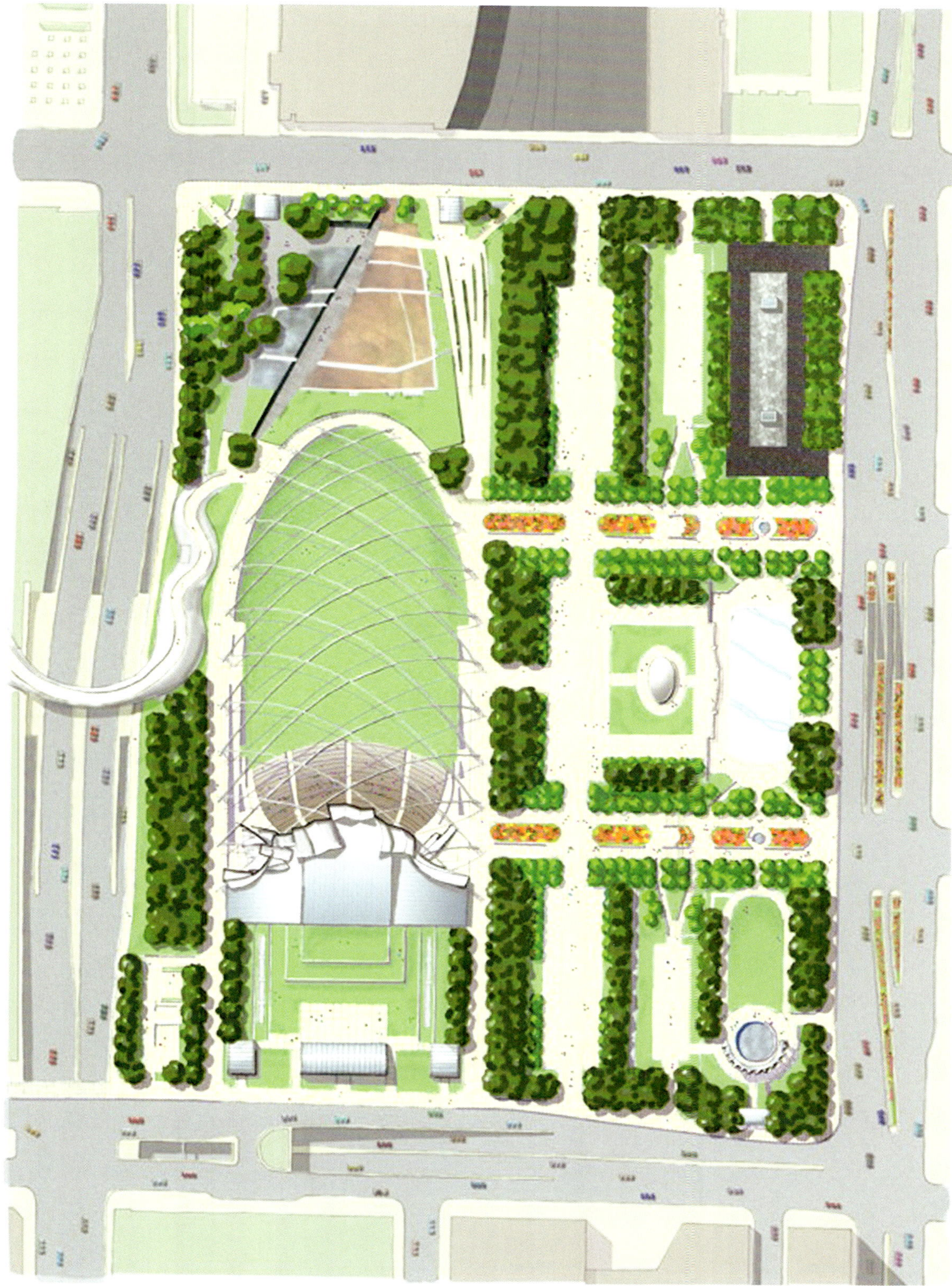

General plan of Millennium Park.

CEO for the Sara Lee Corporation, Bryan is a natural fundraiser, having worked his magic for Chicago's Lyric Opera House and Orchestra Hall earlier in the nineties. As an initial estimate he's angling for around sixty million dollars, although the final sum will be nearly three times that: what attorney Jack Guthman calls "the J.B. dollars."

> "When the Crowns first signed up for the fountain, they couldn't possibly have foreseen what it would become. It's one of those rare instances when the result is actually better than anyone could have imagined."
> Mark Sexton, architect

Bryan called on the Crowns somewhat late in the day. By choice a low-profile family, they have extensive investments in real estate and construction, and they naturally understand the extent and implications of the development taking place downtown. As director of the family's private charitable foundation, it was on Susan Crown's door that Bryan first knocked back in January of 1999. With plans in hand, he was asking the family to sponsor one of the last remaining projects. Ed Uhlir had by now divided the park into a series of "rooms," each accommodating one or more features. The room under discussion was situated on the southwestern corner, and it had already been decided that it should comprise some kind of water feature. But what kind? A fountain to rival the *Buckingham Fountain,* the Versailles-inspired leviathan that's been a Chicago icon for nearly eighty years? Not in the sense of competing, insists Susan Crown, but it was clear from the outset that it must at least equal the *Buckingham Fountain* in ambition. But should it, like the music pavilion, be realized by an architect, or was it more appropriate to appoint an artist?

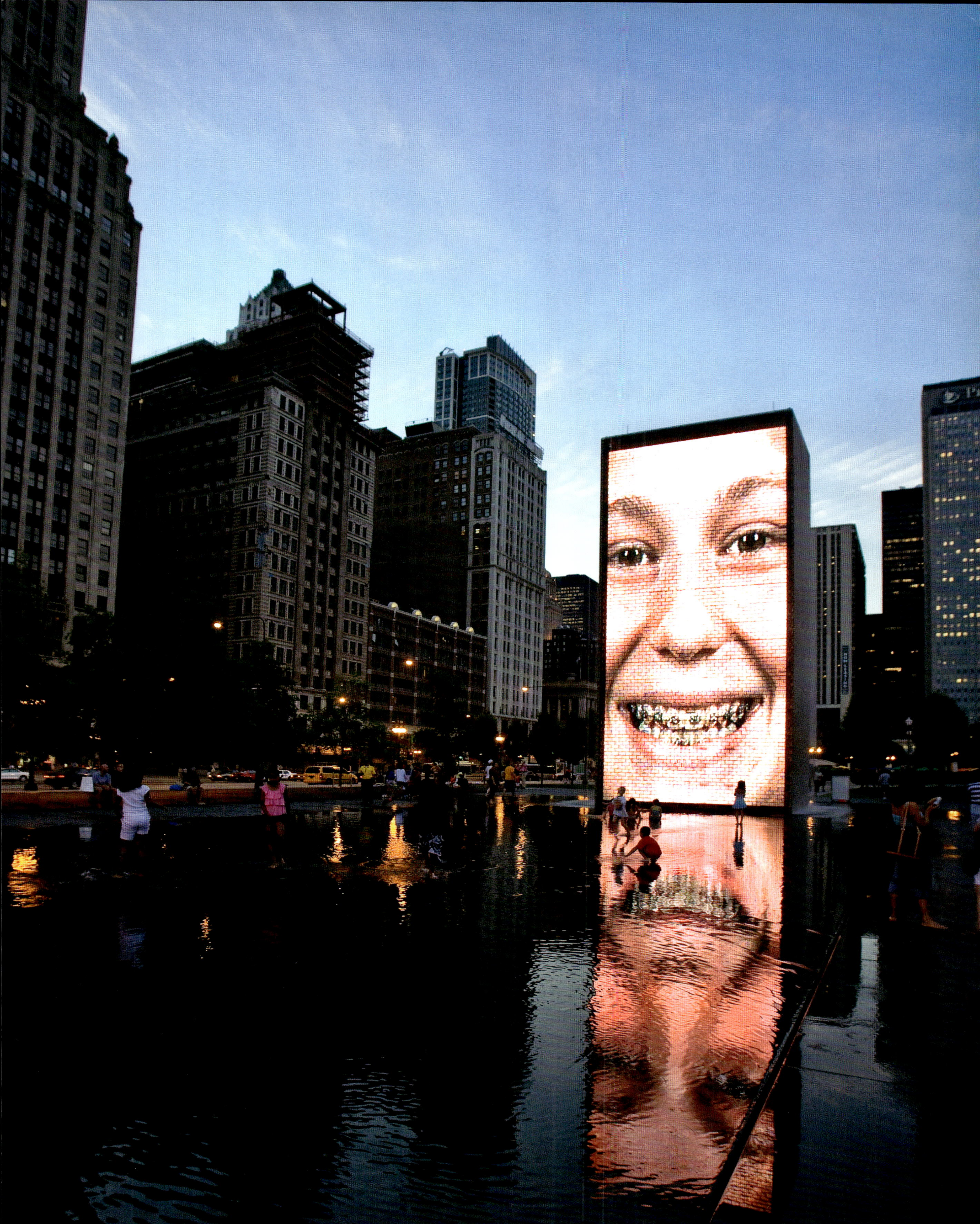

The Son's Tale

The Crowns are a close family, so much so that Lester Crown claims that "when you speak to one of us, you speak to us all." Initially, his son Steve's involvement was marginal, with the other members of the family organizing the search for the right artist and overseeing the preliminary stages of research and development. But Steve was part of the selection panel and was well aware that the family was unanimously behind Plensa's proposal. It was, he says, a surprising choice, but the forty-four-year-old European sculptor who was still relatively unknown in the States so impressed the family that he "came from last to first place almost overnight."

When Steve fully enters the story—towards the end of 2001—there were already questions being raised over the height of the fountain, most especially from the neighboring Art Institute, on whose board Steve sits. The initial budget projections were also higher than expected and there were questions over the directions being taken by the subcontractors. In short, there is a serious danger of the piece slipping out of Plensa's control towards an unspecified end and cost.

Steve's first priority is to confront these complex issues and put the project back on track. It's not an easy task, but—as we will later see—it was his decisive action that saved the day. He introduces the new maxim that henceforth the mission is to build the fountain and leave the design in the hands of the artist.

From now on Steve is involved with every element, from the hiring and firing to the supervision of the fabrication. He sits in on the key meetings and when the artist travels to the various construction sites, Steve goes too. It's an extraordinary commitment for someone who is also running a large slice of the family's multi-billion-dollar business interests.

Understanding the complexity of the project—having a bird's-eye view of all the components, as he calls it—it's Steve who gives the team "permission to fail." He knows that there will be false trails, but also that they are better

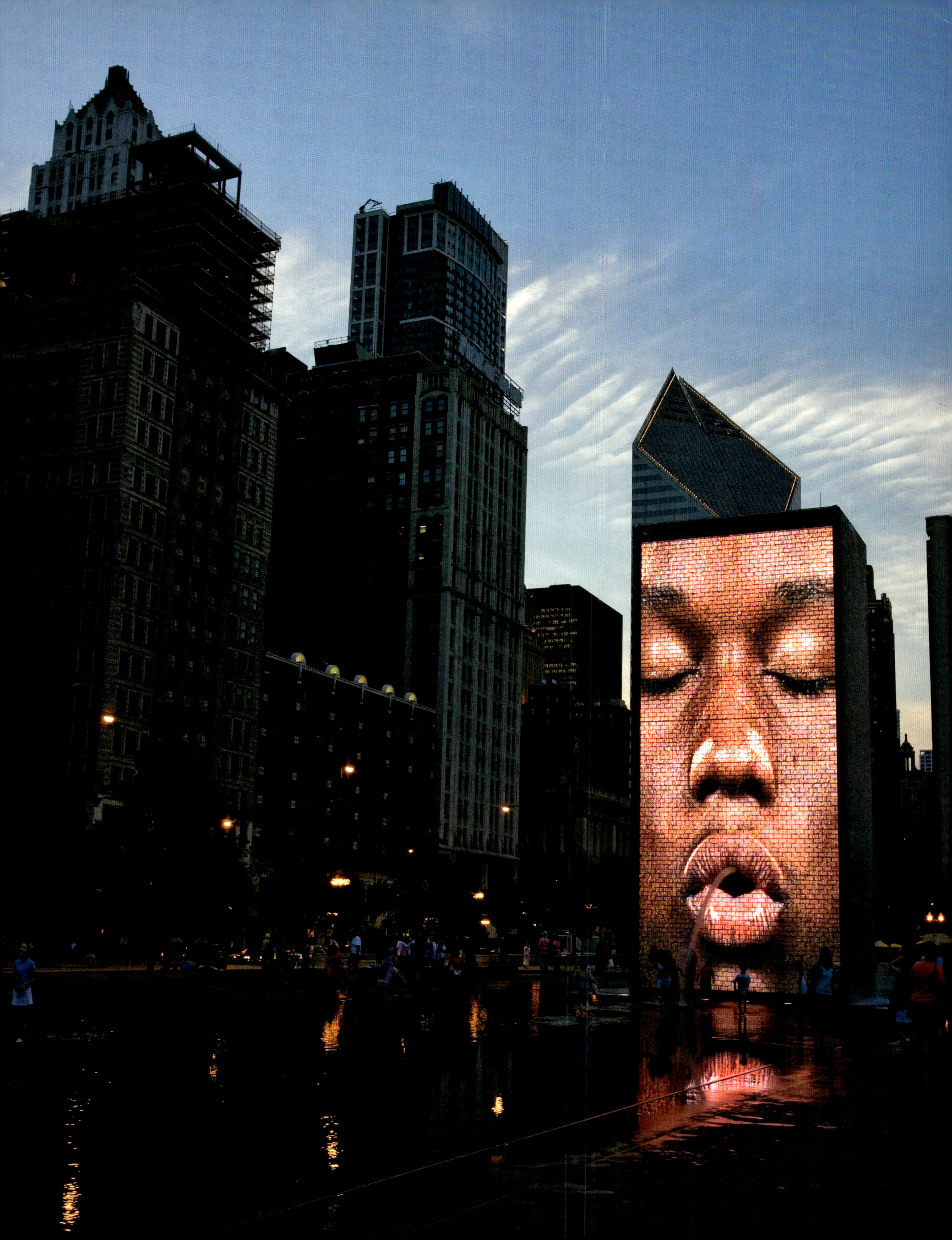

confronted on the workbench or back lot than for them to return as gremlins
to haunt the finished product.

But while he understood the physical structure as well as anyone, he admits
today that neither he nor the family had any idea of the impact the finished
piece would make. "We were happy to help provide something that would last
for our lives, our children's lives, and their children's lives. But never in our
wildest dreams did we anticipate the excitement and sheer joy the fountain
would give."

Steve Crown tells me that initially they would have been happier sponsoring
the ice rink, which was at least a concept they fully understood. Susan tells the
same story, adding that an ice rink directly involves people, which is one of
their prime considerations. But Bryan had proved successful in his quest for
other sponsors and all that remained was this ill-defined homage to water.
Lester Crown, the family patriarch, presided over an informal meeting in their
offices on North La Salle, and the entire family was brought into the discussion.
In the early days, at least, that principally meant his children, Susan and Jim,
but it was a decision that would also involve his other son, Steve, and Jim's
wife, Paula. Feelings were divided, for the foundation's money had not previously been used for arts funding and there were many other uses to which it
could be put. Nevertheless, the family made a commitment to proceed.

At this stage, no one knows the final cost. No one knows who the designer
will be or what form the fountain will take. But having made the commitment,
Lester, Susan, and Jim Crown draw up their general criteria. Foremost, it
should be a fountain for the people, a space that Chicagoans will use. They
foresee it as something timeless and yet reflecting the latest technology;
something that might evolve, that could be updated if necessary in the years
to come; something they hope will redefine what a fountain can be in the
twenty-first century.

> "It all seemed a dream of wonder, with its tale of human energy,
> of things being done, of employment for
> thousands upon thousands of men, of opportunity
> and freedom, of life and love and joy."
>
> From *The Jungle,* Upton Sinclair's classic story of immigrant life in
> Chicago during the early years of the twentieth century.

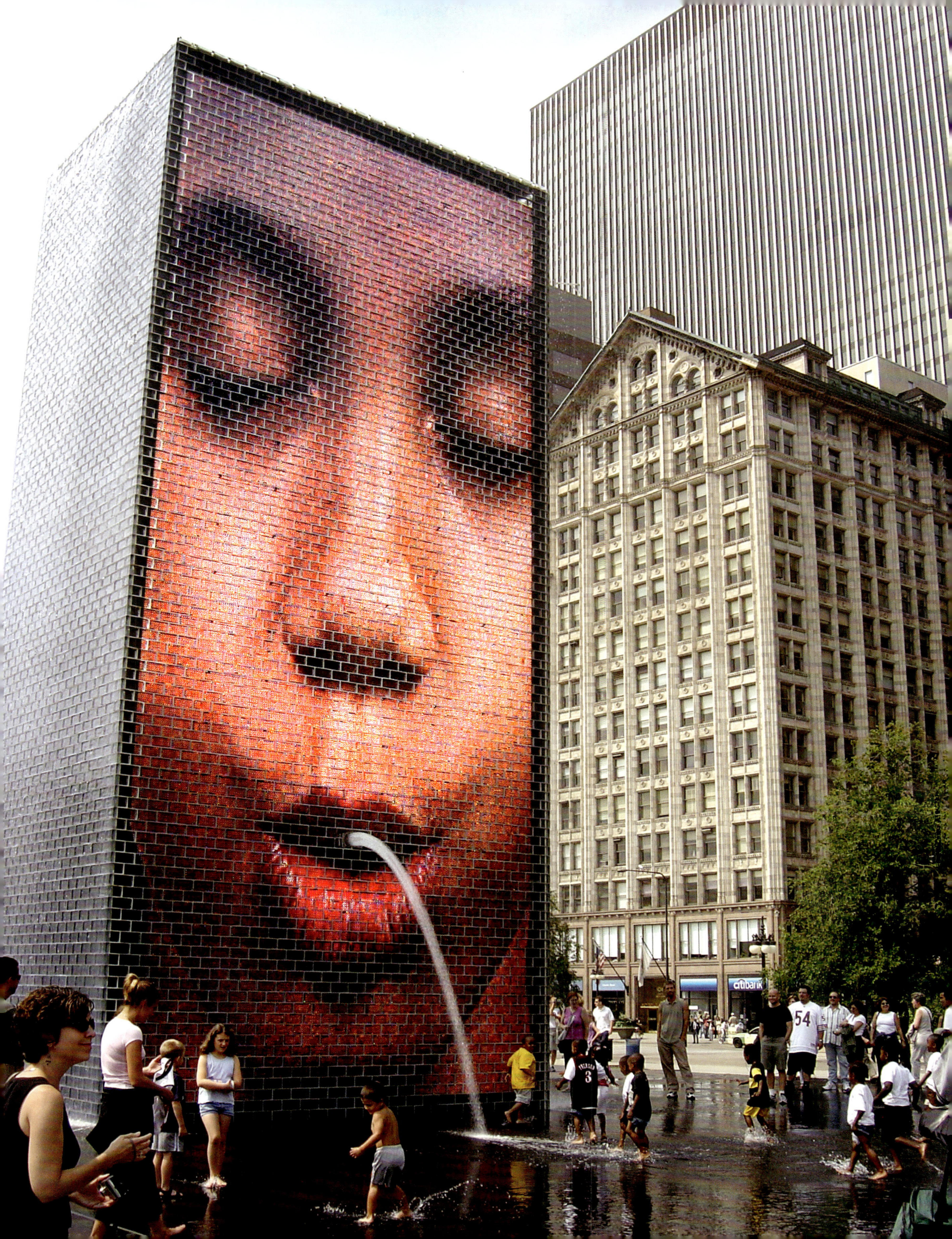

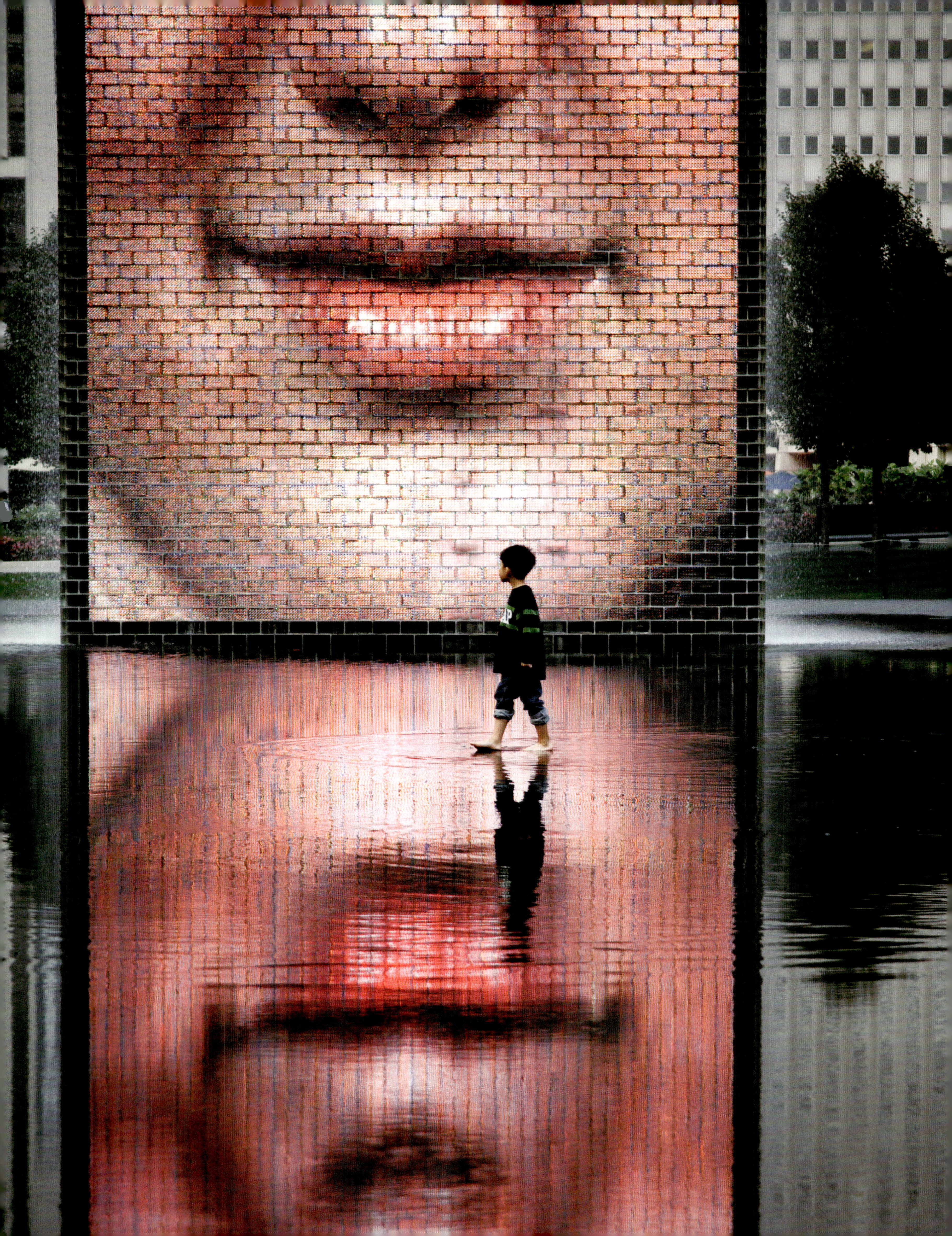

An Absolute Responsibility

Like many other Orthodox Jewish families escaping the impoverishment of Eastern Europe in the late nineteenth century, Lester Crown's grandparents, Arie and Ida, emigrated and settled in Chicago. It's a common enough story: Arie was an itinerant peddler seeking a better life for his wife, daughter, and six sons. But unlike Upton Sinclair's protagonist, the Crowns found that the reality lived up to the dream. Before long they had good reason to be grateful for the opportunities the U.S. had given them.

Lester's father Henry began the family sand and gravel business with his brother Sol in 1919 and, despite the Depression and the war years (Henry served as a Colonel in the U.S. Army, a fact still celebrated by his uniformed portrait in the Crown offices), by the early 1950s the family was already in a position to buy a twenty-three percent stake in the Empire State Building. Over time, the family business had diversified into construction, defense contracting, and real estate, along with sporting and other interests, and had become a multi-billion-dollar empire.

When Lester Crown talks of "the absolute responsibility of giving back to the society," it isn't just words: it's a moral imperative. The family's priorities are Chicago (the city that has become home), the underprivileged in general, and Jewish causes in particular. Over the years, the Crowns have supported Jewish and African-American colleges, schools, hospitals, recreational facilities, and concert halls, while Henry Crown was an early supporter of the civil rights movement. Since the mid eighties the family's private charitable foundation—named in honor of Arie and Ida—has been managed by Susan Crown.

Starting from Scratch

An initial scheme for a fountain does already exist. Even before John Bryan approached the Crowns, the architectural partnership of Skidmore, Owings & Merrill (SOM)—who'd worked on the park and parking lot from the beginning—had been asked to draw up some ideas for a prospective fountain.

Susan Crown recalls that between March and September 1999 the plans evolved from the initial drawings to the maquette stage, but also that she was growing increasingly uncertain about the direction being taken. She defers to Lester, believing that a more creative approach should be taken. Her father agrees: "The way we need to go is to find someone with vision." But at this stage, the balance still leans towards an architectural visionary, or more precisely someone with experience of working with water.

SOM's proposal takes the form of a standard fountain, but with a series of additional features representing the evolution of the city from prehistory to the present: what is essentially a recreational area for children and families. While this fulfils at least one of their criteria, both Lester and Susan see the potential for creating something more innovative—something in keeping with the tone set by other ventures in the park. At a meeting with Ed Uhlir, James Feldstein, and other Millennium Park representatives on September 22, the Crowns announce their intention to broaden the search and seek other design ideas elsewhere, a conviction that is strengthened when Gehry's plans for the music pavilion are unveiled in early November.

A City of Giants

From the outset, the *Crown Fountain* already had a lot of competition, and not only from what was being constructed elsewhere in Millennium Park. Downtown Chicago is a shrine to modern architecture, while its public plazas are littered with substantial artworks by such masters of the twentieth century as Picasso, Chagall, Miró, Oldenburg, and Calder, largely acquired under the city's enlightened "percent-for-art" policy. And that's not even to mention the extensive collection of the Art Institute or the direct comparison that was likely to be made with the nearby *Buckingham Fountain*.

All of this would become part of the challenge, helping to determine the scale and ambition of the *Crown Fountain*. Plensa was later to admit that he remained uninformed about the other projects on site, that the fountain was conceived and developed very much in isolation. But neither he nor the

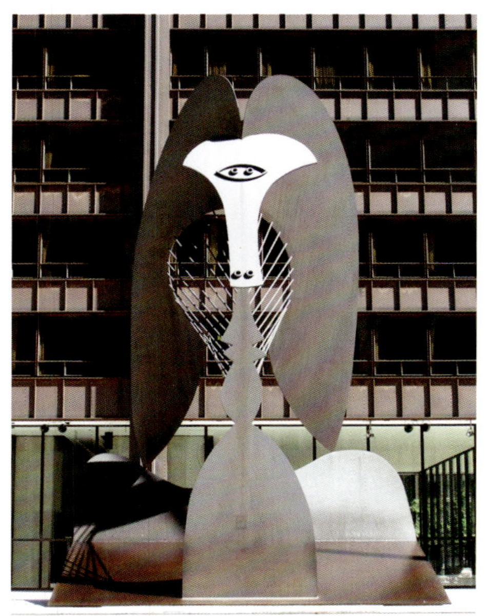

Pablo Picasso's *Untitled,* 1967.

Crowns were in ignorance of the enormity of the challenge offered by the city and in particular by what the Art Institute symbolized. In Plensa's words: "A museum is a place where they preserve tradition, just as the function of the artist is to break down that tradition. Museums and artists are not naturally working in the same direction." Unlike some latter-day Quixote, Plensa would be well aware that the windmills at which he was tilting were indeed giants, and the response would need to be appropriate.

First Steps

As she readily admits, although experienced with other aspects of the foundation's activities, Susan Crown is not an expert on contemporary art and initially thought in terms of commissioning an architect. The family has been building for three generations and has a good working knowledge of construction in general. When it comes to water, the Crowns know where to find the latest innovations and the first place they look is in the hotels and casinos of Las Vegas, including the spectacular new water display at the Bellagio designed by Los Angeles-based water engineers, WET Design. But their brief remains open, with Lester and Susan adamant that the solution they are seeking should be like no other fountain in existence. But where do they begin looking for something that doesn't yet exist?

Among others, the family turned to Bob Wislow of U.S. Equities Realty, the company that was project-managing those aspects of the park sponsored by private interests. Wislow had been actively involved with contemporary art since co-founding Sculpture Chicago in the eighties, an initiative that sited temporary installations on the narrow extension to Grant Park that ran beside Michigan Avenue. A family friend, he was delighted to join an ad hoc advisory group that included Richard Gray, Alan Schachtman, and Ed Uhlir.

Central to this informal circle was Robert Stern head of the architecture school at Yale and a friend of Susan's since her college days. Stern had been Susan's first port of call and had agreed to draw up a short list of prospective architects. Meanwhile, art consultant Emily Nixon was assisting Wislow in assembling

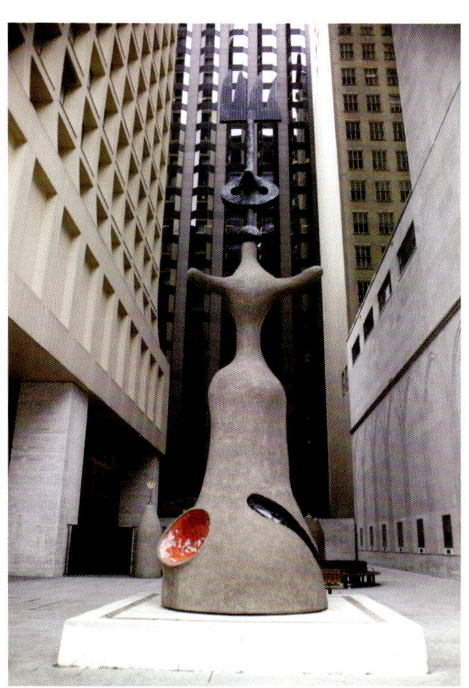

Joan Miró's *Chicago,* 1967.

prospective artists. But it fell to another family friend, Jack Guthman, to throw
Jaume Plensa's name into the hat.

The Collector's Tale

Jack Guthman's office is everything you'd expect of a high-flying U.S.
lawyer—and then some. We're on the twenty-eighth floor and two windows
give onto a panorama that stretches from the Wrigley Building to the Michigan
Lake shoreline. On the wall hangs a Rauschenberg screen-print. It's eight-
thirty in the morning and Jack's already taking calls from behind his large
desk. He has his back to the lake, so I guess the view is all for my benefit.

He comes over to join me, modestly protesting that his part in the story
is a small one. Back in the fall of 1999 he'd been keeping up with the
developments in Millennium Park through his old friend at U.S. Equities,
Bob Wislow. One day Wislow called to say that the Crowns had agreed to
finance a fountain. Wislow was aware that Jack was a fellow collector of
contemporary art and asked to run a list of potential designers by him before
it was presented to the Crowns. Although today he can no longer remember
exactly who was included, what struck him at the time was that half of them
were architects. So Jack called Wislow back saying, "Bob, it's supposed to
be a sculptural piece, so why not focus on having more artists on the list?"

Now, it just so happens that Jack owns a work by Jaume Plensa, bought
from his first show at Paul Gray's Chicago gallery in 1996. And by another
coincidence, Jack, Bob Wislow, and their wives had been together in Paris
two years previously, when Wislow had almost literally stumbled upon a
retrospective of Plensa's work at the Jeu de Paume. And Plensa makes
fountains. Although Jack isn't sure if the artist works with water, he clearly
recalls seeing pictures of the light beam "fountain" the artist had recently
installed in Jerusalem.

Wislow agrees to support Plensa's inclusion in an extensive presentation
for Susan Crown. In a curious corollary, she was later to comment that, of

the one thousand images she saw in Wislow's offices that day, "the piece
that I kept returning to was Jaume Plensa's light sculpture in Jerusalem."

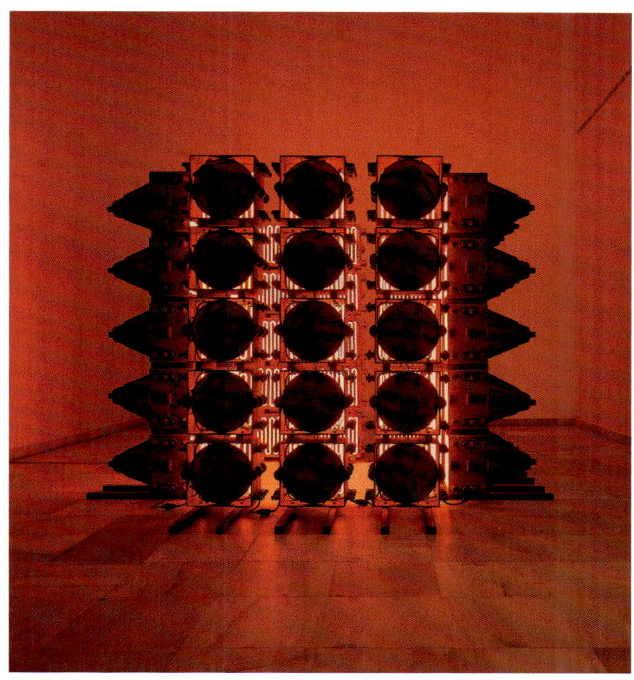

Jaume Plensa's *La Neige Rouge,* 1991, the earliest work in the
decade-long evolution that led to the Crown Fountain.

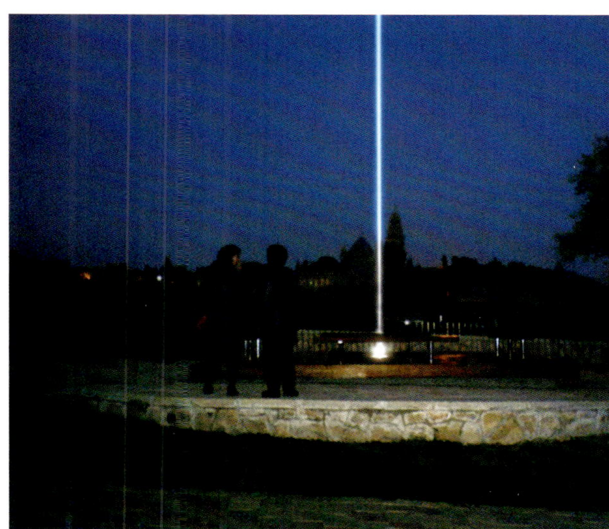

Jaume Plensa's *The Bridge of Light,* 2002, Jerusalem.

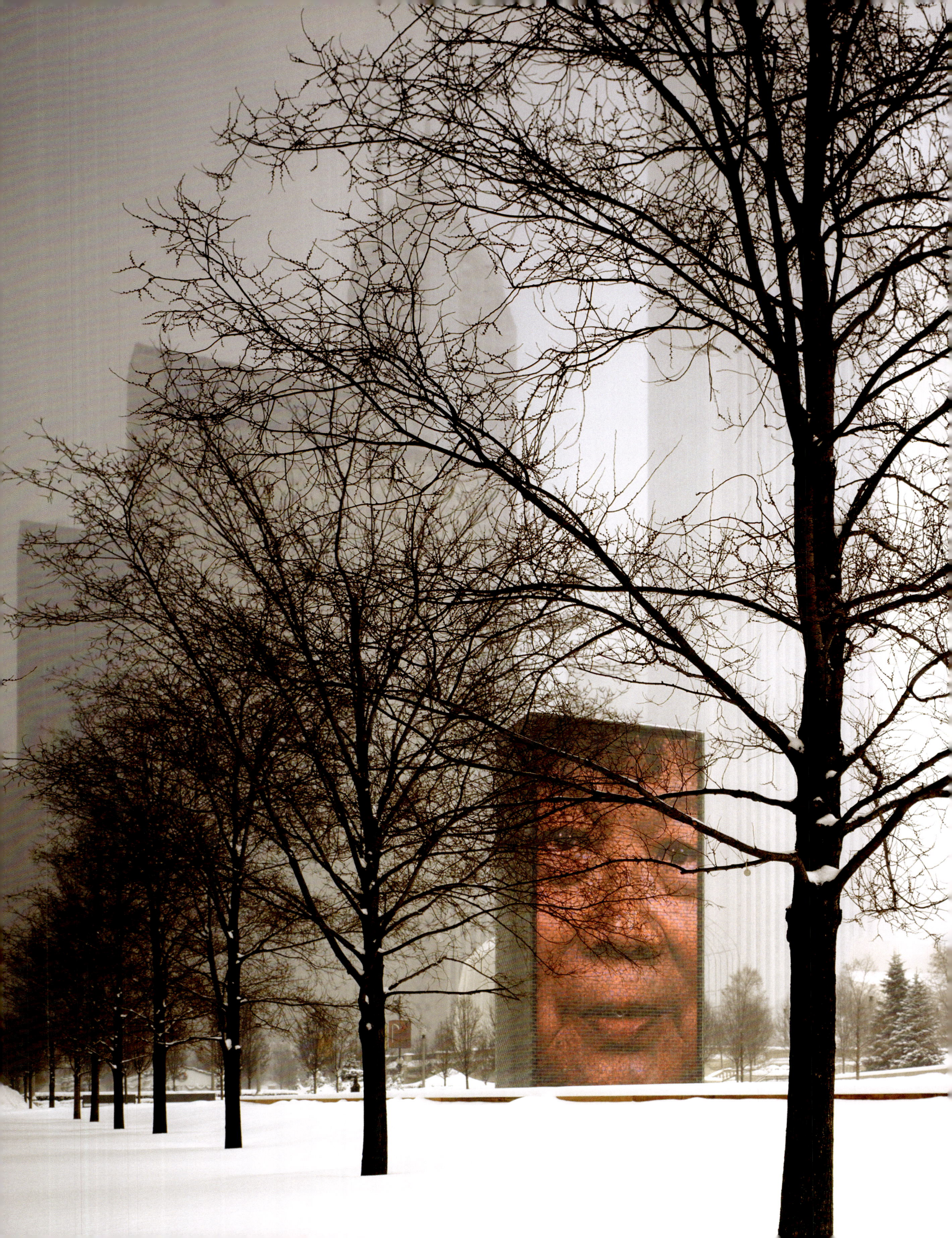

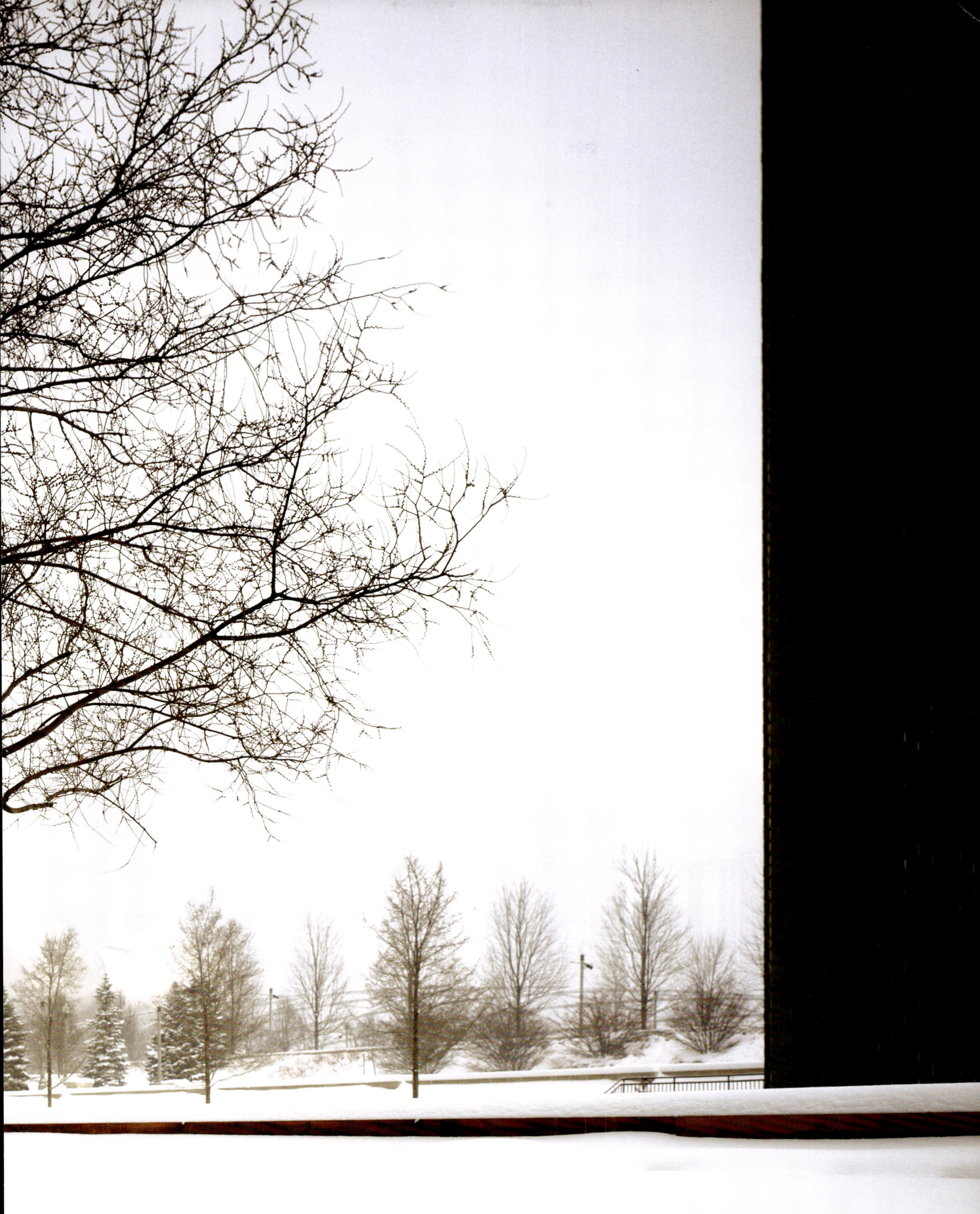

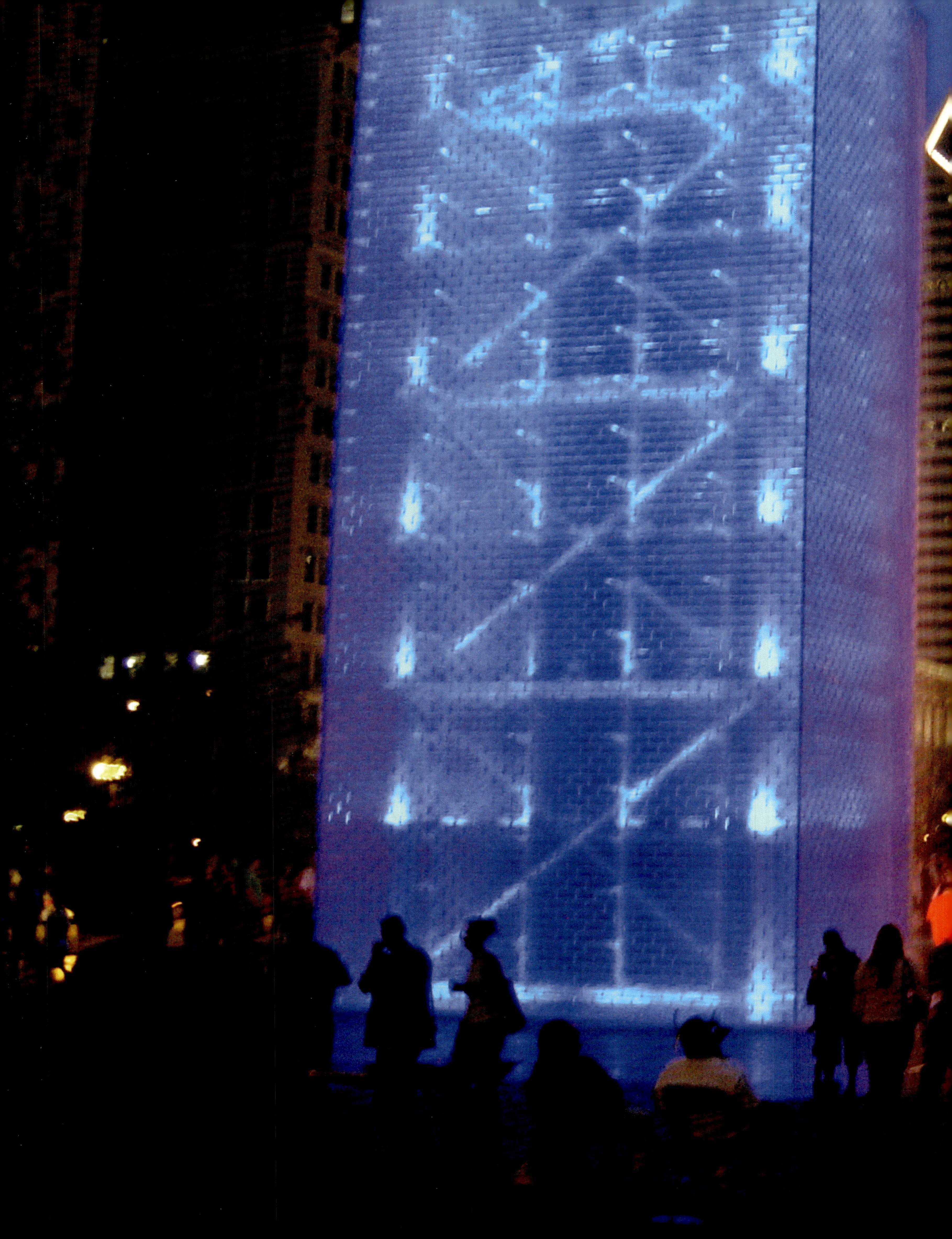

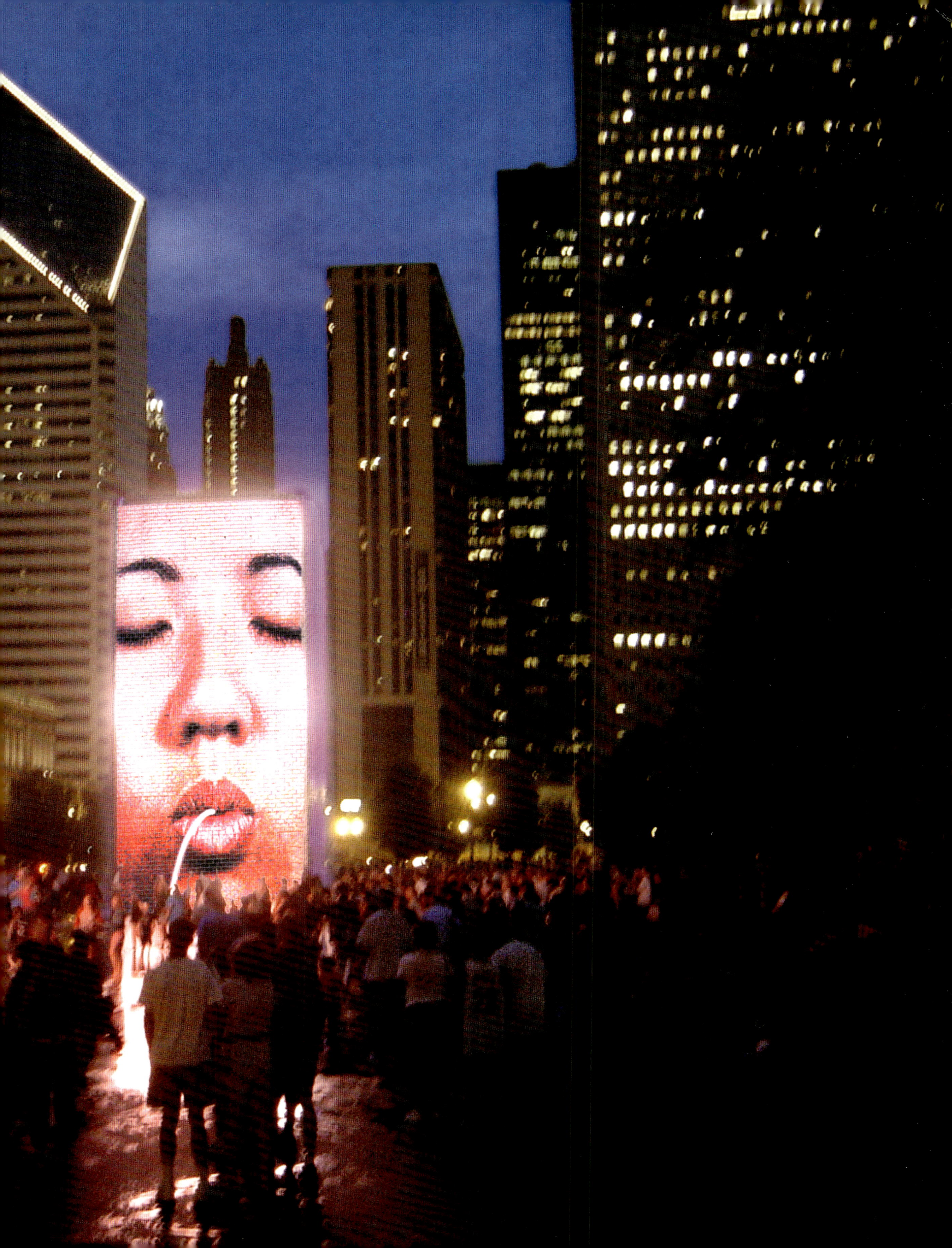

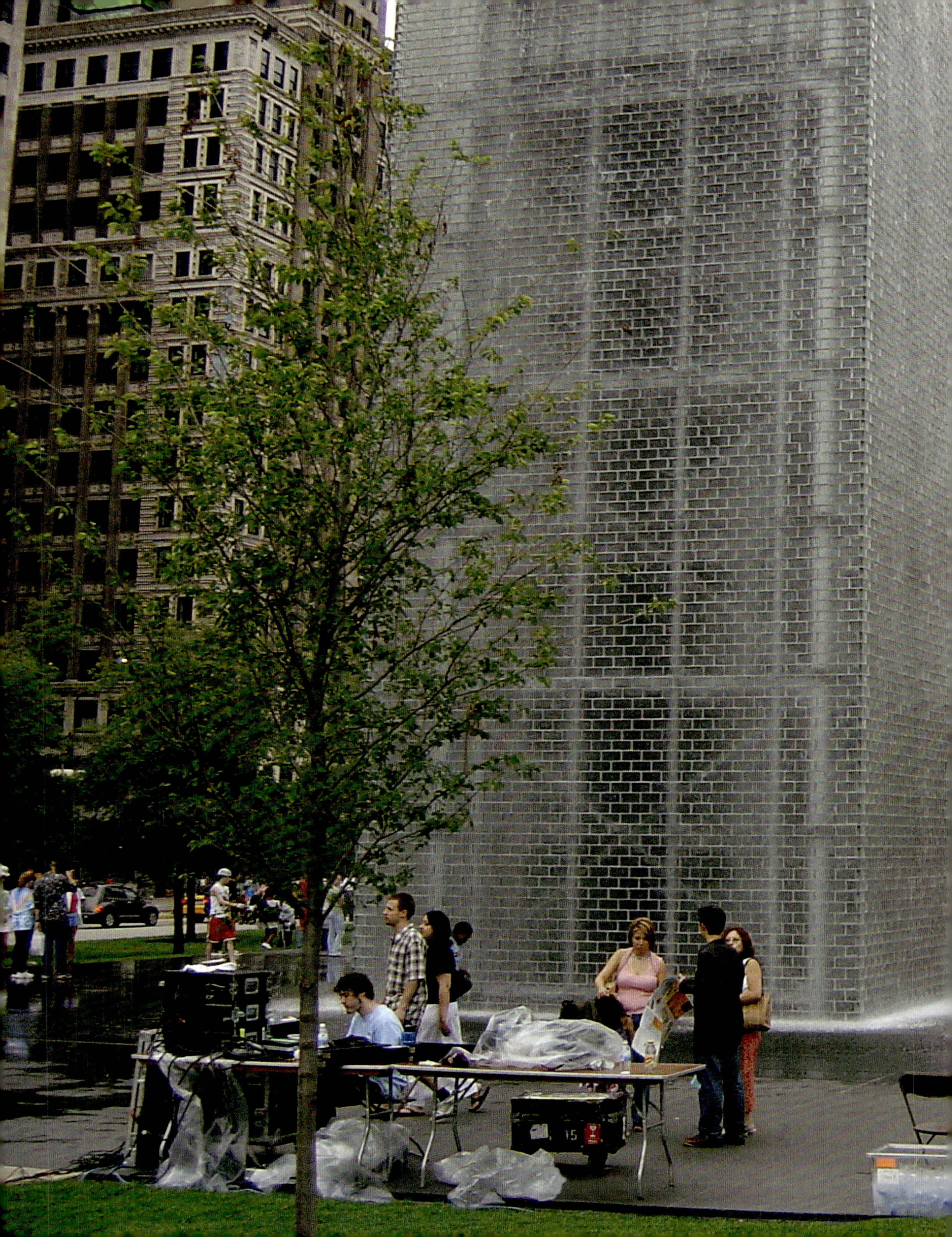

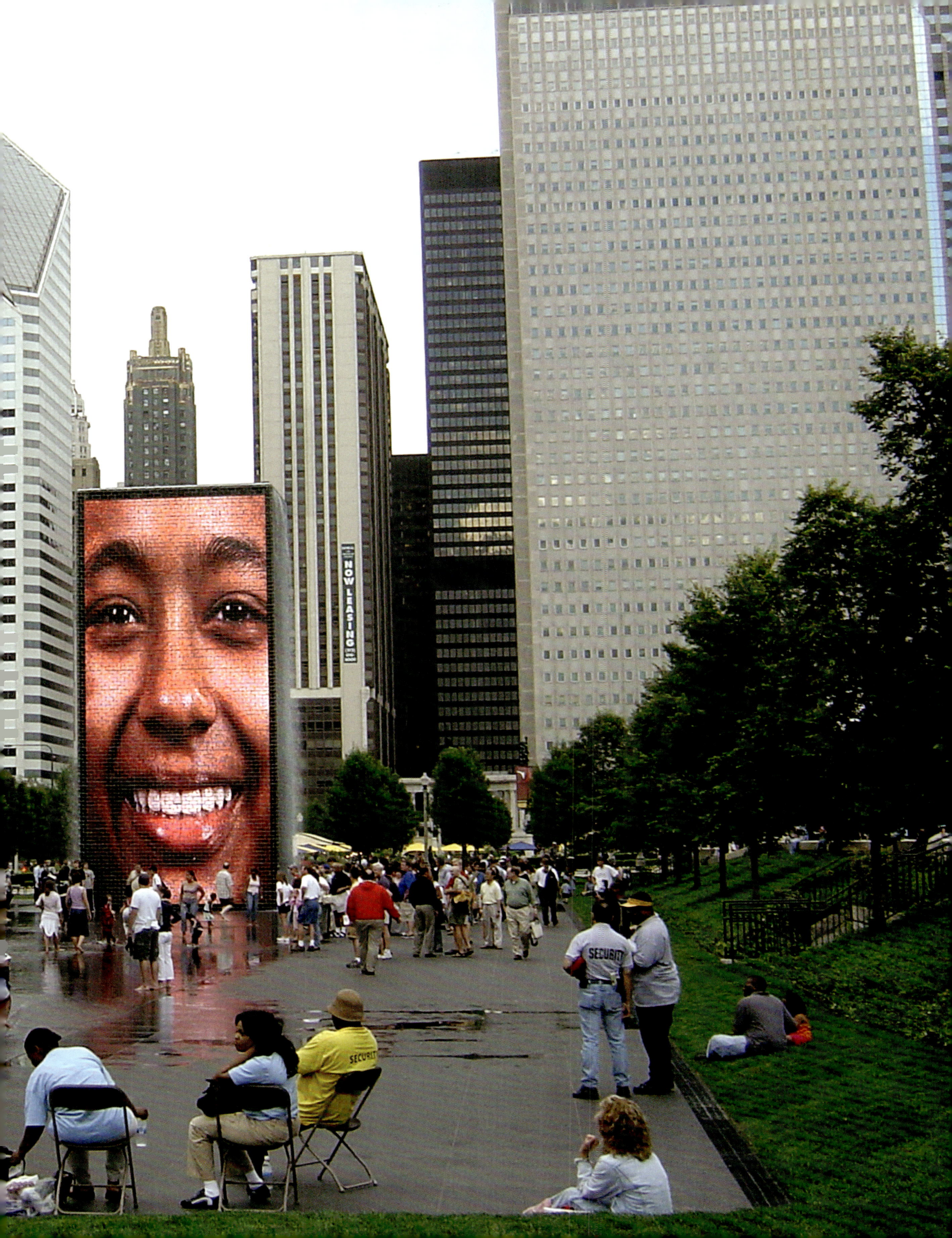

NOW LEASING
SECURITY
SECURITY

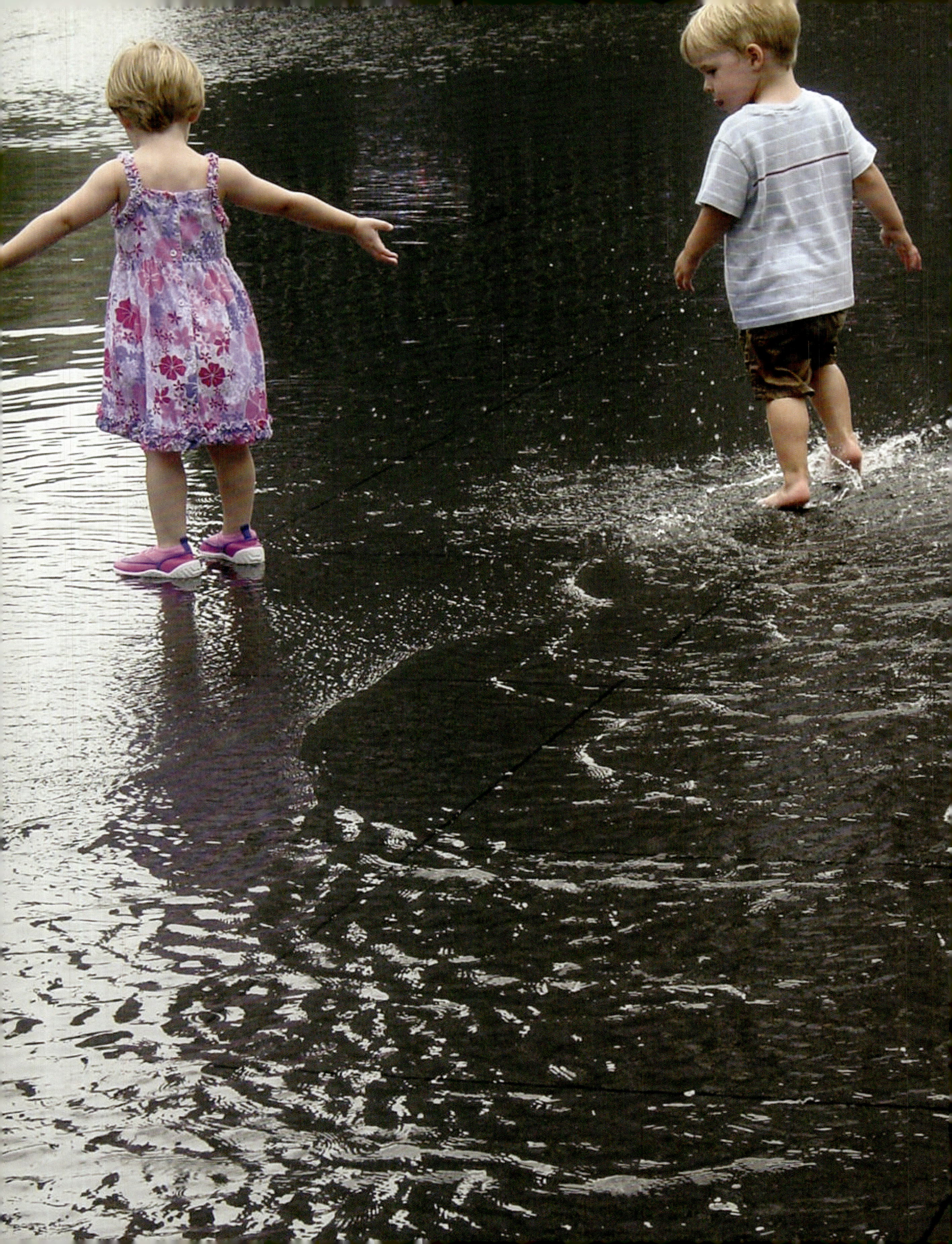

3

The Race Begins

It's now January 2000 and Jim Crown has come up with the idea of a design competition. Following the presentation of the prospective candidates in Wislow's office, Susan Crown has reduced the initial list to just three names. One of them is Plensa's and Paul Gray passes on the news to the artist in Barcelona. Although widely recognized in Europe, and having produced public projects in many other parts of the world by this time, Plensa is still relatively little known in America and the competition is tough. Robert Stern is pushing for the veteran architect Robert Venturi. Then nearing his seventy-fifth birthday, Venturi is one of the leading exponents of the eclectic Postmodern style, although this would be his first fountain. The third nominee is Maya Lin, another alumna of Yale and a former classmate of Susan Crown. Lin is internationally renowned for her *Vietnam Veterans Memorial* (1982) in Washington, D.C., a seventy-five-meter-long granite wall bearing the names of the fallen. But in Montgomery, Alabama, she'd also designed a fountain for the *Civil Rights Memorial* (1989), a cause close to the late Henry Crown's heart.

That same month, all three are individually invited to Chicago to meet the Crown family and to visit the site. Despite working on a major exhibition for Madrid's Reina Sofia National Museum that will open in just three weeks, Plensa flies out on January 13 for an initial conference with the family. During the meeting Lester Crown takes the artist to one side and tells him that he's expecting something "unforgettable": the exact same word that Wislow has used to describe his recollections of Plensa's Paris show during his discussions with the Crowns. From the artist's perspective, the meeting couldn't have been more encouraging.

> "One of my first meetings with the Crown family and its advisors took me to Millennium Park, to the site where the fountain was to stand. The enormous visual power of Chicago and the family's enthusiasm had such an energizing effect on me that ideas for the project immediately began to germinate in my head and take root in my heart, despite the tremendous challenge that this invitation had placed before me."
> Jaume Plensa, April 2000

Plensa's ideas came fast and furious, and he called upon Paul Gray to help sift them into a manageable form. To remain in the running, he needed to deliver a concrete proposal by mid April. But while the basic form rapidly materialized, there were simply too many tangents, too many starting points, too many references, and too many histories to compress into a single model. From the beginning, Plensa made a mental distinction between form and content. The form would furnish the "body" of the piece, the necessary armature to physically construct the fountain, its pipes and tanks, the glass towers, the shallow reflecting pool that would form the heart of the plaza, and the LED screens upon which his images would play. Nobody had put these elements together before, but the technical problems still lay in the future. All this comprised the body of the piece and there would be specialized technicians to find the necessary solutions.

The Gallery's Tale

With offices in Chicago and New York, Paul Gray joined his father's gallery in 1982 and now largely runs the business originally started by Richard Gray twenty years before. Although he didn't give Jaume Plensa his first solo showing in Chicago until 1996, Paul says that the gallery had been keeping an eye on his work since the mid eighties, but adds, "He was always too busy in Europe to fit us in."

The first thing he points out is that, with the exception of a handful of individuals, most people's perception of the project began when the *Crown Fountain* was already complete. And to begin with a *fait accompli* and work backwards is perhaps to miss the roller coaster ride of the true story. The gallery had been involved with the Millennium Park project from the outset. Richard was sitting on its art advisory committee, but this effectively precluded him from proposing any of his own gallery artists. On the other hand, Paul had been instrumental in introducing Plensa's work to Jack Guthman, and it would be Guthman's comments to Bob Wislow that ensured Plensa's name went on the list.

Paul says that during his first telephone conversation about the fountain, Plensa was in turn excited by the enormity of the opportunity and daunted by the realization that it was certain to go to someone more famous. After several hours of intense conversation, the artist reached the conclusion that it was all or nothing; that the proposal would have to be something "totally amazing" or he would be simply wasting his time.

Knowing both the project and its key players better than Plensa, Paul assumes the role of friend, councilor, and trusted advisor, and the two work closely together over the following three months, perfecting the form of the all-important presentation. Paul remembers Plensa returning to Chicago in April 2000 with his laptop and the minimalist wood-and-Perspex model, which now sits in Steve Crown's office. But as Paul says, "the Crown family were as much taken with Jaume himself, with his sincerity, with his willingness to take creative risks, and with the way he'd begun by taking a long, historical look at the meaning of fountains."

In the following months and years, Paul continues his role as close friend and advocate. He attends endless team meetings with the artist, interpreting the nuances of at times fraught confrontations as the project takes shape, falters, and then regains momentum. There are times when the artist is convinced the project won't materialize and Paul is there to reassure him. He accompanies him on the many trips around the country to source or supervise the manufacture of the various components. But he says that while Plensa may have needed a helping hand in the darker hours, he never needed any creative help. "Creativity he has in abundance—I think he is a genius."

Back to the Roots

Plensa was not overly concerned by the body: his thoughts dwelled on the soul. What he thought of as the soul was in part the images that would fill the screens and animate the space, although from the earliest computer-generated impressions we can see how far these images of people and nature were refined in the years to follow. But beyond that was the quest for something far less tangible, and to pursue that we need to travel back in time with the artist.

To be a European, and more so to come from the Mediterranean, is to walk with history. It is not to be taken lightly, this weight of history that hangs around our necks. As a student living in a village near Cambridge, I rented a cottage whose beams were erected long before Columbus was born. And when I moved with my Catalan wife to Barcelona, we considered buying an apartment facing Santa Maria del Mar, the sailors' church where Columbus gave thanks on returning from his first voyage to the New World. Such facts of history are inescapable.

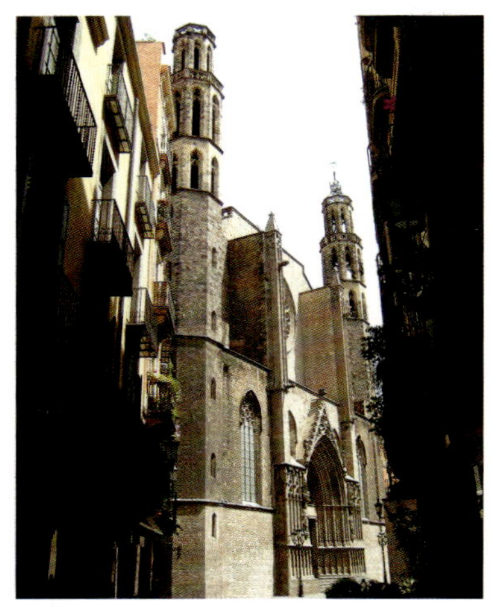

Santa Maria del Mar, Barcelona.

People so far removed in time that we dare not even call them ancestors. And yet the way they conducted their lives still impacts upon us. Not only do we walk their streets, drink our aperitifs in their squares, live on the foundations of their homes, travel from their cities, and arrive at their ports, but their thinking also permeates our very souls, is embraced in our language, in our street signs, in our city names. On the very day in 1492 that Columbus finally set sail, Ferdinand and Isabella set about expelling the last of the Moors from Spain. But something of the Moorish sensibility remains; it's married to the culture. So it ripples back in time, and cities, streets, and squares with five hundred years of history—and sometimes two thousand years—seem more

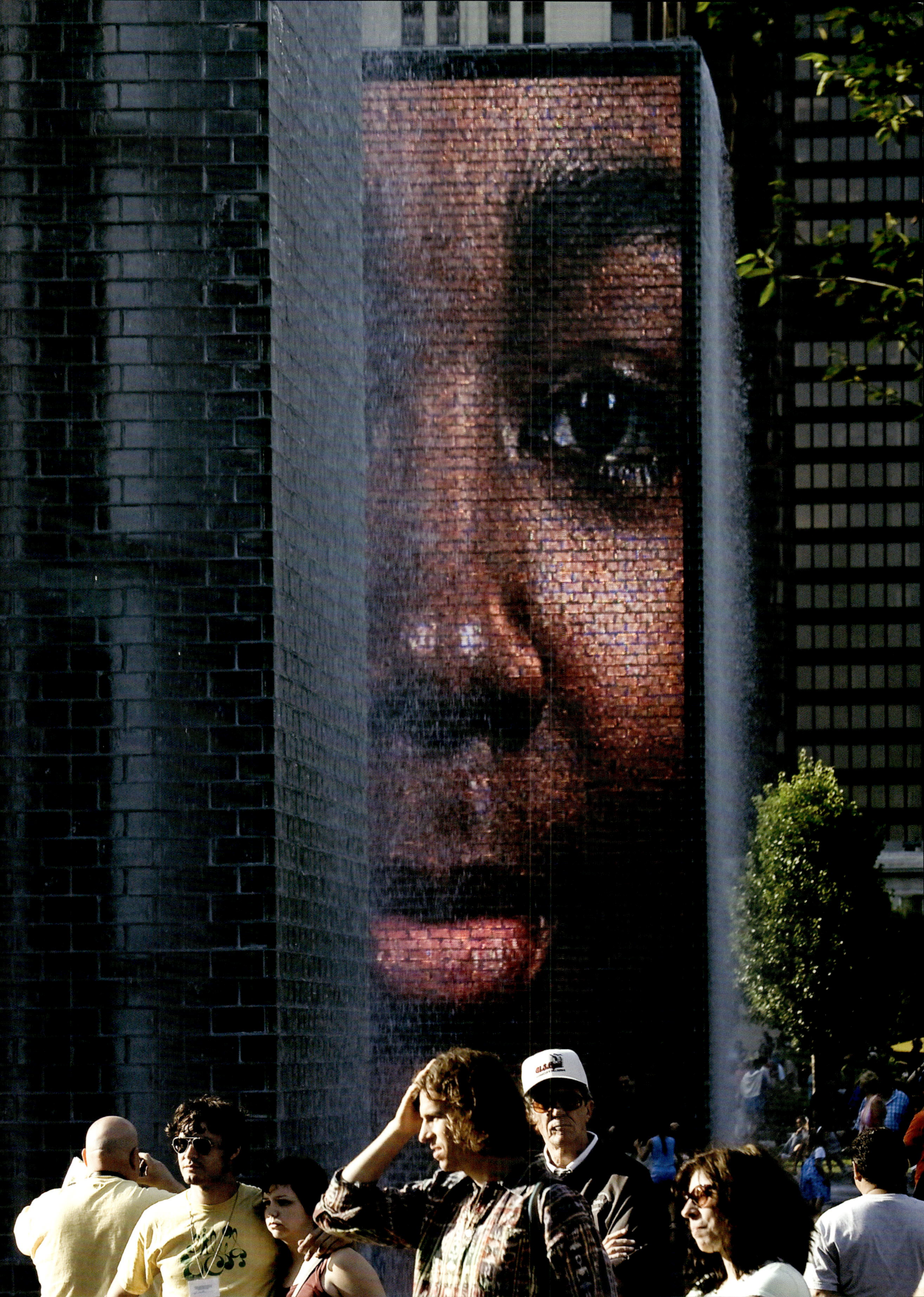

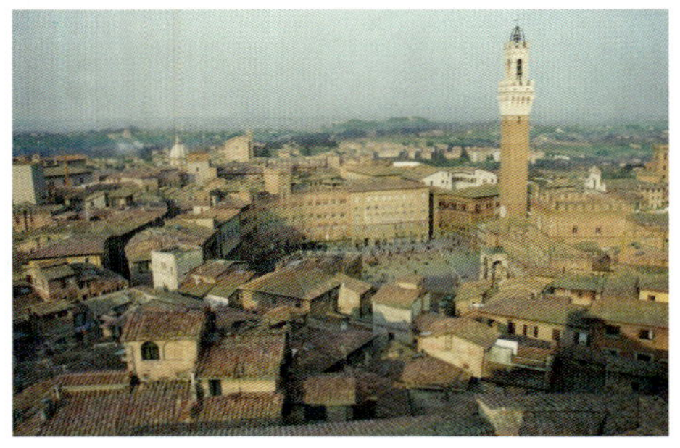

Siena, with its Piazza del Campo.

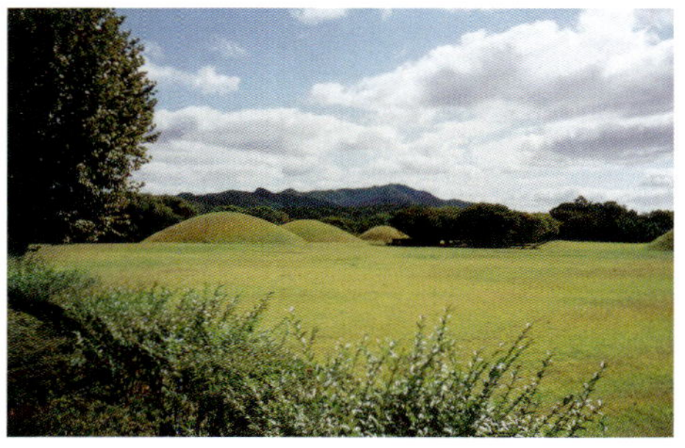

2,000 year old burial mounds in Kyongju, South Korea.

familiar, more *simpatico,* than the urban, modernist spaces built in our own lifetimes.

Take Santa Maria del Mar. Buried below its small square are the remains of those who died during the siege that ended on September 11, 1714. It is not a somber square, but it demands a sense of reverence. And not only for the national heroes who lie beneath its stones: the foundations of the buildings themselves demand respect, dating back to the thirteenth or fourteenth centuries. The lives that people lead before us, and the traces they leave behind, do count for something.

We are sitting at a table in Plensa's garden and I'm telling him about Kyongju, the ancient capital of what is now South Korea. Plensa likes the story, so perhaps it's worth repeating here. In the very center of the city lies a vast, two-thousand-year-old burial ground with some twenty tumuli: giant mounds of earth like small hills shrouded in grass. Despite its age, there's something almost contemporary about its minimalist construction, and the combination of form and an awareness of its history inspires a sense of serenity and calm in its many visitors. My point is that although you couldn't set out to build a space like that today, you could learn from it, abstract some of the basic principles. Plensa smiles and responds with a single comment: "Exactly!"

This, in part, was what Plensa was trying to communicate in that first presentation. That there are certain squares or meeting places that are charged with an aura, that interact with people in specific ways. Some encourage quiet introspection. Others produce the bustle of human contact, of commerce, of exchange. Still others are for relaxation and social intercourse.

We have journeyed to those squares together, sitting over a whiskey in the quiet of the artist's garden. He has taken me to Marrakech and to Siena's Piazza del Campo, and I have countered with tales of Esfahan and Persepolis, each of us savoring the particular nuances and magic of each space. And space here is the operative word. He is not talking of buildings, of architecture, of stone or concrete, but rather the empty spaces they embrace and which human beings populate. Or not, for here is the corollary. In the twentieth

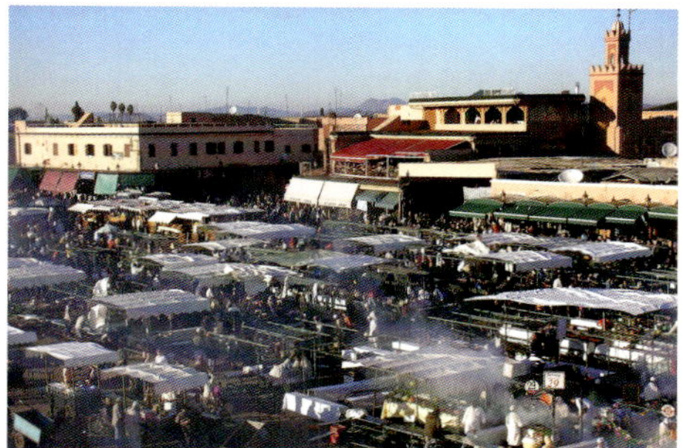

Jamaa Al-Fna square, Marrakech.

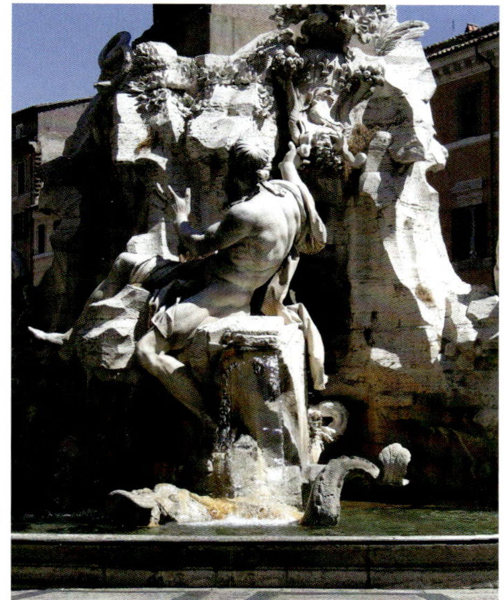

Fountain of the Four Rivers, Gian Lorenzo Bernini, 1651.

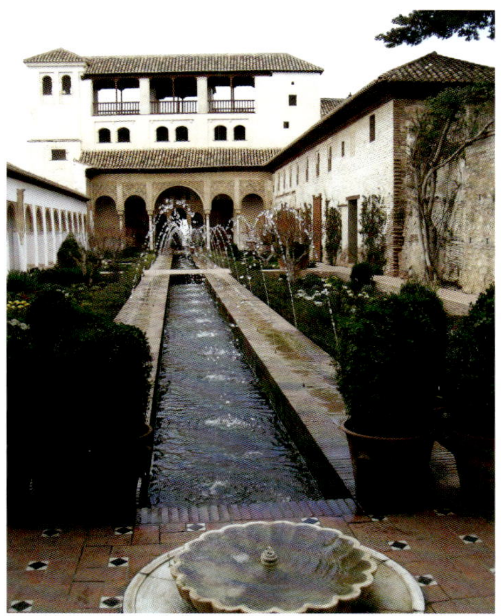

Alhambra, Granada.

century, with the best of intentions, we tried to rid ourselves of this baggage. "Less is more," said Mies van der Rohe. But in other hands, less became simply less. When we point to the landmarks on our skylines and say it's a "Libeskind," a "Foster," or a "Pei," we refer to the buildings, not to the spaces. Space has become the negative, the remnant, the leftover. The zero space around the perimeter, the gap in between. The shortcut between A and B.

Similarly, Plensa wanted to return to us the original meaning of "fountain" and the ways in which water was revered when civilization was in its infancy. When cities were first raised out of the desert and water was precious. When the inundation of the Nile meant life. When local gods resided in the bend of a stream or a mountain spring. Fountains came to preserve, embody, and celebrate those primitive but essential roots. Beyond their utilitarian ends, fountains were meeting places where the carved gods, nymphs, and gargoyles proffered the water of life: majestically, sensually, and at times mockingly, as is the way of our old gods.

Bernini's *Fountain of the Four Rivers* in Rome was not only a great work of art. It marked the survival of what Jung called the "primitive psyche," a largely unconscious expression of the last vestiges of our ancestral and animalistic past. On the other hand, the fountains in the Alhambra Palace in Granada were neither principally symbolic nor aesthetic, but were designed to humidify the air, cooling the fierce summer heat of southern Spain and creating a "paradise on earth" for the Caliph. Even the abundant food on his legendary table owed its existence to the Moorish watercourses that still irrigate one region of Valencia and to this day remain regulated by a tribunal first set in place by Spain's Arab rulers in the tenth century.

Walking on Water

Plensa has a specific dream. It's one he's had since childhood and any analyst would find it a gift. He wants to make it possible for people to walk on water. This is no messianic complex; nevertheless, like our earlier encounter with transubstantiation, neither can we completely dismiss its wider cultural significance. Water frequently figures in the biblical stories, which in turn were adopted by artists as their principal subjects, from the more dramatic interventions (the Flood or Deluge; the parting of the Red Sea) to the more intimate (the apostles casting their nets into the Sea of Galilee). Prominent among these, of course, is the episode of Christ walking on the water, one of the most haunting images of the New Testament. The illusion of standing on the sea is easy for a painter to achieve—but it's a whole different problem for a sculptor. Even after Plensa has built his shallow pool, he needs people to want to enter, to want to walk upon the water.

How impoverished, therefore, are the trickles and pirouettes substituted by modern architects, whatever the scale. All the more so when they serve only as an entrée to some anonymous office block, an afterthought around which no one gathers, beside which no one contemplates, and by which no one is inspired.

> "… a tale told by an idiot,
> full of sound and fury,
> signifying nothing."
> Shakespeare, *Macbeth*

Plensa wants to restore the fountain to its rightful place. Not at the periphery but at the center of people's lives. A fountain to which people effortlessly gravitate in a space that is welcoming. A beacon that reaches out with its celebration of life. A place for everyone with the traditional idea of water as the axis around which life turns.

There is just such a fountain in Plensa's hometown of Barcelona. It stands at the foot of the Monjuïc hill and was built for the Great Universal Exhibition of 1929. It's not a completely appropriate model, for its contrived dancing jets of water, colored by a pageant of changing lights and augmented by music, are not what he has in mind for the *Crown Fountain*. Nevertheless, on hot summer nights vast crowds of people make the pilgrimage to Monjuïc to sit and relax in the cool moist air. And an equivalent space, with an equivalent response, is what he hopes to achieve in Chicago.

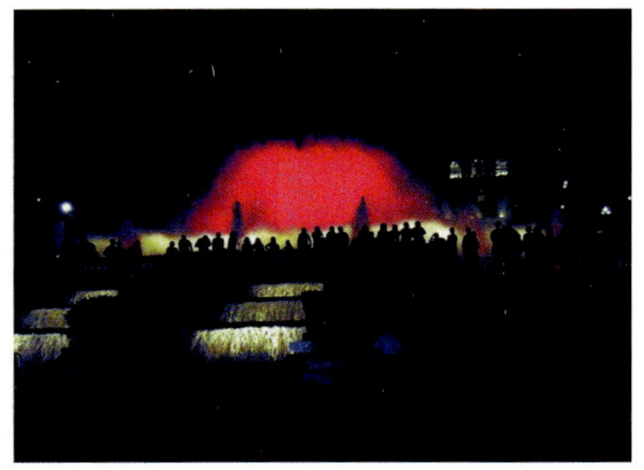

Monjuïc Fountain, Barcelona.

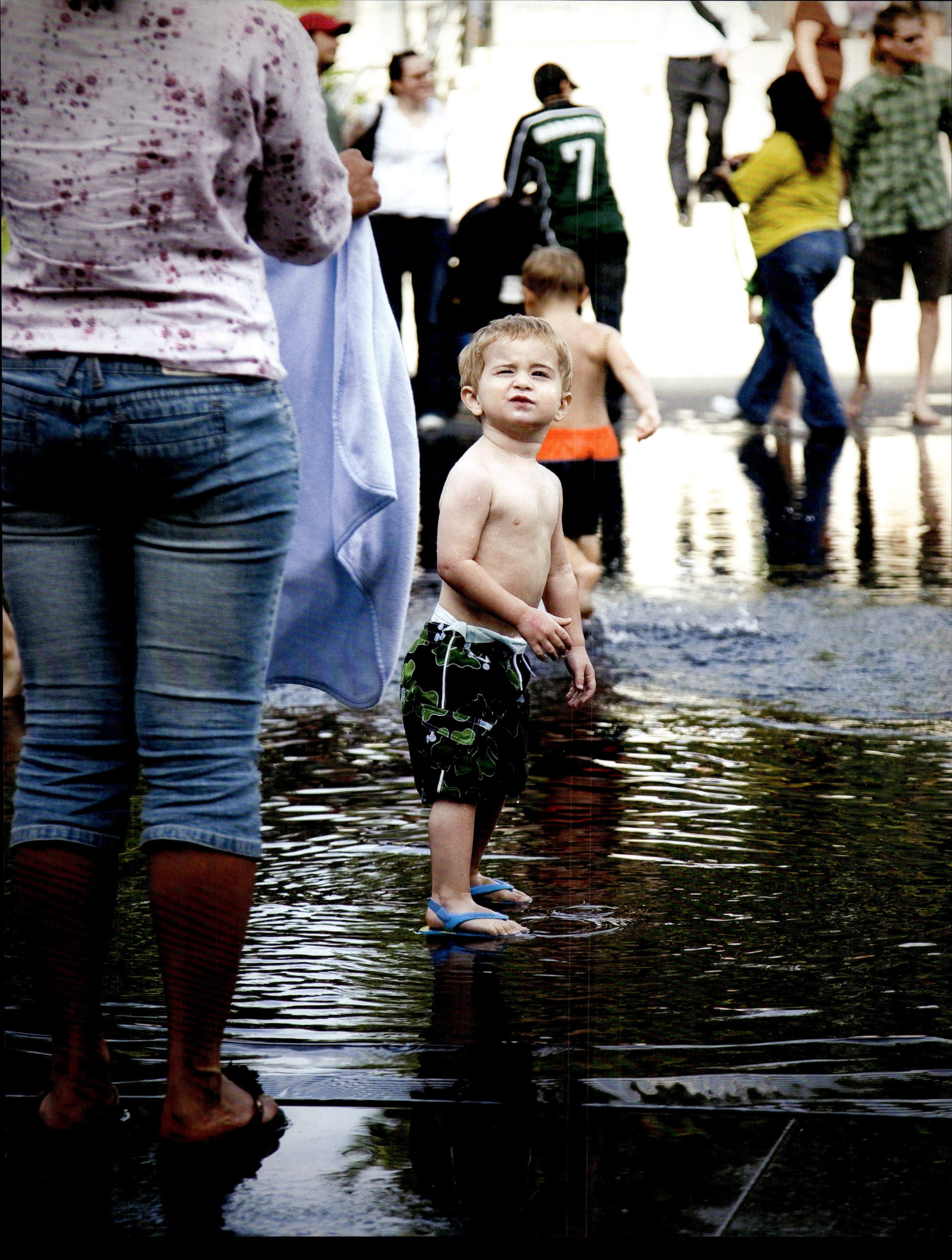

Ambitious stuff. But neither Plensa nor the Crowns want to reference in any obvious way the great fountains of the past. This much is clear: Plensa has to begin over. To make a truly twenty-first century fountain he first has to strip down the entire concept, spreading out the components on his workbench. He then has to reassemble it anew, and the tools he uses to represent his ideas are Photoshop and PowerPoint.

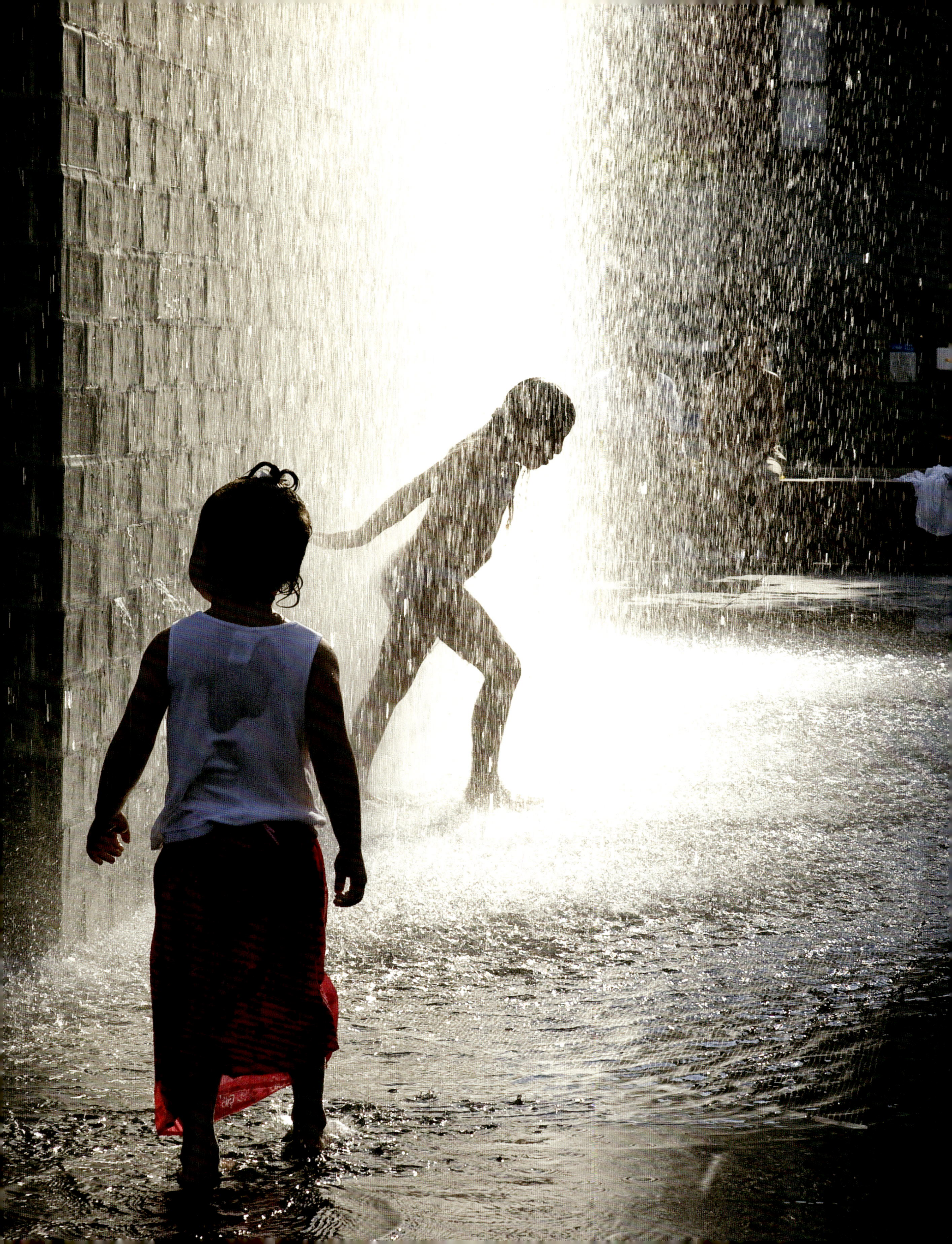

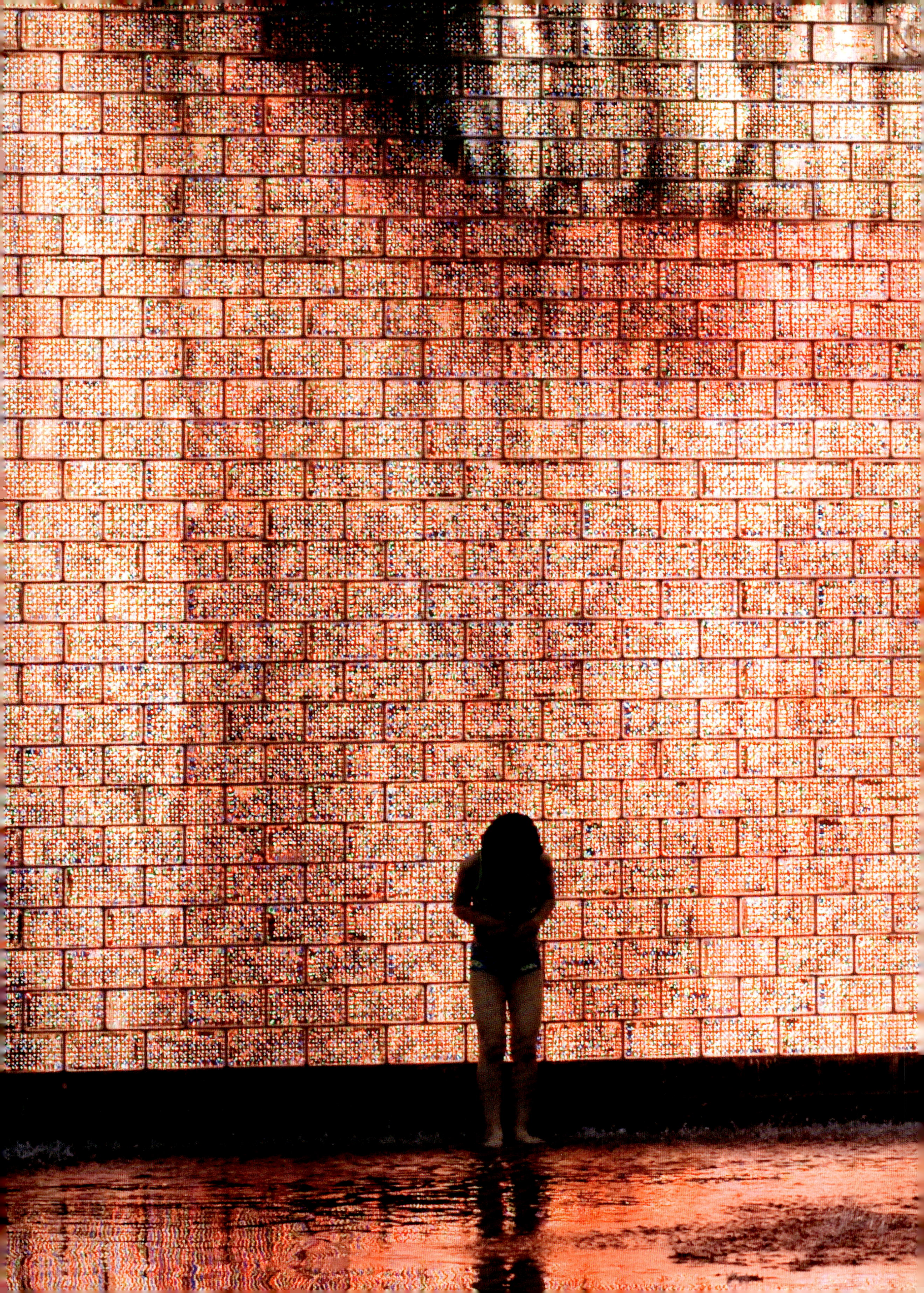

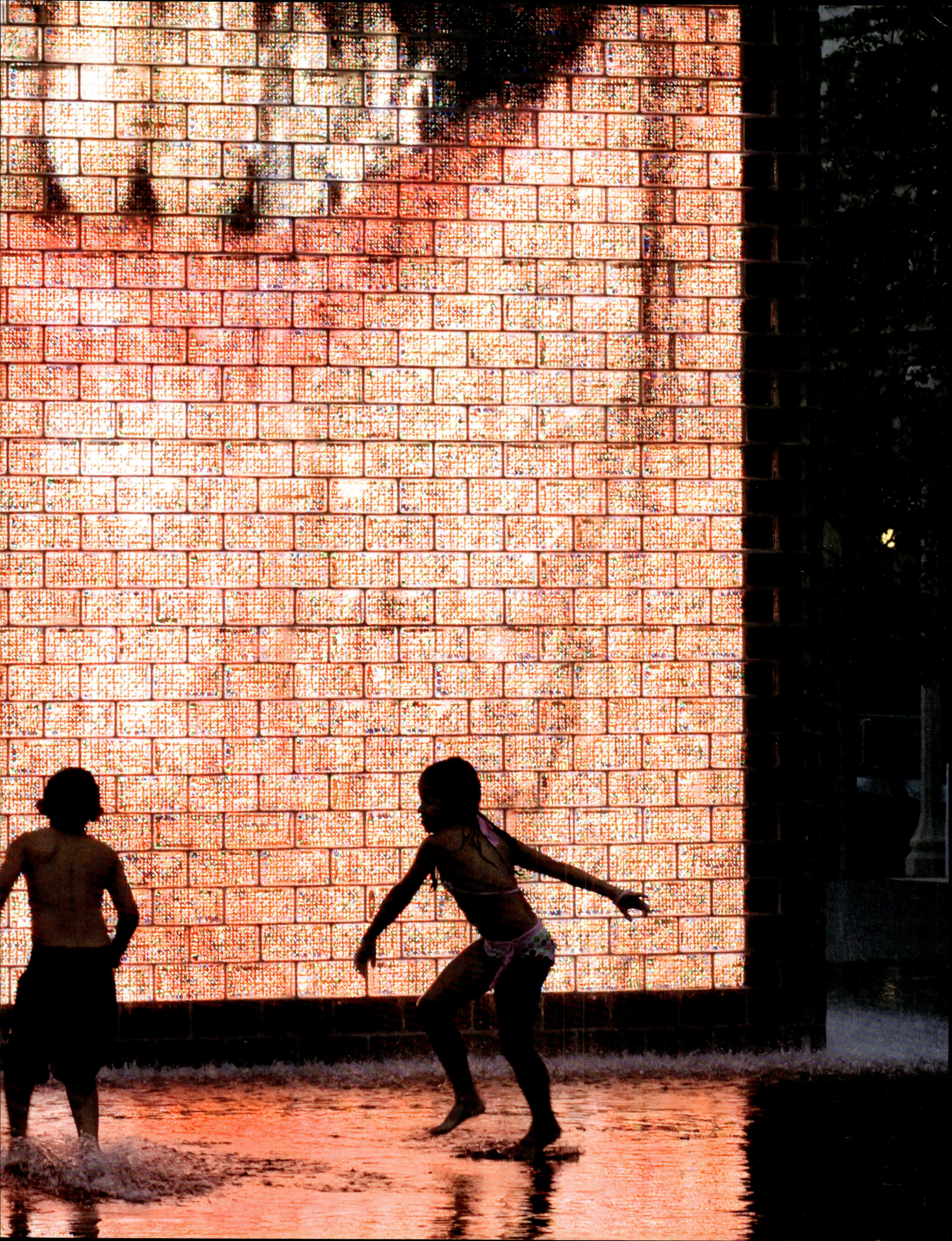

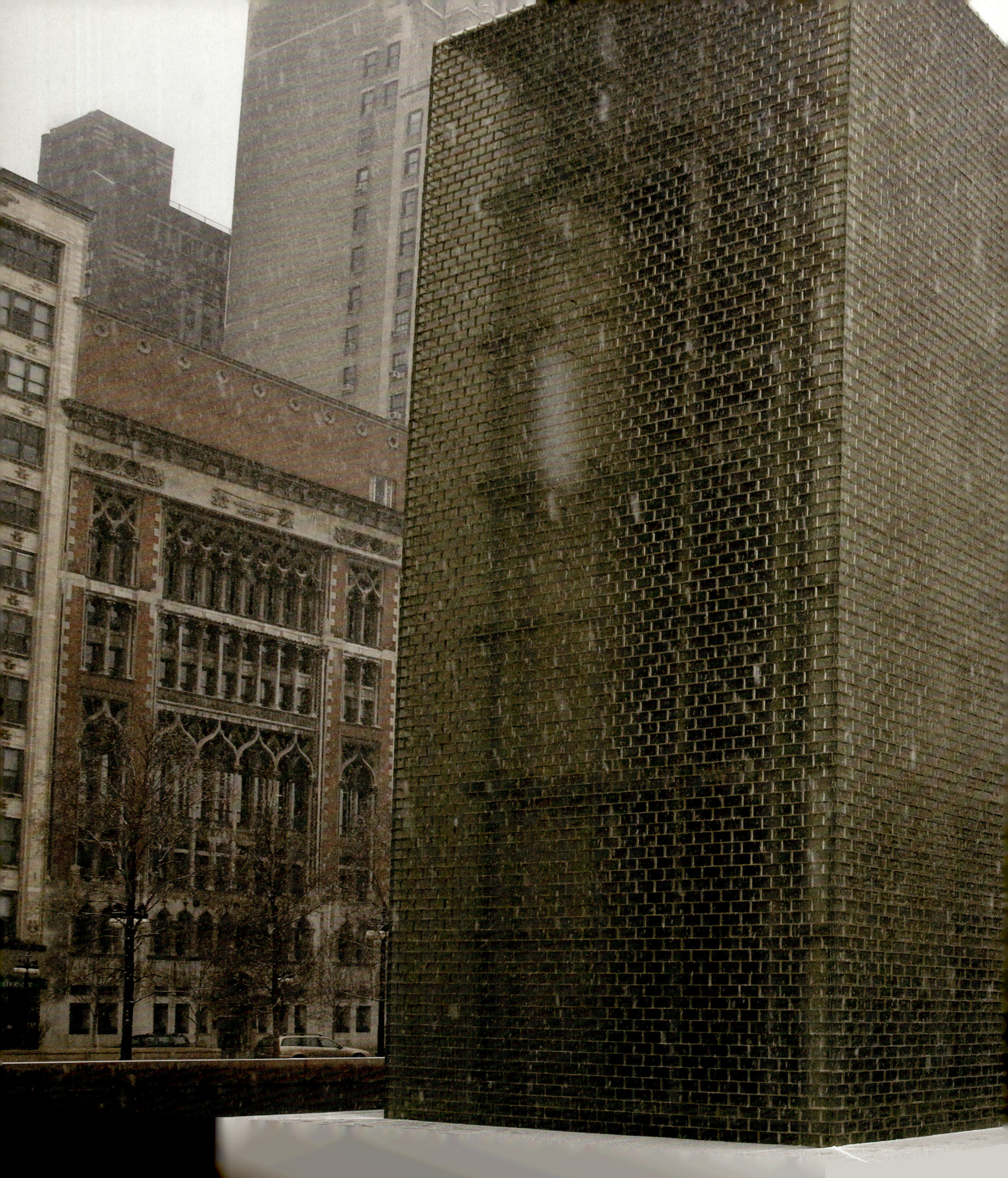

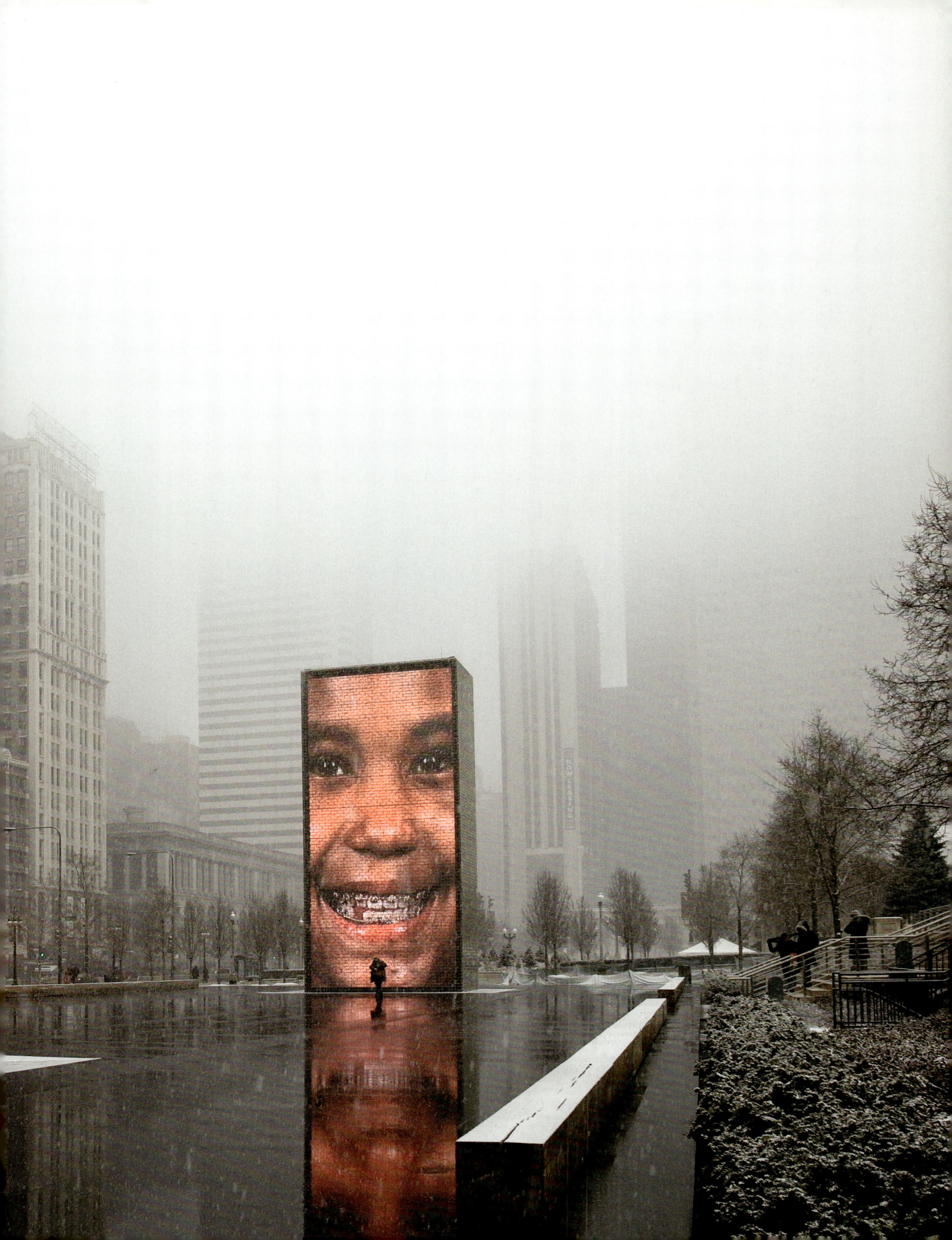

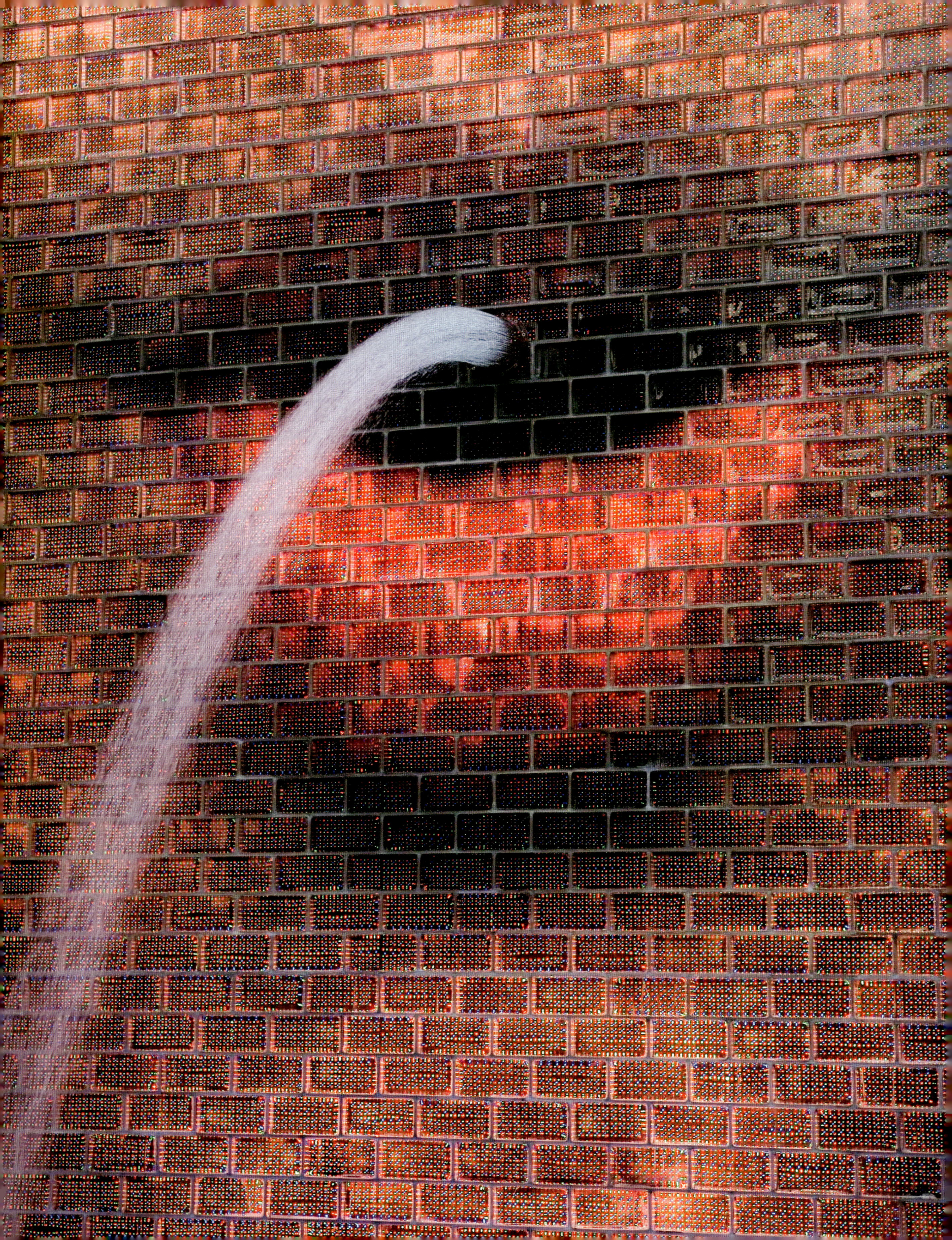

4

The Game Plan

Plensa finally made his presentation on April 19, 2000, before a panel that included Lester, Susan, Steve, Jim and Paula Crown, and representatives of the park and of the mayor's office. Earlier that same day both Lin and Venturi had made their pitches. Lin's proposal was for a characteristically low, horizontal design, with slow-moving water, although the artist hadn't advanced beyond the concept of piece. While admired by the Crowns, the consensus was that it lacked drama, that it was, by her own admission, "low-key." Nor did it meet their specific criteria for a unique piece reflecting the twenty-first century. Venturi, however, went for verticality. There was to be no actual water, but lighting would create a virtual fountain that continued to function through the harsh winter months. But again, it was conceived as a monument removed from its audience, a giant phallus more to be admired than used. What's more, at 150 feet the structure would rekindle those old objections to the construction of obtrusive buildings, most especially as this corner of the site actually borders Michigan Avenue and is cheek by jowl with Chicago's somewhat elitist Art Institute. Just across Monroe, the Art Institute was also built on forbidden turf and raised some objections of its own back in the 1890s. But it seems to have become used to its privileged isolation and, as time will tell, is somewhat particular about its new neighbors.

By the afternoon, and with only Plensa's proposal still to come, the Crowns are considering reopening the competition. They reconvene in the North La Salle offices and as Plensa is invited to present his ideas, the mood is sober.

But Plensa's presentation isn't simply a maquette; it's an entire game plan, a metaphysical barrage of sources, images, and meditations that fundamentally don't answer but rather ask the question: "What could a fountain be?"

> "No man ever steps in the same river twice, for it is not the same river and he is not the same man."
> Heraclitus, ca. 535–475 BC

It's worth spending a moment looking at that proposal. It begins with the planet Earth, passes by way of Heraclitus, Lao-Tse, the Buddha, and Babylonian mythology to an examination of water as the origin of life, its place in nature and as a source of nourishment. It switches from water as a reference to nature in an urban environment, to public spaces, to the history and evolution of fountains. And that's all before addressing the *Crown Fountain,* which Plensa at first approaches through the abstract notion of meeting points, interaction, and purity of form. And then, under the banner "A Fountain for the Whole World," he unveils the actual piece.

Although the presentation is largely schematic, the Crowns get a pretty good idea of the finished product. Or the body at least, for Plensa is already using that somewhat esoteric distinction. As Jim Crown will comment later in our story, the soul would take a lot longer to understand.

By the end of Plensa's presentation, the mood has changed completely. In Susan Crown's words, "We were all so excited!" Despite a slight apprehension over the dignity of the waterspout that will emerge gargoyle-like from the mouths on the twin LED screens—a doubt that will only be set to rest once the fountain is actually realized—no one is more captivated by the artist's performance than Lester. In the end it's the singer as much as the song, for the Crowns are entranced by the artist's enthusiasm, imagination, verve, and sheer breadth of vision.

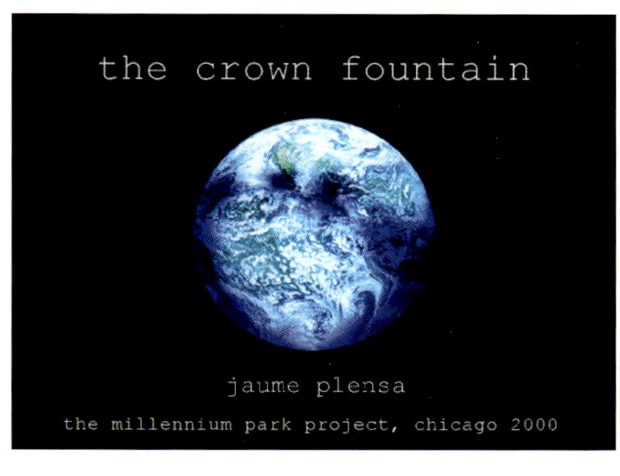

the crown fountain
jaume plensa
the millennium park project, chicago 2000

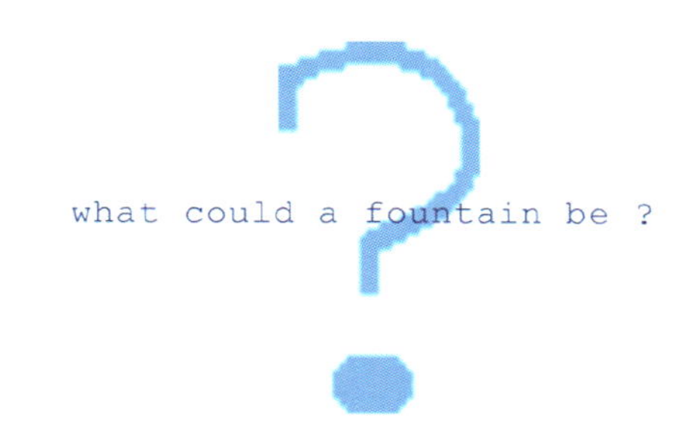

?
what could a fountain be ?

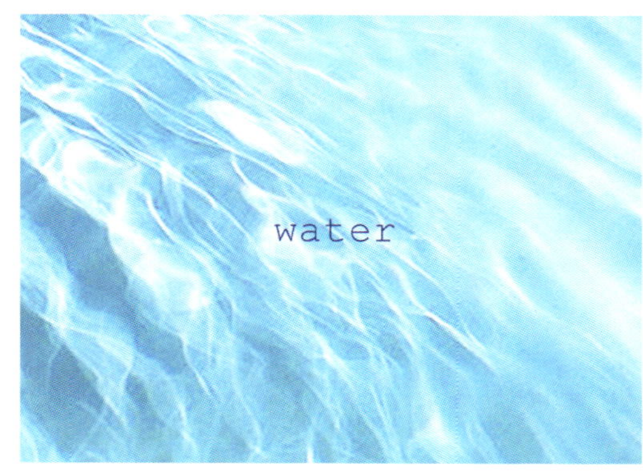

water

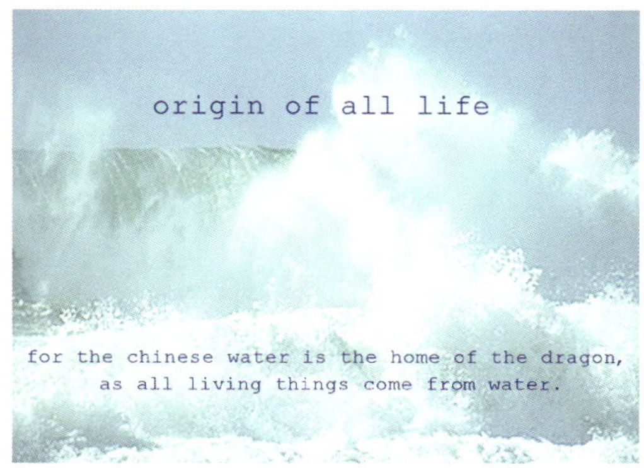

origin of all life
for the chinese water is the home of the dragon,
as all living things come from water.

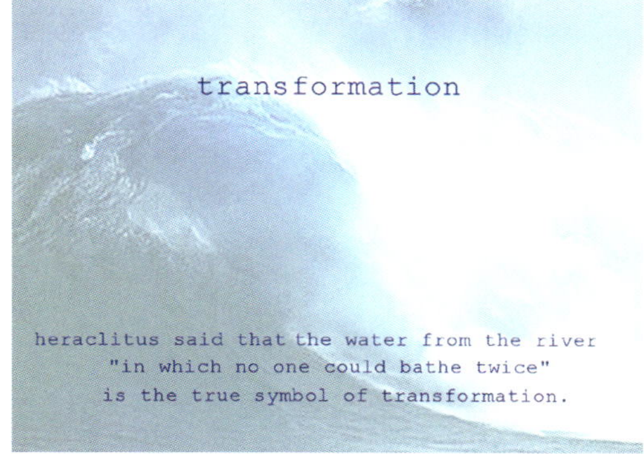

transformation
heraclitus said that the water from the river
"in which no one could bathe twice"
is the true symbol of transformation.

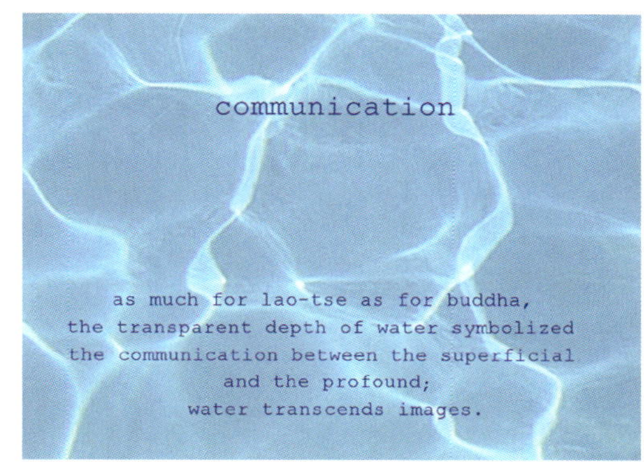

communication
as much for lao-tse as for buddha,
the transparent depth of water symbolized
the communication between the superficial
and the profound;
water transcends images.

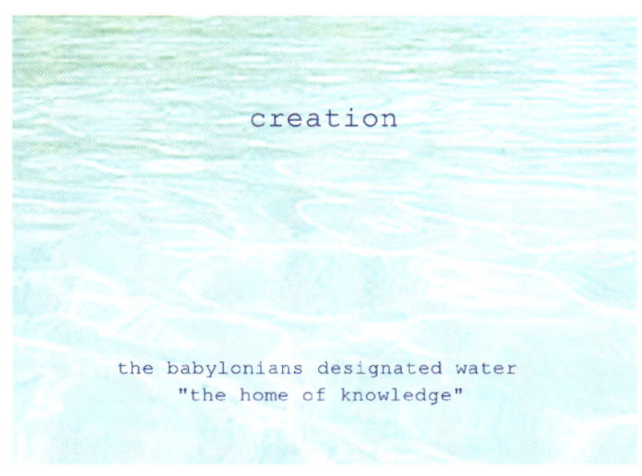

creation
the babylonians designated water
"the home of knowledge"

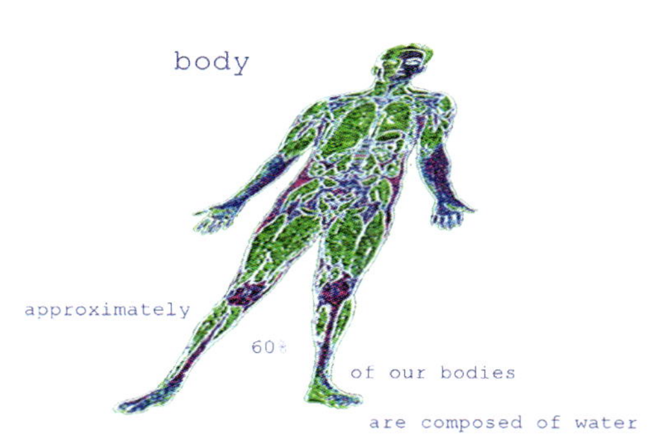

body
approximately 60% of our bodies
are composed of water

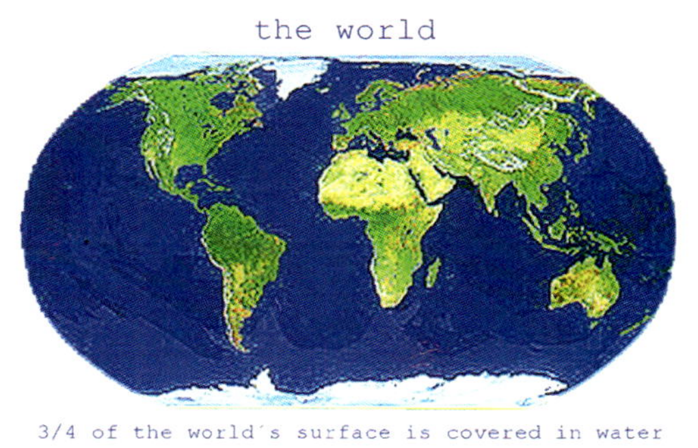

the world
3/4 of the world's surface is covered in water

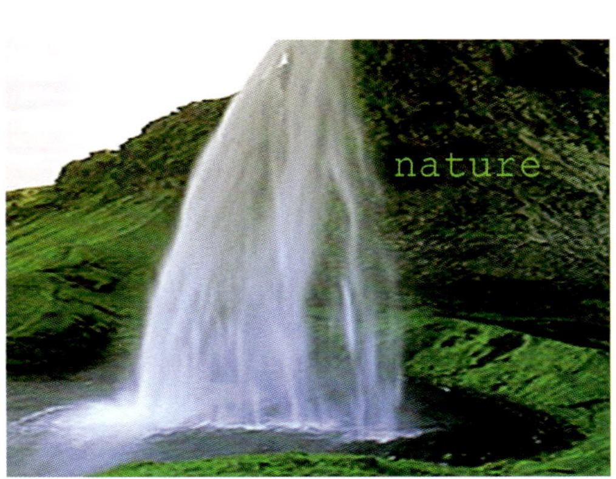

nature

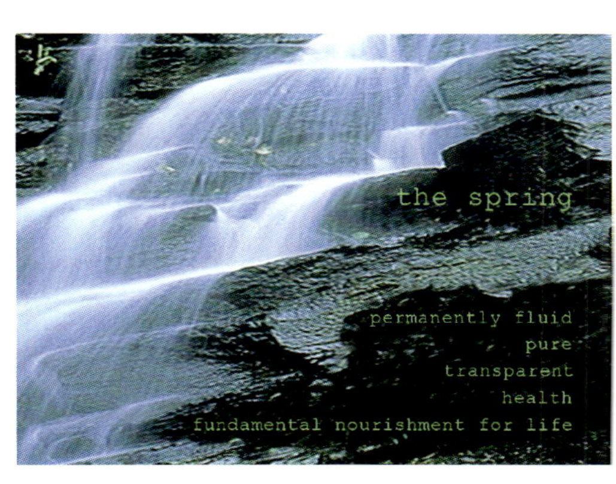

the spring
permanently fluid
pure
transparent
health
fundamental nourishment for life

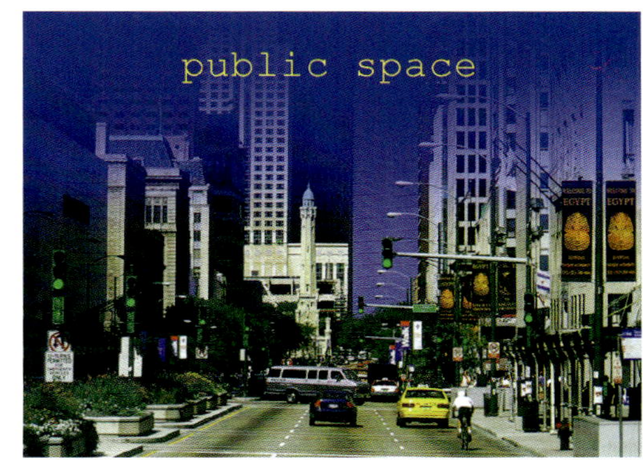

public space

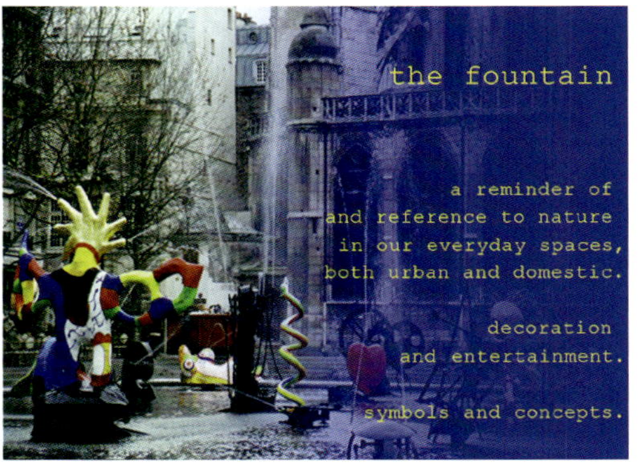

the fountain
a reminder of
and reference to nature
in our everyday spaces,
both urban and domestic.
decoration
and entertainment.
symbols and concepts.

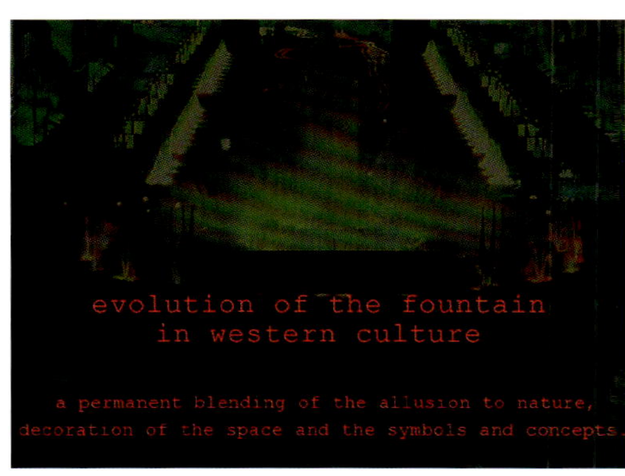

evolution of the fountain
in western culture
a permanent blending of the allusion to nature,
decoration of the space and the symbols and concepts.

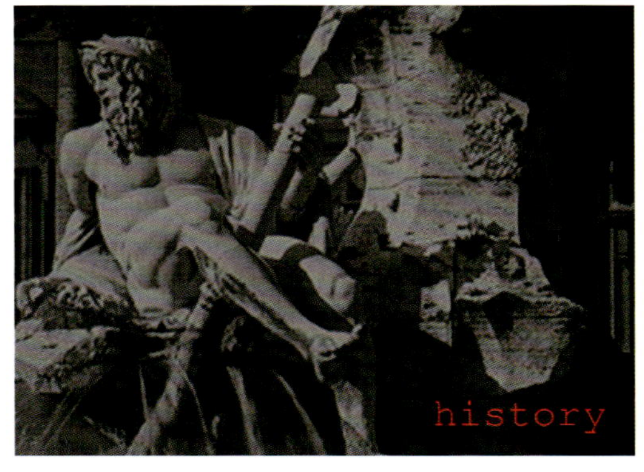

history

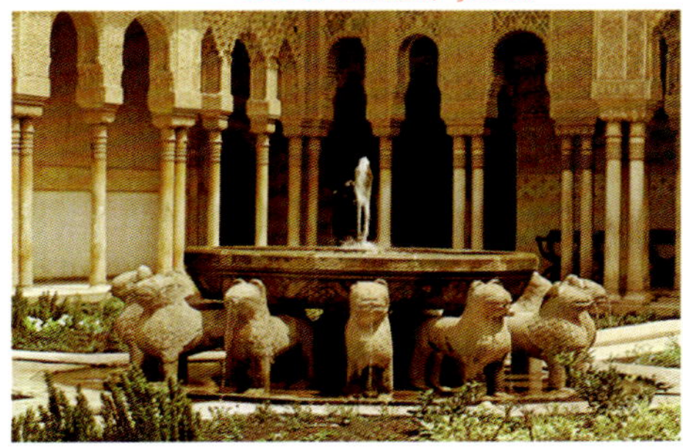

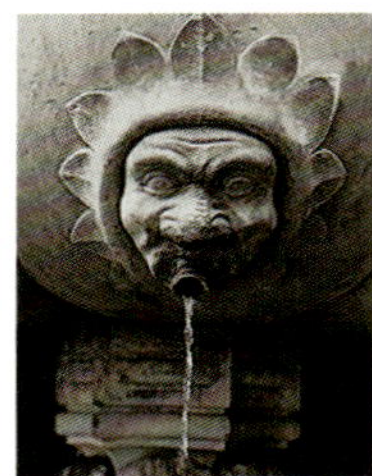

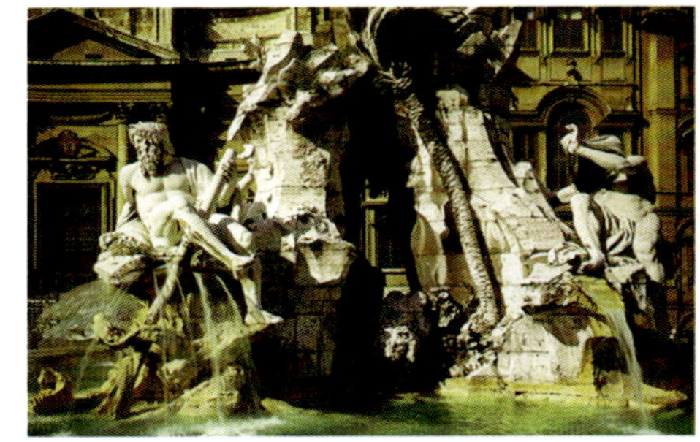

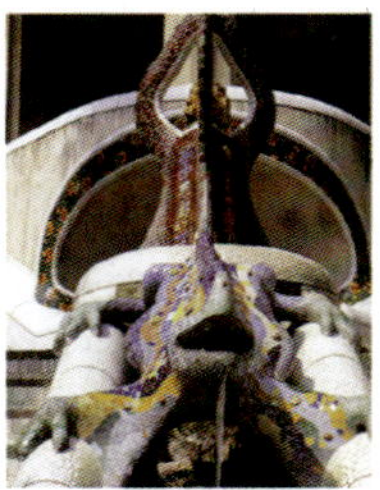

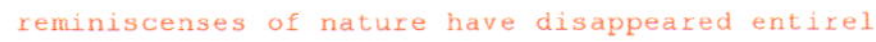

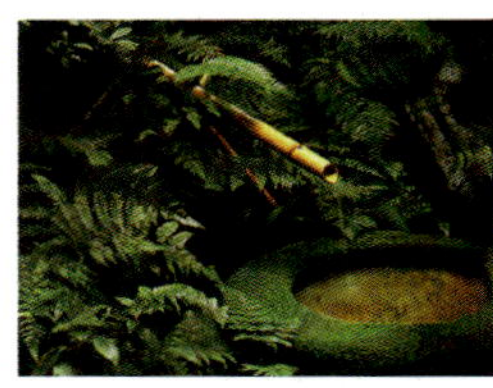

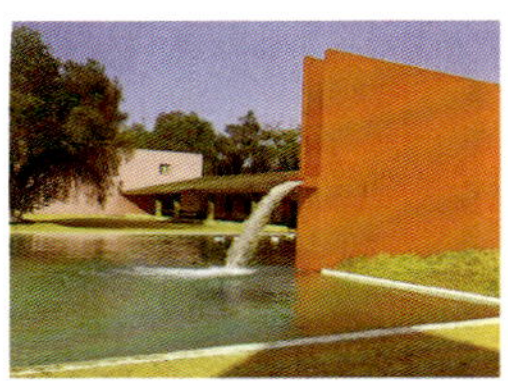

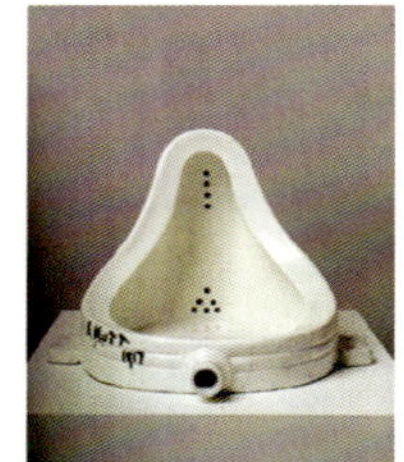

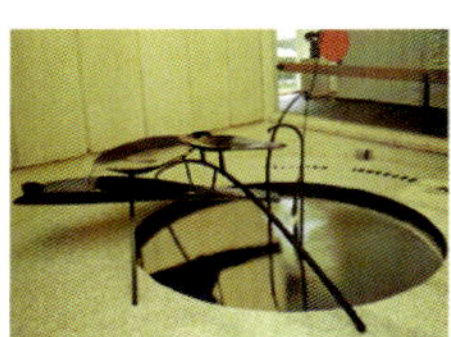

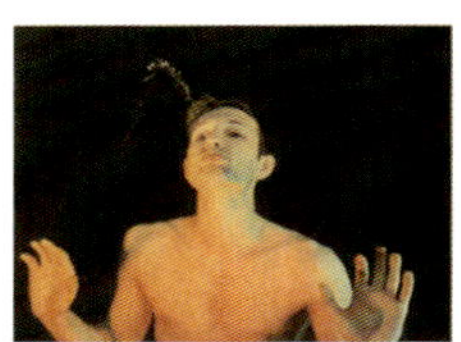

21st century

the crown fountain

fundamental ideas for the project

the fountain as autonomous work, existing both
physically and conceptually for itself.

to recover the relationship between memory,
decoration and concept incorporating the main
idea of global communication.

falling water like a natural spring.

purity of form and movement in the fall of the
water.

to return the concept of the fountain to the
public space.

to create a magical and interactive space
between the spectator and fountain.
a place for reflection and entertainment.

incorporation of digital images.

images of human faces, bodies, the world,
nature, etc..

meeting point.

permanent collaboration between
the art institute of chicago, the museum of
contemporary art, etc. and with other cultural
and social institutions throughout the city.

the crown fountain
is not just
a fountain for chicago,
but one for
the entire world.

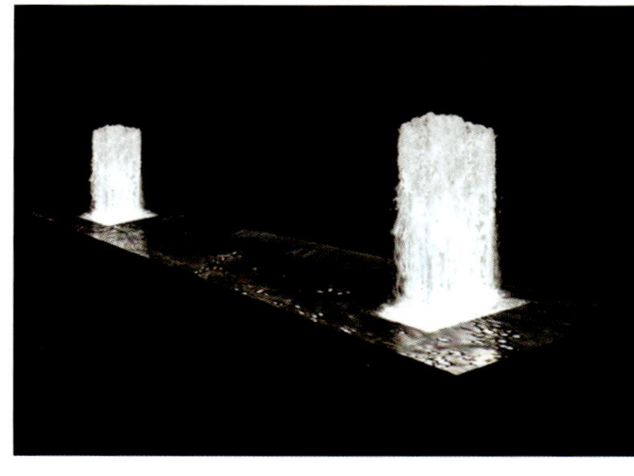

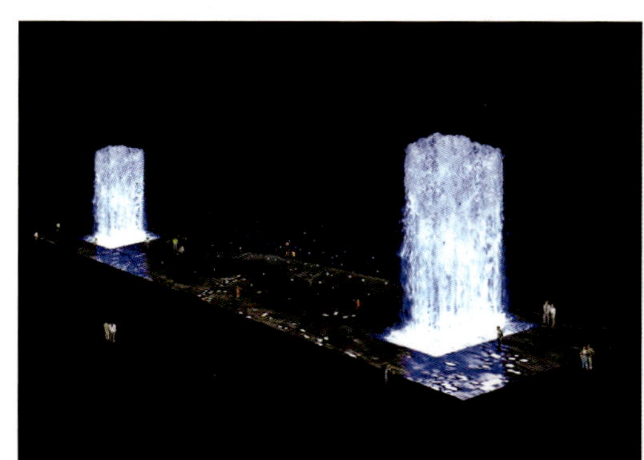

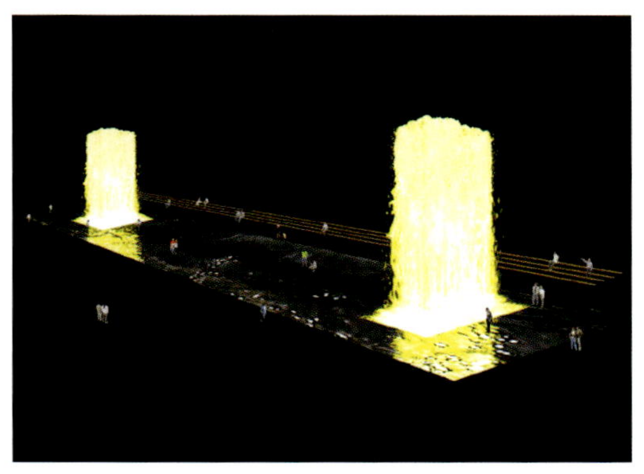
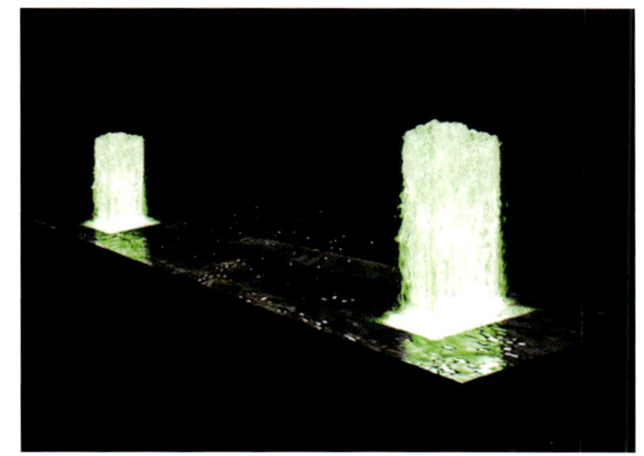
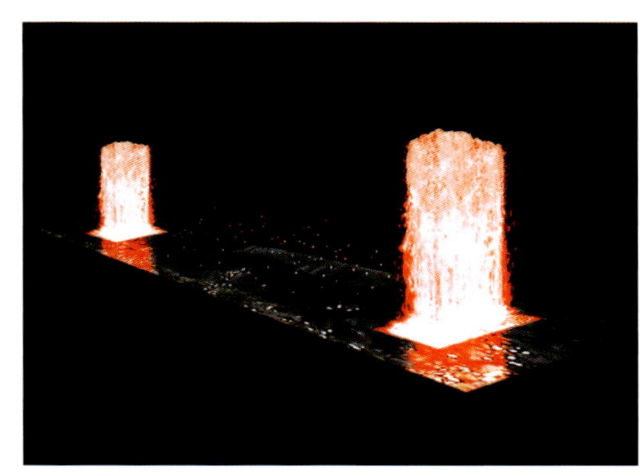
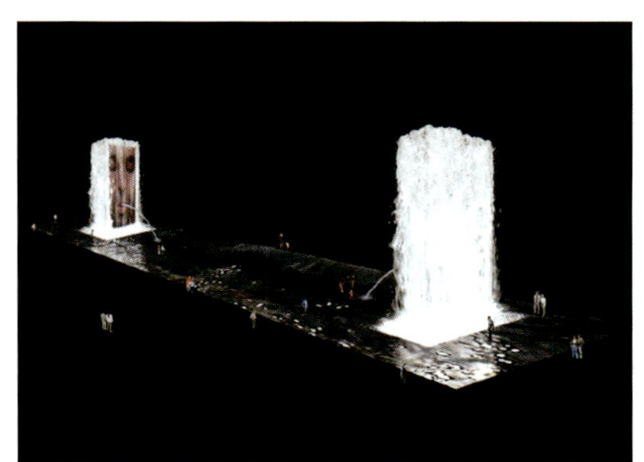
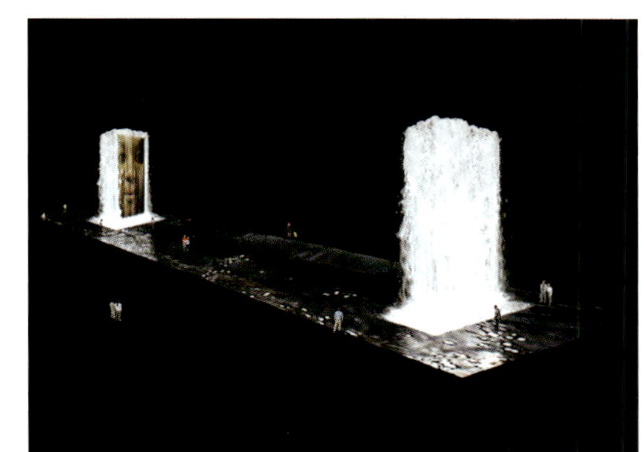
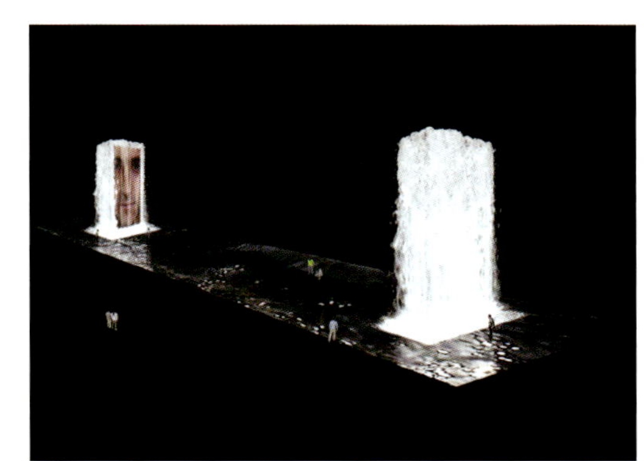
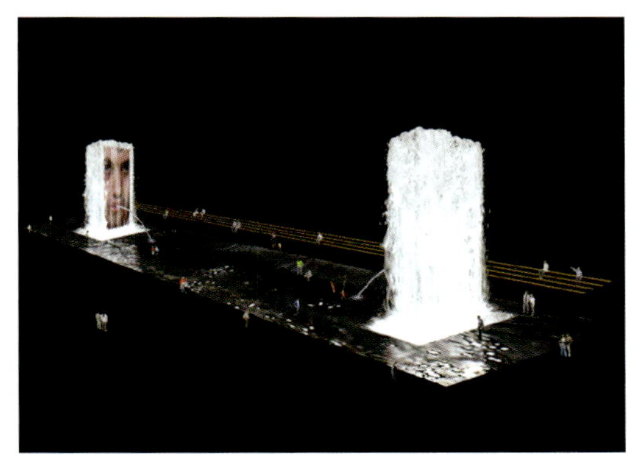
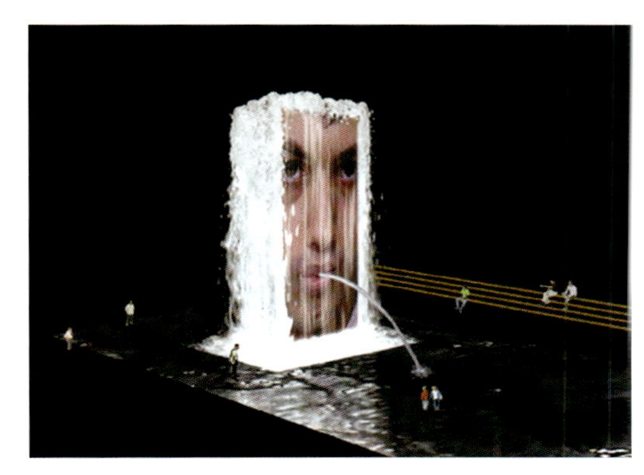
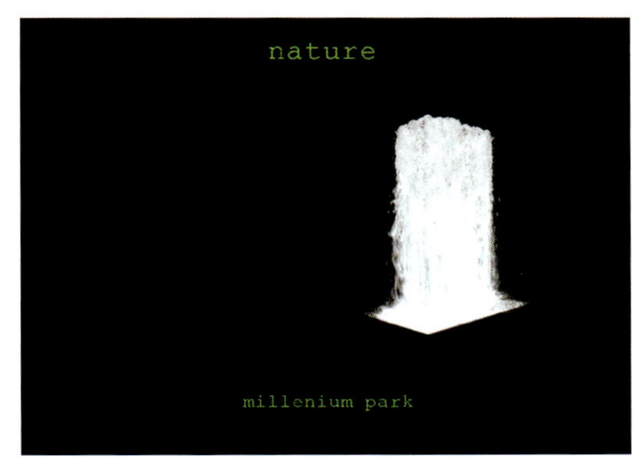

nature
millenium park

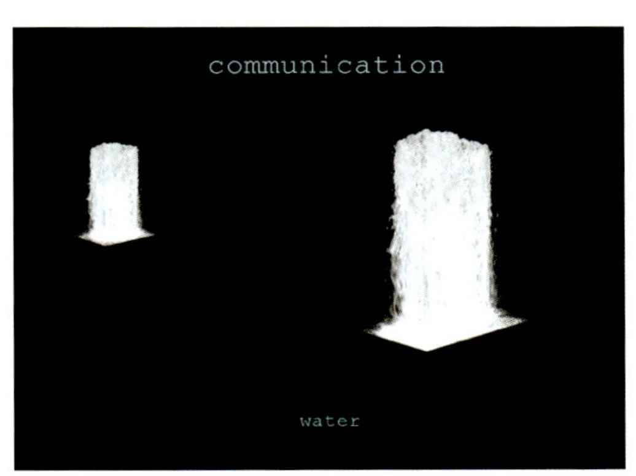

communication
water

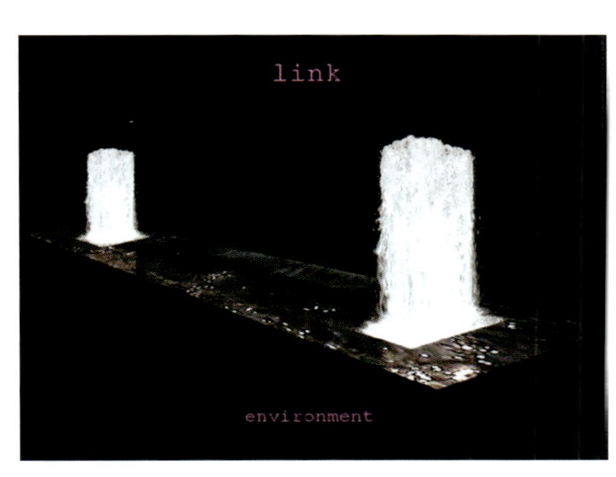

link
environment

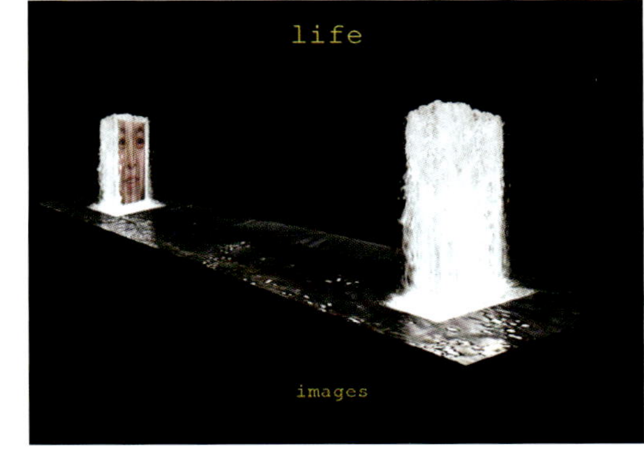

life
images

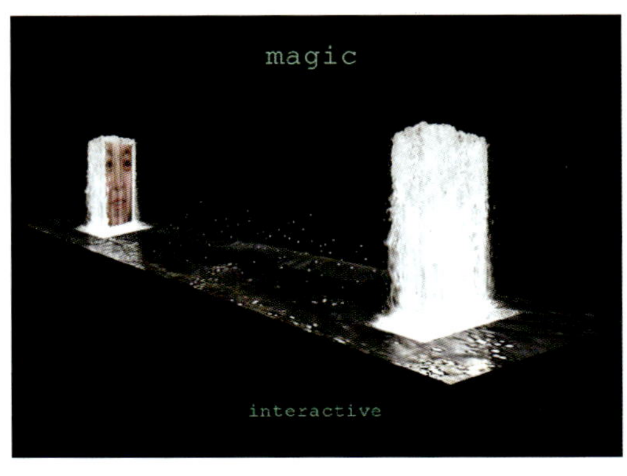

magic
interactive

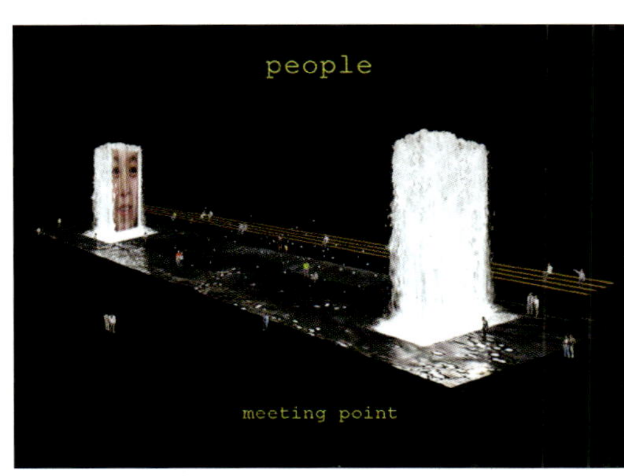

people
meeting point

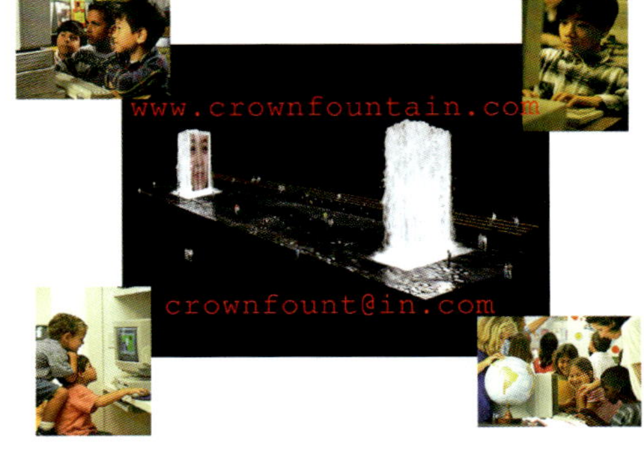

www.crownfountain.com
crownfount@in.com

A Fountain for the World

The family lost no time in confirming their decision. On April 20 at a lunch in the La Salle offices attended by Lester, Susan, Jim, and Paula, it fell to Paula, herself an arts and architecture graduate and a keen participant in the selection proceedings, to read out a letter addressed to the art committee of the Millennium Park Foundation. It had been, she stated, an evolutionary process, but the family found Plensa's work "compelling in a number of ways."

> "The design is the opposite of static. It is organic, complex, and flexible in terms of ideas, presentation, and even weather conditions. It has elements of classic Palladian symmetry, yet it incorporates an advanced technological design that pushes the boundaries of the materials… It features water—a most basic and essential life element—integrated with [the] most sophisticated technologies. It is contemplative [and] provocative. It brings nature into the core of our city, both physically with water, and virtually with images and light. The design makes our mind[s] reach beyond the conventional, yet it is so accessible and tactile. From afar, the Fountain has the elegance of a Miesian tower, yet up close has [the] detail of Richardsonian Romanesque architecture. Plensa's fountain communicates to the world that Chicago is not static. It is global in its reach."
>
> From Paula Crown's letter to the Millennium Park Foundation, April 2000

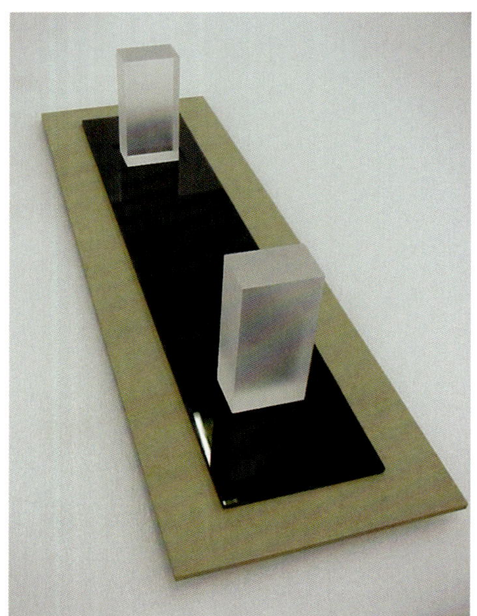

Jaume Plensa's original model for the *Crown Fountain*, 2000.

Almost as an afterthought, the letter to the art committee adds: "We hope you will find Jaume Plensa's design … as compelling as we have—enjoy."

But Millennium Park's own committee is not the only one whose approval is needed before the project gets the green light. In the weeks to follow, Plensa's proposal must run the gauntlet of all the city's planning bodies. Susan Crown recalls that the reaction at this early stage was almost universally supportive, but the proposal is so radical that it inevitably finds detractors—Michael Lash of the Public Art Committee, for one.

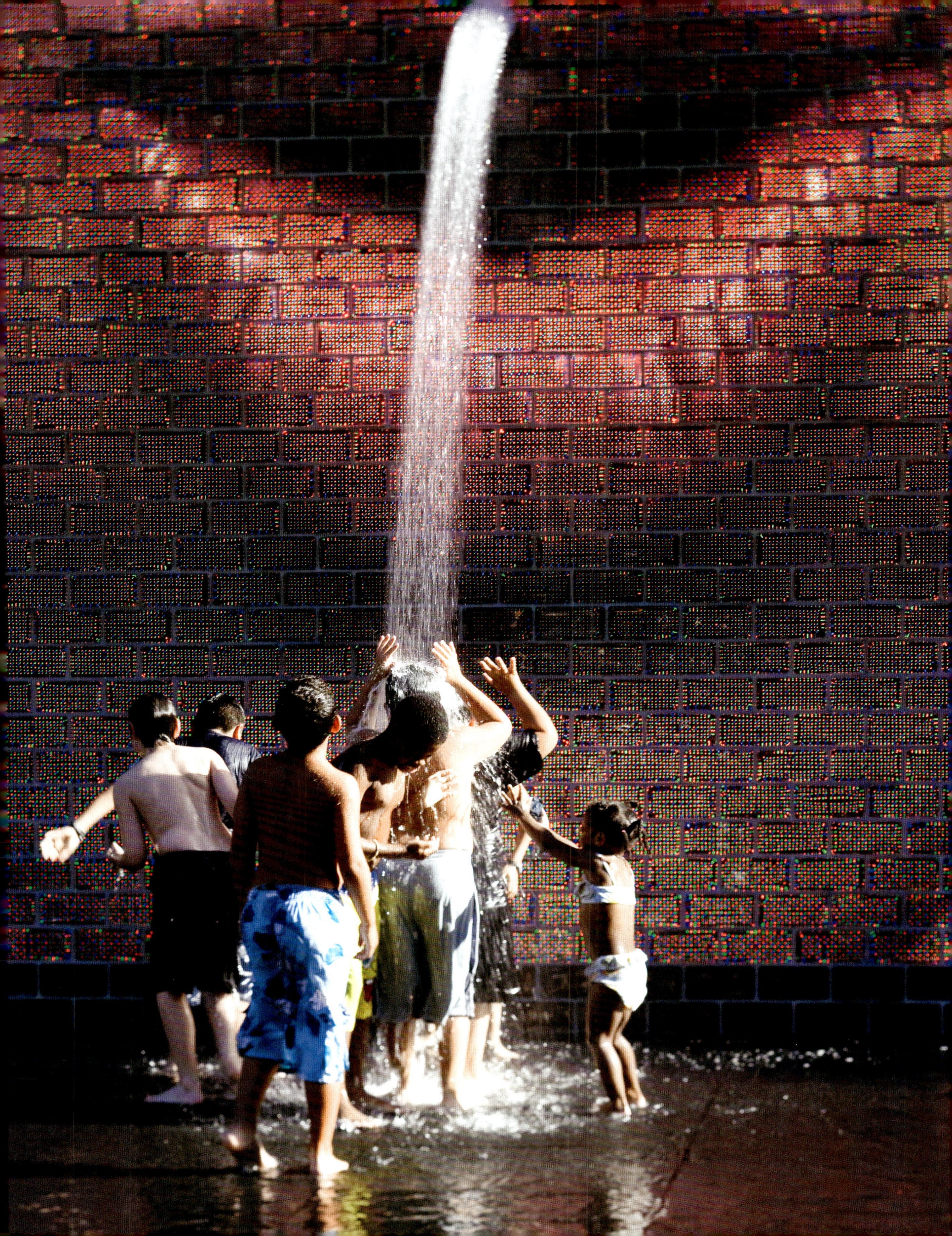

Mayor Daley's reaction perhaps best typifies these early responses. At the formal presentation meeting, attended by Lester and Susan Crown, Plensa, Wislow, and various representatives of the park, the mayor expresses his enthusiasm for the innovative design. At the end of the meeting he turns to Lester and thanks him profusely for "all you are doing for the city." But although this was the first formal presentation, Mayor Daley has kept up with developments through Ed Uhlir. And despite his upbeat reception, there are doubts about the appropriateness of the giant screens. The mayor is also concerned by a First Amendment issue—the possibility that at some future date the LED screens could be deemed a public forum. It's a concern that leads to the implementation of careful controls governing the use of imagery and a special provision within the park's constitution to vet any future changes.

But as Paul Gray says, "such initial reservations were to be expected with a proposal this innovative." Lester Crown's challenge had been "to dream something new" and Plensa had risen to it. Except that, at this point, the *Crown Fountain* was still *only* a dream. Plensa is a sculptor and is well versed in working with a wide range of materials, from the cast iron of his pieces from the late eighties and early nineties, to resin, glass, alabaster, bronze, light, sound, and water. But he is no engineer, nor is he an architect, and it will take the skills of an entire team to translate his dream into concrete reality.

Refining the Dream

The dream had really begun seven years earlier with the installation for the Henry Moore Sculpture Studio in Dean Clough. Although formally quite disparate works, both *Twins* and the *Personal Miraculous Fountain* find their echo in the schema for the *Crown Fountain*.

> "*Twins* grew out of a relationship to the place. It was an acknowledgment of the lives of those people who had worked in the mill or in the area—their names coupled with the kinds of diseases created by nineteenth-century industrialization. Small elements, which taken together make a more complex

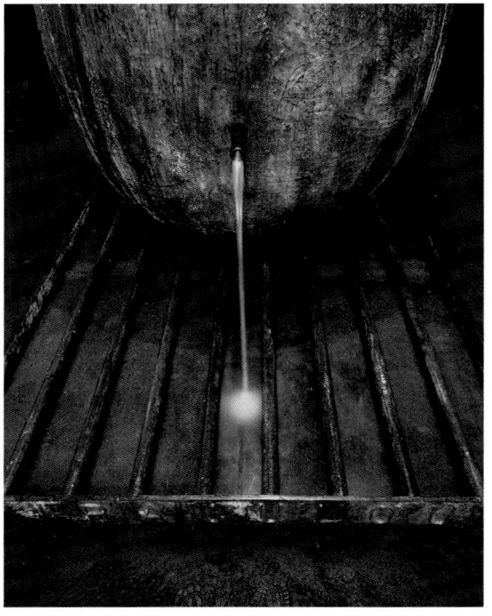

Jaume Plensa's *The Personal Miraculous Fountain*, 1993 (detail).

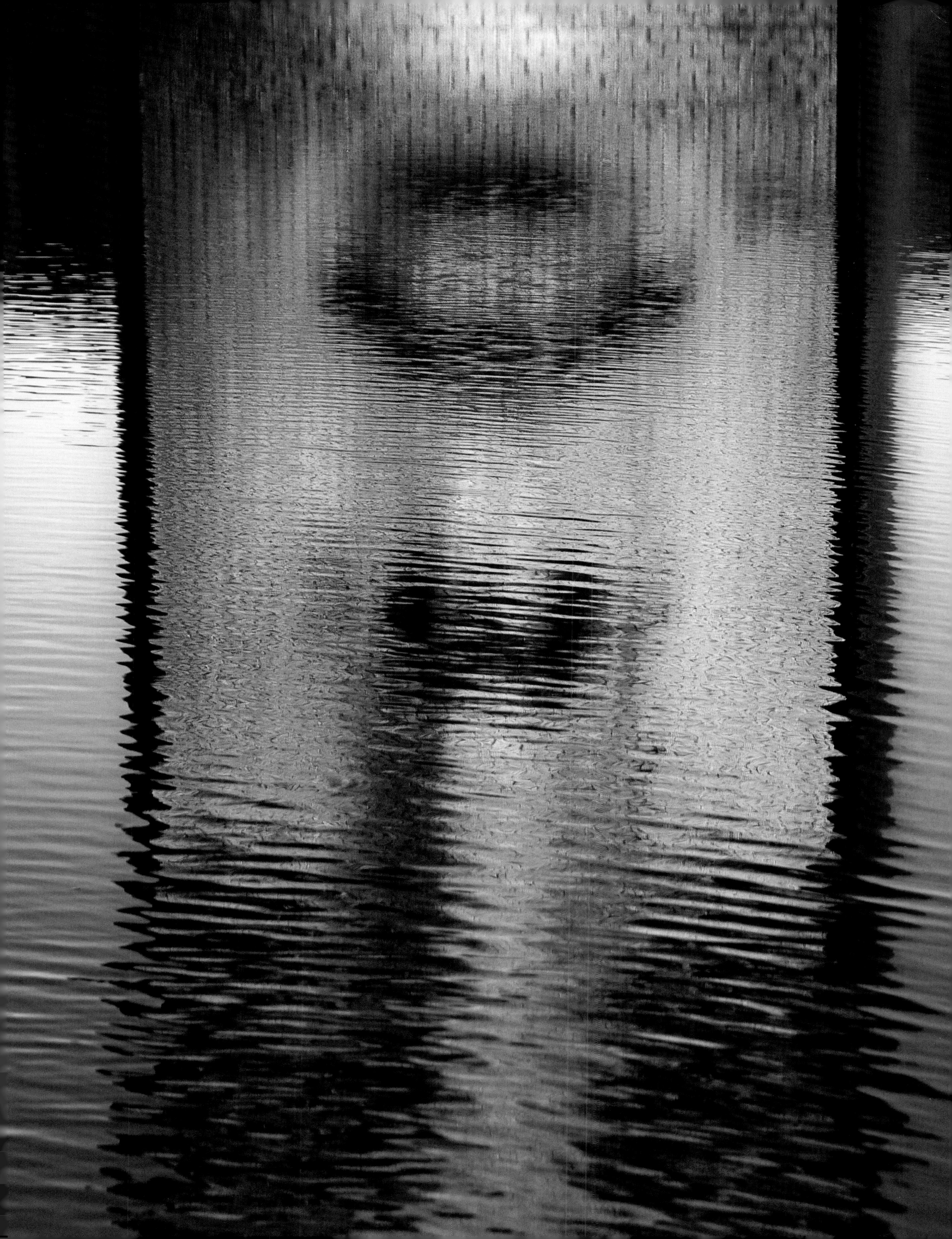

body, a society. And the fountain had quite a different aspect.
All the elements of my work today were already there. For
example, *Twins* had two parts, and the idea of duality was
something I have come to explore a lot in recent years. In the
Crown Fountain, the concept is exactly the same as the
Personal Miraculous Fountain, but combined with the duality
of *Twins*—the idea of a conversation between two elements. So
Dean Clough was quite seminal, even if I was just beginning to
explore these ideas and at a largely unconscious level.

It was there that I also began to explore the idea that humidity
could become an element in the work. The floor of the space
where the *Miraculous Fountain* was installed was covered
in soil—one hundred tons of it. And soil absorbs moisture, so
that the atmosphere became completely saturated and water
continually ran down the blinds on the windows. In the *Crown
Fountain* all of these elements come together."

Jaume Plensa

But the Dean Clough installation was only one step on the long journey to
the *Crown Fountain.* At the Jeu de Paume show, both Wislow and Guthman
had been impressed by a slightly earlier work, *La Neige Rouge* (1991). This
was the first piece to have a tower-like structure, almost a cabinet, that people
could enter. Materially it was closer to *Twins,* in that it was made from cast
iron and extremely solid, but its interior contained red neon lights, which
paradoxically gave the impression of heat, that the core of the iron was liquid
and molten like a bleeding wound, but also fertile like a womb.

The work had in fact grown directly out of the artist's experiences in the foundry.
For several years he had been working with cast iron, traditionally regarded
as an inferior material by artists, but celebrated by Plensa for its similarities
to the Earth's magma and lava flows—its bleeding wounds—and so evoking
the natural process by which its molten core mutates into the intransigent
and all-too-solid mountains. He had become aware of the strange alchemy
that possessed the metal at high temperatures, of how its mass appeared to

become weightless and was transformed into pure light. In his own words, it would become "pure form, but also formless." *La Neige Rouge* attempts to capture that experience by contrasting the solid superstructure with the "molten, formless" interior. In so doing, it anticipates another of the *Crown Fountain*'s concerns, which is for the cascading water (that at night can be turned glowing red by the interior lights) to dissolve the forms of the towers. Or rather, for it to create a "purity of form" governed by gravity and the dictates of the laws of nature.

Water Always Falls

In contrast to the traditional model, Plensa is adamant that there should be no upward jets of water in his fountain, for the simple reason that in nature water always *falls* in response to gravity. For Plensa, the upward jet that so distinguishes the nearby *Buckingham Fountain* typifies a certain artificiality, a bravura display of our technical ability to master the forces of nature. But as he made clear in his initial presentation, Plensa's conception of a fountain is for it to exist in harmony with nature, to evoke nature: Niagara Falls on Michigan Avenue.

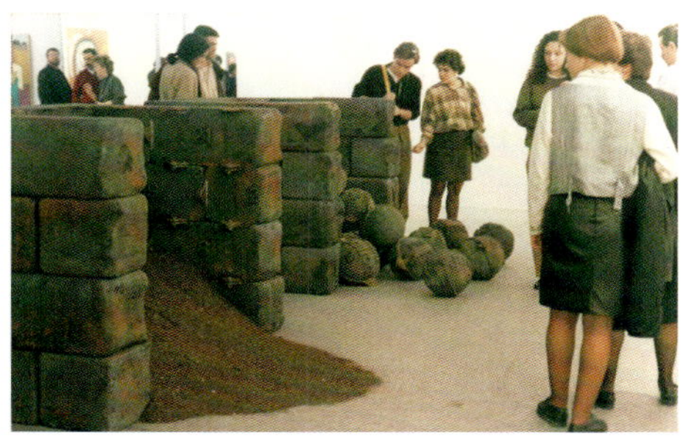

Jaume Plensa's *Prière* at ARCO, Madrid, in 2000.

Looking back on those earlier cast-iron pieces, it strikes me now how physically robust they were. The first piece I ever saw was *Prière* (1989) on the stand of Plensa's gallery at the ARCO art fair in Madrid. In part, what made these twin, massive iron bunkers stand out was the simple fact that every other gallery had brought light, easily transportable works. But not Plensa! Simply by virtue of *Prière*'s existence the work referenced gravity, making you aware of the pull of the Earth beneath your feet and the fragility of the floor upon which you stood. It was one big arrow and it was pointing downwards.

> "With the two towers the water is always falling. At the same time it dissolves the structure of the towers, making them one with the landscape. I very quickly realized that the towers would blend with the architecture of the city, but that the falling water would integrate them into the landscape, so giving more

emphasis to the faces. The towers are like two transparent houses that people might inhabit, but at moments they become something else, something with a soul, and these faces appear out of the normal architecture of the city."
Jaume Plensa

Answering a Question with a Question

Even the opening salvo to his presentation finds a precedent in his earlier work. How typical of Plensa to begin not with a statement, but with a question: "What can a fountain be?" In works from 1992, such as *Firenze II,* the artist actually cast a question mark in aluminum. A similar form, though on a far grander scale, was originally proposed for the BBC building in Portland Place, London. That it was rejected in favor of another of Plensa's installations is in itself interesting, coinciding as it did with the beginning of the Blair government's attempts to restrict the BBC's independence and freedom of speech.

The installation for the BBC in London has a singular form: a cone, like a giant megaphone, that points skywards. Like the light beam he installed in Jerusalem, and similar works in Auch in France and Gateshead in the north of England, it embodies a sense of our reaching for the stars. More specifically, Plensa comments that traditionally God speaks to man from on high, and in these works he is looking to reverse this, to have man speak to his gods. But what questions do we ask in our post-Nietzschean world?

Towers and cabinets began to make a frequent appearance in his work from 1994, together with the exploration of translucent materials. The starting point was again *La Neige Rouge* and the foundry experience of working with molten iron. Plensa describes the concept as an attempt "to return to the origins of the world, to those processes that brought the mountains into being." But this is also fused with the experience of working with water at the Henry Moore Sculpture Studio. Water was something new in Plensa's work. It was a fluid just like the molten iron, but a transparent fluid. And the problem of how to fix this transparent fluid in a sculptural form became something of an obsession.

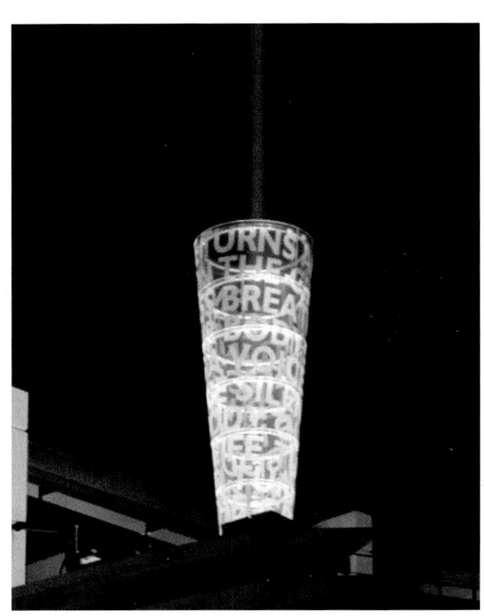

Jaume Plensa's *Breathing,* 2006, for BBC Broadcasting House, London.

»Alle Kunst ist der Freude gewidmet.«

"All art is dedicated to joy."

Friedrich Schiller

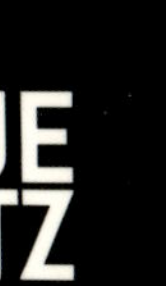

Wir freuen uns über Ihr Interesse an unserem
Buchprogramm. Der Hatje Cantz Verlag zählt mit
seinen hochwertigen Publikationen und exklusi-
ven Collectors' Editions seit über 60 Jahren zu den
renommiertesten Verlagen für Kunst, Fotografie
und Architektur. Wenn Sie regelmäßig über unser
Gesamtprogramm informiert werden möchten,
schicken Sie bitte die Karte ausgefüllt an uns zu-
rück. Oder besuchen Sie einfach unsere Website
unter www.hatjecantz.de.

Thank you for your interest in our book program.
With high-quality publications and exclusive Collectors' Editions, Hatje Cantz has been one of the
most renowned publishers of art, photography,
and architecture for over sixty years. If you would
like to receive our free catalogue, please fill out
and return this card. For more information please
visit our website at www.hatjecantz.com.

Bitte schicken Sie mir | Please send me

☐ **Ihren kostenlosen Verlagsprospekt** |
your free sales catalogue

☐ **Ihren E-Mail-Newsletter** |
your E-mail newsletter

Name | Name

Straße | Street

PLZ, Ort | City, Zip code

Land | Country

E-Mail | E-mail

Antwortpostkarte

Hatje Cantz Verlag
Zeppelinstraße 32
73760 Ostfildern
Germany

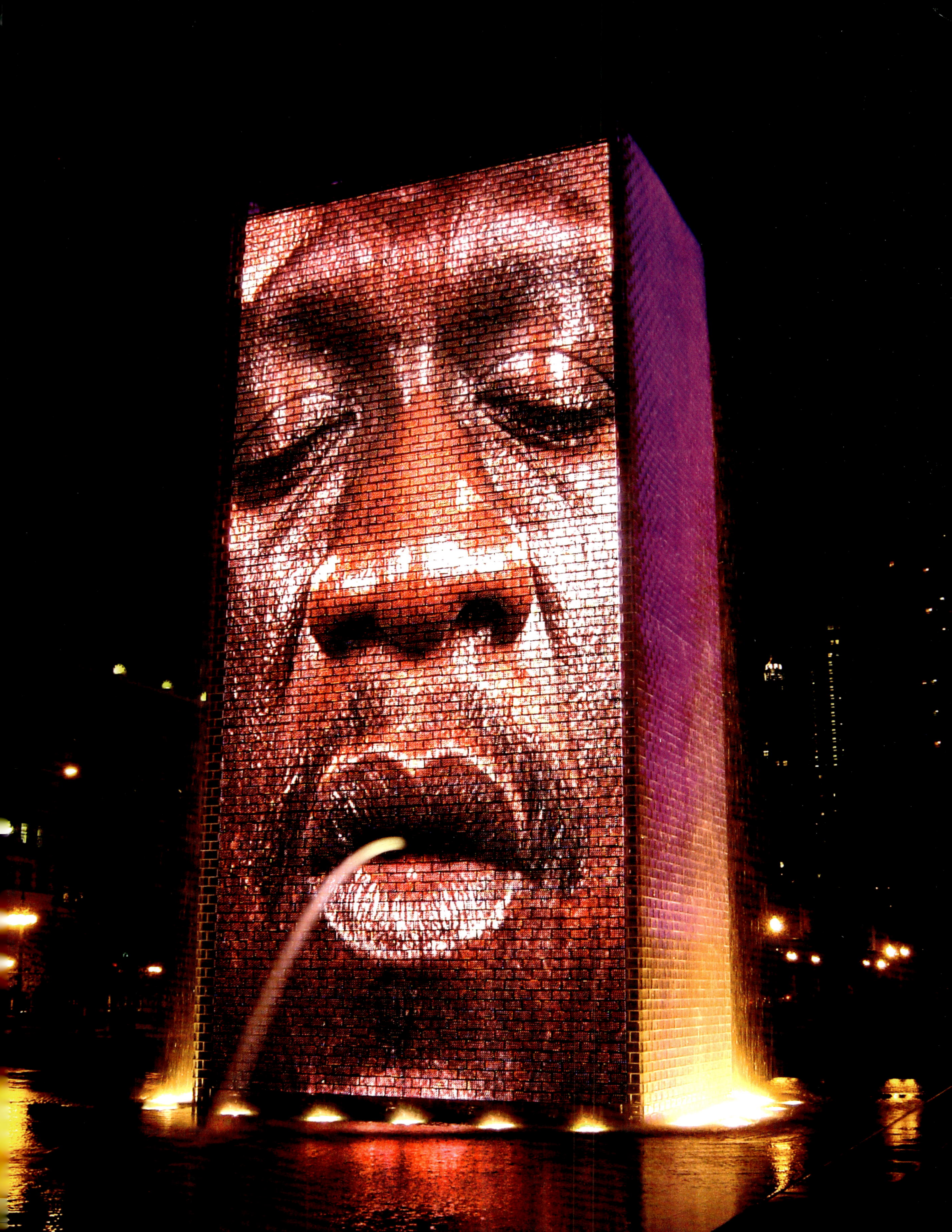

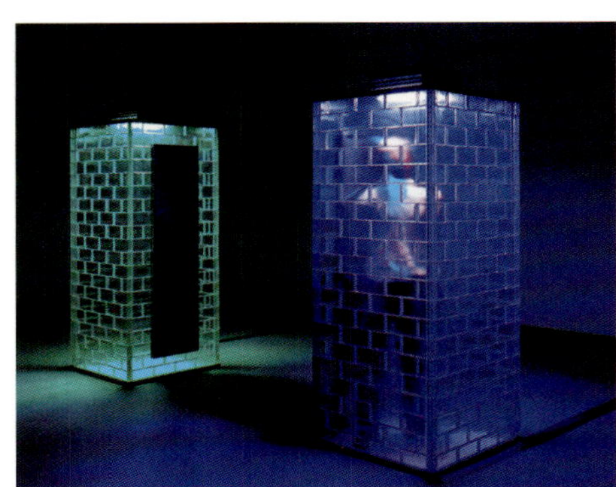

Jaume Plensa's *Song of Songs I, II, 2004.*

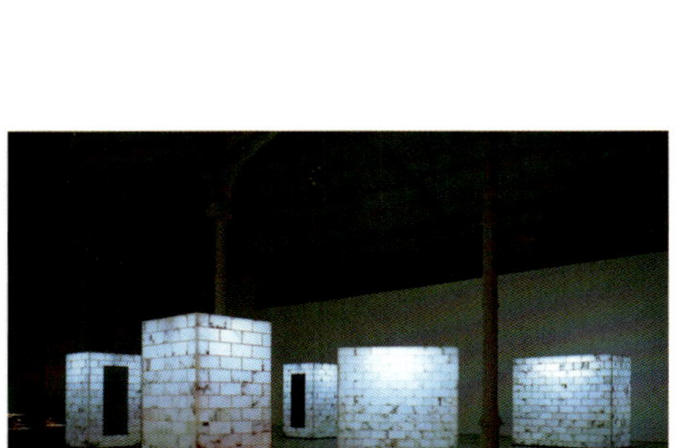

Jaume Plensa's *Love Sounds,* 1998. These translucent "cells" made by Plensa in the late nineties clearly anticipate the towers of the *Crown Fountain*.

Plensa at first started working with resin, then with alabaster, and finally with glass. Alabaster is a natural stone, semi-transparent when cut into thin tiles. Resin, of course, is an artificial product that sets through the chemical reaction between two agents. But glass resembles iron in that it begins as a hot liquid, then cools into a solid state. Also like iron, once cooled it can no longer be worked. It took Plensa several years to make that link and to discover his transparent "iron."

However, even in the earlier resin cabinets Plensa was experimenting with different forms of construction. One saw the inclusion of words—quotations from Shakespeare's *Macbeth*—cast onto relatively large resin panels, a development of the practice originating with the iron pieces such as *Twins* and which continues in various forms to this day. Another variation saw the cabinets built from resin bricks, very much as the towers of the *Crown Fountain* are constructed.

Love Sounds (1998) is a series of five such cabinets—or cells—crafted from alabaster. Lit from within, they also contain recordings taken from the artist's own body, which at times resemble nothing so much as the sound of rushing water as blood is pumped through a main artery. Visitors are invited to enter and immerse themselves in the experience. But from the outside, the aspect is somewhat different. What we see is the distorted juxtaposition of a human figure within a glowing tower of "glass" bricks: the exact progenitor, in fact, of the towers of the *Crown Fountain*.

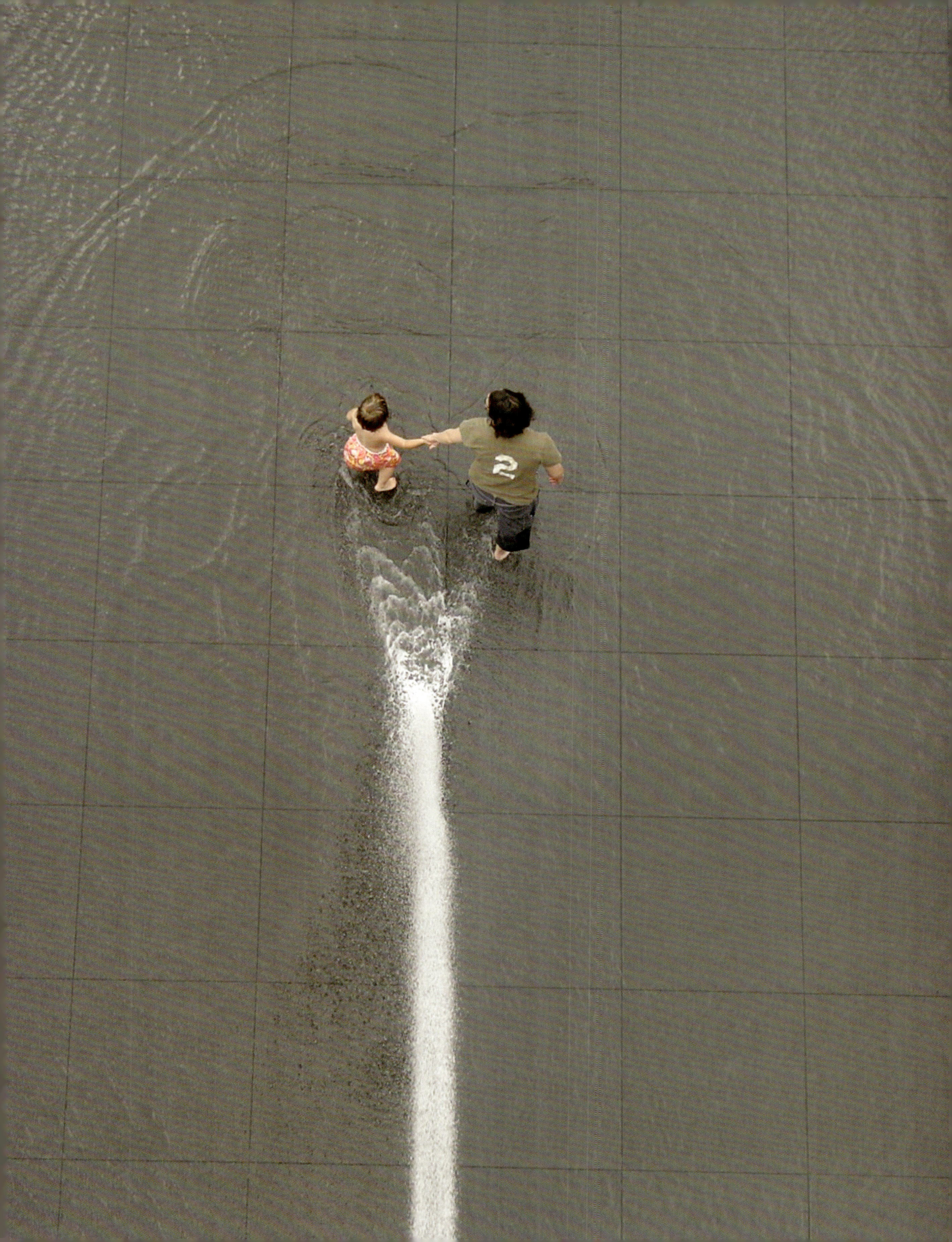

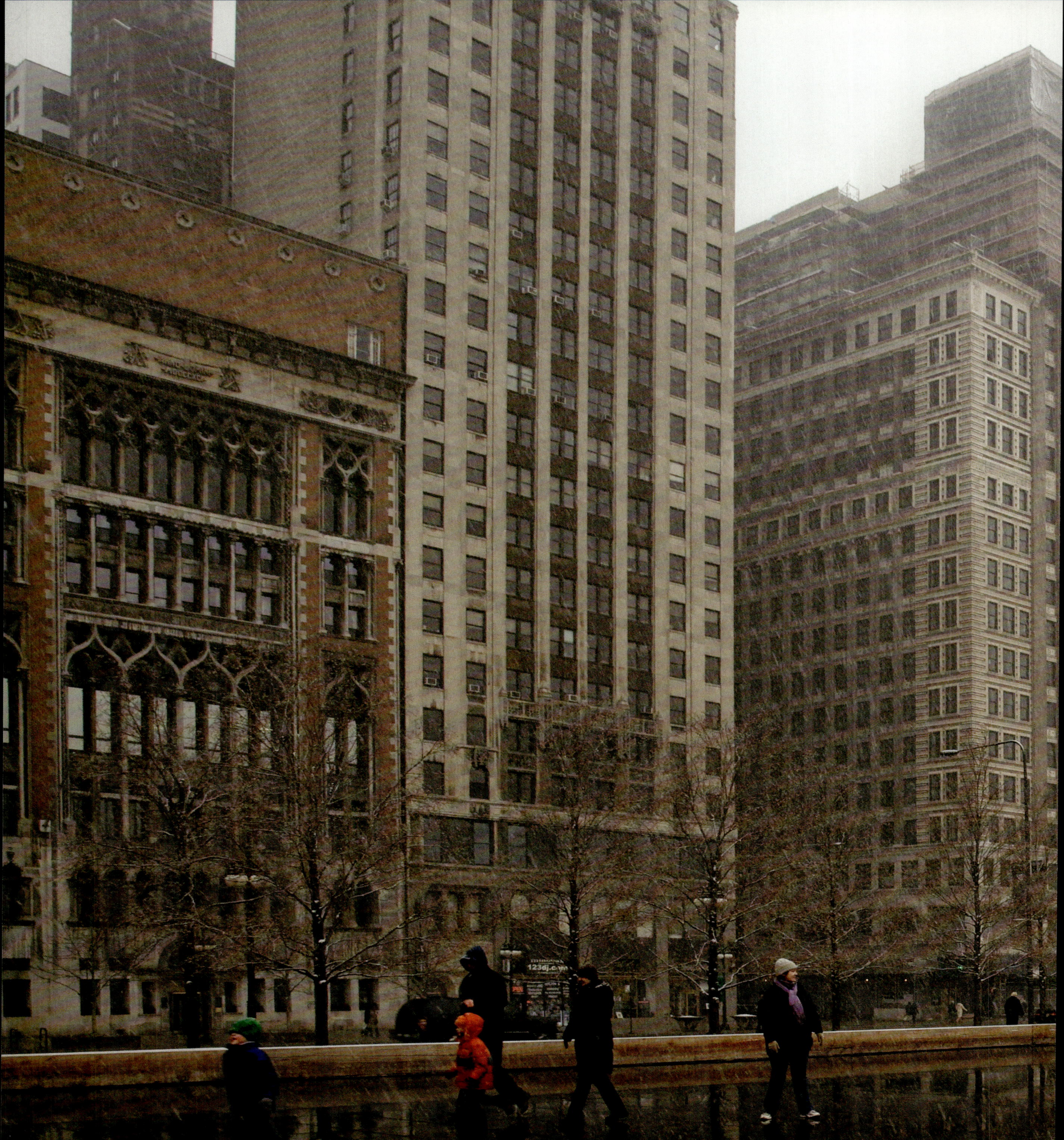

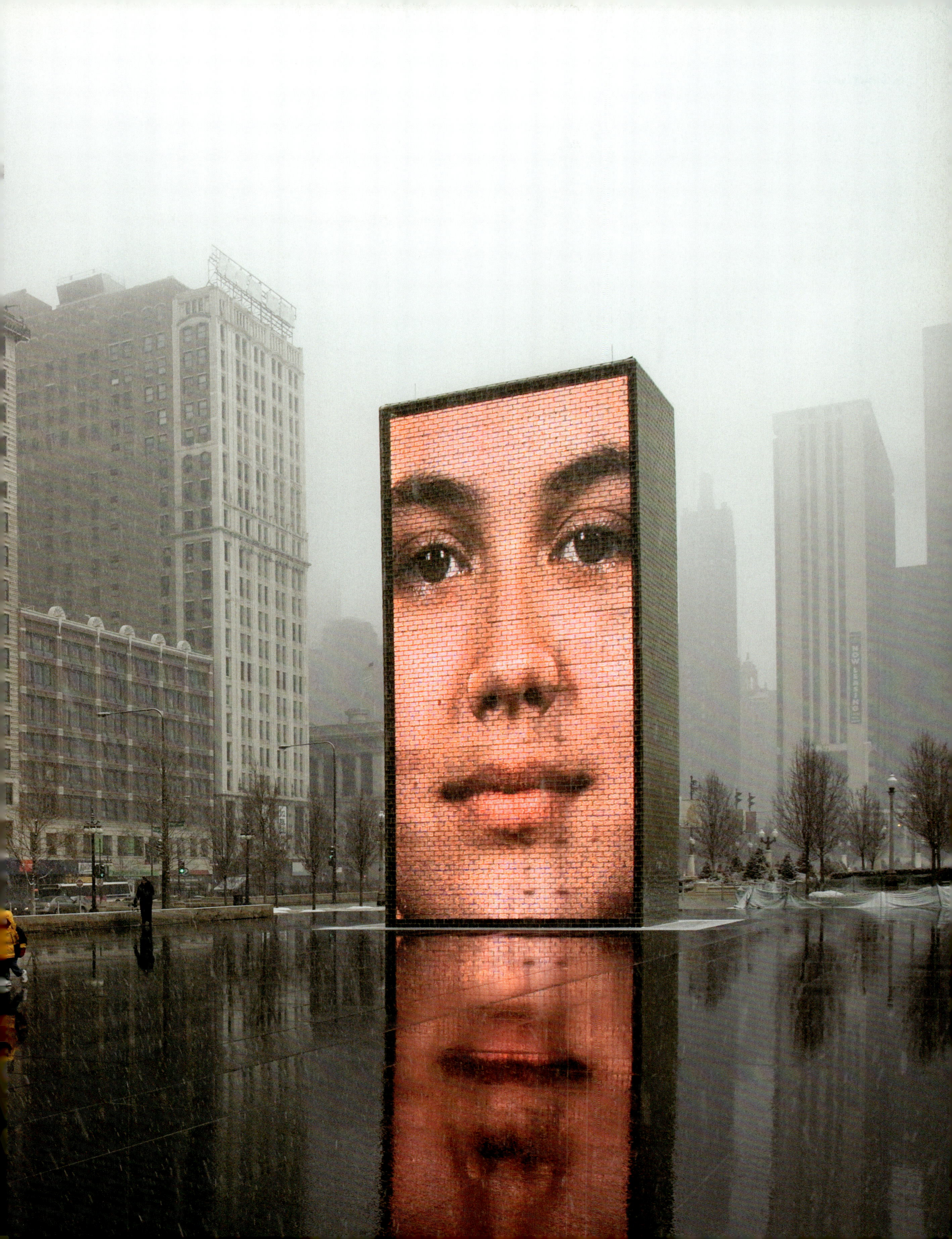

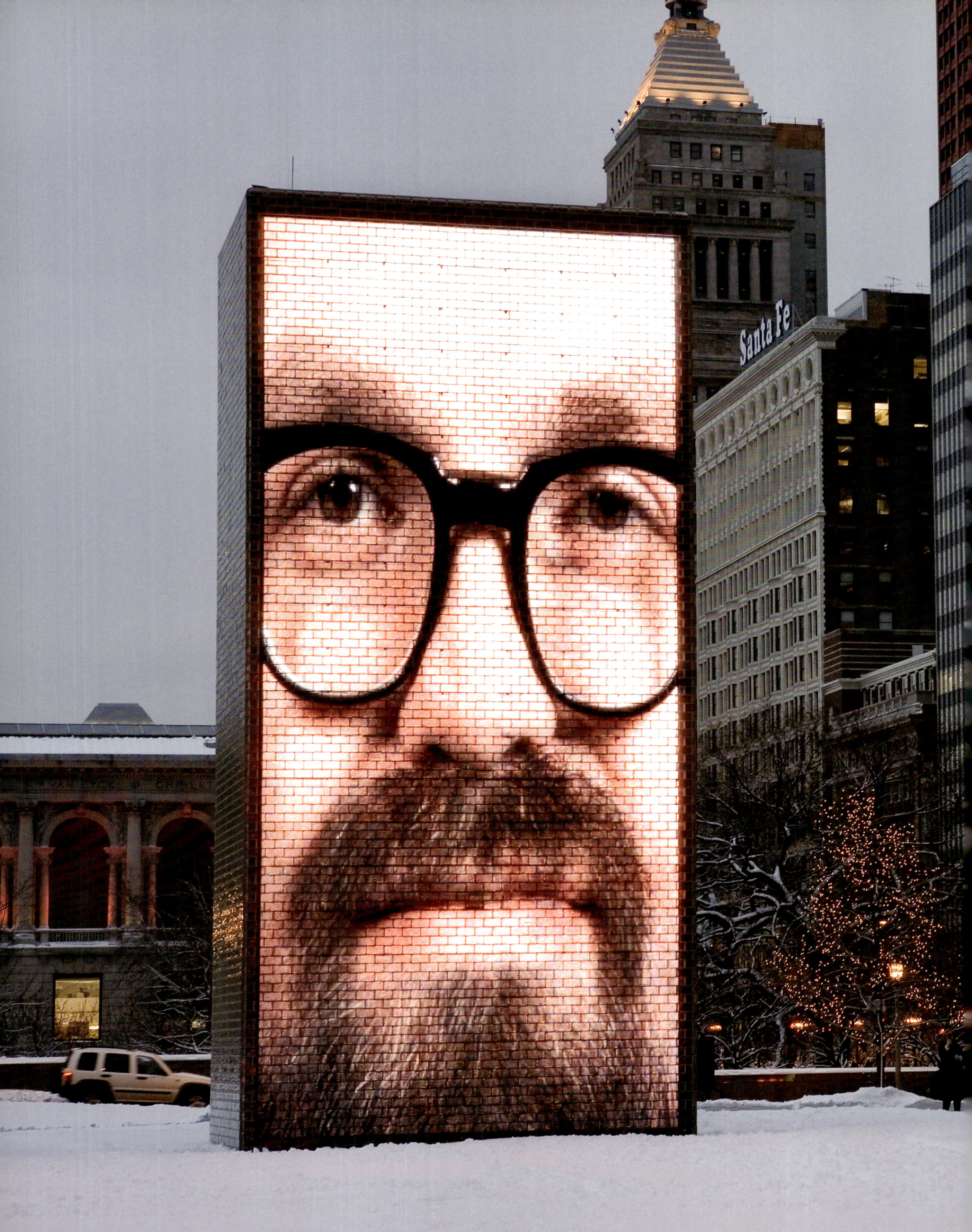

Santa Fe
VAN BUREN   CHASE

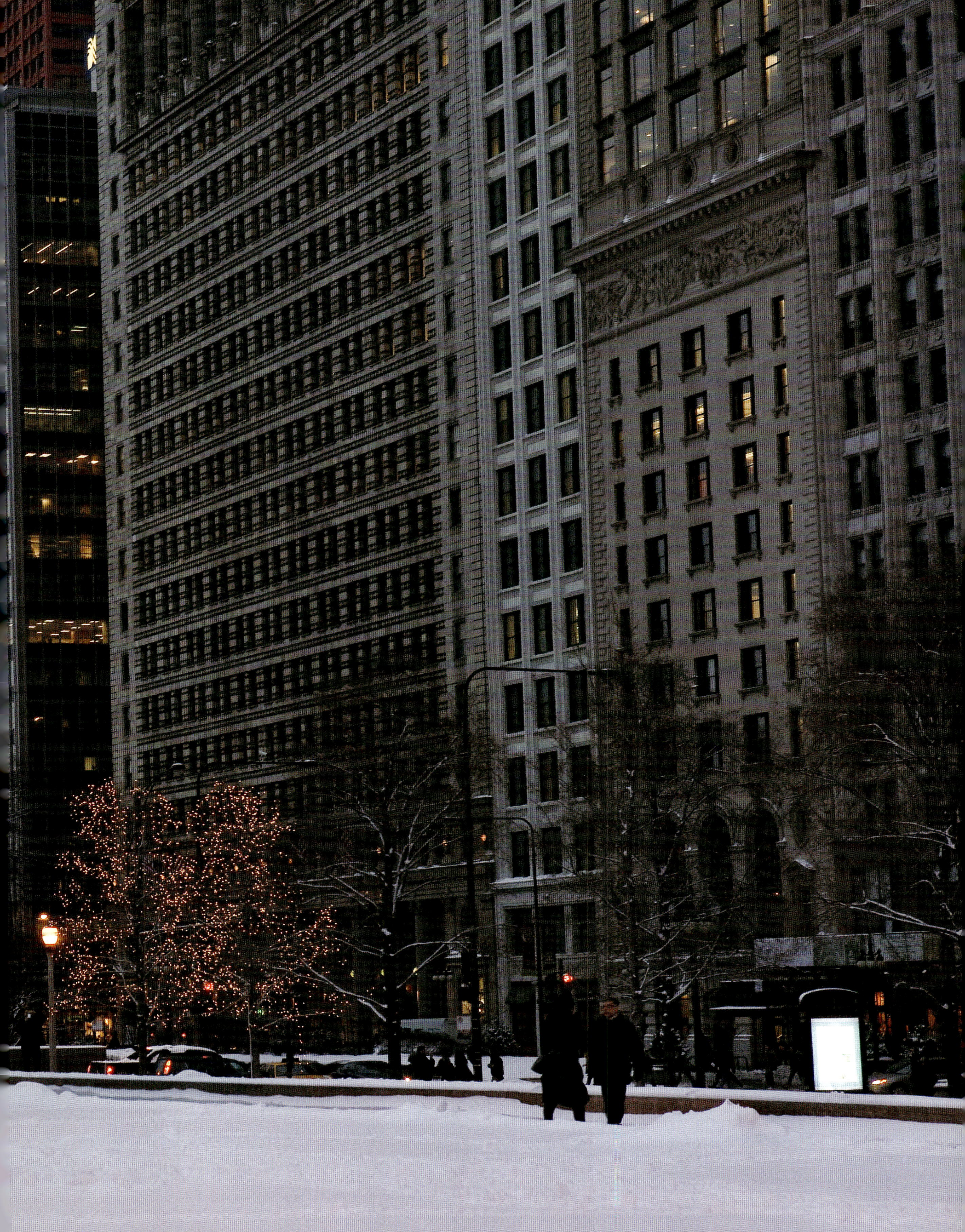

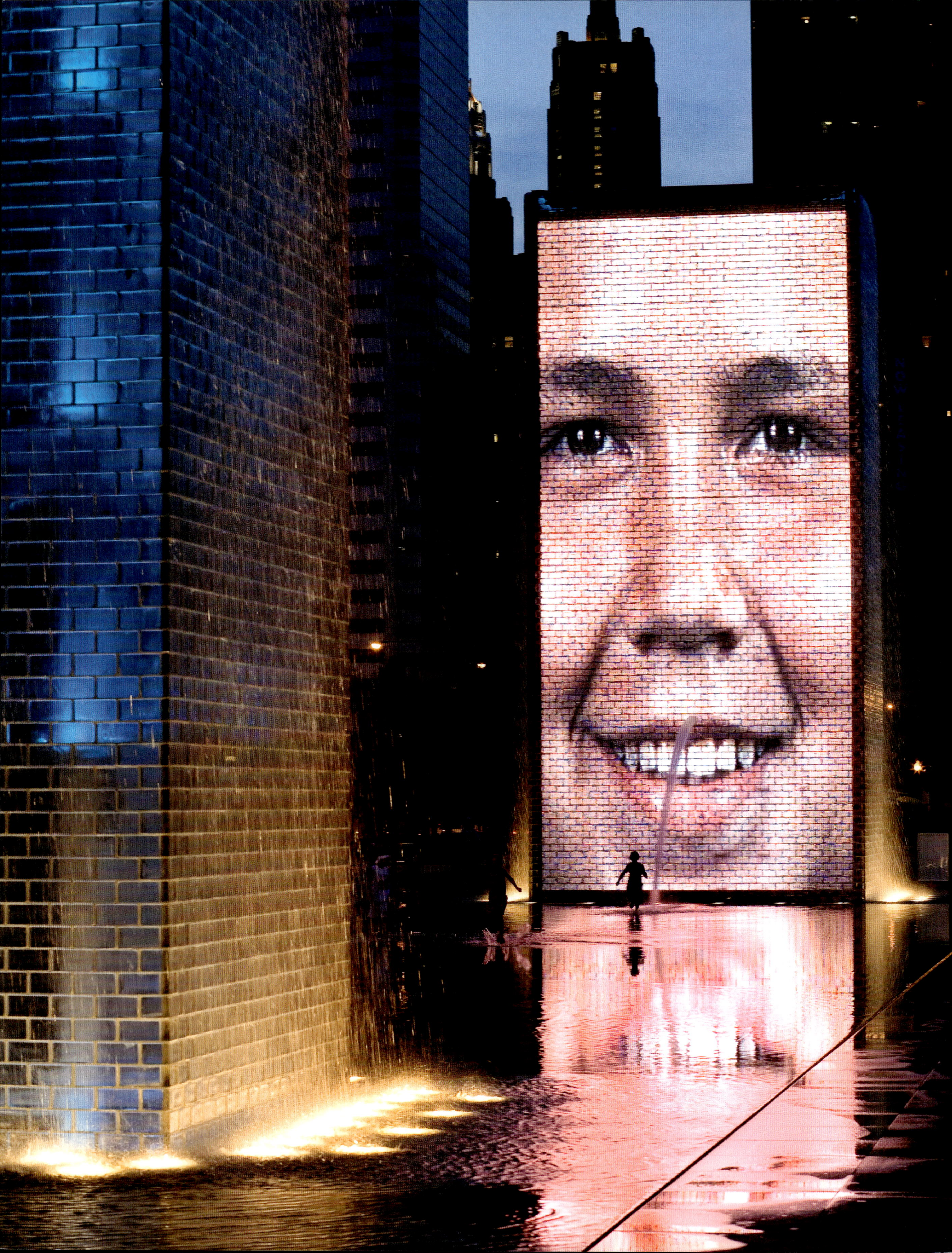

5

Getting the Show on the Road

Plensa's initial presentation consisted of a series of graphics and a live commentary that was, by everyone's account, a virtuoso performance. But it was only a starting point, a preliminary visualization of what was, by his own account, "still only a dream." The all-important question had yet to be answered: would the fountain actually work? As the project progressed, the responsibility for pursuing the technical aspects came to rest increasingly with the team of engineers and water specialists that had been appointed by U.S. Equities. There were structural considerations, complicated by the fact that the project was sited above a parking lot that simply wasn't designed to bear this kind of load. But there was also the question of combining diverse and potentially problematic elements, not the east of which was an extensive electrical system within an installation that was virtually all water.

It took until the late summer of 2001 for the team to conclude that the fountain was feasible and for the Crowns to decide that the time was right to present the project to a wider audience. Plensa set about creating a more sophisticated computer animation, a three-dimensional realization that left Heraclitus and Lao-Tse on the cutting-room floor, but which gave a far clearer picture of the aesthetic detailing, the scale, and the positioning of the fountain in relation to its allotted site. In fact, the basic specifications had changed remarkably little in the eighteen months since his first presentation. The twin towers would be fifty feet tall, twenty-three feet wide, and sixteen feet deep, and made of glass bricks. The 232-by-48-foot reflecting sk n pool would be constructed

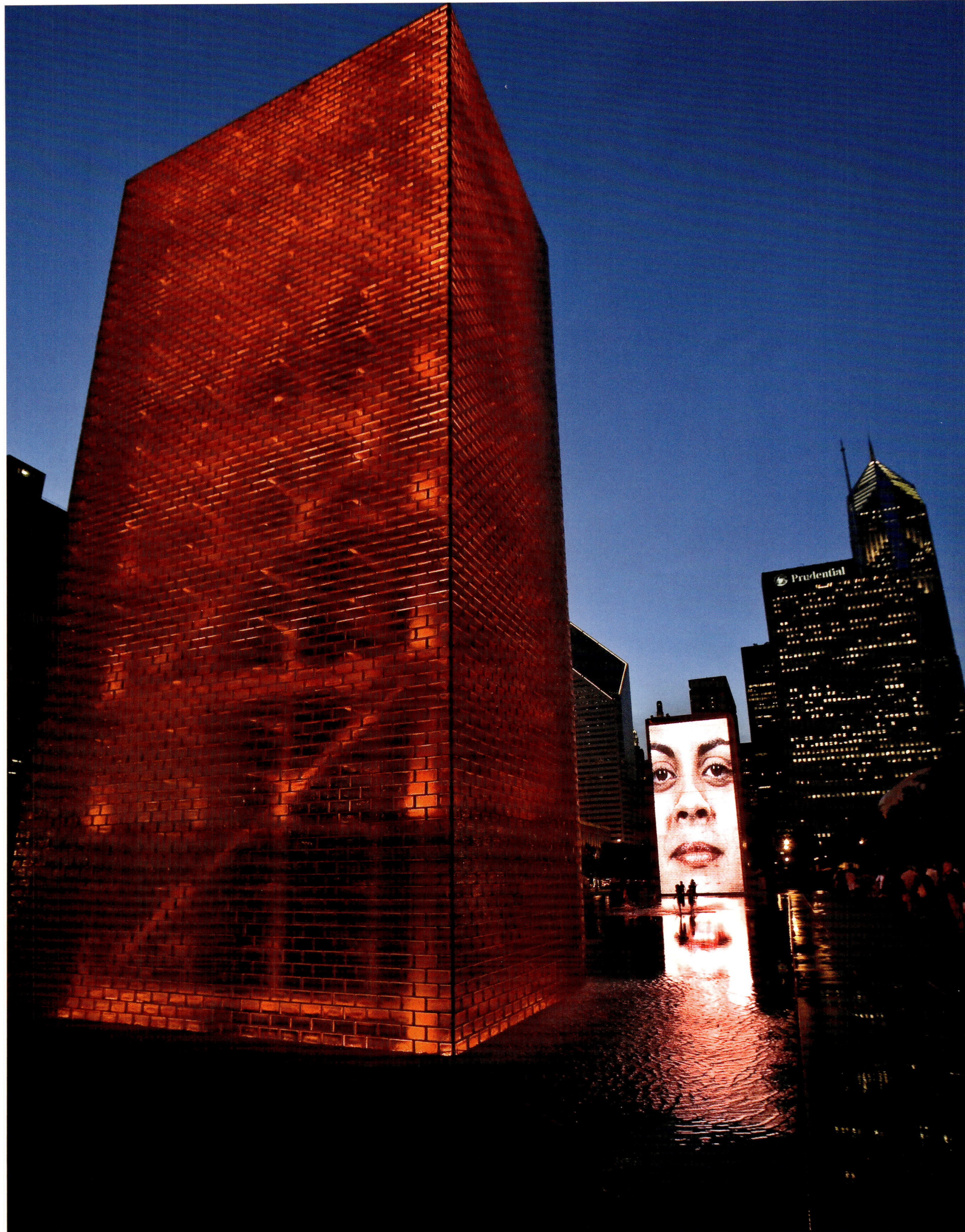
Prudential

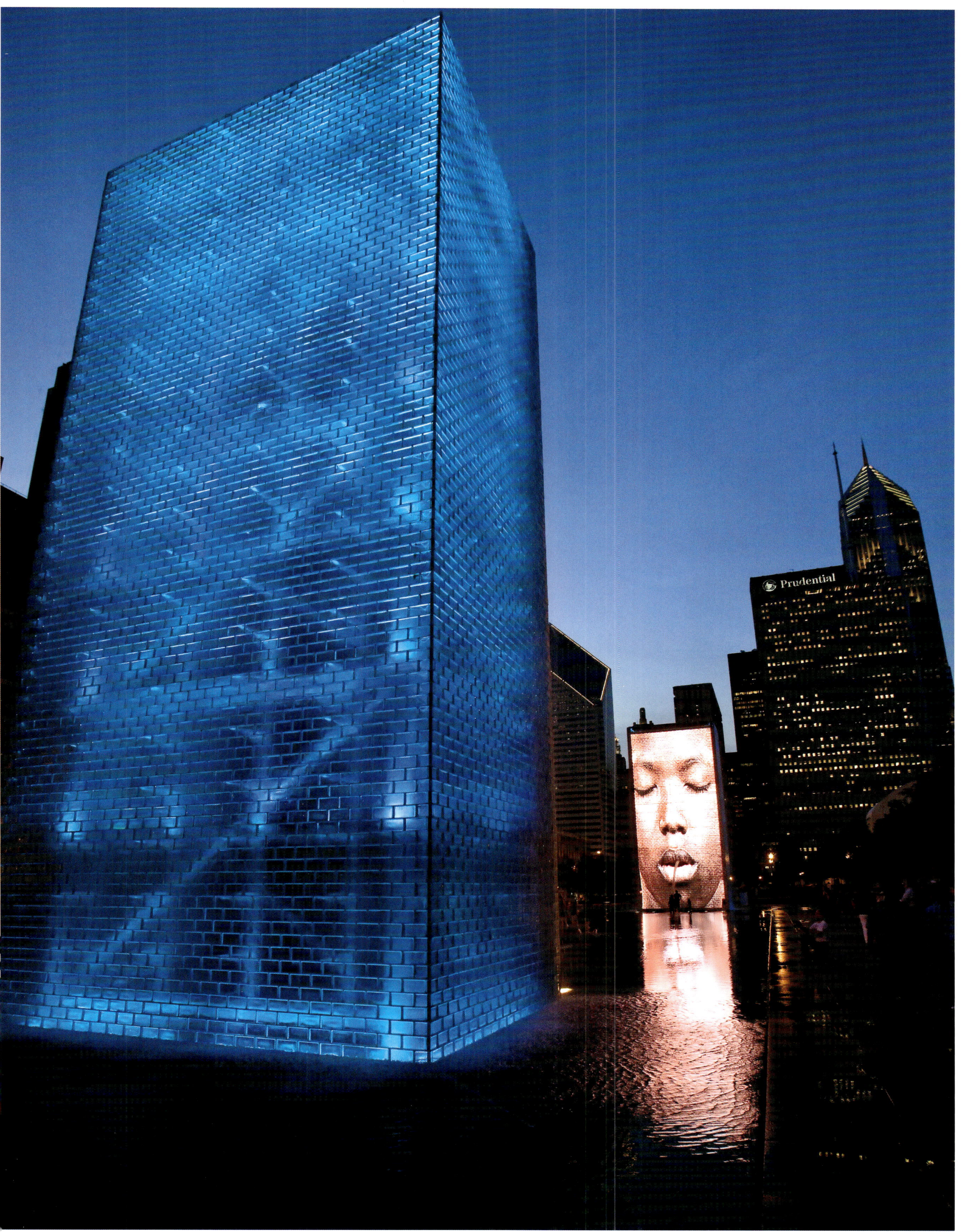
Prudential

out of black granite. There was to be seating set back from the two longer sides (later changed to benches made of solid cedarwood from British Columbia). Water would constantly flow down three faces of the towers, while the fourth would regularly spout water synchronized to the images, followed by a brief cascade. At night, colored lighting from within the towers would illuminate the curtains of water. An archive of faces would be created for the LED screens, one that could continue expanding over time to reflect the evolving demographics of Chicago. The fountain would be linked to the web, and therefore accessible worldwide, with the provision to change the color of the nocturnal lighting by popular demand.

Going Public

The second presentation was made at the Art Club of Chicago on October 4, 2001: the day the *Crown Fountain* finally went public. As reported by the Chicago Sun-Times the following day: "A new piece for Millennium Park was announced [yesterday]—a fountain with twin towers of cascading water to rise more than three stories over a rectangular pool just three millimeters deep." The tone was more factual than enthusiastic, and reflected the climate of the moment. Millennium Park was in mid-stride and receiving more than its fair share of negative press. It was a moment when nobody seemed sure where to pin his or her colors.

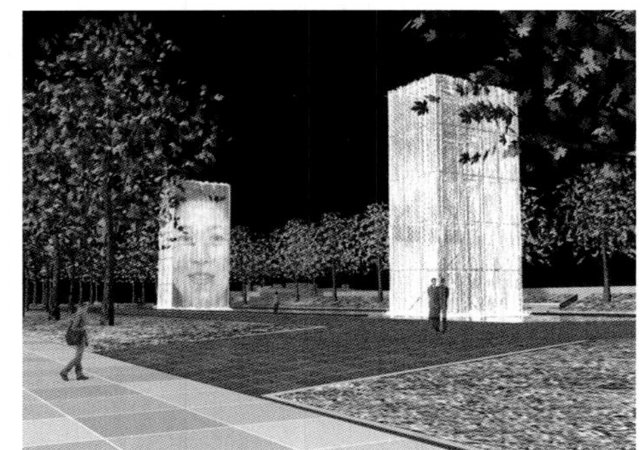

Not all of Plensa's ambitions proved viable. Largely for reasons of cost, the web link and ongoing image archive were shelved. Nevertheless, those that made it to the finish line remained absolutely faithful to the artist's original conception. To view the computer animation, and to swoop bird-like around the site, it was easy to imagine that all the problems had been solved. But, of course, they hadn't.

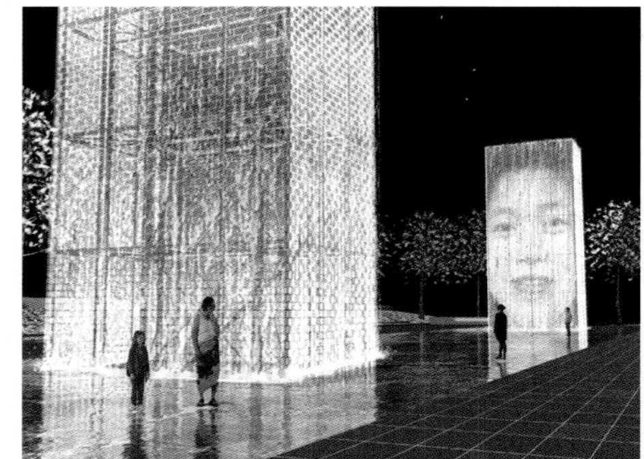

Dog Days

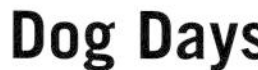

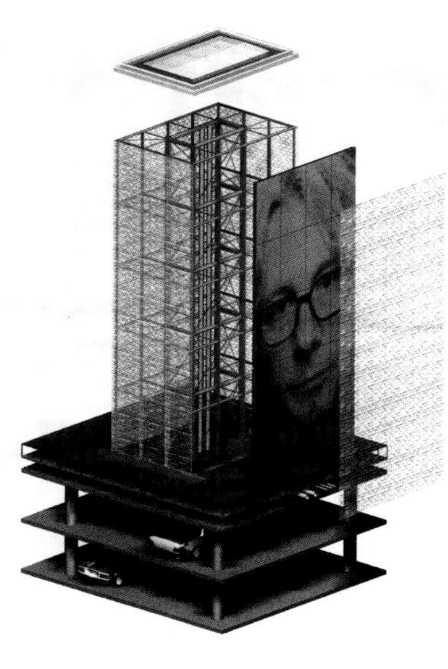

The job of gathering the team had fallen to Bob Wislow of U.S. Equities and his Senior Vice President, Roark Frankel. Frankel was to handle the more hands-on tasks, steering a diverse group of specialists towards achieving a common goal. Principal among the technical team were the same water engineers whom the Crowns had admired back in Las Vegas and who were considered the world's most innovative water specialists. All the participants had worked on larger projects before, although not involving the specific problems posed by the *Crown Fountain*. Similarly, everyone was used to working in partnership with professionals from other disciplines. So it's difficult to know just why the project started to go so badly wrong.

It wasn't the high point of the *Crown Fountain* story and, in all, it set the project back by almost two years. Nobody quite seems to agree on what happened, but it appears that suddenly no one was listening to the artist. Plensa's original "dream" had been set aside and the water specialists returned with a version of the fountain that had been reconfigured in a parallel universe.

One of the problems seems to be that the companies chosen by U.S. Equities are all large. They tend to see the fountain as just another project and the artist as an unnecessary obstruction standing between themselves and the client. They have their own ways of working, their own tried and tested solutions. The only problem is that they are not Plensa's.

> "These large companies never understood that this was an art piece. The original water company, for example, whom I had worked with for two years, when they came to make their final presentation I discovered they'd changed my towers into something resembling pyramids. And in the center they'd put jumping jets of water! Well, I suppose they thought the pool looked empty and that water runs more easily down sloping walls, but that wasn't my concept. This was in the middle of a big meeting and it developed into yet another fight."
>
> Jaume Plensa

And there are other clouds on the horizon. Some people believe the expanse of black granite will create a "hot spot" in the city, absorbing solar radiation by day and releasing it by night. Others believe that the images on the towers will prove a distraction to traffic on nearby Michigan Avenue. Still others hold that the benches will attract homeless sleepers and skateboarders, or that the towers are out of proportion.

With Steve Crown now taking the lead role, the family steps in to defend the project and answer its critics. Some have genuine doubts and it's a question of reassurance, reason, and persuasion. In answer to the height question, at Uhlir's suggestion they even build a mock-up of one tower in scaffolding and invite the doubters to view it. But elsewhere the criticism has a more political edge. Millennium Park is Mayor Daley's baby: it's high profile and a lot is riding on its success. The fountain is only one aspect of the park and is not being funded from the public purse. Nevertheless, it is arguably the most controversial of the individual projects. The music pavilion arises from a long history of trying to locate a permanent music shell in Grant Park, while the *Lurie Garden* offers no conceivable threat. But the *Crown Fountain*… Ah, that is a different matter! Was it in fact a fountain or a multi-dimensional entertainment center more appropriate to Disneyland? Was it a building and therefore in default of those 1836 city bylaws? And was it based on a technology that would soon become dated and reduced to nothing more than a monument to a bygone era?

Throughout much of the twenty-month period that the fountain was in the hands of the first team of engineers, the Crown family had been reluctant to go public, and the air of secrecy that surrounded the project can only have helped its critics. At an even later stage, with objections to its height now coming from James Wood, president of the Art Institute, and with a new estimate well exceeding the original budget, even Lester Crown faltered, suggesting to Plensa that the towers could be scaled down. Plensa considered for a moment, then gave a reply that has since entered into the folklore of Millennium Park. "If you can scale down Chicago, then I can scale down the fountain." Lester couldn't, and so Plensa didn't either.

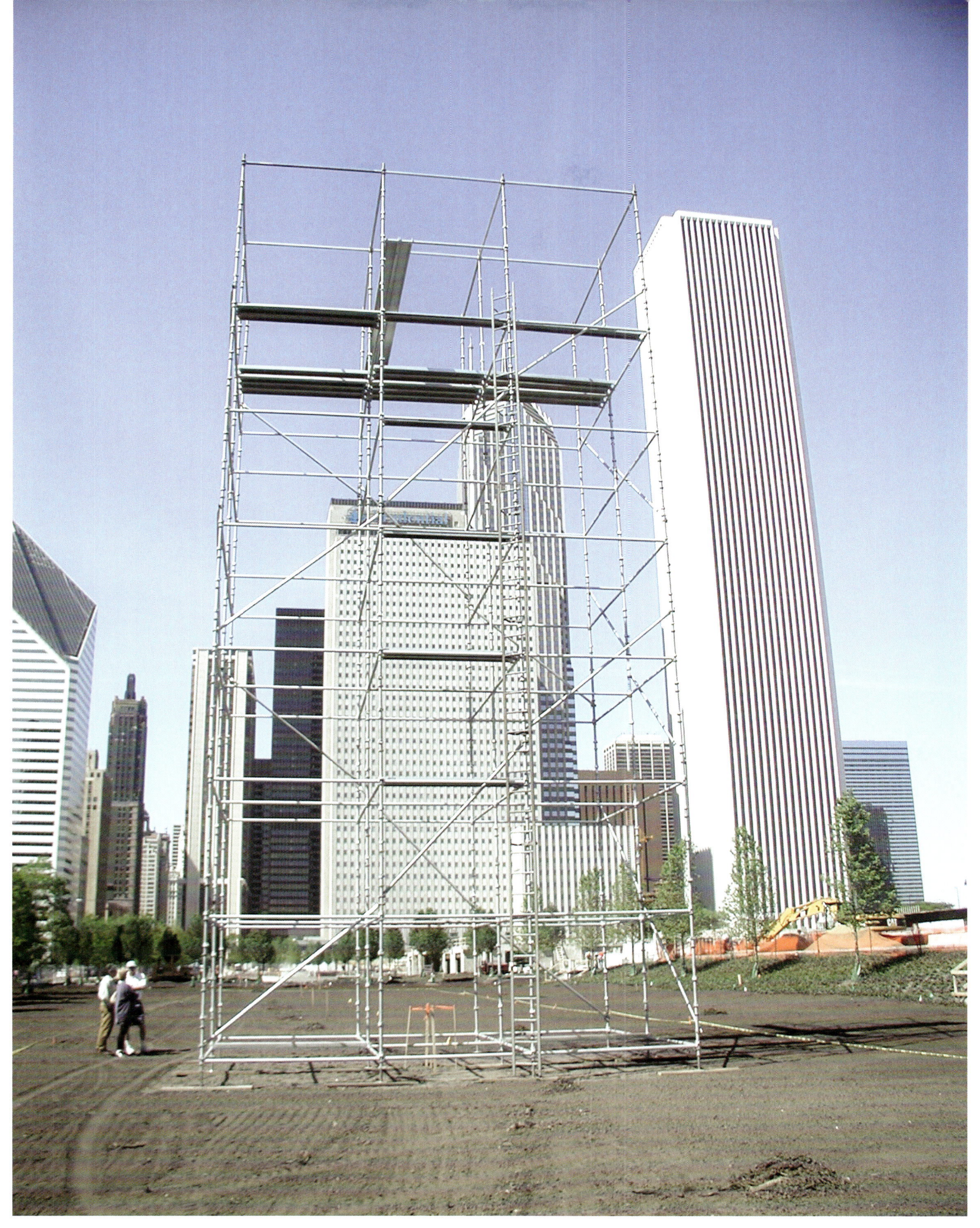

"On May 29, 2001, Jim Crown, Alan Schachtman, Susan Crown, Paula Hannaway Crown, and Paul Gray accompanied me to see the mock-up construction and check its proportions in relation to the site."

Jaume Plensa

Despite Lester's momentary hesitation, it was the agency, patience, and faith of the Crown family that carried the day. Plensa recalls that "the Crown family, who after all were providing the money for this tremendously ambitious project … constantly defended the piece, both with the politicians and the technical team. They were unbelievably supportive."

A Voice in the Wilderness

Throughout this time, Plensa was making frequent visits to Chicago to attend meetings and generally keep watch over the project's progress. But he was still based in Barcelona. He still had commitments to meet, work to make, and exhibitions to install. He still had an obligation to his studio assistants, who were largely engaged with other projects. In the first two years of the new millennium, he participated in over twenty group exhibitions worldwide and had solo shows in galleries and museums in Madrid, Bilbao, Malaga, Salzburg, New York, Berlin, Santiago de Compostela, Barcelona, and Ljubljana, and was preparing a further eight shows for the following year. It was a punishing schedule, but although Steve Crown had belatedly stepped in to hold the fort, Plensa still needed to be sure his voice was heard in Chicago.

> "The Crown family didn't want to go public until everything was resolved, not only technically, but also in terms of all the political infighting. There seemed little point in offering it up to public debate until we knew the project was able to proceed. But during that period it was shown to quite a wide audience, representing many different interests, and I think that eventually helped me to realize how best to communicate the piece in all its complexity. So, it wasn't a public debate as such, but there was a lot of valuable discussion with representatives of the community."
>
> Jaume Plensa

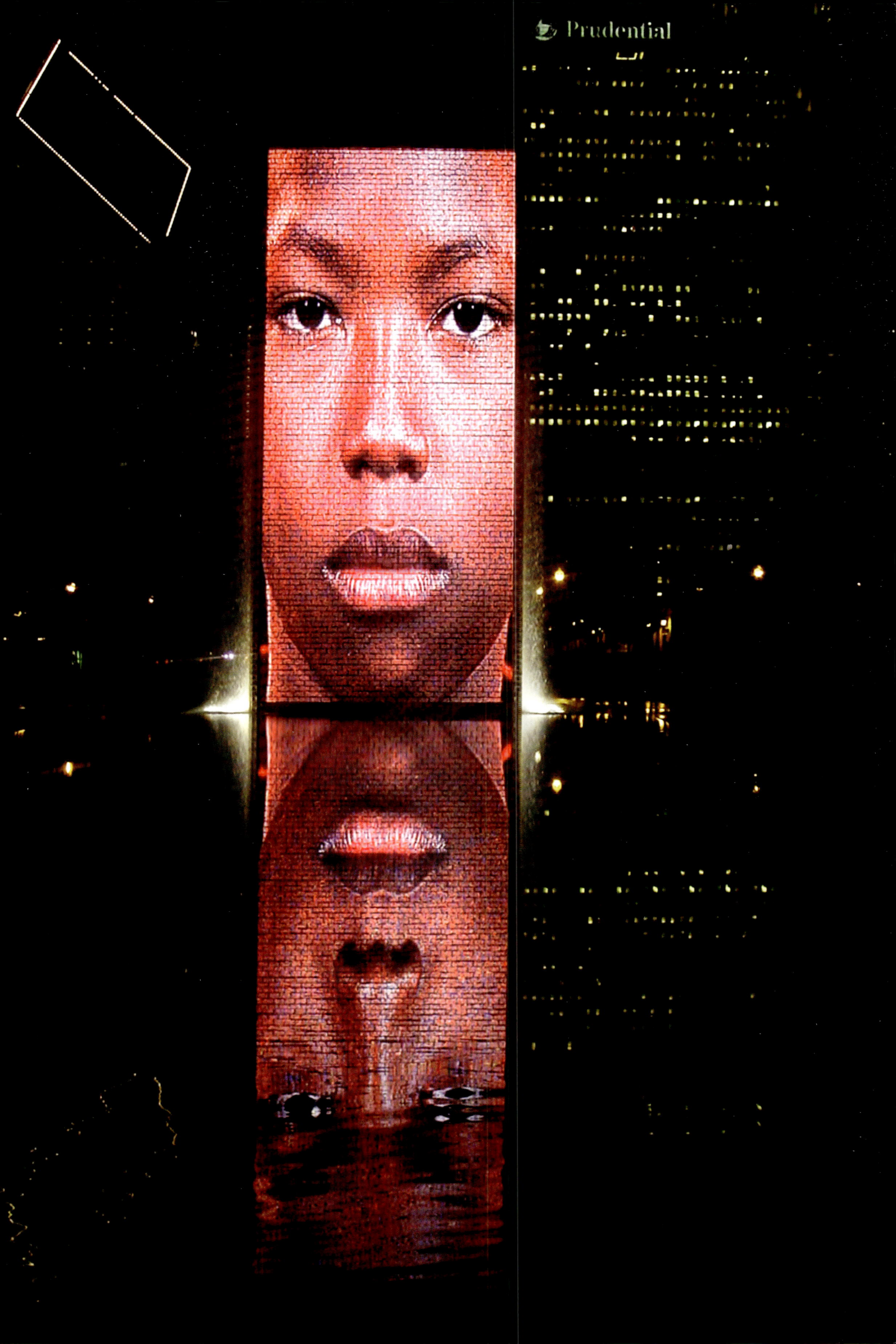

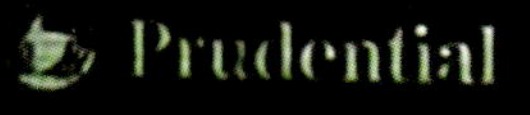
Prudential

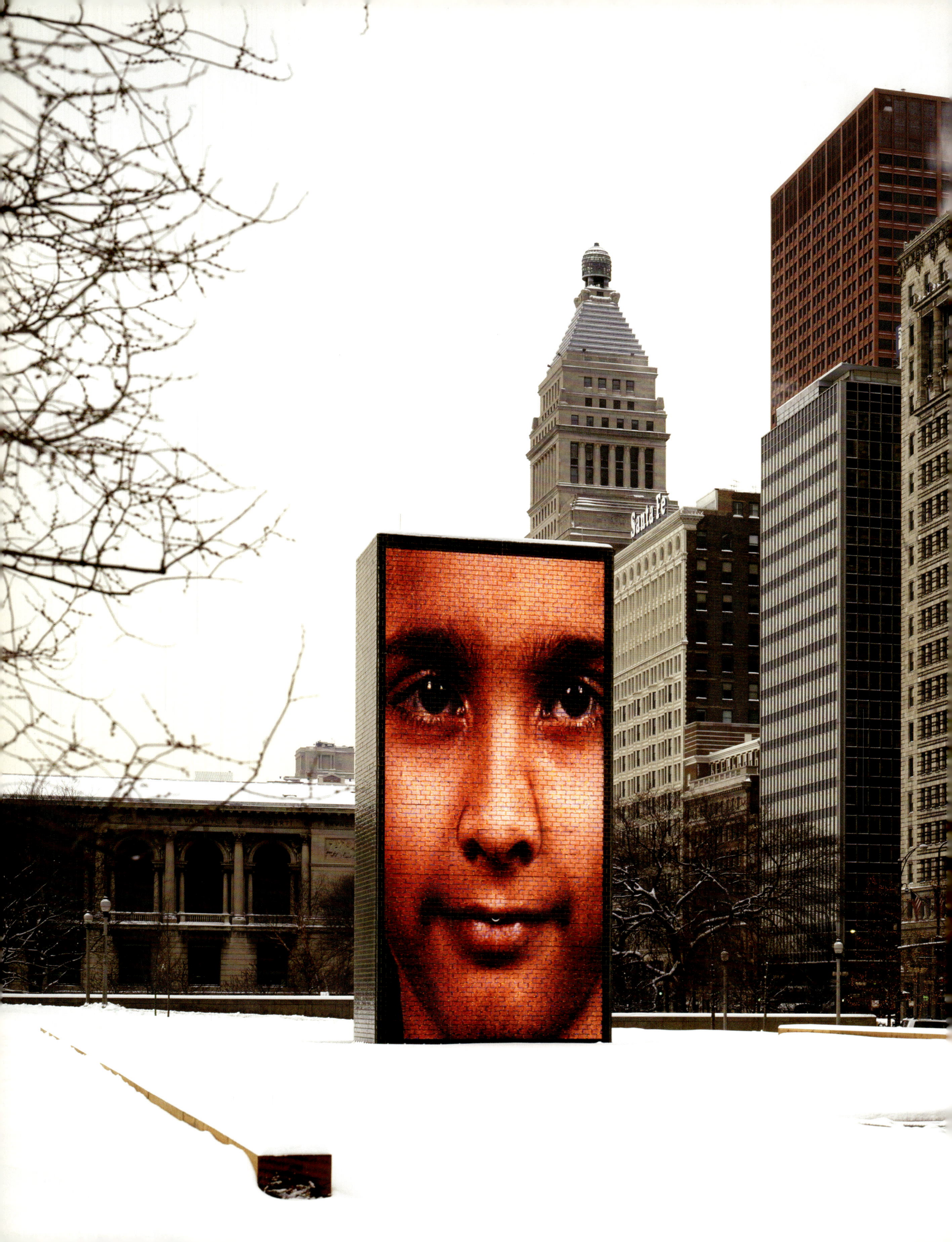
Santa Fe

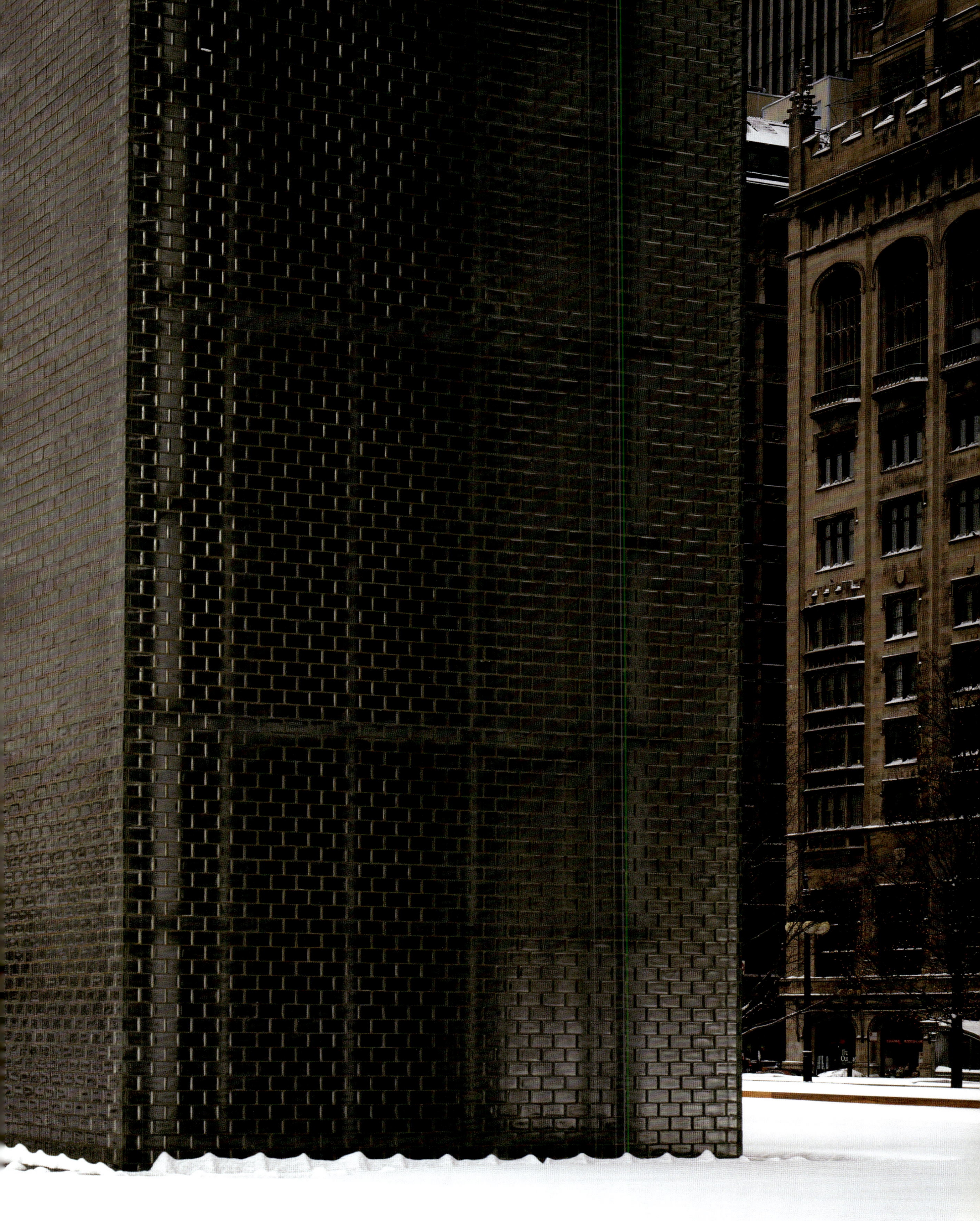

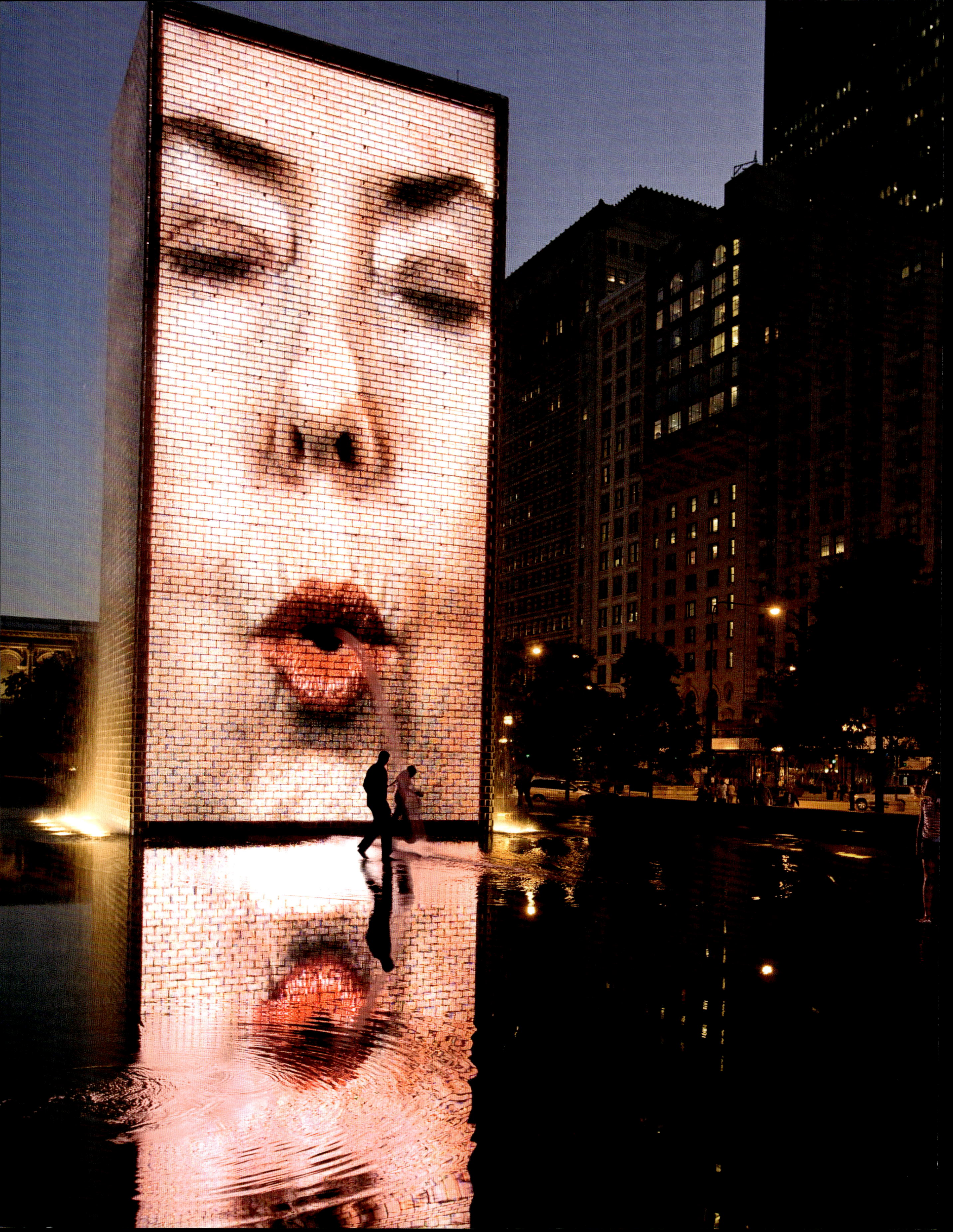

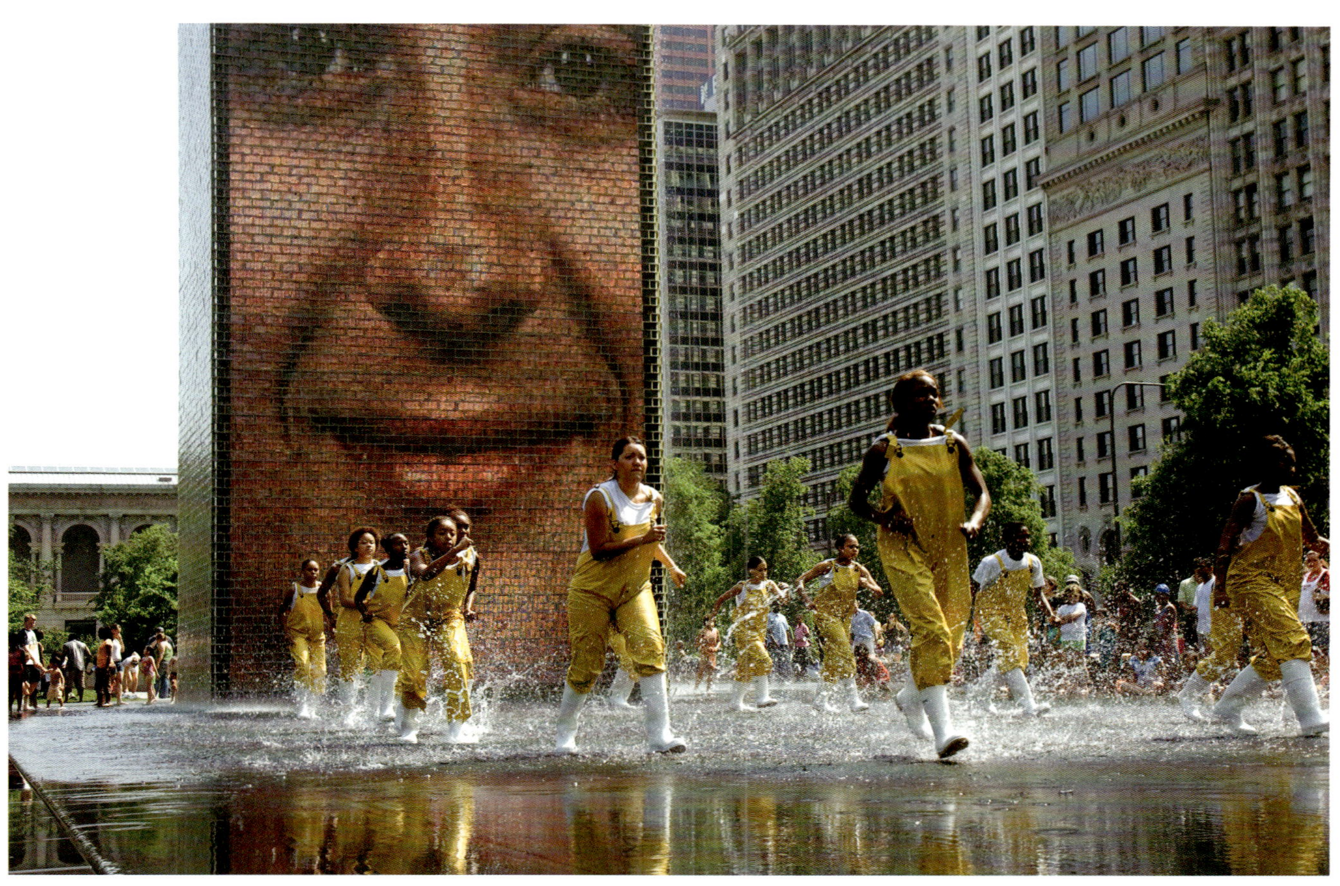

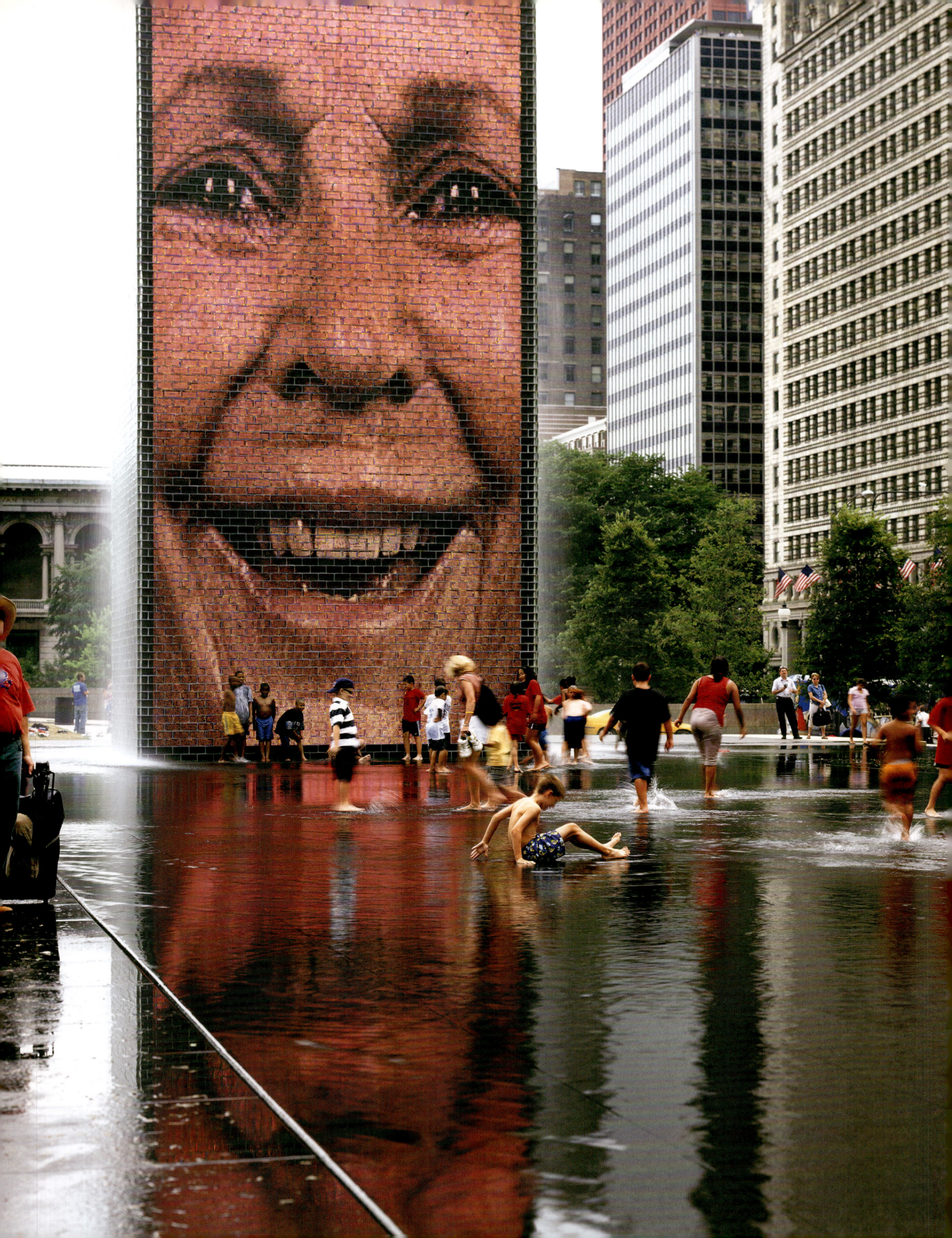

6

A Space for People

Let's return to Ljubljana for a moment. Although I'm not aware of it, by the time of our preliminary visit in March 2001 Plensa is already one year into the Millennium Park project. And when not actually in Chicago, he is talking by telephone with Paul Gray at the gallery. We are in Slovenia for just two days and on the second evening we retire to a bar, where we are discreetly supplied with endless vodkas as the ideas flow. Plensa gives himself over entirely to the project in hand as we indulge in flights of fancy as to what form the exhibition might take. We conclude that one entire venue might be empty and given over to sound. In the cold light of day it proves totally unrealistic, but shows that Plensa's mind was exploring the idea that space was for people, not simply to be populated by objects. It's the same idea that he's trying to get across in Chicago, that the space around and between the towers should be left empty. A space for people.

A New Start

Things came to a head over the Christmas–New Year period 2001. There was no personal rancor, Plensa insists, but quite clearly the project wasn't working—or not in the direction the artist wanted. It's not an unprecedented situation. Many artists find their initial conception sidelined by the inevitable constraints of budget, time frame, politics, and the sheer complexities of scale and communication. Plensa's team is doing their best, but with the urgency to complete the project on budget and on time, and with so many fingers in the technical pie, the proposals for the completed structures simply aren't what the artist intended.

He has to consider the obvious choice: to accept a compromise or to walk out.

It has happened before. The classic example must be Jørn Utzon's design for the Sydney Opera House, a groundbreaking construction that has since become a symbol for the city, a UNESCO protected building, and an influence on many future architects. And yet the building that was originally sketched out on the back of an envelope saw its architect abandon the project after disagreements with both the city and the engineering team assigned to it. There is a salutary lesson here. Despite conceiving one of the world's most iconic buildings, Utzon never won a major commission again.

The same fate could await Plensa, and there are sleepless nights. As he frequently confides to Paul Gray, his ultimate fear is that the project will never be realized, that the accumulated misunderstandings and escalating costs will force the Crowns to withdraw. But it was Steve Crown who came to the rescue. Apprised of the gravity of the situation by U.S. Equities and assessing the proposals on the table, with the family's support he made the decision to keep faith with the artist's original vision. It was the ultimate vote of confidence, for it meant dismissing the existing team, writing off two years' budget, and starting over again.

Larger Goals and a New Team

Not all was lost, for a lot of practical information had been gathered over the previous months. But the change of team meant courting a potential public relations disaster at a time when questions were already being raised with regards to the park's schedules and expenditure. It can't have been an easy decision, but Steve Crown had the foresight to "focus on the larger goals," as Roark Frankel would later comment.

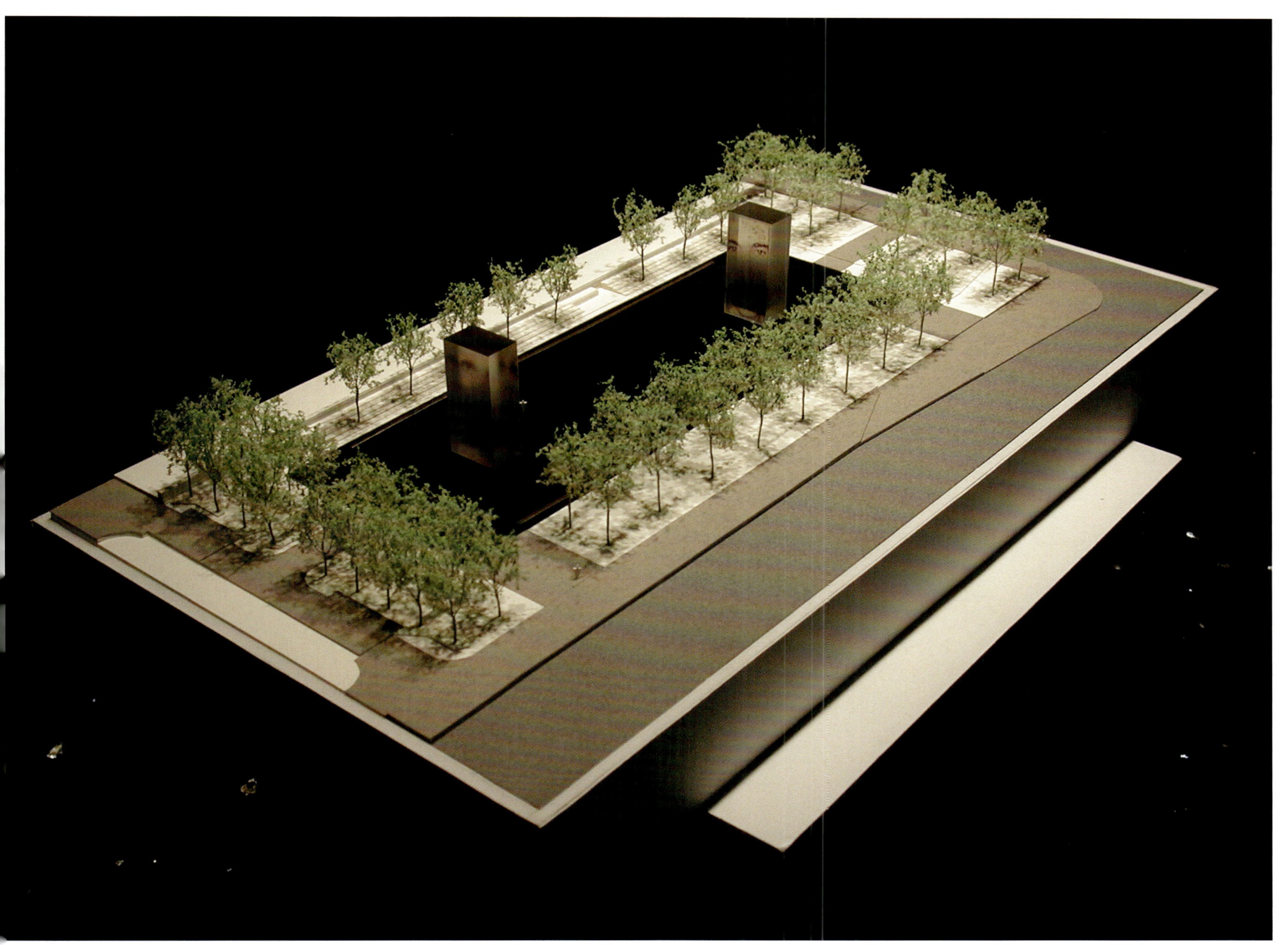

Krueck & Sexton's final model.

If there was one defining moment when the project found its feet and picked up momentum, this was it. Finding themselves back in the driver's seat, Bob Wislow, Alan Schachtman, and Roark Frankel of U.S. Equities were instructed to propose a new team. And this time they thought small. Well, smaller. The mistake had been to take on big companies that sought a direct relationship with the client. So, why not use smaller companies who were prepared not only to listen to the client, but also to work alongside the artist? Companies for whom this was not simply another job, but *the* job. Steve Crown was adamant that they use local firms wherever possible, not only as a vote of confidence in the city, but because, "when there's a problem, you can just walk down the street, knock on their door, and get it sorted out."

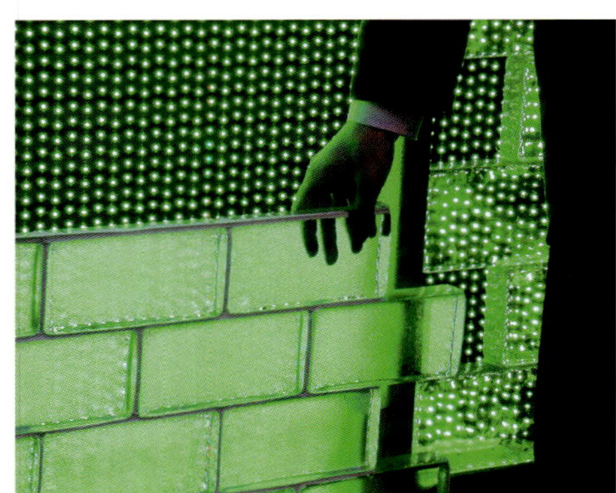

It wasn't possible to source all the expertise locally and the net had to be thrown wide, with various contracts going to companies across the continent, but the architects who are appointed in February 2002 are a relatively small, Chicago-based partnership. Ronald Krueck and Mark Sexton have several things in their favor aside from their relatively intimate scale. As Frankel wrote in an e-mail to the artist, "Without trying to be too much of a cheerleader, I'm confident that you'll be very excited by their work, their experience with glass, structure, and detailing and, most importantly, their respect for your work and what you are trying to achieve here in Chicago."

On March 12 Plensa is in Chicago for yet another meeting, this one attended by Steve Crown, U.S. Equities, and the architects. Immediately there's an "interactive chemistry," as Frankel puts it. It's Mark Sexton who will work most closely with Plensa and he seems to understand what the project requires. Initial ideas are thrown around and then, as Steve Crown says, "an unusual thing happened. Mark turned to Jaume and asked, 'Is this what you had in mind?' It was the first time that the artist had been asked!"

There's only one problem: initially, Krueck and Sexton aren't sure they want the job. Although they've worked on many varied projects, including most recently the Spertus Institute of Jewish Studies, also on Michigan Avenue, and the restoration of the Mies van der Rohe buildings on Lake Shore Drive, the partners see themselves primarily as initiators, designing projects from

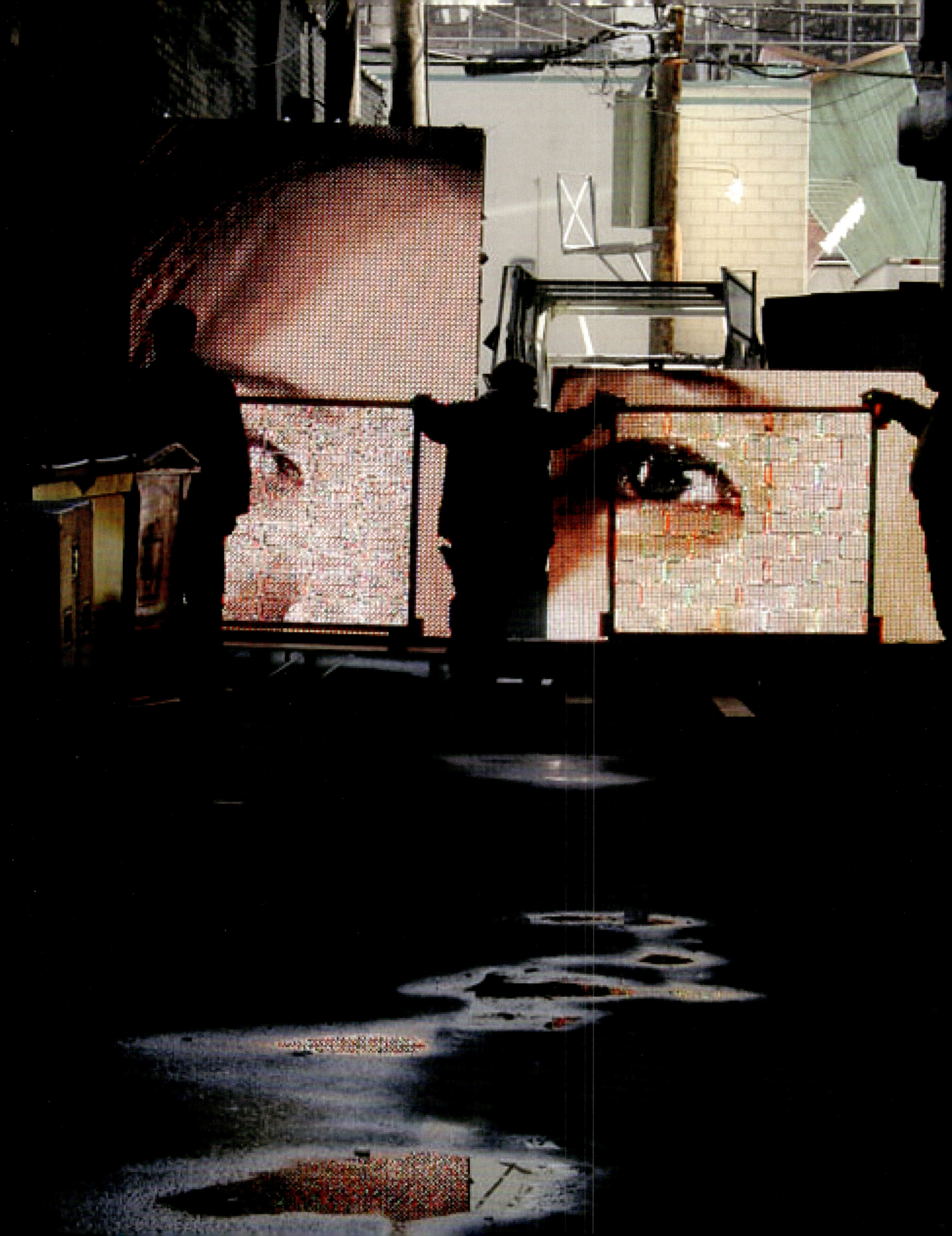

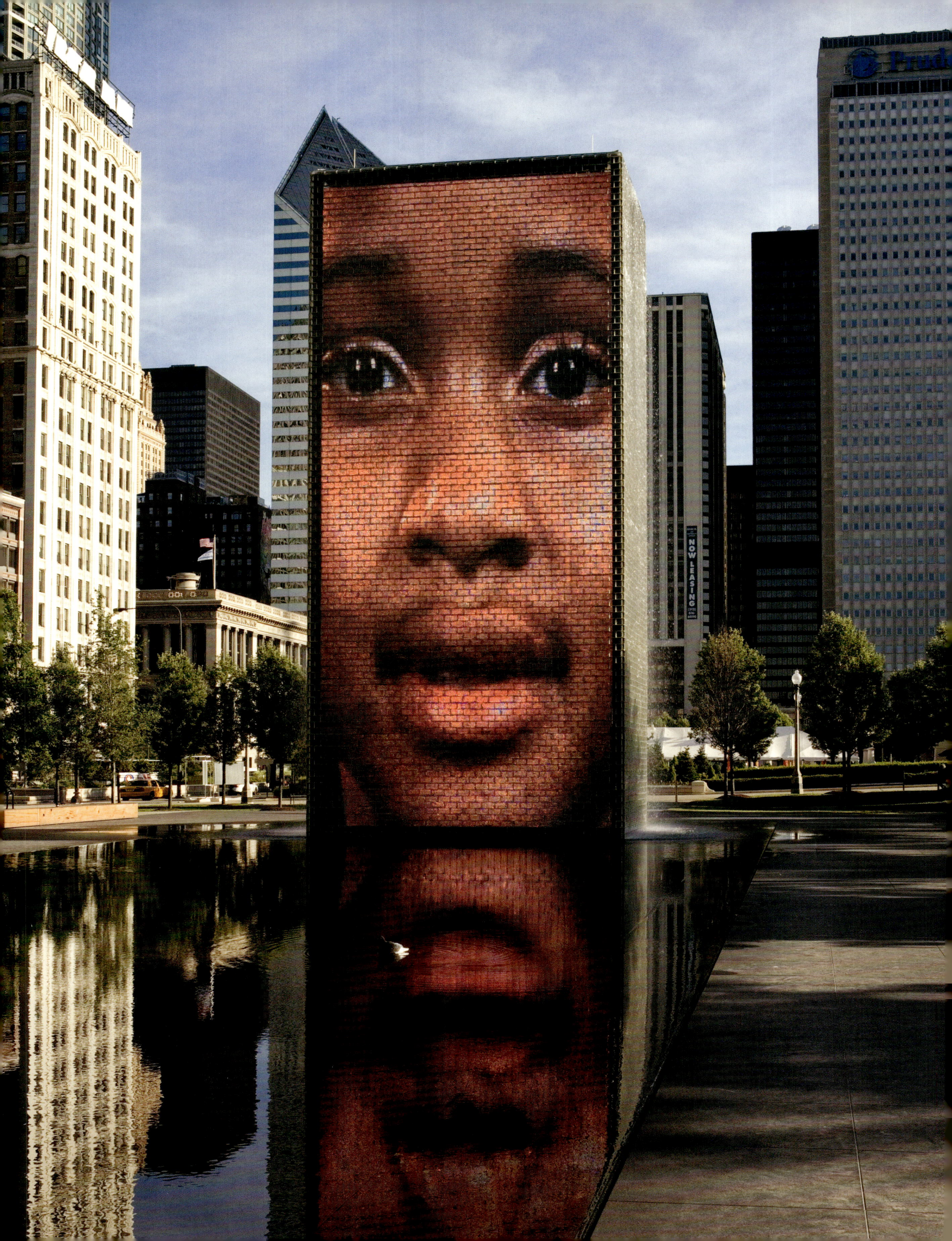

the ground up. And it is clear that in this case Plensa's design concept
needs to be respected to the letter.

The Architect's Tale

"When we were approached in January 2002, we were offered
a clean slate: only later did we hear that another architectural firm
had been involved before us. But because we are a design
firm, when we were first presented with the idea, the initial reaction
of my partner and I was—do we really want to do someone else's
work? The artist had already developed a very strong concept,
including the computer animation. But we looked at it and
thought, although there are some very strong design ideas here,
the artist didn't necessarily have the experience to put them
together. And, you know, every client has an initial idea that they
want fulfilled. So although we were at first reluctant, we agreed
to meet with Jaume. We were intrigued, let's say, because it was
one of those things that's a little bit out n left field.

We also thought, if we take on this project we are going to have
to deal with the ego of the artist, because most of the good ones
are like that. Likewise, Jaume was thinking much the same about
working with us! But when we met him for the first time it was
quite a different story. He does have a position and a strength,
but he was not an egotist. Quite the opposite. He was always
open to ideas—he listened. It was such a joy to work with him
because he had incredible insight! It developed into the story of
an architect and an artist coming together to create something
neither one of us could create independently. The concept
didn't get better, but the end piece did."
Mark Sexton, architect

With Krueck & Sexton tentatively onboard, and with their advice, U.S. Equities
has already begun work on the other players that would make up the new

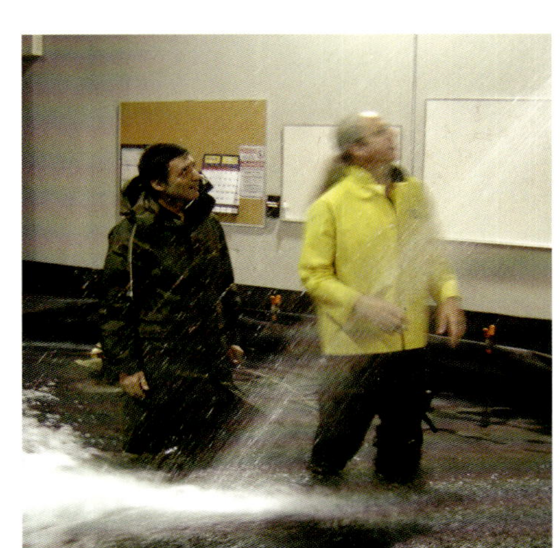
Checking the gargoyle with Larry O'Hearn.

team. In fact, like an arranged marriage, the prospective team is already largely in place by the time Plensa attends the meeting of March 12.

It was to be a marriage made in heaven, with Sexton and Plensa hitting it off immediately. Plensa was later to tell the architect that his role was to be simply a translator. Then with typical grace and humility he adds: "But like you are translating a Greek play. It needs someone with a special creativity, sensitivity, and a fundamental understanding of the entire concept." Despite his initial reservations of working to someone else's plans, Sexton grasps the potential. As he says, "We understood the complexity from the outset: the challenge was in making it look effortless."

The following morning Sexton, Krueck, and Plensa have a date with the rest of the team that develops into a workshop and runs throughout the afternoon. By six in the evening it's clear that everyone is pulling in the same direction.

The team now covers many of the key components. The water features will be handled by Crystal Fountains of Concord, Ontario, who have recently completed projects in San Francisco and Pittsburgh. The lighting is by a local firm, Schuler Shook, who have already worked on several of Chicago's key art projects and are well known to the architects. The structural engineers are Halvorson Kaye, also Chicago-based, with Tim Kaye having already worked with SOM. Environmental Systems Design will handle the air cooling and plumbing, having recently renovated Chicago's *Buckingham Fountain* and Shedd Aquarium.

In the weeks and months to come they will choose Baltimore-based About TWF as the back-room boys who will design the computer programs that control all the image and lighting sequences. BARCO, from Utah, will take on the manufacture of the specialist LED screens that sit inside the glass towers, while Pierini, a local firm, will handle the supporting steel structures. International Granite and Marble, another Chicago-based company, will install the flawless black granite for the pool area, which is eventually sourced in Italy. And after interviewing dozens of potential manufacturers it is decided that L.E. Smith Glass, a hundred-year-old family firm from just outside Pittsburgh, is uniquely equipped to produce the individual glass bricks.

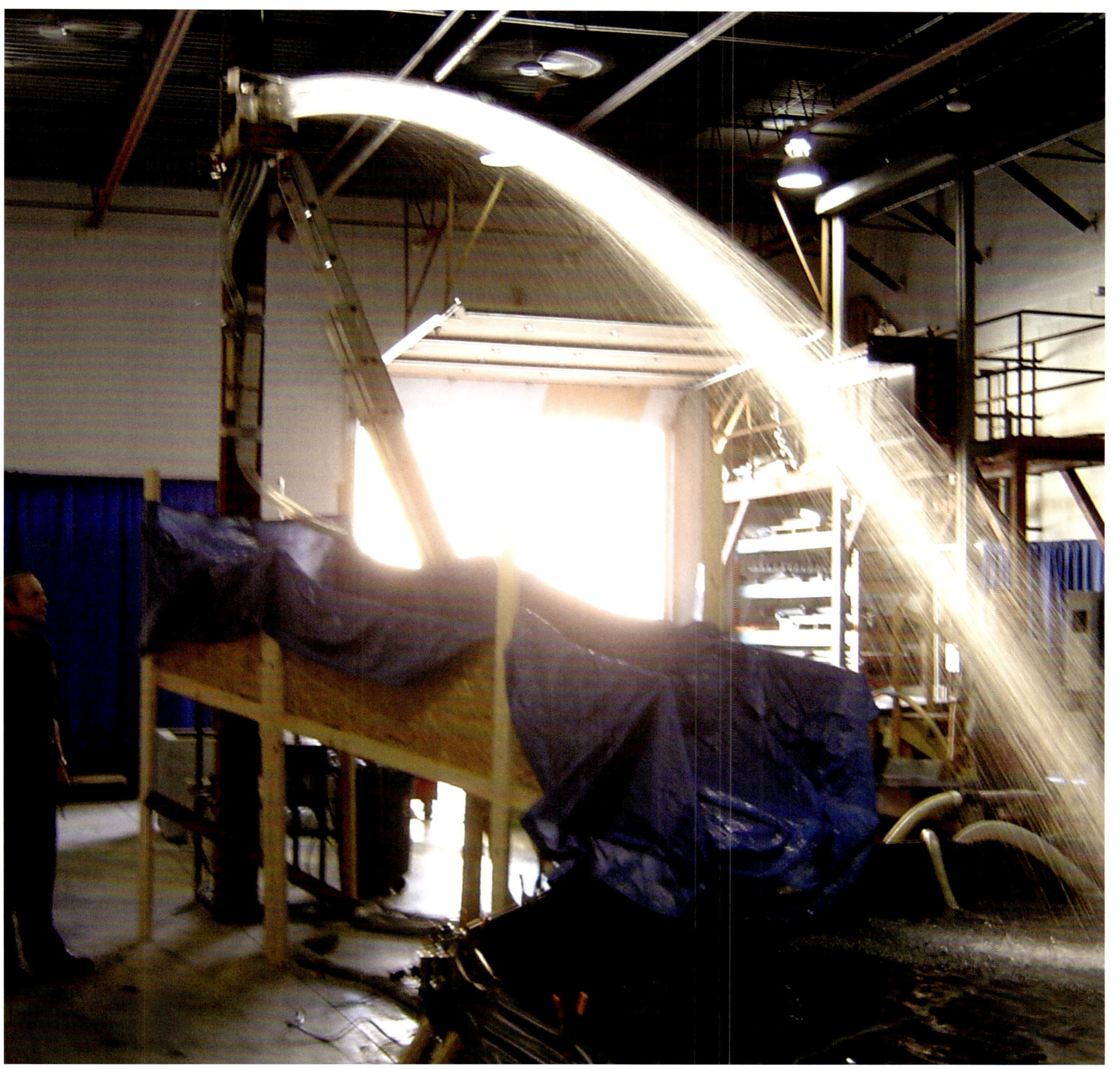

"On December 1, 2003, Roark Frankel and I went back to visit
Larry O'Hearn in Concord, near Torontc, this time with a very
important reason: the gargoyle. The nozzle was designed and
developed not just for aesthetics, but also for safety. The magical
caress of the water on our heads was fantastic. We were the first
to experience what would later become a collective celebration
of life."
Jaume Plensa

It's a long list of names, but it gives some idea of the complexity of the operation. Each specialist area has to confront hundreds of individual problems, many unique to the project. And every single element has to be designed, tested, and perfected. Crystal Fountains, in particular, have to resolve a series of key issues. The first is how to ensure the towers are perfectly level, otherwise the curtains of water will fall unevenly. It's basically a problem for the engineers, for the structures sit astride the concrete and steel armature of the underground parking lot, which, unlike solid ground, is prone to movement. They have to make the water fall vertically yet avoid the force of impact incurred by a fifty-foot drop. (After much experimentation, the answer proves to be a curved top combined with a natural effect whereby the water ripples down the sides of the towers.) They also have to figure out how to make safe the pressure of the gargoyle spout without diminishing its visual impact, as in their first trials the water pressure flattens a 250-pound adult. And most of all, in tandem with BARCO they must devise how to deliver the water spout in a way that doesn't leave a black "hole" in the video image.

The instability of the site also presents a further problem, for the artist's original vision calls for a 9,324-square-foot reflecting pool with just a minimum "skin" of water: something that had not been attempted before, never mind over a preexisting structure. Of course, the pool isn't quite what it seems, for beneath the 250-pound granite slabs lies a two-foot-deep reservoir with sensors to help maintain the pool's water level while recycling eleven thousand gallons through the towers every hour. The very fact that the site is prone to movement creates a huge challenge for the water engineers. They must work with the stonework installers, the architects, and the other engineers in creating a suspended floor that will be level to within a fraction of an inch across its entire surface.

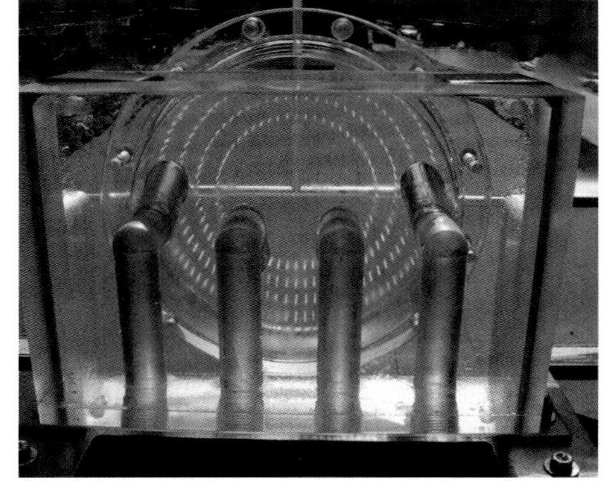
Detail of the gargoyle nozzle.

Not Just Another Brick in the Wall

They used to say there are eight million stories in the Naked City. There may not be as many in the *Crown Fountain,* but to follow just one simple element from beginning to end illustrates how complex each of the developmental stages was. It was Mark Sexton who told me the history of the glass bricks and I give all credit to him for turning a technical discourse into a voyage of discovery.

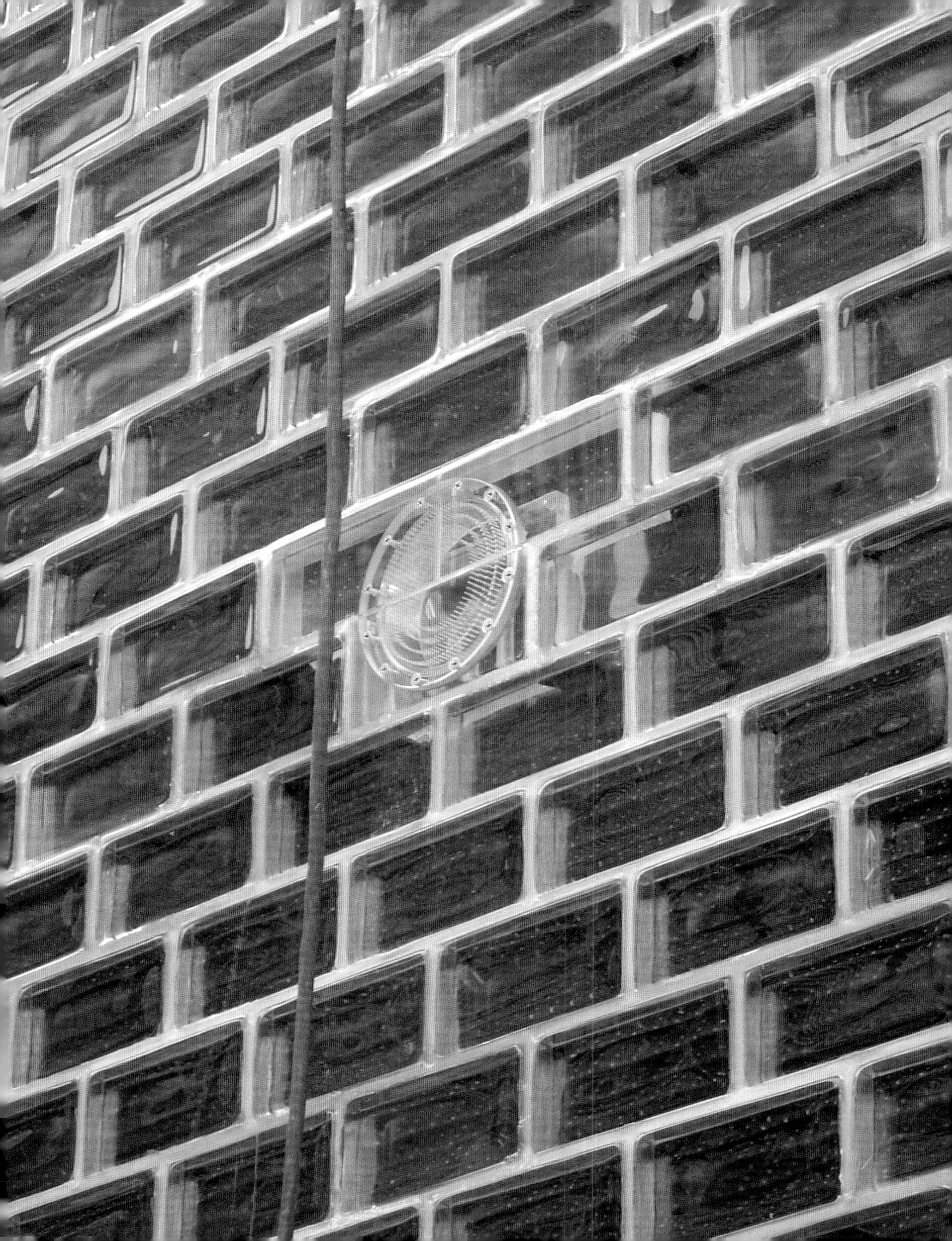

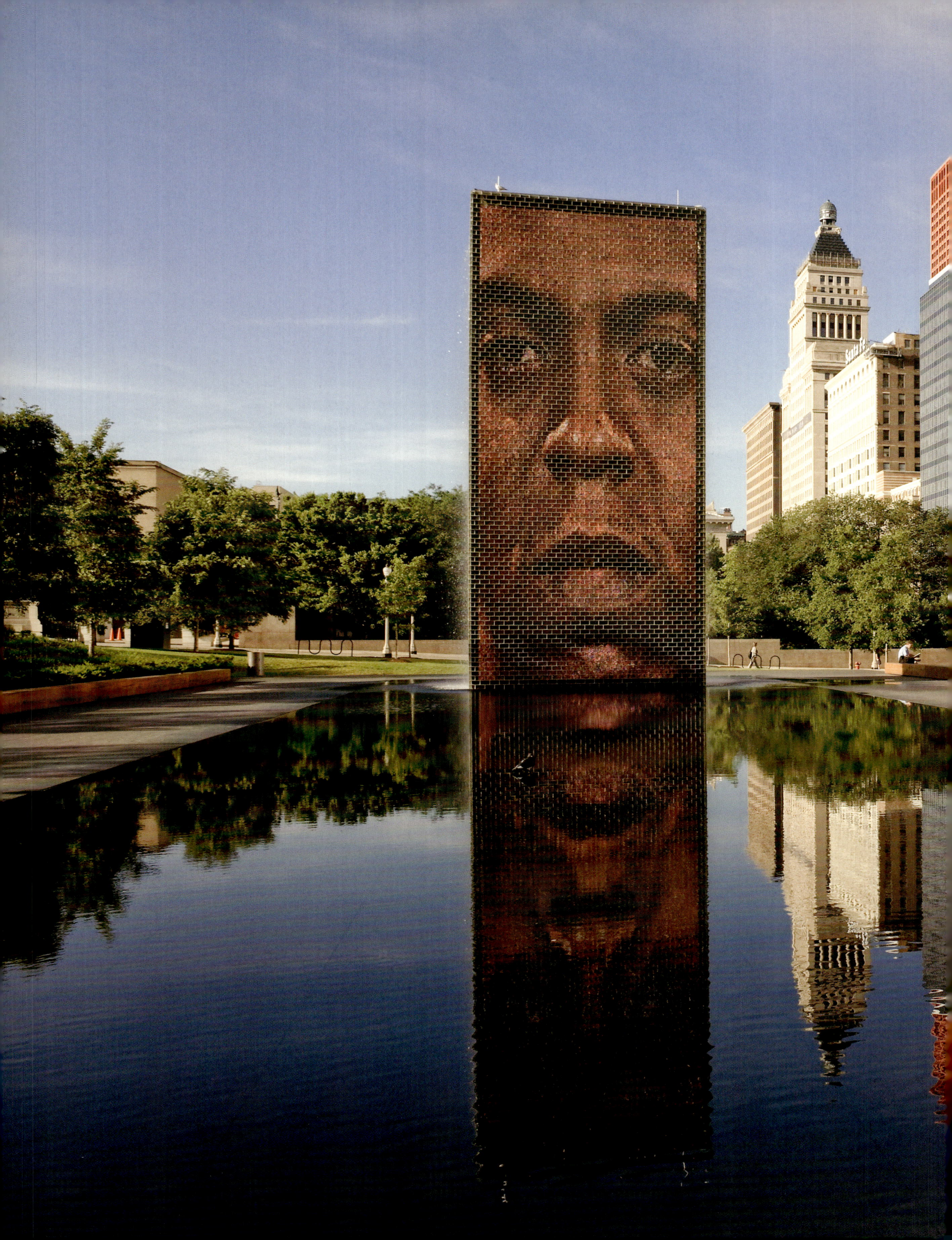

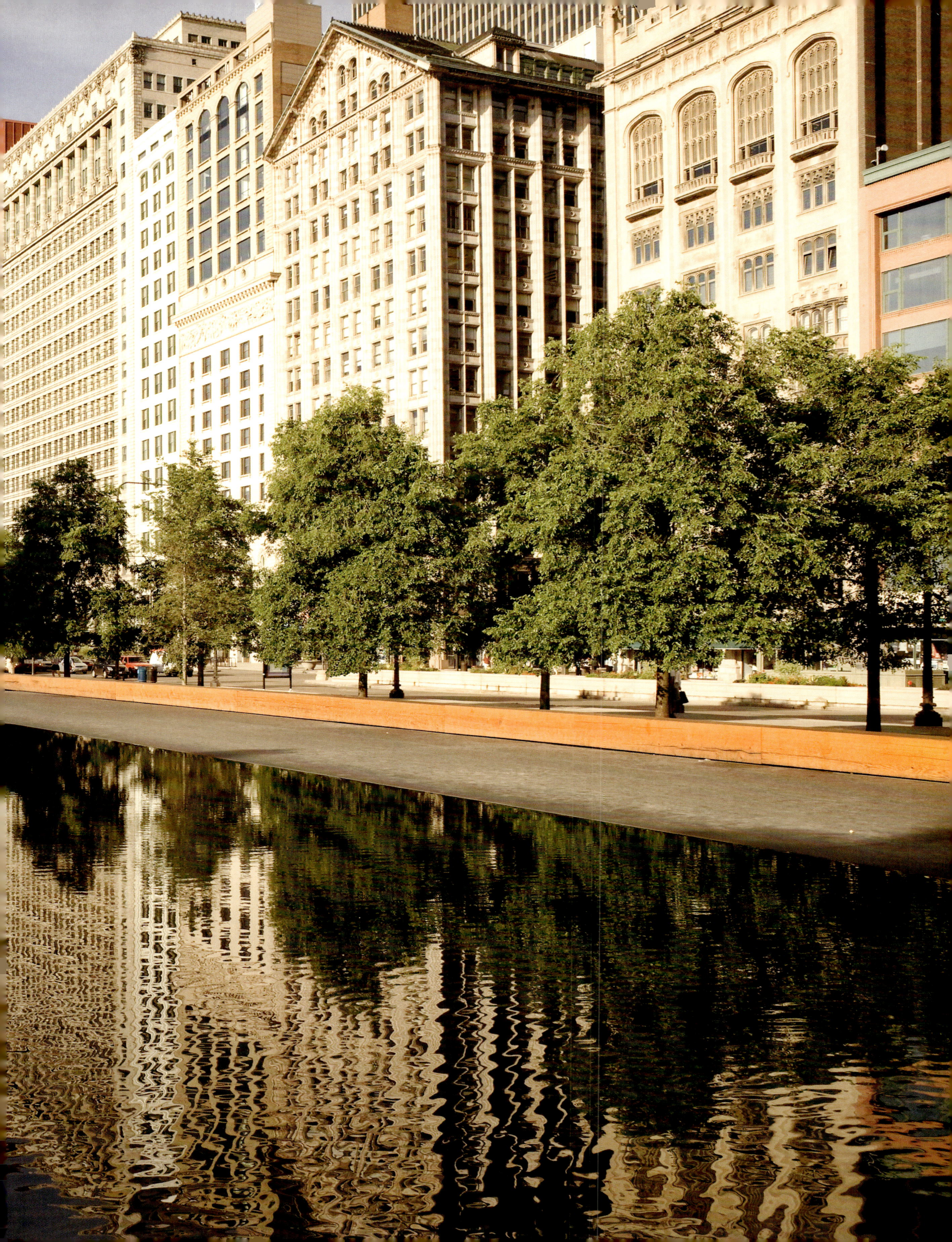

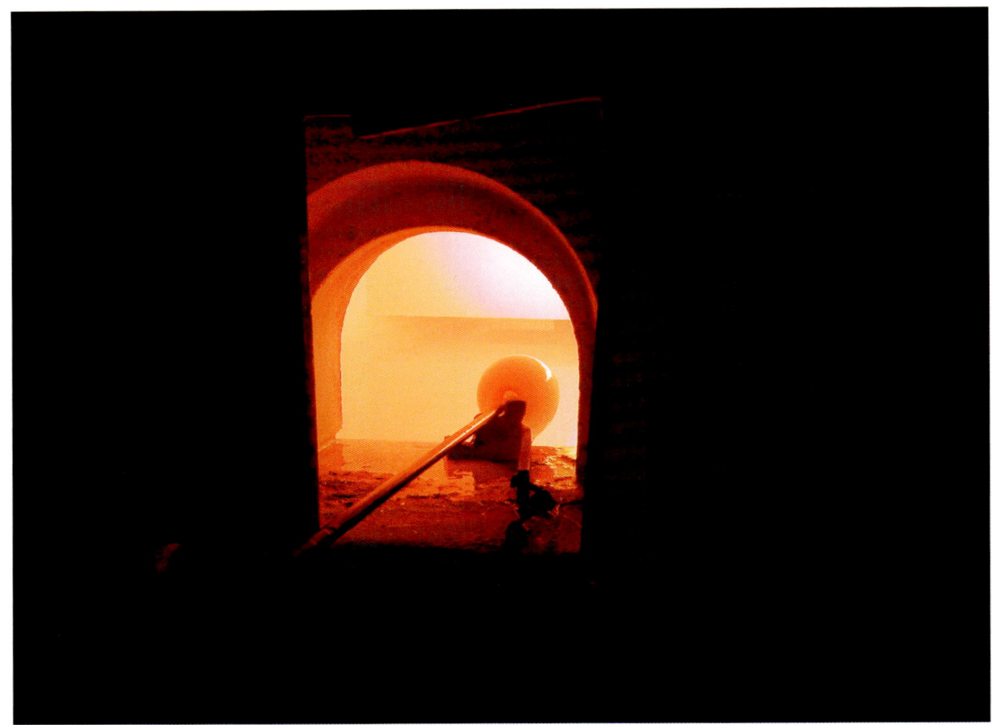

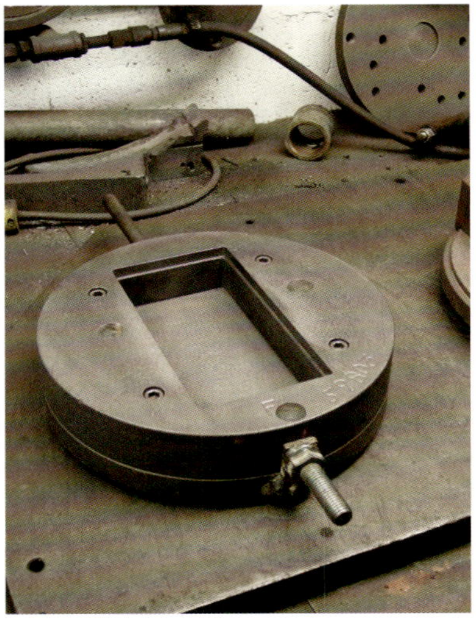

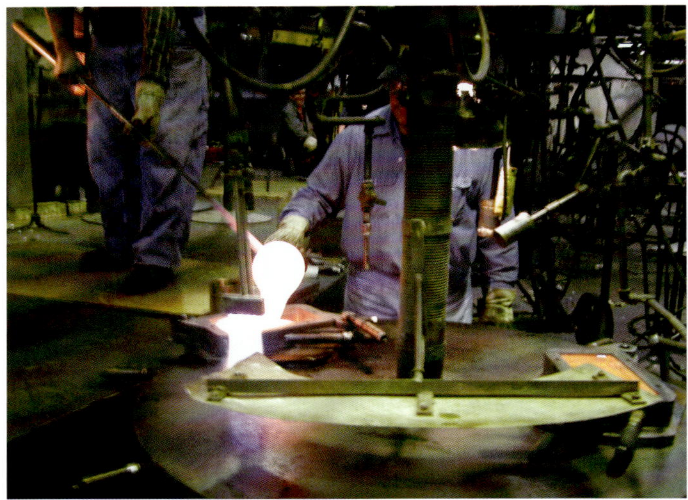

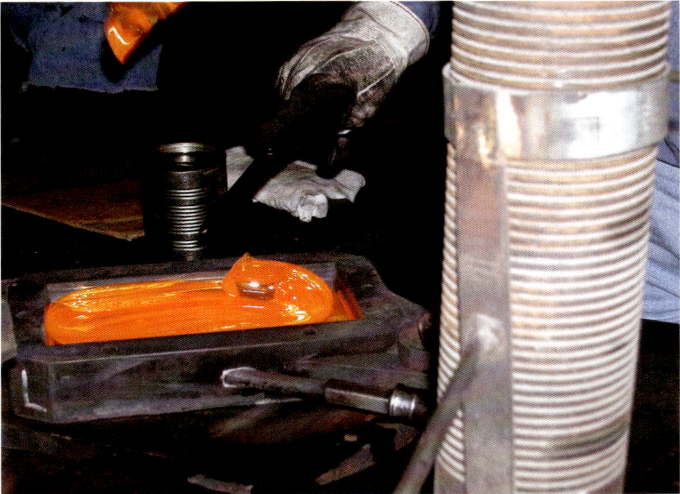

"The old L.E. Smith Glass foundry proved to be fascinating!
At the beginning of October 2003, Roark Frankel, Mark Sexton,
and I traveled to Mount Pleasant near Pittsburgh to meet Norm
Pennington. To see the glass bricks for the first time was a
revelation. During the following weeks, the company cast the
22,500 ten-pound glass bricks needed to cover the towers."
Jaume Plensa

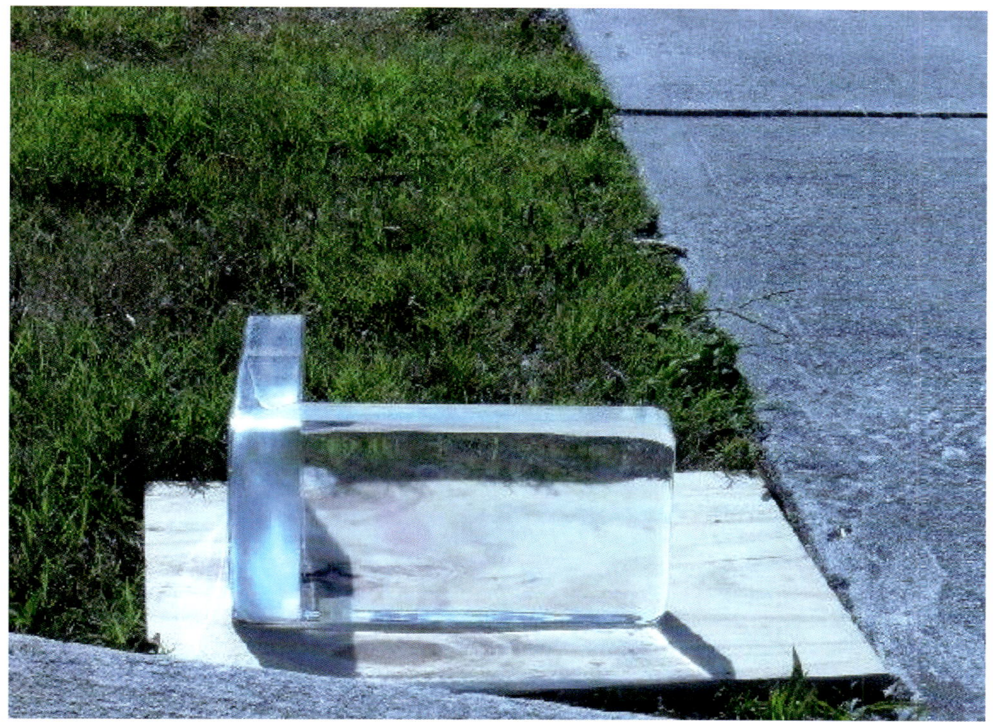

I am holding one brick in my hand. It's a sensual object, not unlike a gold ingot, but despite a weight of ten pounds, at first sight it doesn't look much aside from its startling clarity. Plensa has worked with glass bricks before, but nothing quite like this. This has been handmade by the small firm outside Pittsburgh, using a mix of exceptionally iron-free silica sand and soda to create the purest water-white glass. The mix first needs to be heated to 2,600 degrees Fahrenheit. Then it takes two men to each pour separate amounts of the liquid glass and a third to ensure the exact measure that creates a slight lip and meniscus where the surface rises fractionally above the cast iron mold. Next the mold is transferred to an oven at 1,100 degrees, where it is left to cool gradually to avoid cracking or internal stress. Although twelve men are assigned to the job, only 350 bricks can be produced in a day. And they will need 22,500 for the *Crown Fountain*.

It's not only a science: it's an art. And one of the sadder footnotes of this story is that this expertise—accrued over a century—was lost when, shortly after, the company became insolvent. The *Crown Fountain* was its last major commission, but remains a tribute to a small, family-run company that, despite its hard-won skills, was unable to survive the realities of cheaper, mass-produced competition.

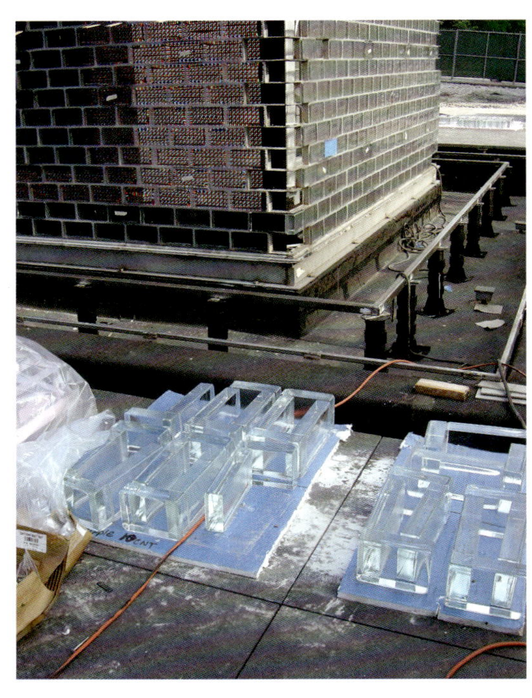

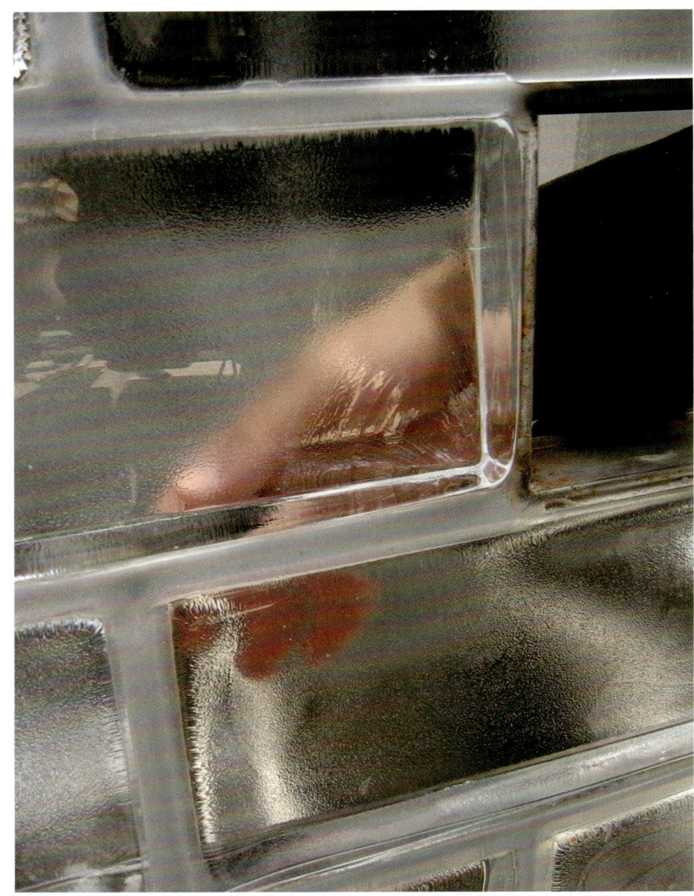

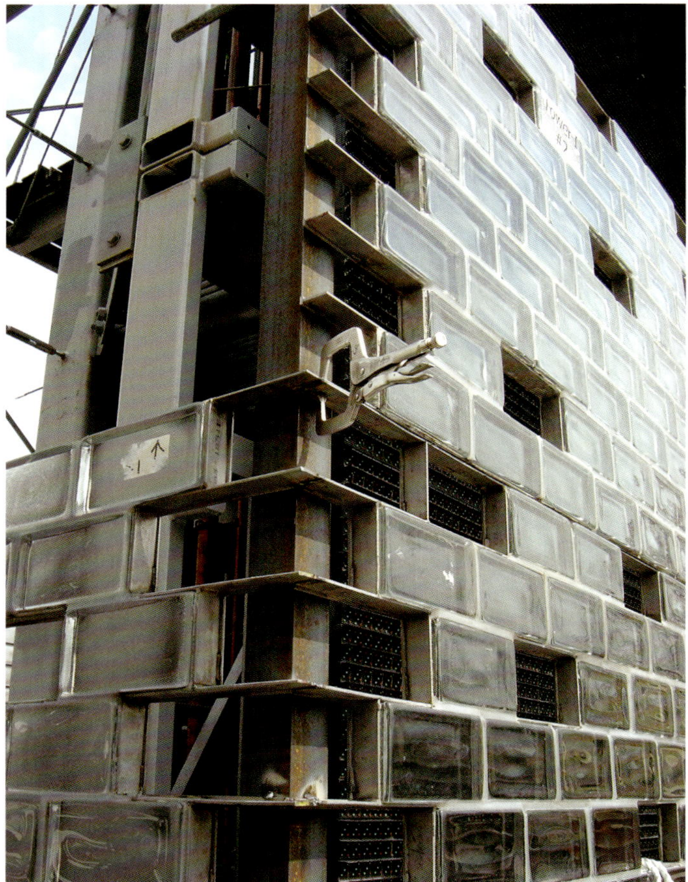

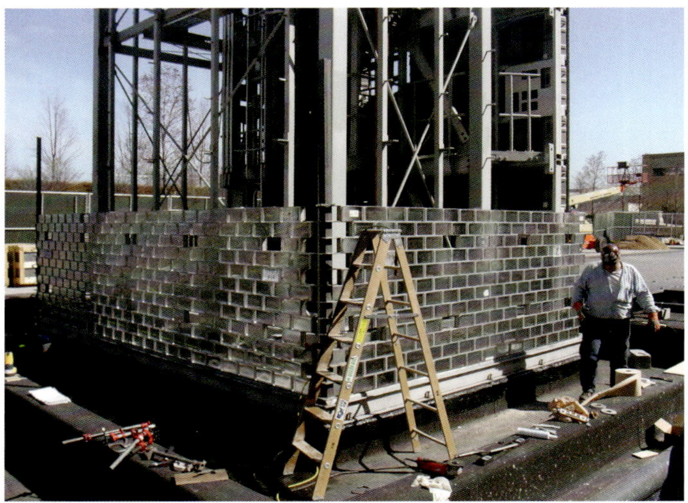

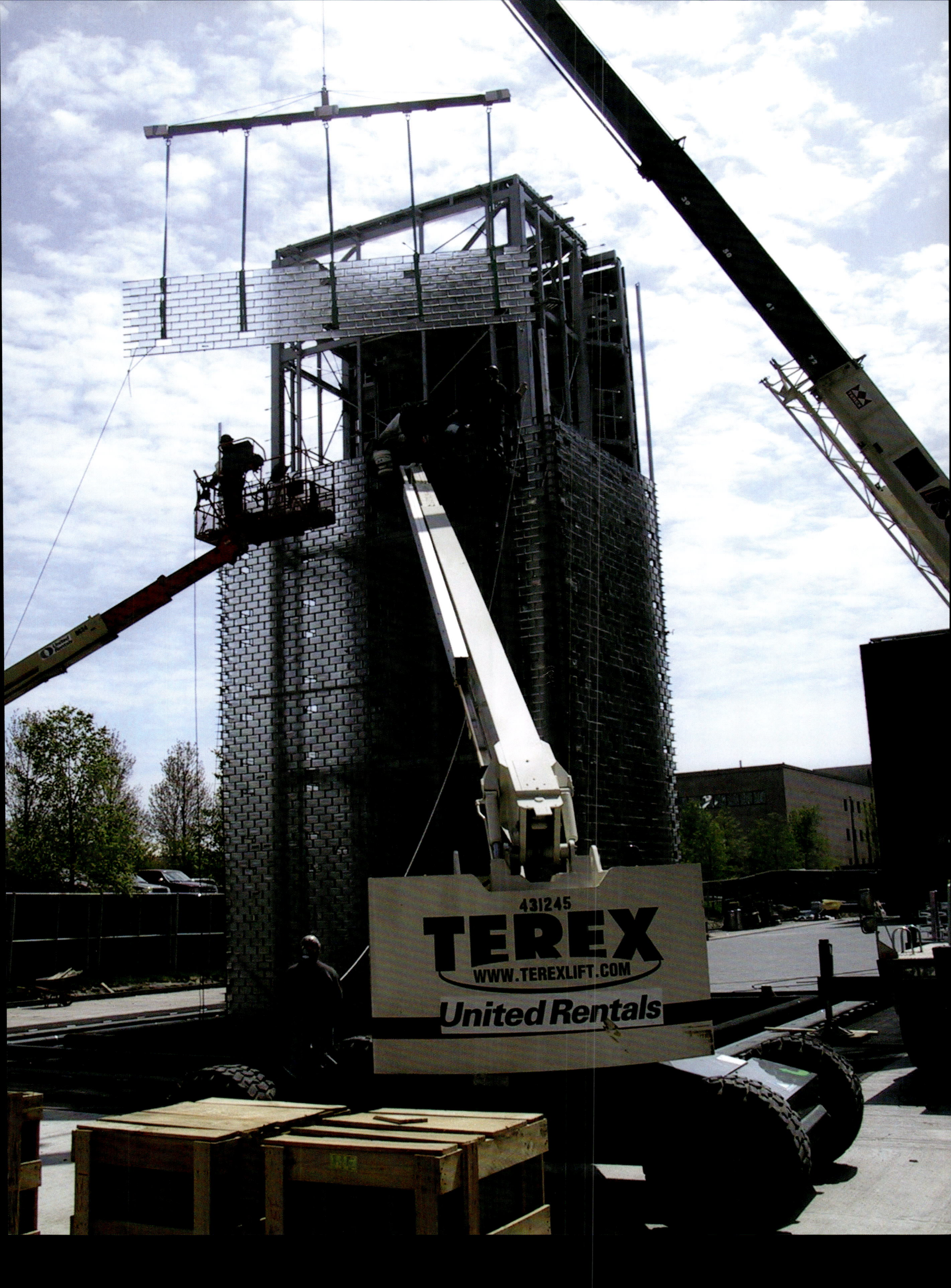

431245
TEREX
WWW.TEREXLIFT.COM
United Rentals

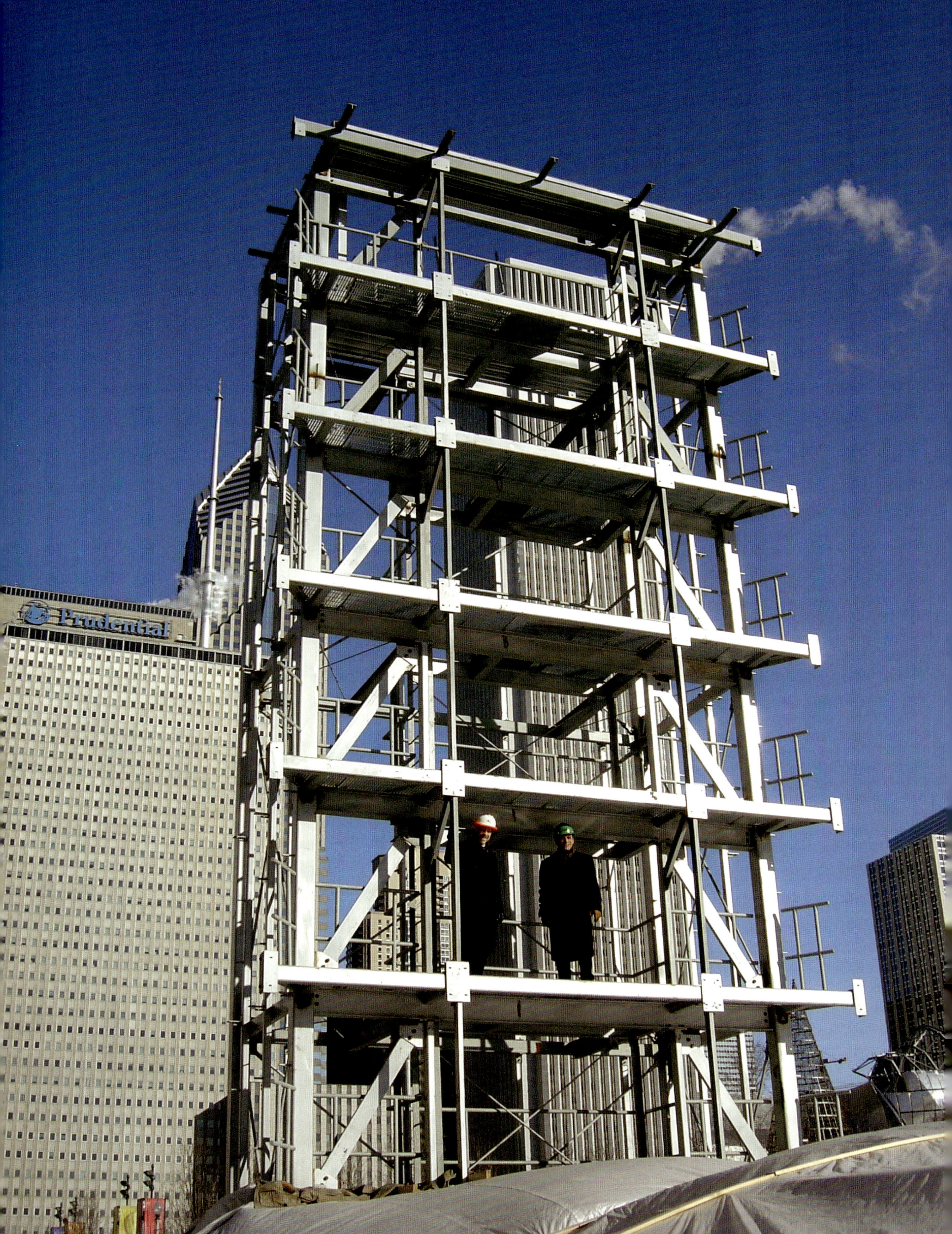
Prudential

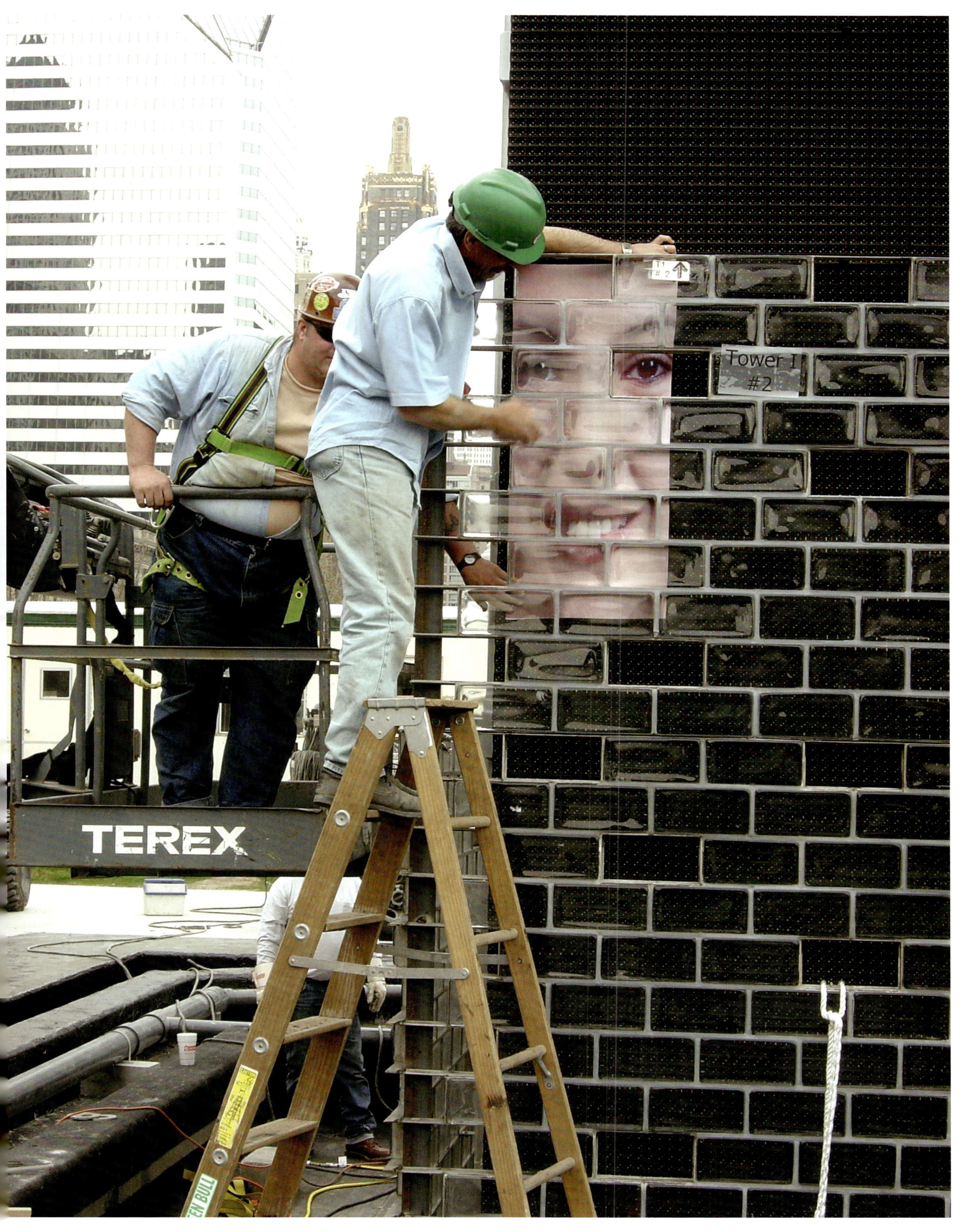

TEREX
Tower I
#2

The brick I'm holding is for the façade that covers the LED screens, and to prevent image distortion each and every one must be near identical and free from any imperfections. For the other three sides of the towers the surface is textured, giving the opacity that will conceal the internal structures while still conducting the colored light that illuminates the towers by night. Still others have rounded edges to perfect the vertical corners of the towers or for controlling the water flow over the top. Rounded steel would have been more expedient, but Sexton is obsessed with preserving the integrity of the artist's original concept. A glass tower is a *glass* tower. And he is fortunate in still having a company that can deliver the goods.

"Although clay bricks had been around for upwards of ten thousand years, there was no history of putting glass bricks together. Not on this scale. We had to invent it from scratch."
Mark Sexton, architect

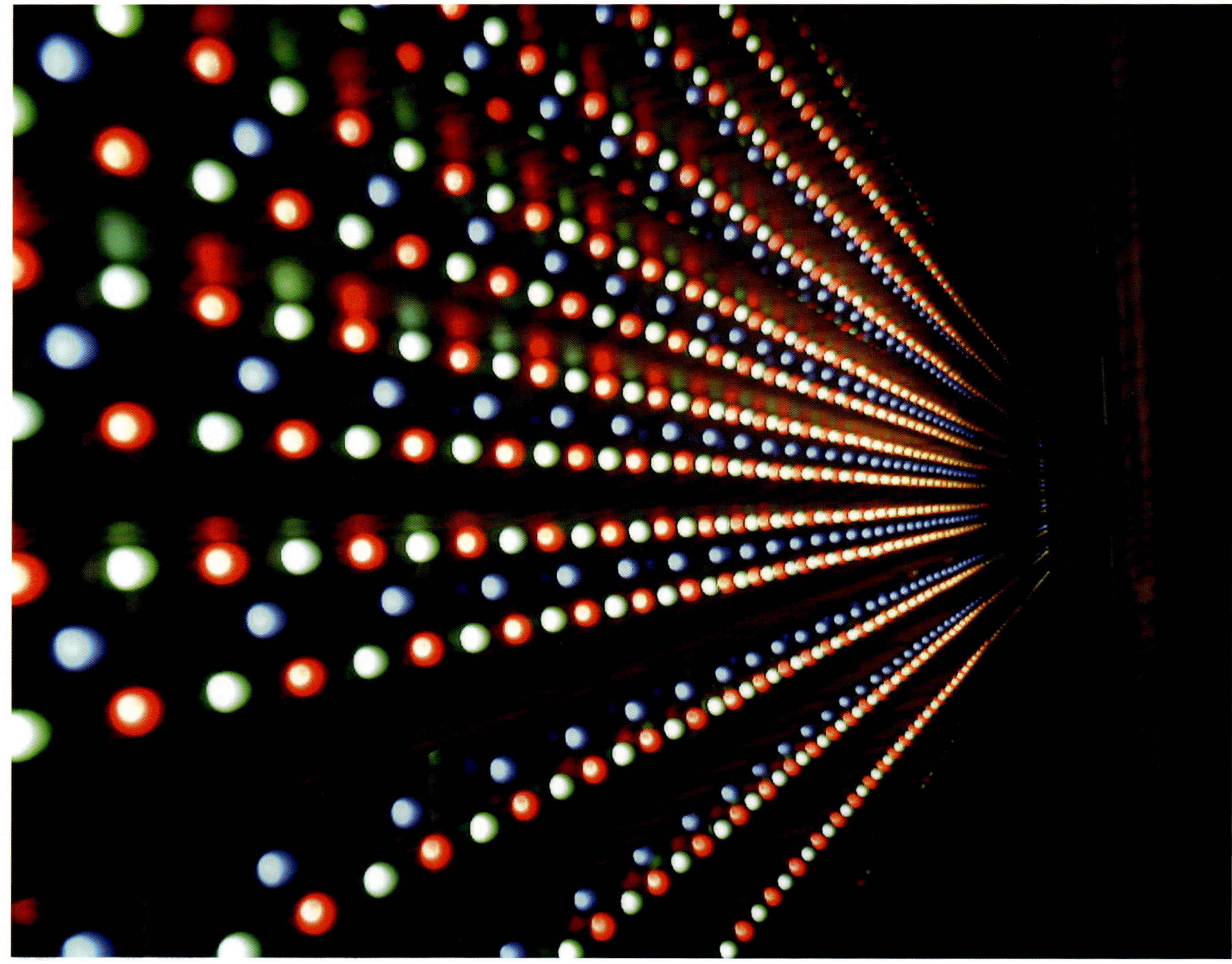

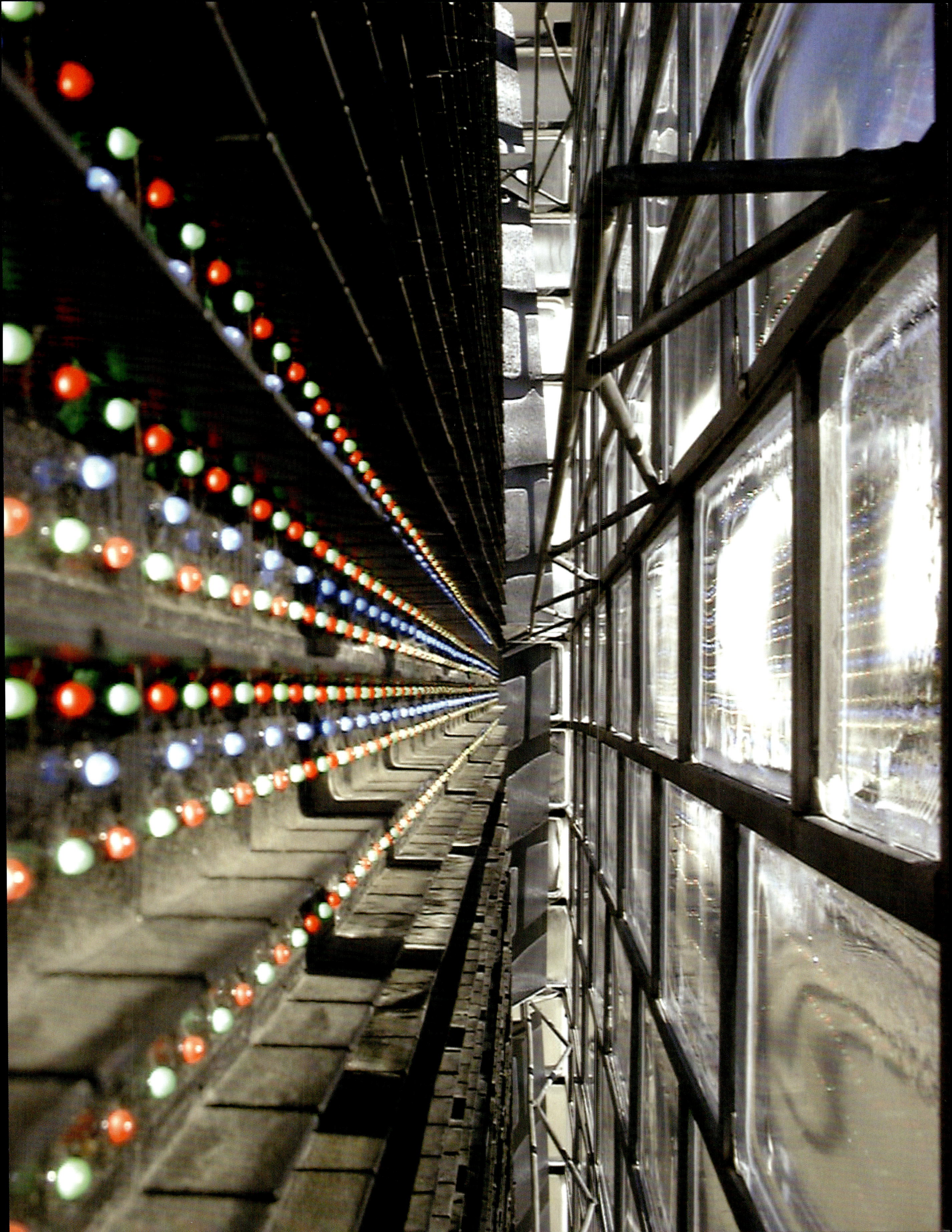

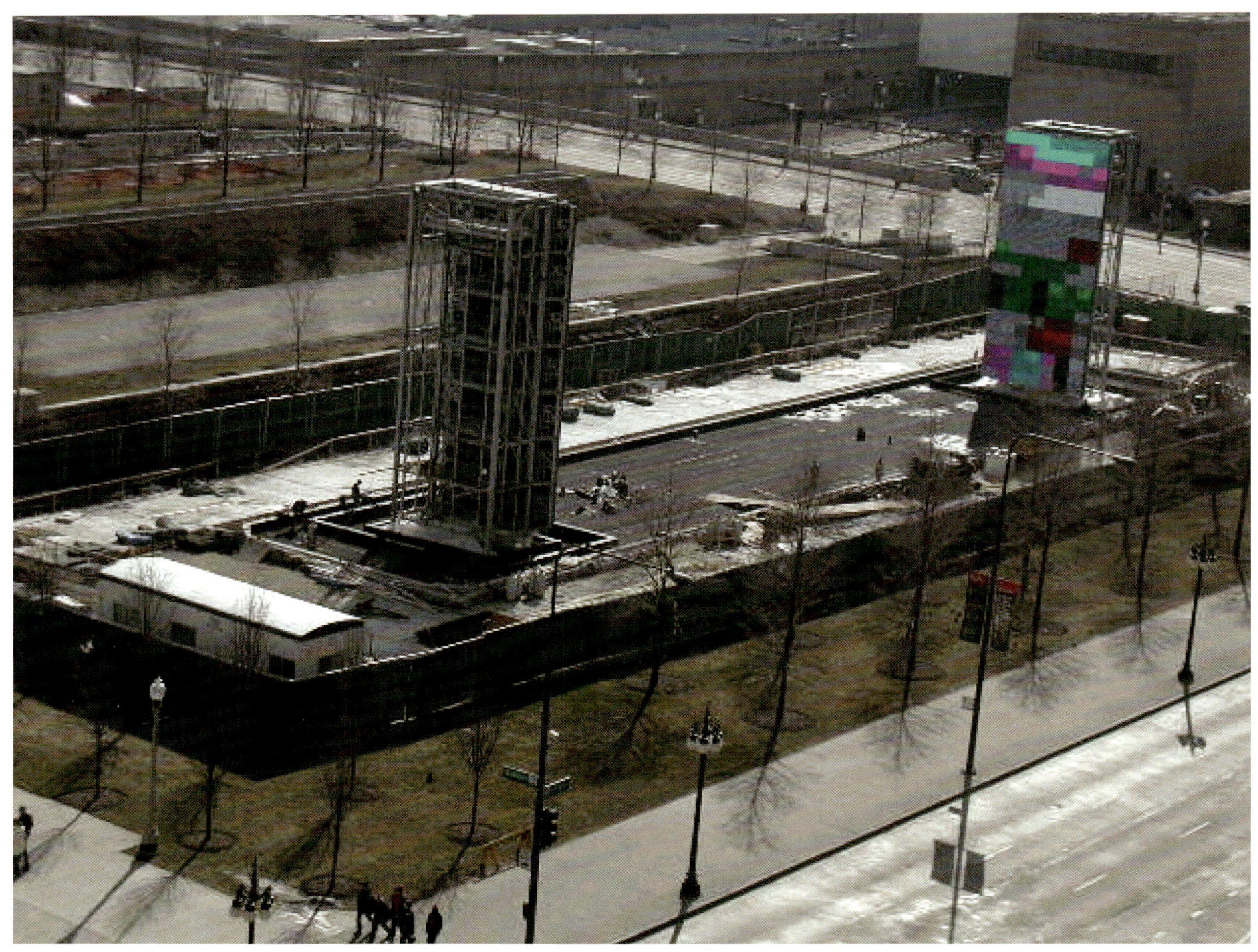

The problem is that no one knows quite how to assemble the bricks to make the two transparent "houses" that are part of the artist's dream. Plensa's previous cabinet pieces are relatively small, but Sexton recognizes from the outset that an unsupported fifty-foot-high, glass-brick wall is untenable. Moreover, at just over an inch, the bricks are relatively thin in comparison to their length and width, a limitation imposed both by the manufacturing process and by the need for perfect transparency. Technically, they are closer to tiles than bricks and therein lies the problem.

Much time is spent devising alternative approaches. One early solution is to epoxy the bricks together in one-meter sections, then bind them tightly with a compression ring. They make a mock-up using wooden blocks, but while they're presenting it to Steve Crown it simply explodes under internal tension.

Also, the artist's concept is for the individual glass bricks to be staggered—literally like conventional brickwork—but this further complicates any thoughts of assembling them in modules. For once, Plensa is prepared to accept a compromise. Seeing that his dream of pure glass towers isn't working, he decides it would be acceptable for the bricks to be supported by a steel frame. But the architect says no, realizing that to introduce an obtrusive latticework would fundamentally undermine the original concept.

Then one day Sexton observed an unexpected phenomenon. He was holding one brick and noticed that, seen through the glass, his fingers disappeared. No matter how he angled the brick, he could see nothing of the hand that was holding it. It was simply the effect of internal refraction, but it opened up a whole new possibility. If the steel too would magically disappear, why *not* slot the glass bricks into a massive grid?

The first steel grid sections are manufactured and together with samples of the bricks are shipped out to another company for assembly in Florida, where they are simply glued into place and pointed with silicone. Everybody visits for the trial run and this time the mock-up works perfectly.

The Soul in the Machine

Throughout the entire period that the "body" is being perfected, a quite separate development is taking place. It was U.S. Equities' idea to involve the School of the Art Institute of Chicago. Initially it was to locate a "translator": someone who spoke the hi-tech language of contemporary video and who could communicate Plensa's ideas to the engineers. Tony Jones, the school's president, refers them to Professor Alan Labb, who mediates with the technicians and resolves the initial specs for the most appropriate

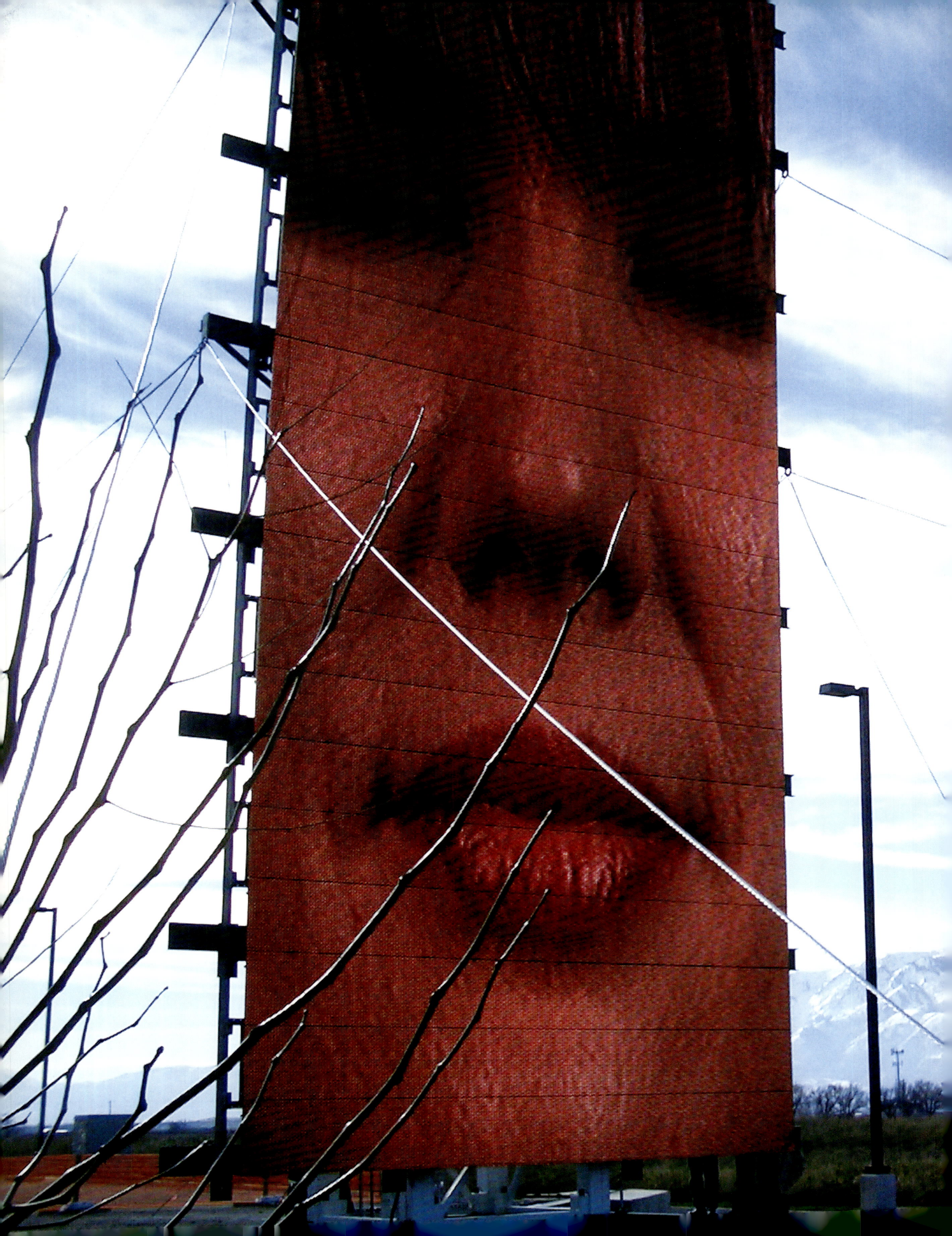

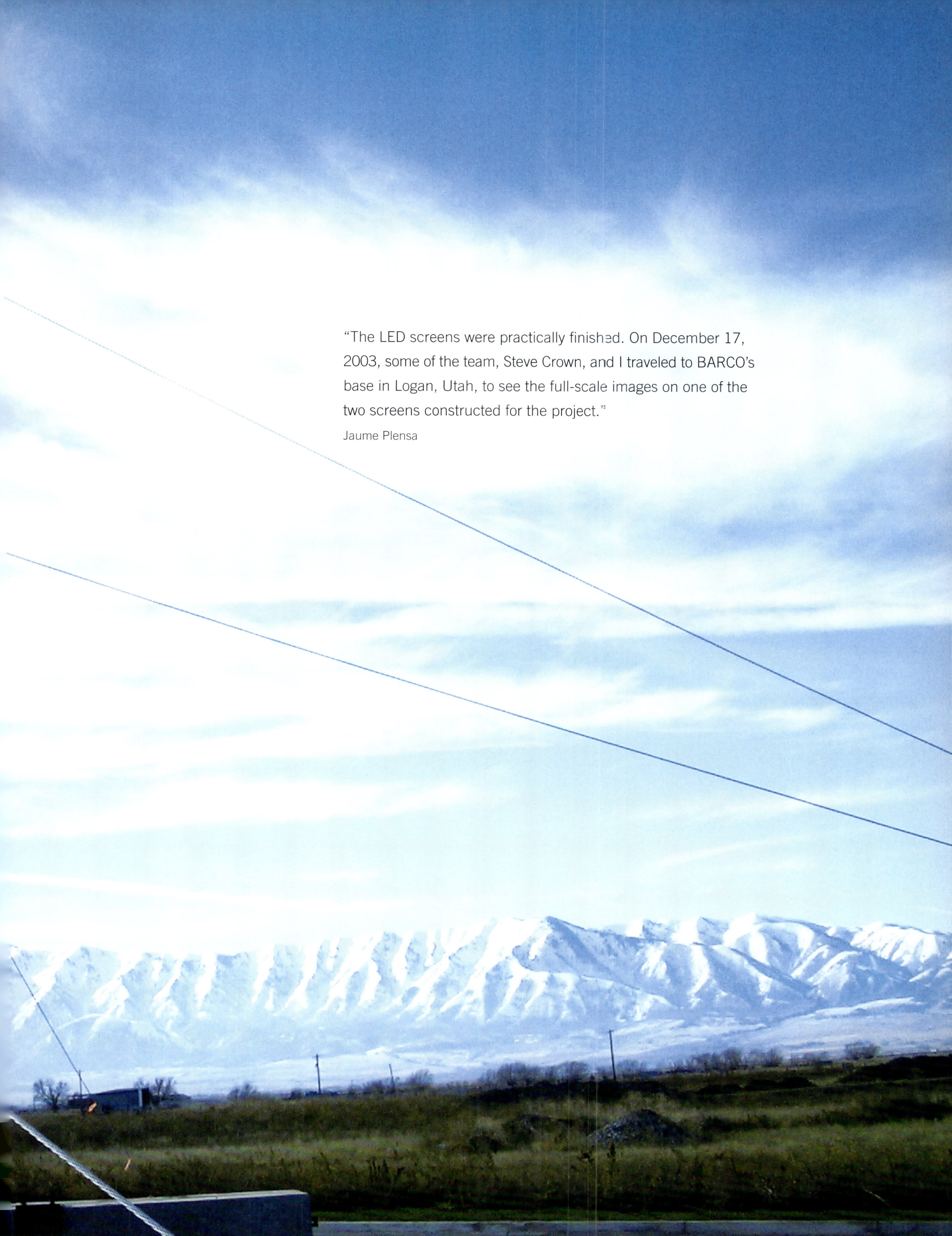
"The LED screens were practically finished. On December 17,
2003, some of the team, Steve Crown, and I traveled to BARCO's
base in Logan, Utah, to see the full-scale images on one of the
two screens constructed for the project."
Jaume Plensa

high-definition format. In Labb, Plensa discovers another kindred spirit and before long the school is given the job of constructing the video archives. Professor John Manning is also brought onto the team, Labb likening their roles to producer and technical director.

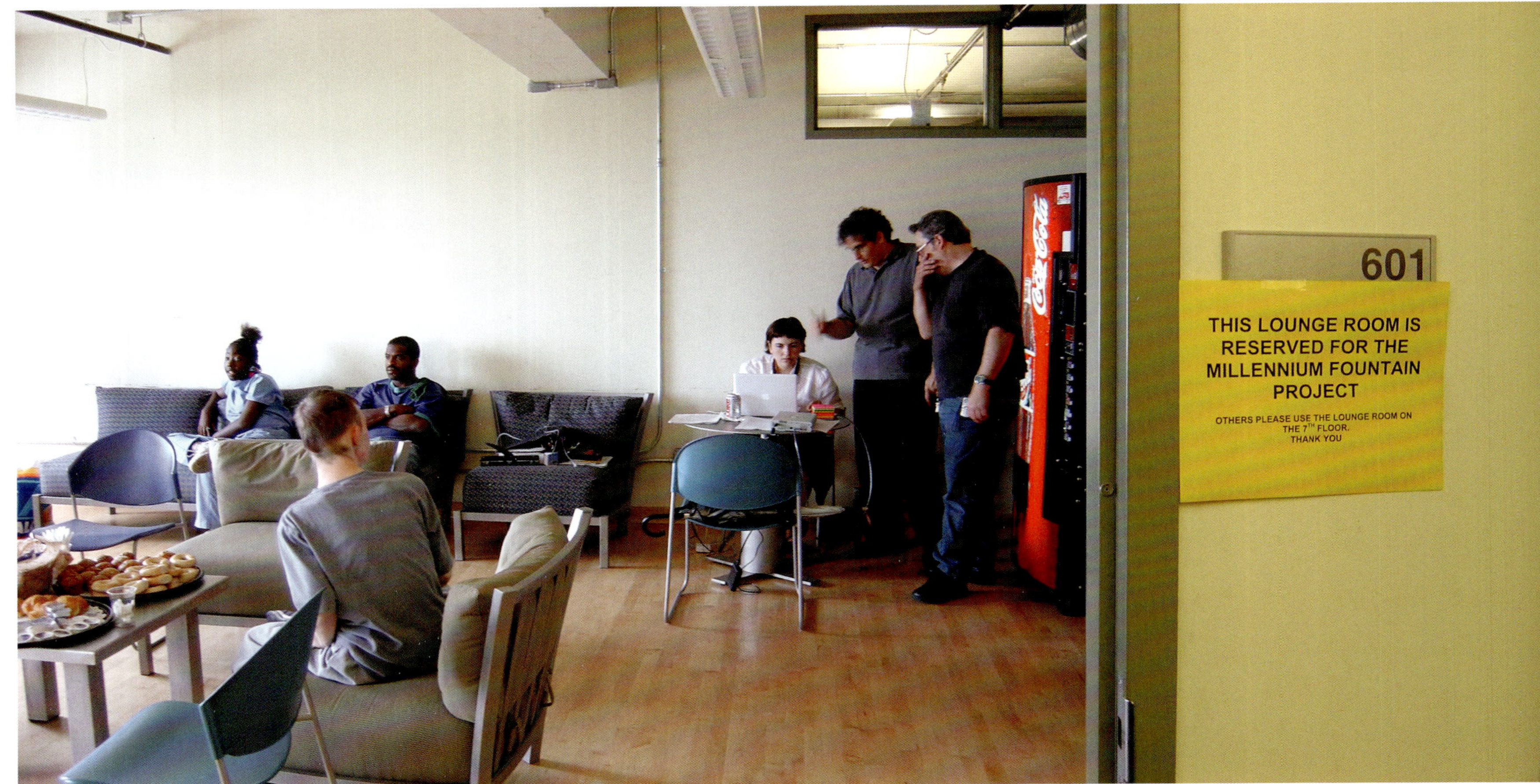

"Tony Jones, director of the School of Art, enthusiastically accepted our invitation to collaborate in the creation of the image archives, and to that end he asked professors Alan Labb and John Manning to take charge of the project with the help of a select group of students.

After several months of working on the content, we installed our film set and office in the school, and for over two years we filmed and post-produced the faces that would finally give life to the *Crown Fountain: the Soul*."

Jaume Plensa

The Video-Maker's Tale

John Manning turns up in a tee shirt with the slogan "No Comment," which is in stark contrast to the effusive Chicagoan who's keen to share his experience of working on the project. We meet outside a coffee shop that's just alongside the School of the Art Institute and across the road from the *Crown Fountain*. John began as a video artist back in 1976, the pioneering days when lots of technical solutions needed to be ad-libbed—a background, he says, that prepared him for the job in hand. Nowadays he's an assistant professor at the school and together with Alan Labb and a large number of the students, he's originated the picture archives for the fountain.

Initially, the two towers were to display identical images, but Plensa quickly evolved the idea of the screens being in dialogue with each other except for the moments when the faces give way to scenes of nature. John and the students have made these too, traveling around the neighboring states to fulfill Plensa's exacting brief for the one hundred images of rivers, streams, and waterfalls. He's not been involved in the initial stages, but he's directed much of the studio work and has handled all of the postproduction.

Most of the actual filming has been done over the summers of 2002 and 2003, but when all the one thousand or more faces have been compiled, it takes him a whole eighteen days just to review the material. "It was an incredible experience," he tells me. It was also rewarding for the students, who were thrilled to work on a "real" project, something that wasn't just a school exercise, but which would become a permanent part of the community.

The first problem is one of simple logistics. To record more than one thousand faces will take several months of filming over two years, but the conditions have to remain controlled and consistent. A room in the school is set aside as a studio, and powerful lighting and a camera are installed. But this is no ordinary camera. To achieve the quality of image and resolution, Labb recommends they hire the same model as used on the latest *Star Wars* movie. A second, more portable video camera is acquired so that Manning and the team can head off to the country on weekends. Then there are the computers, five of the latest G5 Macintoshes with sufficient additional hard drives to store and manipulate vast amounts of data.

Each sequence consists of a four-minute, slow-motion clip of the subject's face, followed by a separate clip where the lips pucker. The timing has to be exact or the puckering won't coincide with the waterspout. The positioning of the subject also has to be exact, for although the image can be resized vertically and horizontally, the position of the mouth and eyes must conform to a predetermined grid.

The camera has been designed for the wide-screen and thus needs to be tipped vertically to produce images in the format of the towers. This would be easy enough with a pocket digital, but this camera is big. And as there's no tripod produced for this unusual orientation, a rig has to be improvised to support the weight and stabilize the shot. But the rig isn't exactly mobile. So they come up with another improvised solution: a dentist's chair that allows the subject, not the camera, to do the moving.

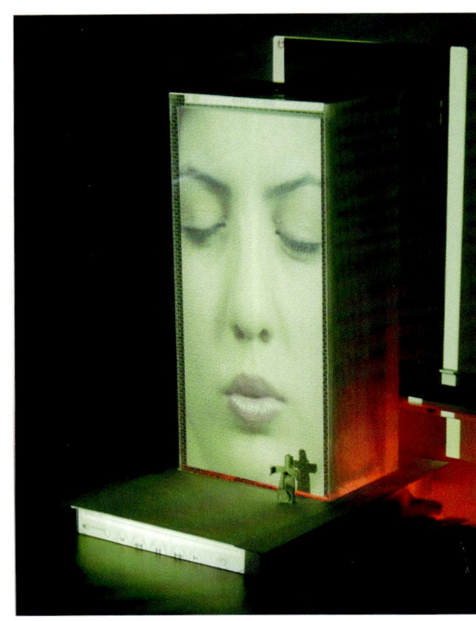

They are also constructing two sets of each video sequence. During the winter months, when the water is cut off, the puckering lips become redundant and are edited out in a procedure that will be programmed into the master computers. It is a consideration to which the artist has given much thought, for he wants the "fountain" to continue functioning even when the water features have shut down.

The second problem is how to gather over one thousand people whose faces truly represent the demographics of Chicago. A mere two hundred years old, by definition the city is an admix of immigrants, where the local Native Americans have been joined by Europeans, Hispanics from Mexico, the Caribbean, and Central and South America, Asians, and African Americans migrating from the southern states. Impressed by the true cosmopolitanism of the city, Plensa intends to make the fountain a celebration of its people.

The Art Institute team comes up with the ingenious solution of approaching the city's numerous community-based organizations and enlists the help of

community-consultant Sara Livingston and graduate student Mery Palarea.
In a process that is largely self-selecting, some seventy of these organizations
eventually yield the twelve hundred volunteers who will submit to the rigors
of filming under the bright lights. To achieve consistency, the technical
requirements are demanding, resulting in a six-page, two-hundred-item
checklist to be followed by the teams of students. Although the actual filming
takes only ninety seconds, the slightest error or movement will be magnified
on the fifty-foot screens, so the volunteers must be held completely still save
for the smiling of the lips and the blinking of the eyes. And, of course, the
all-important denouement, when the volunteers are instructed to close their
eyes and imagine blowing out a birthday candle.

Of the twelve hundred archives assembled, around eighty percent are deemed
usable. But the real work is only just beginning. According to Manning, the
vast majority of the time is spent in postproduction: slowing each image to
exactly four minutes, resizing it to the master grid, and color-correcting it.
In the end, they have assembled eighty-eight hours of material on seventy
thousand gigabytes of disk space: the equivalent of over one hundred thousand
CD-ROMs or a stack of disks over four hundred feet high.

And there's a footnote. All of this equipment—including the second video
camera, the computers, and the editing, storage, and postproduction facilities—
remain with the school, a gift from the Crown family. Moreover, the project
has forged links between the school and the city administration, and over
the next couple of years its students will use their newfound resources in
producing state-of-the-art presentations for the city.

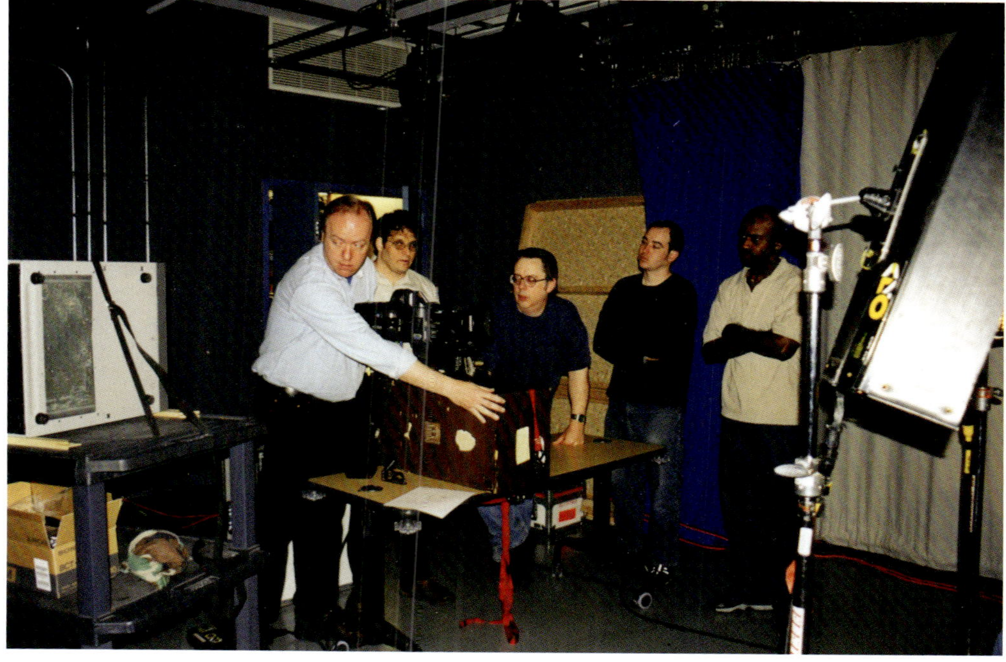

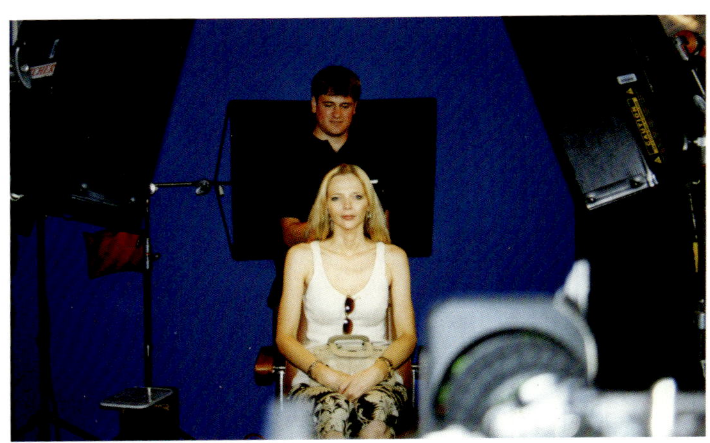

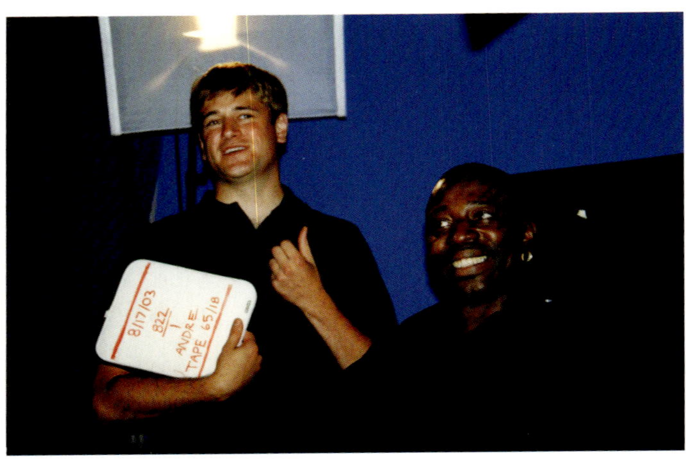

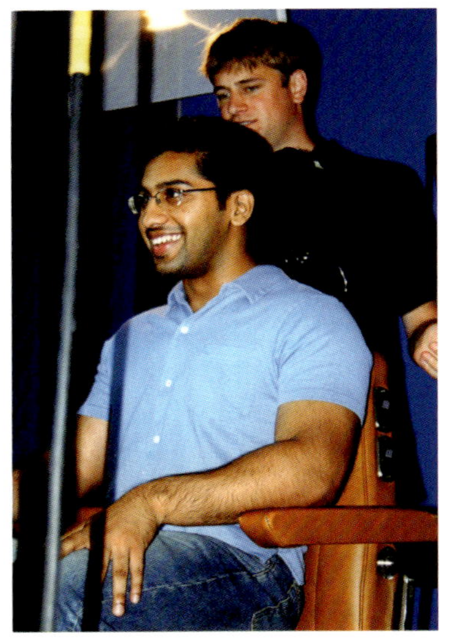

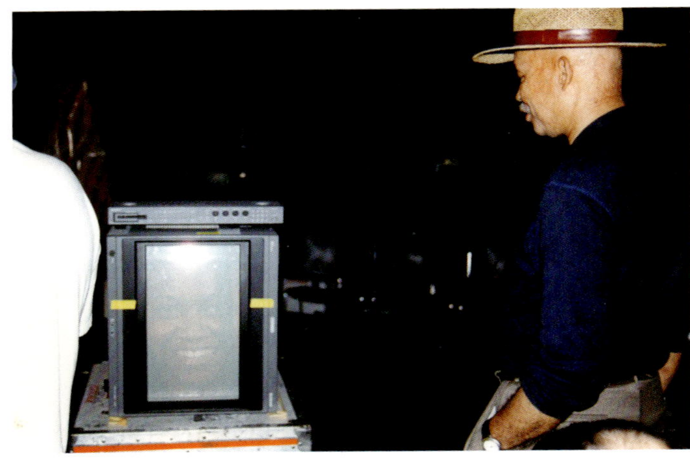

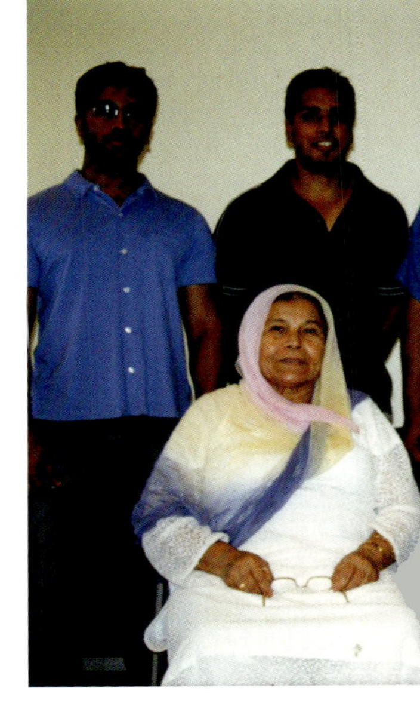

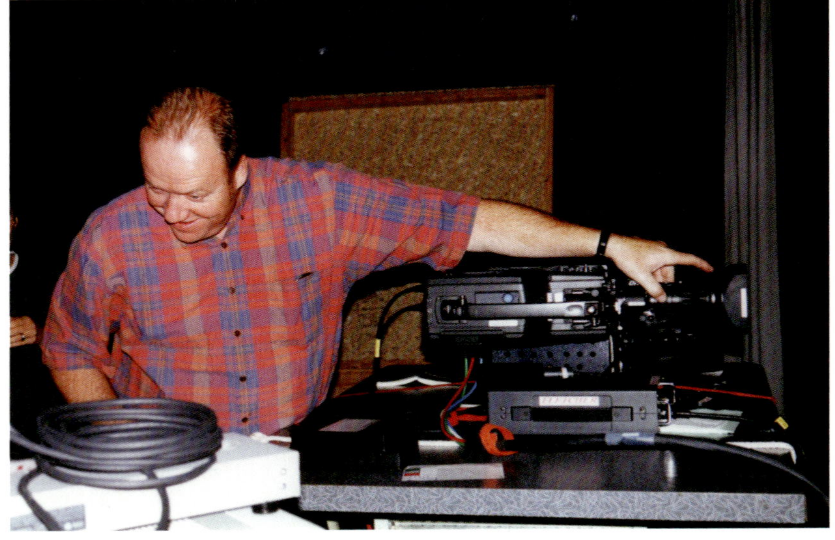

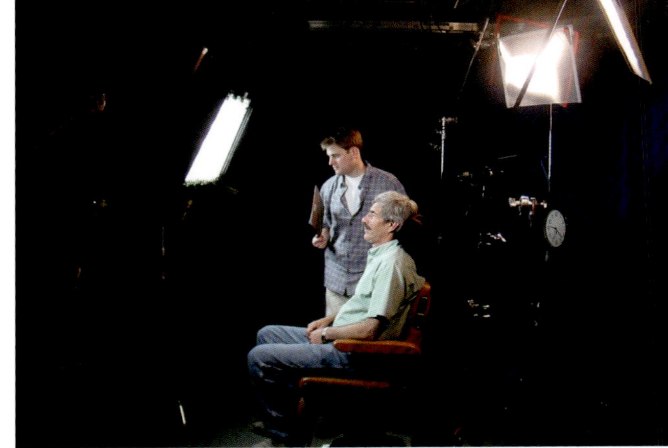

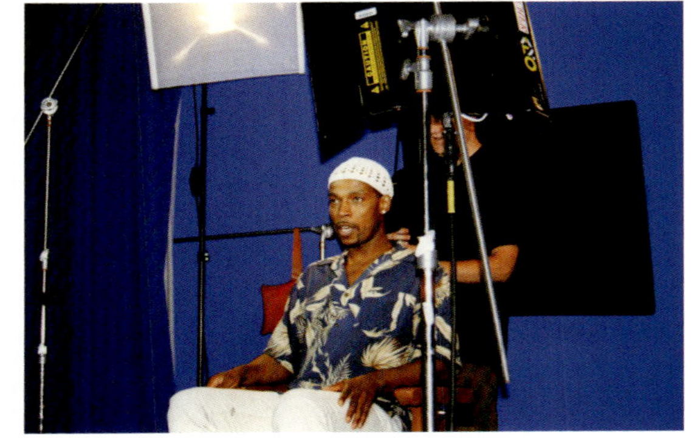

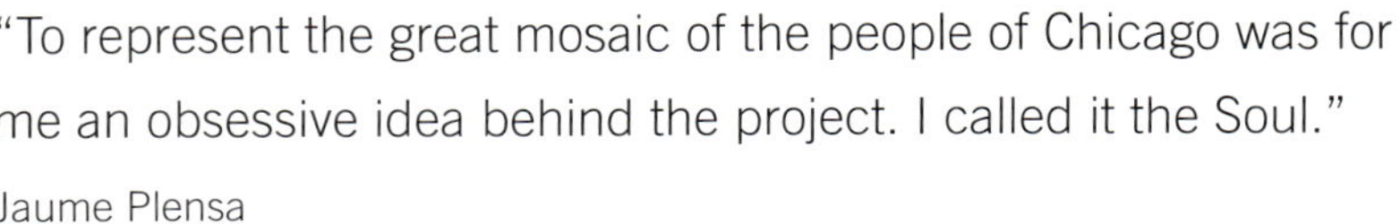

"To represent the great mosaic of the people of Chicago was for
me an obsessive idea behind the project. I called it the Soul."

Jaume Plensa

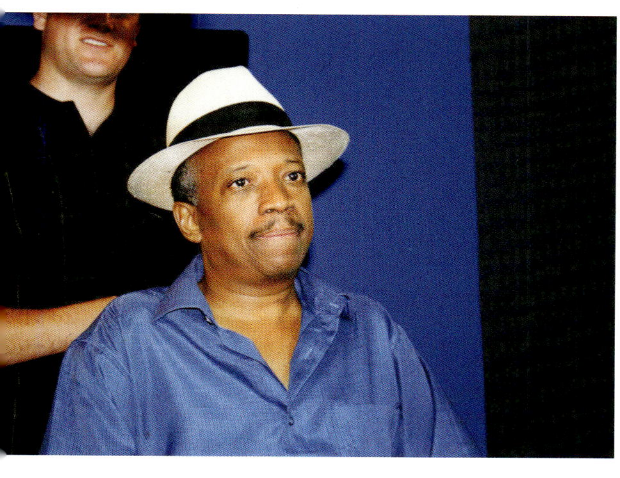

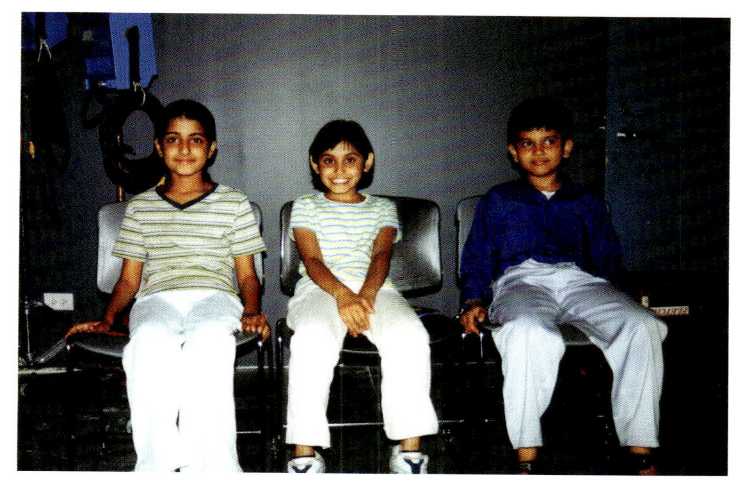

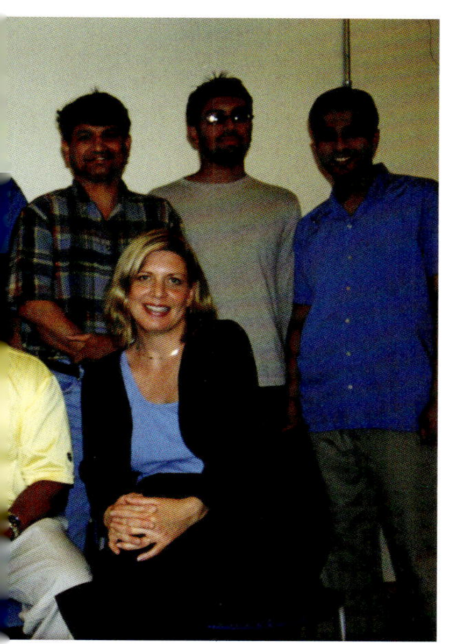

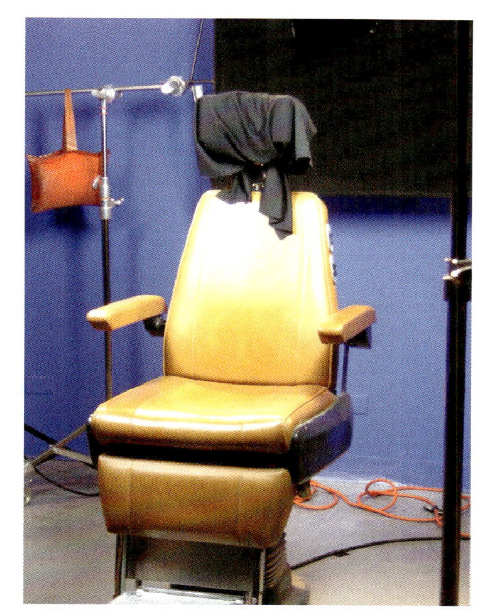

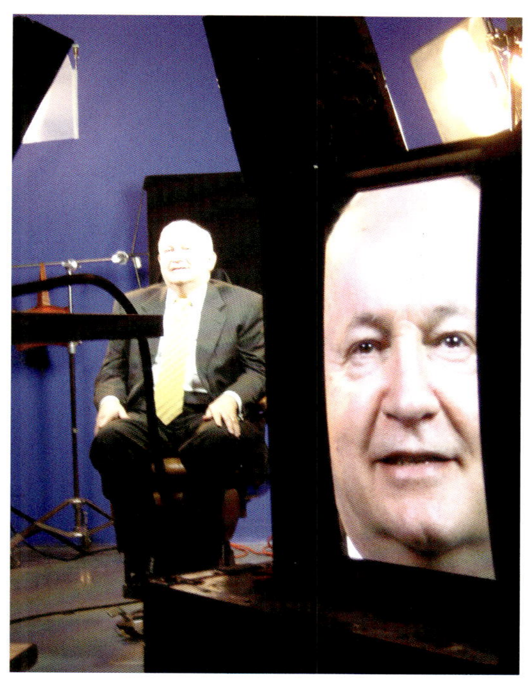

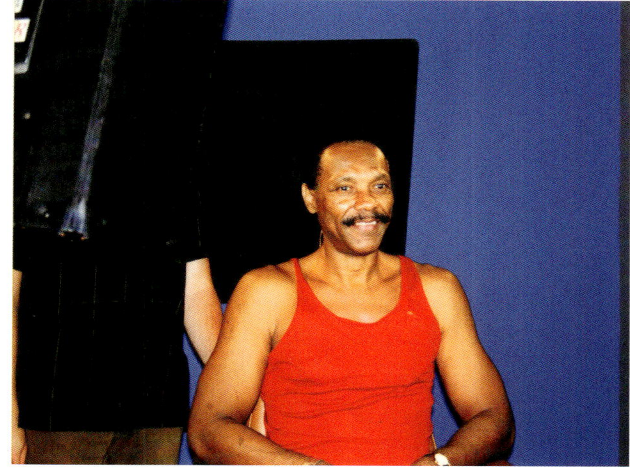

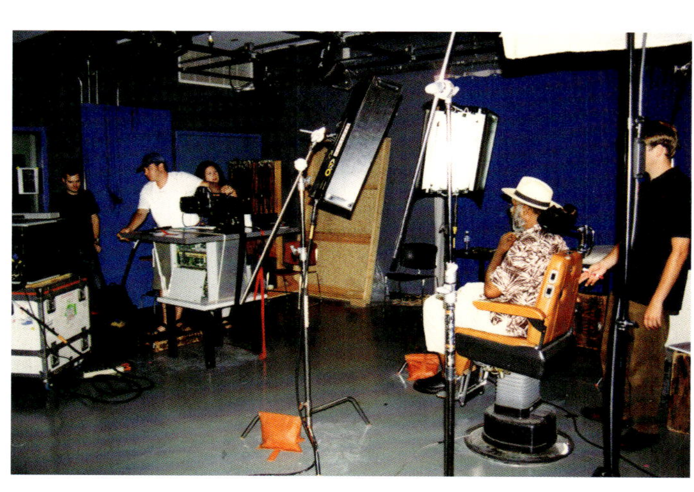

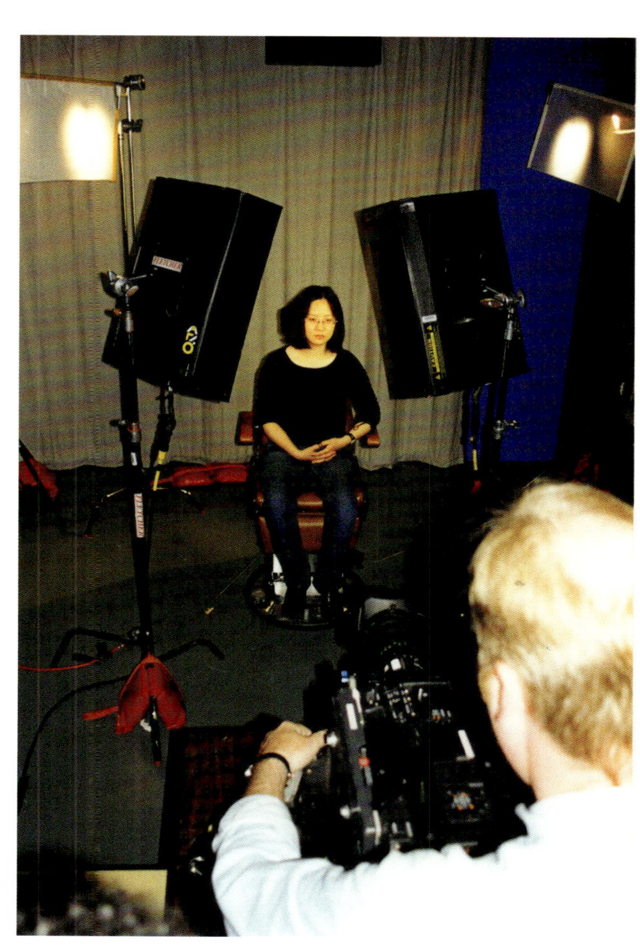

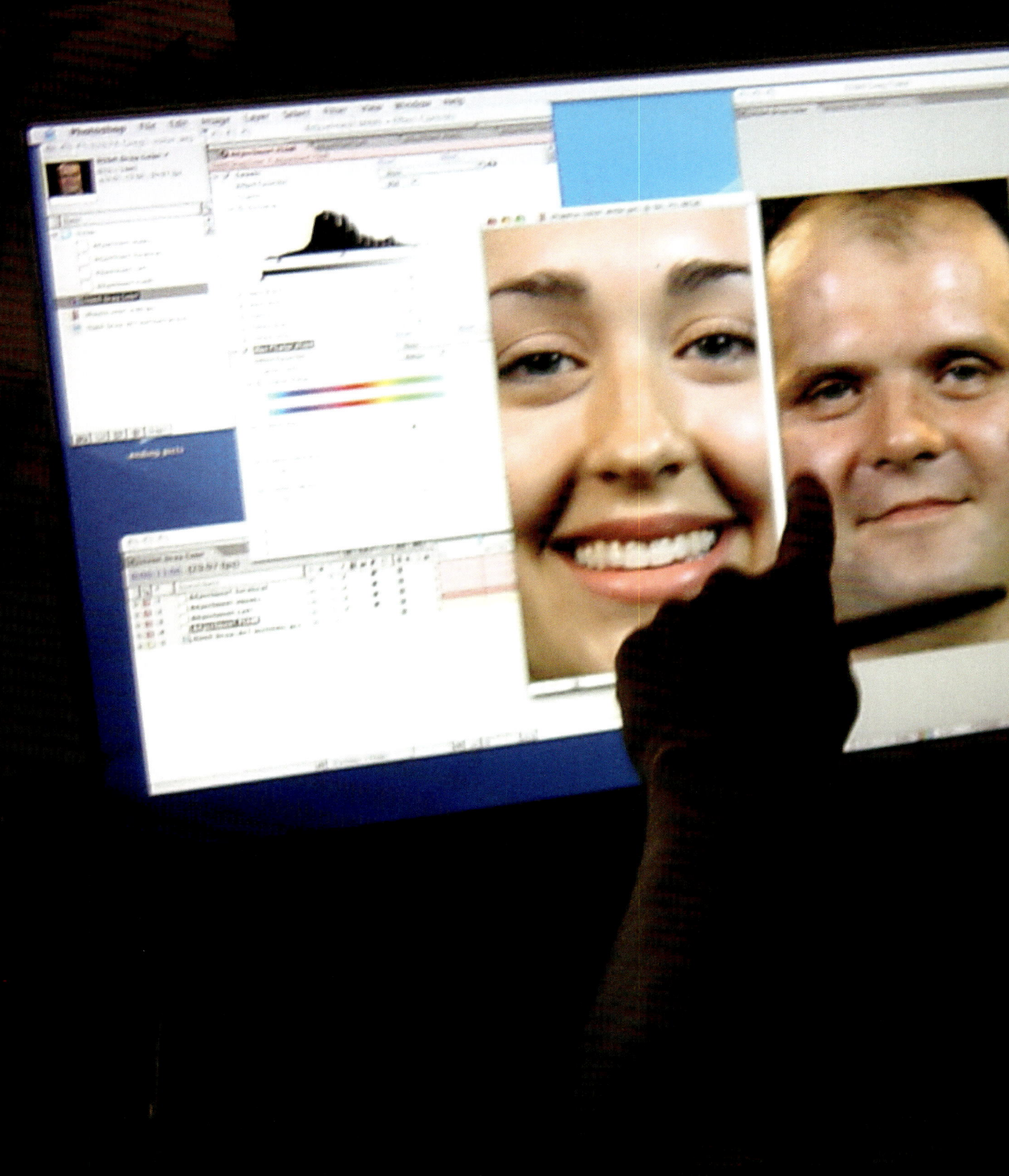

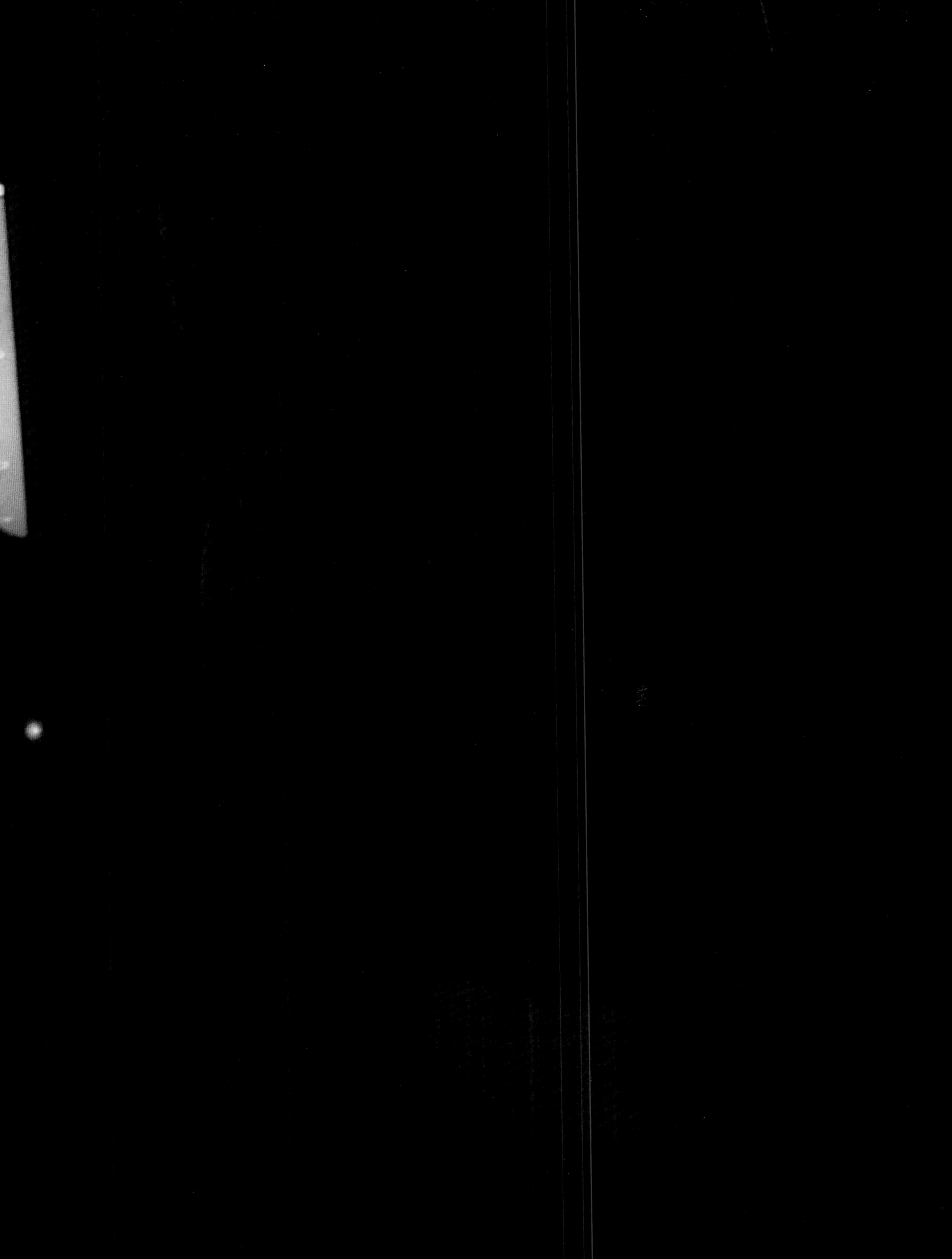

1 Black = 30 seconds
LIGHT TOWER = RANDOM WITHOUT RULES (8 COLORS)
LIGHT POOL SCREEN = WHEN 1 ROW IS ON IS ALWAYS THE MOST EXTERIOR ONE
GARGOYLE EFFECT = TRY TO USE ONLY 1 or 2 LIGHTS (EXTERIOR POOL)

FACE 4 + 1 GARGOYLE = 5 min.
NATURE = 3 min.

THE CROWN FOUNTAIN, LIFE SEQUENCES
Chicago, July 1 2004

Artist's final draft of the computer image sequence.

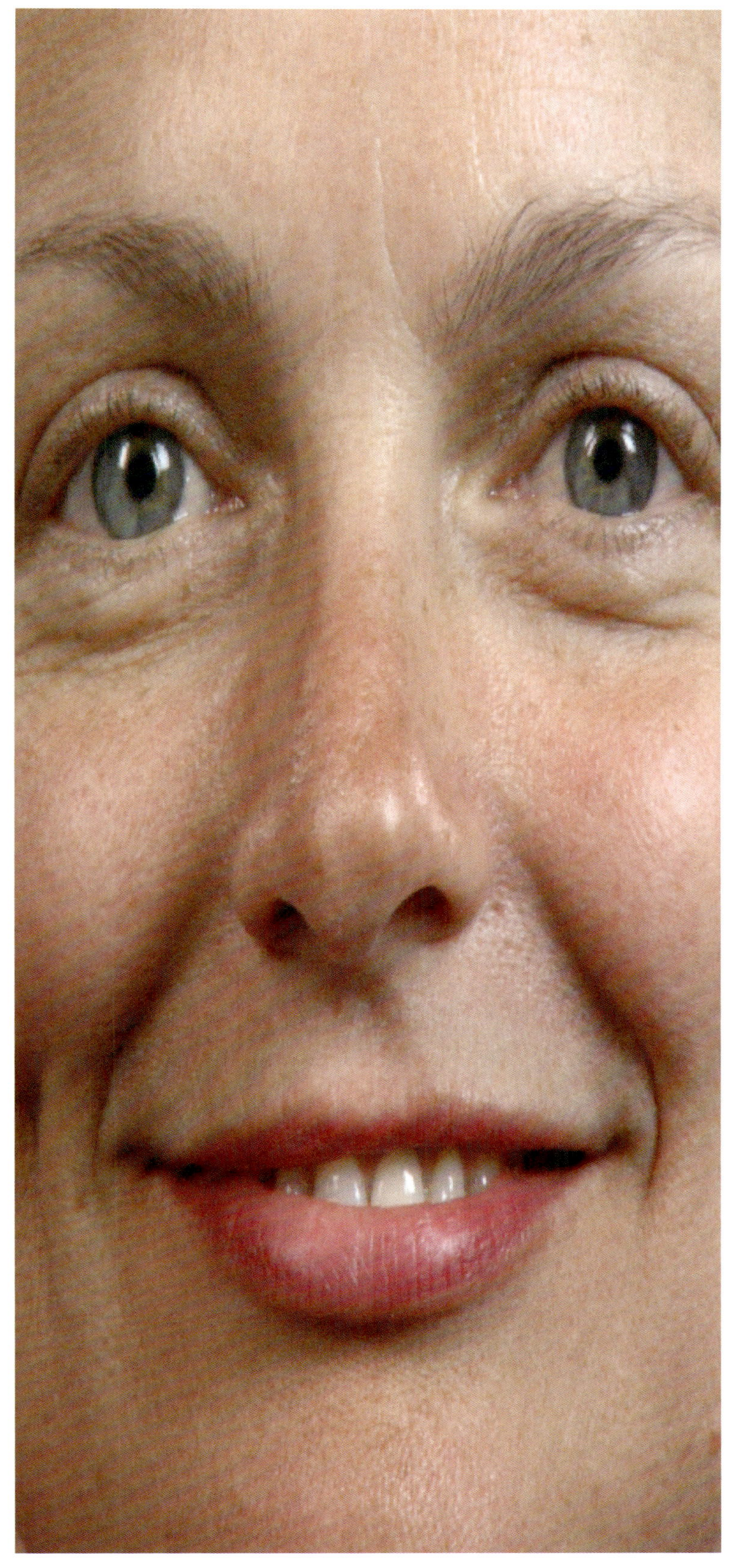
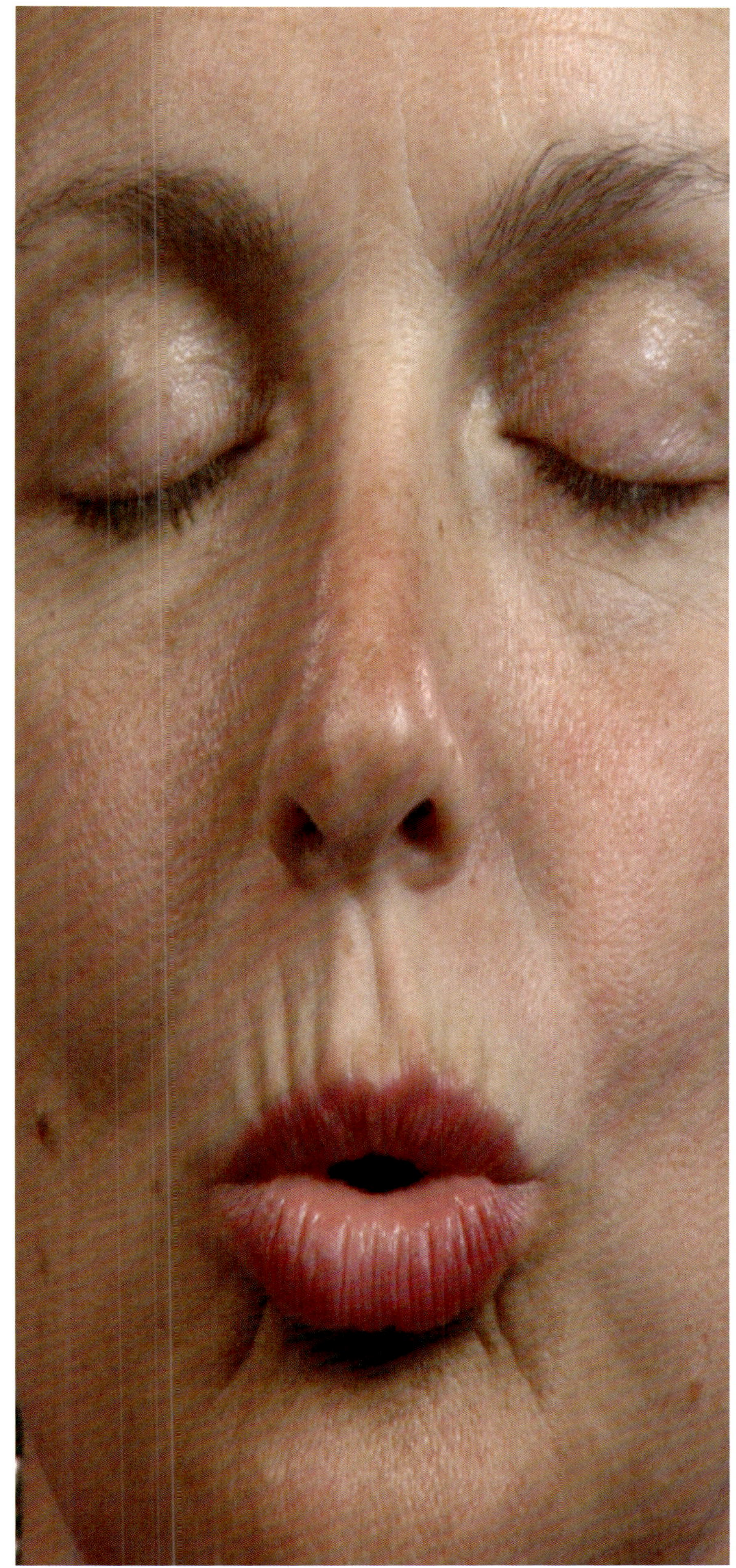

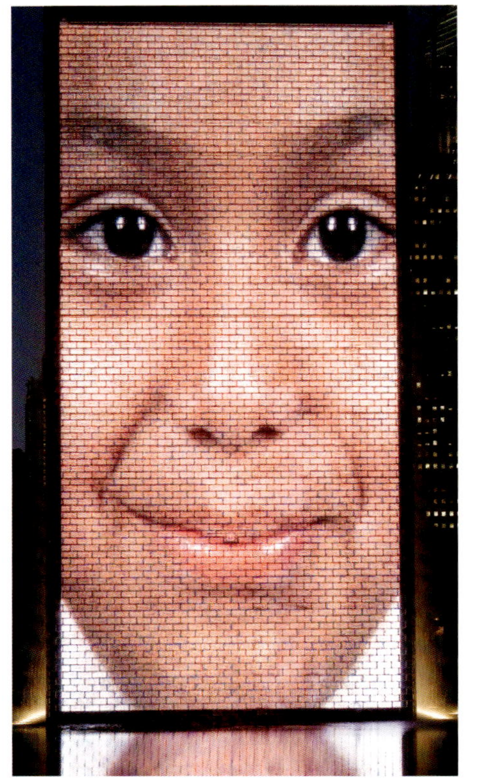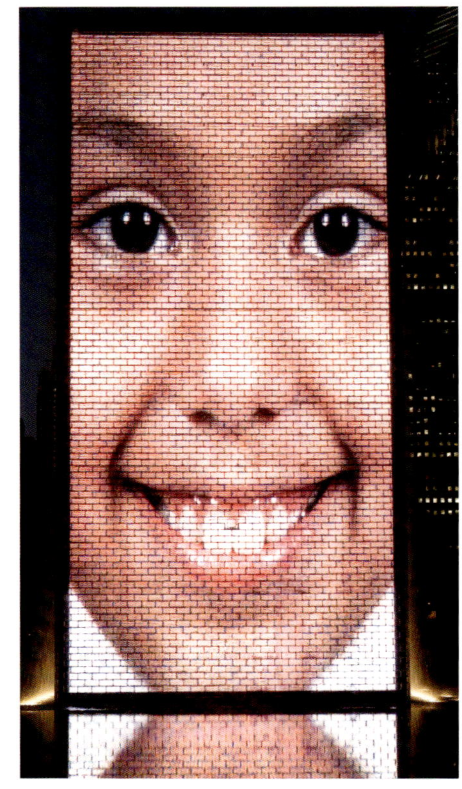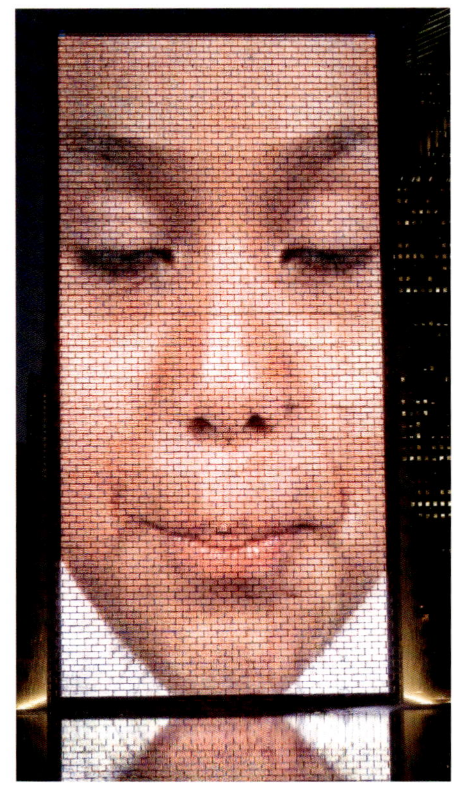

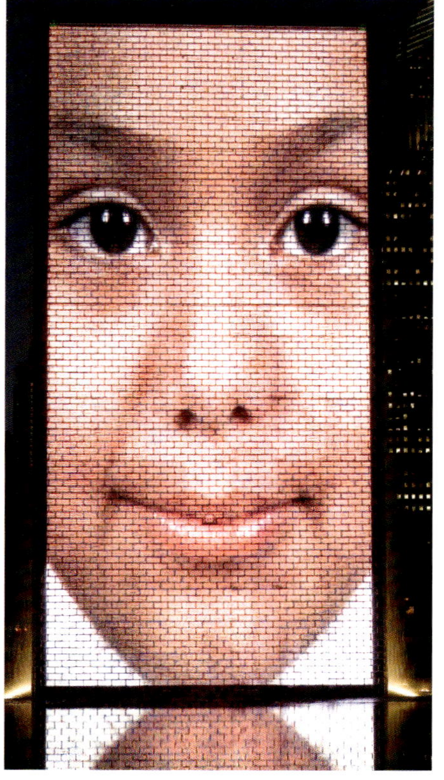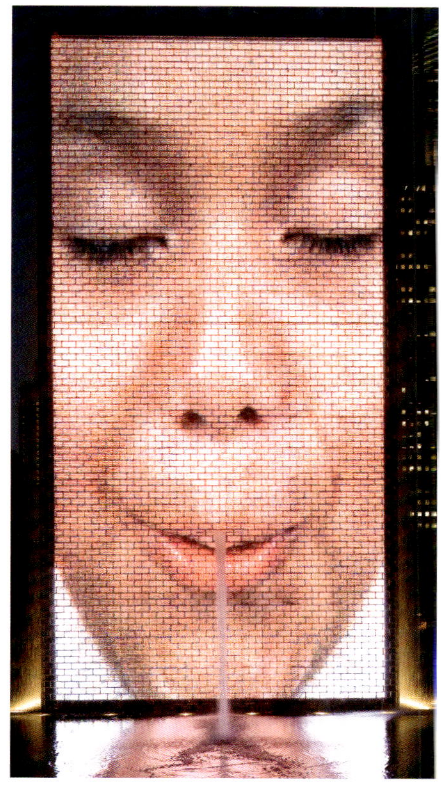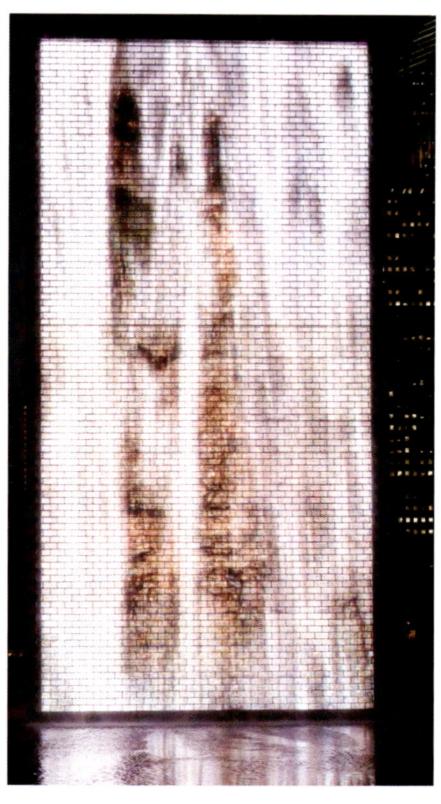

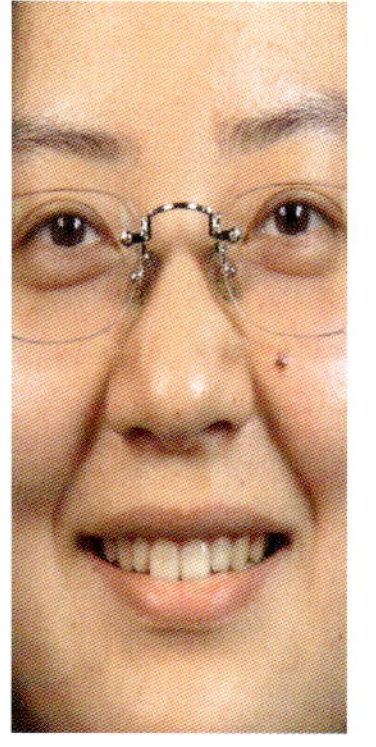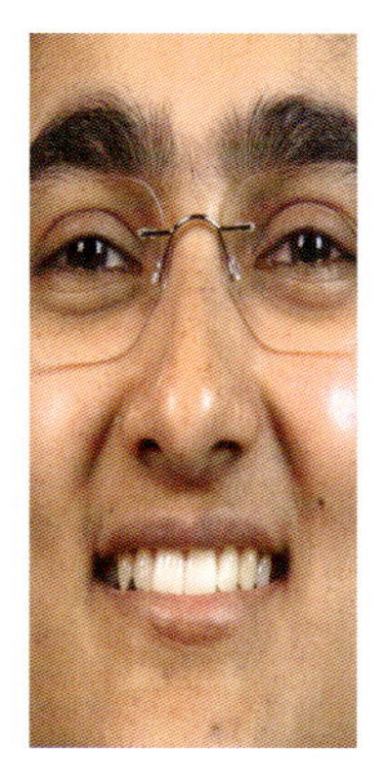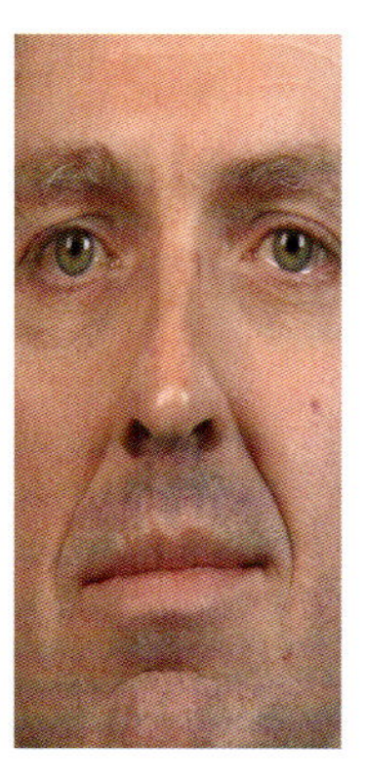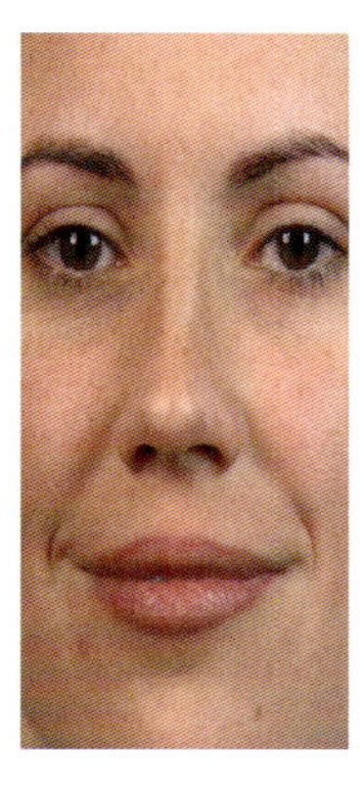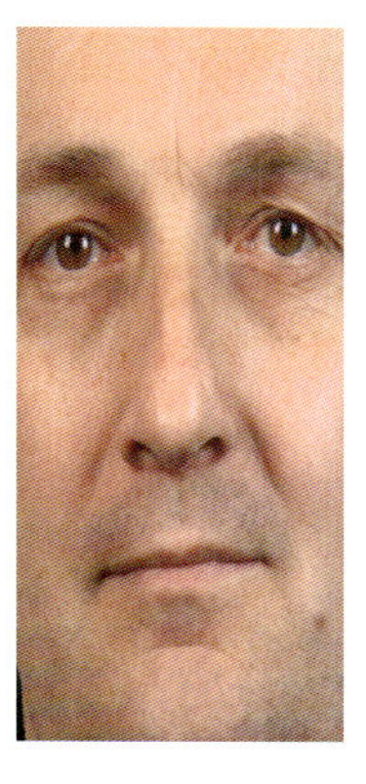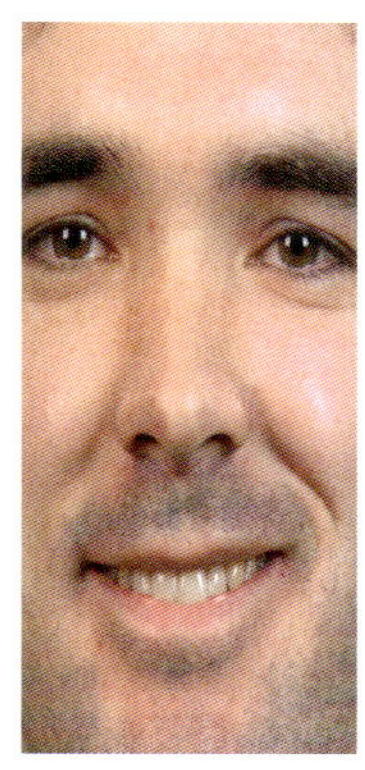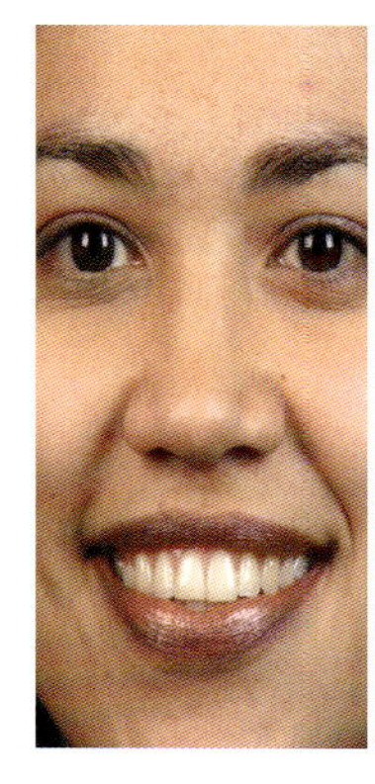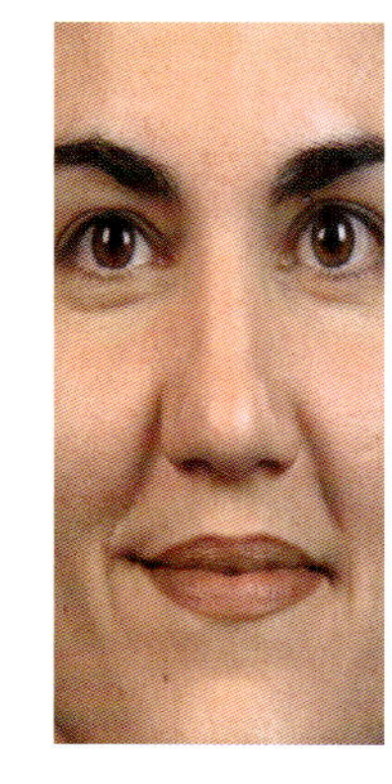
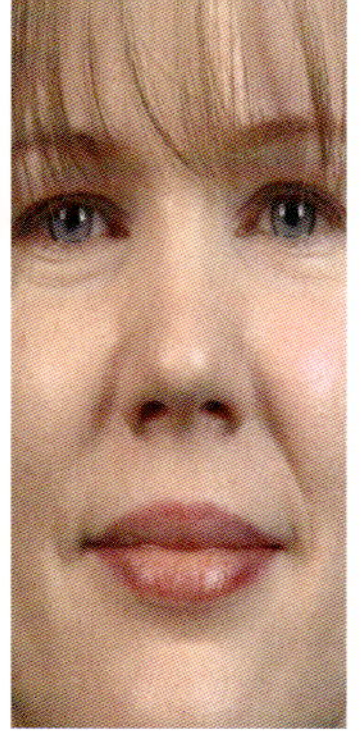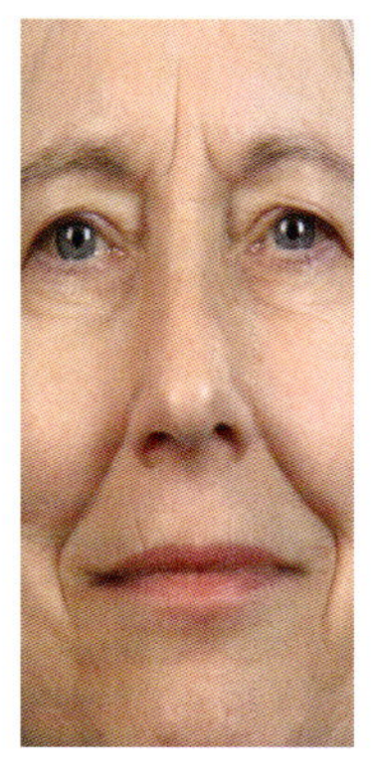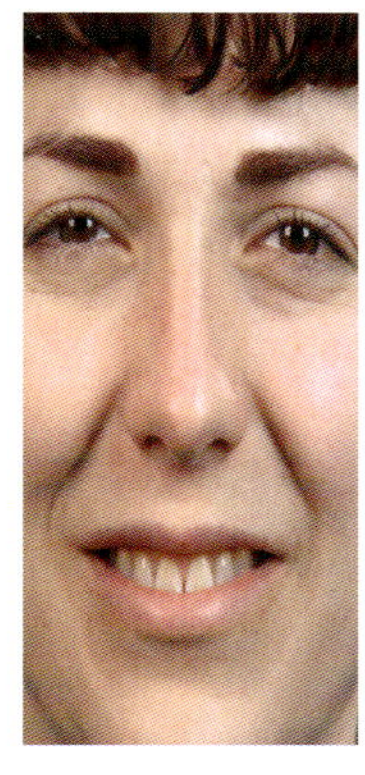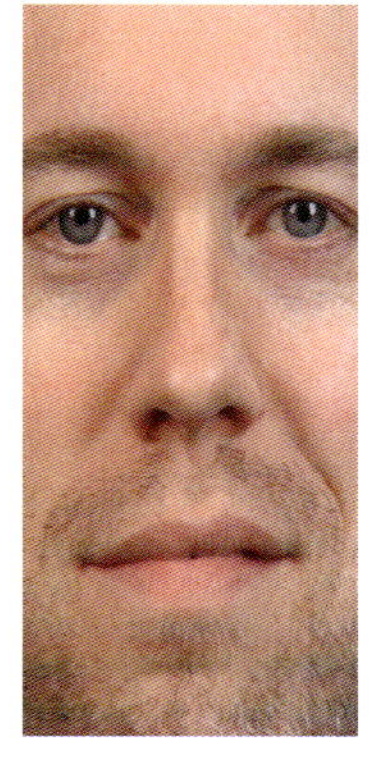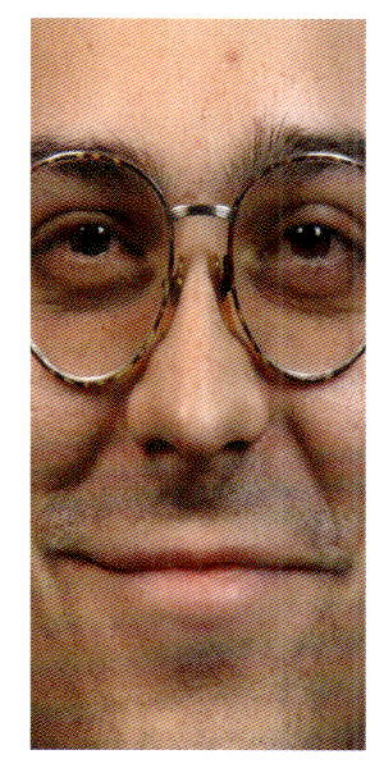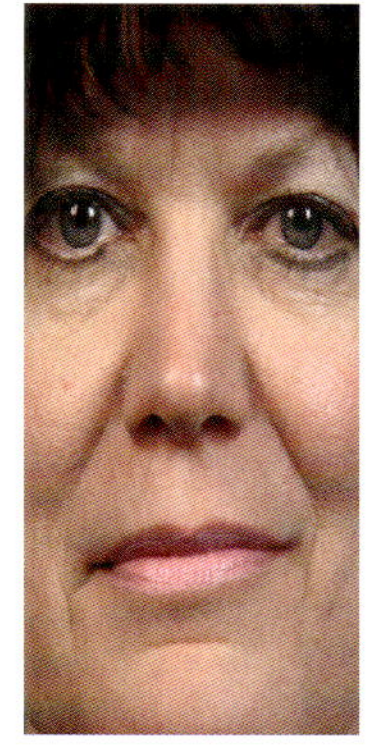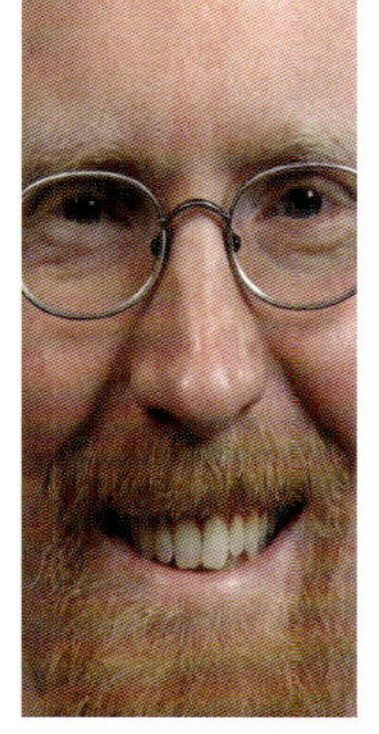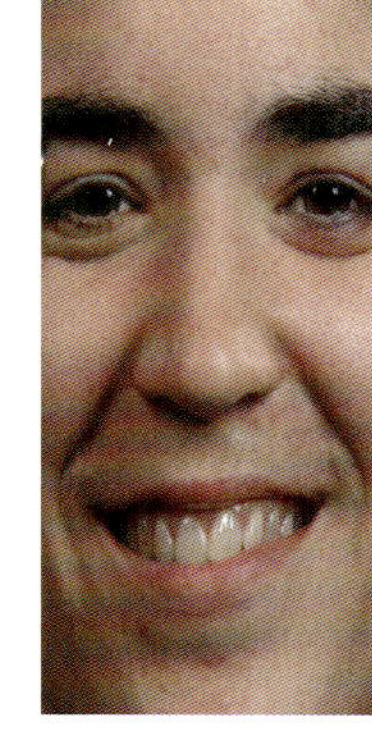
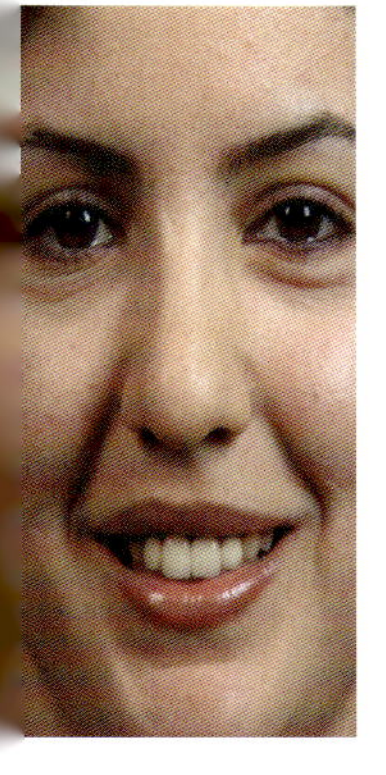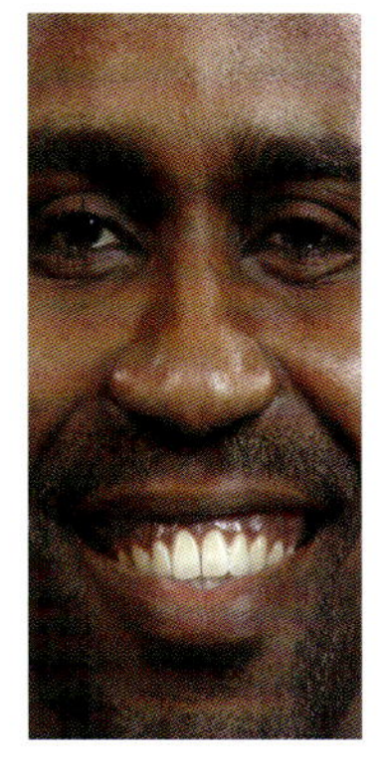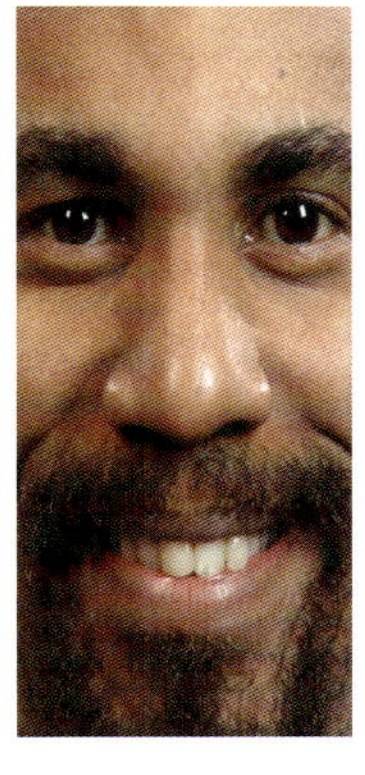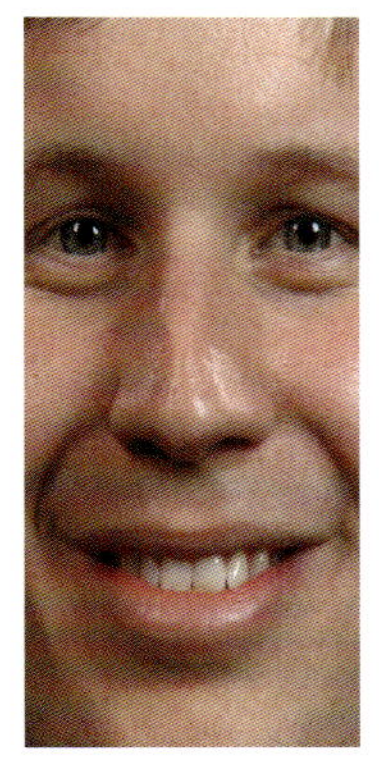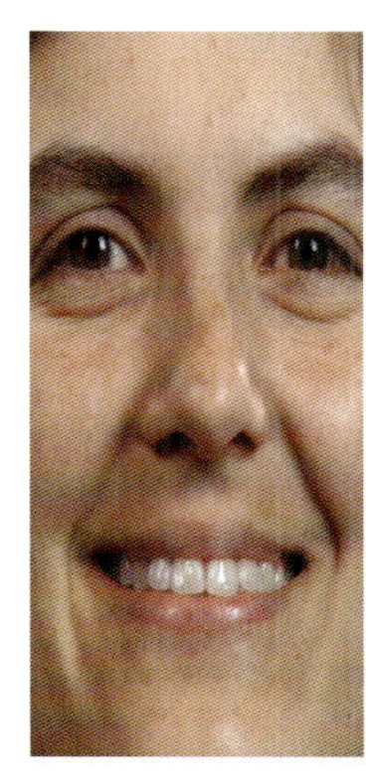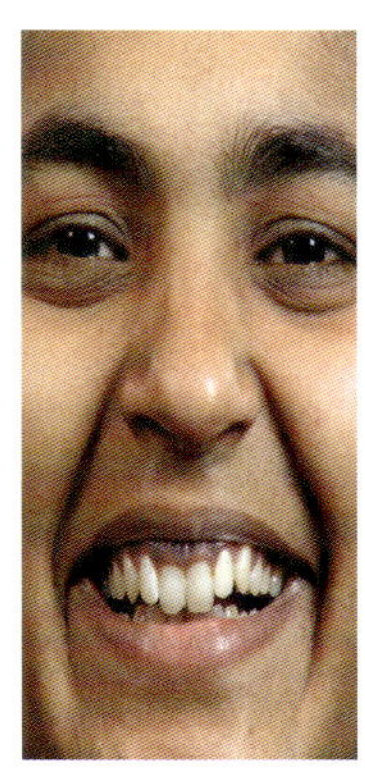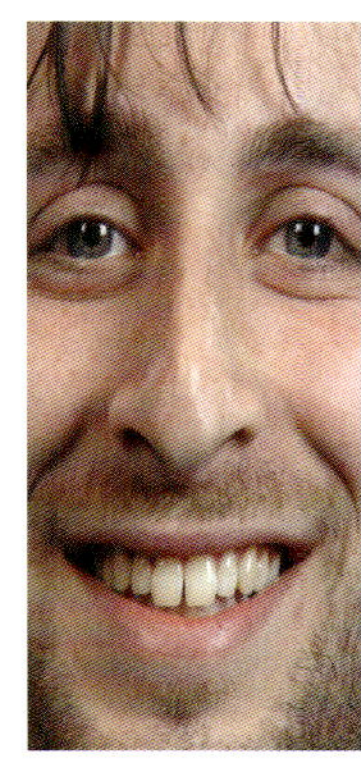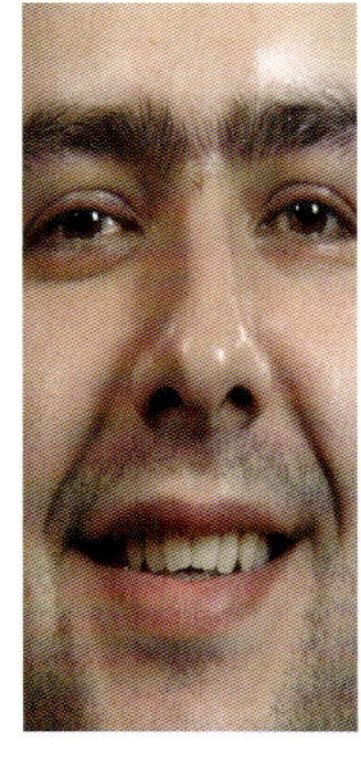
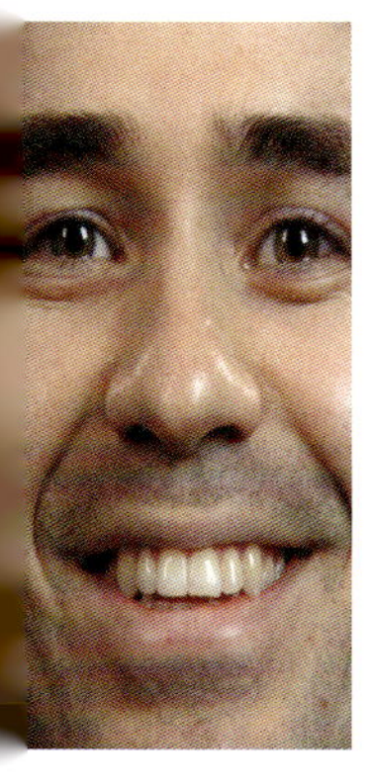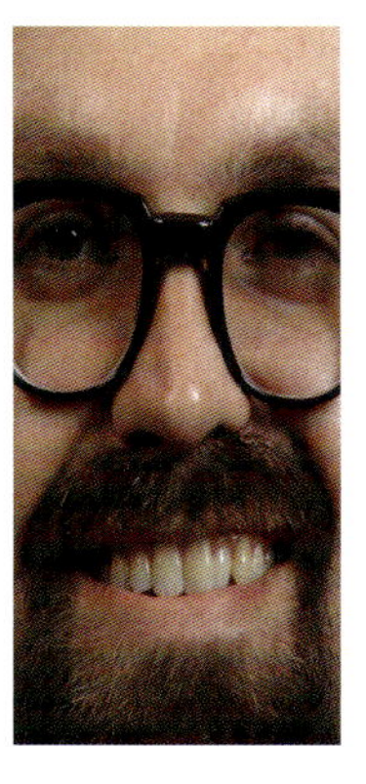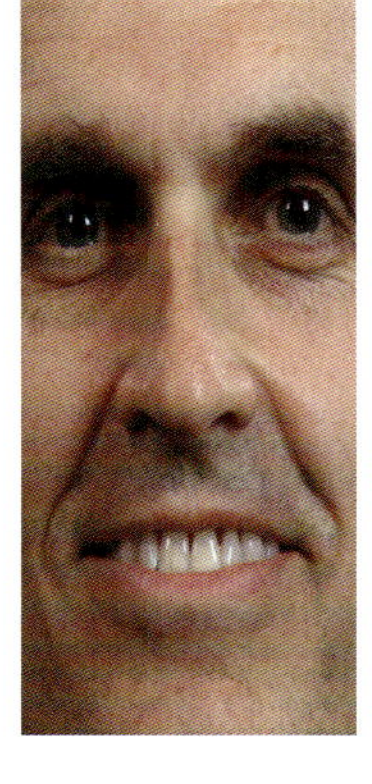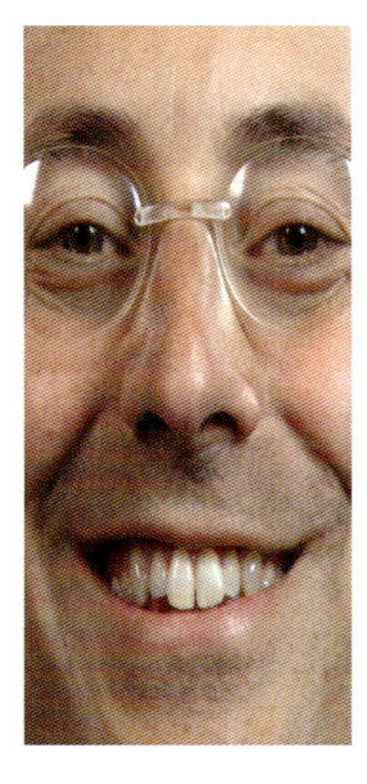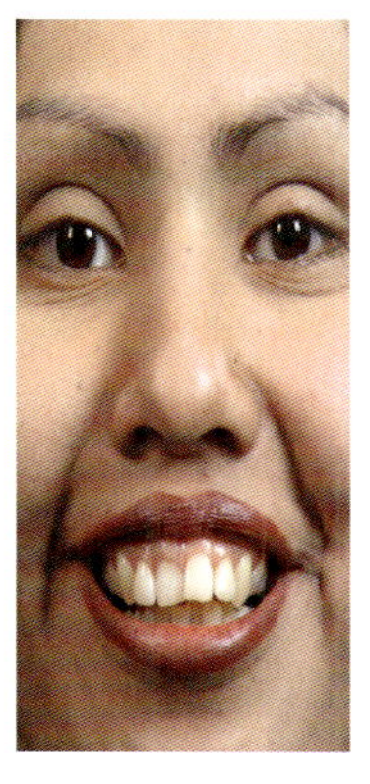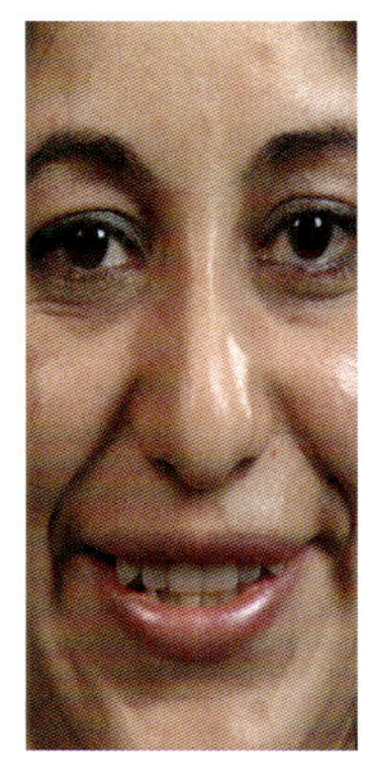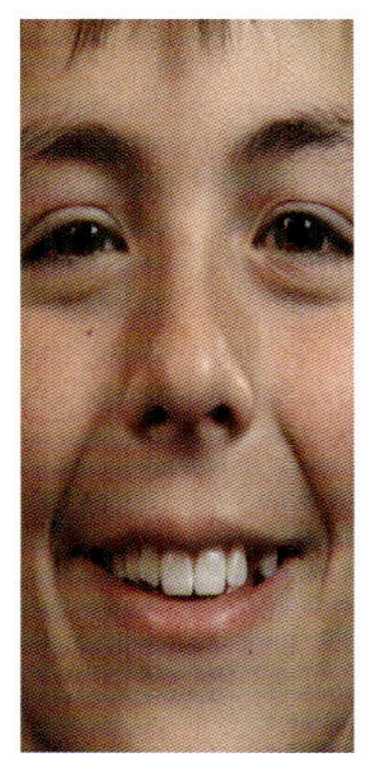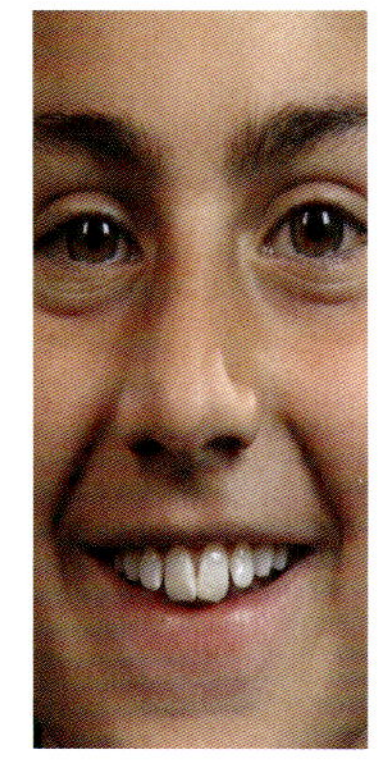

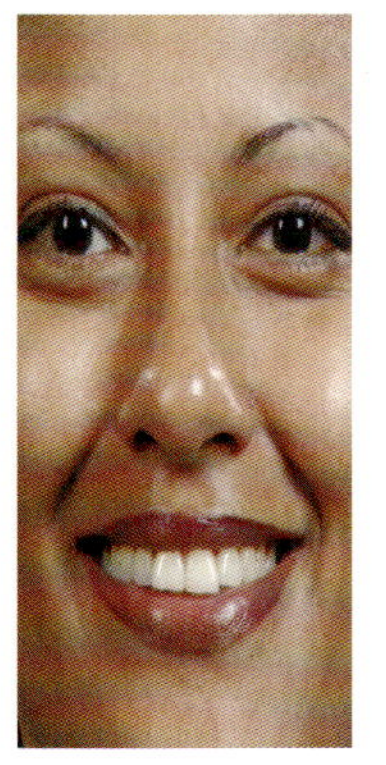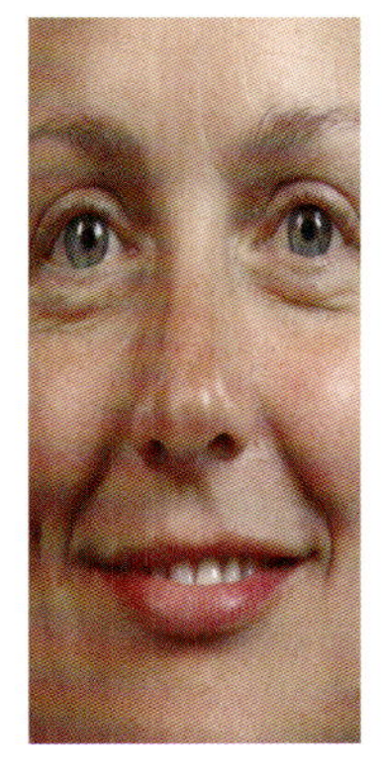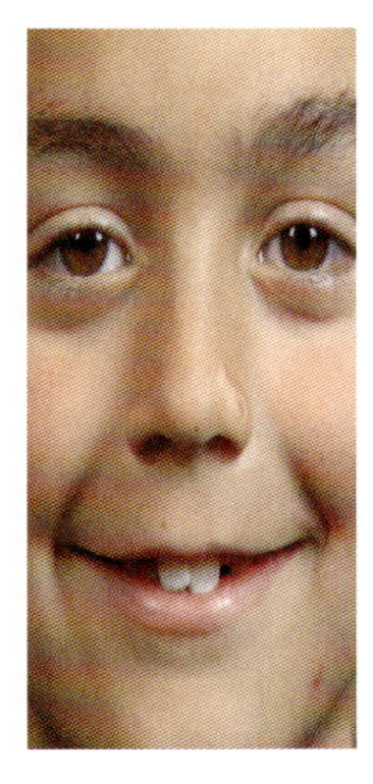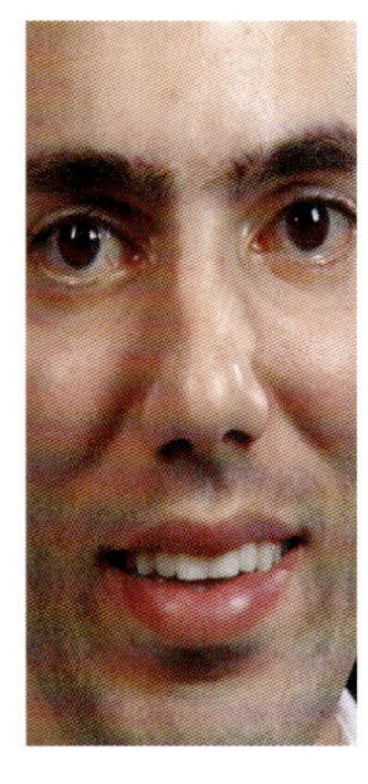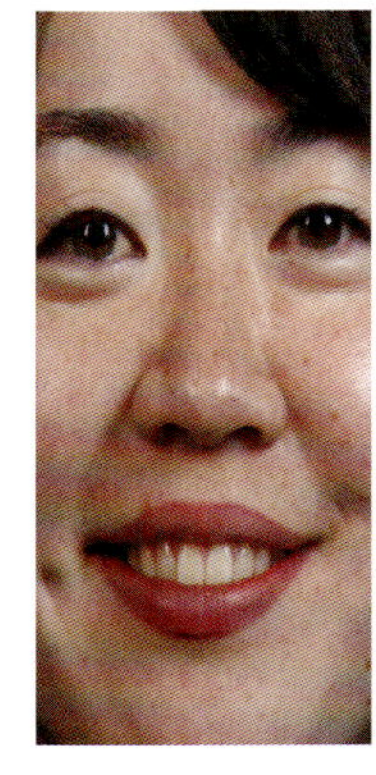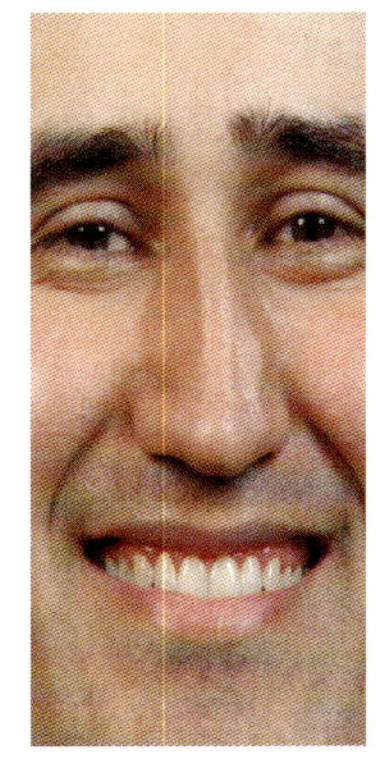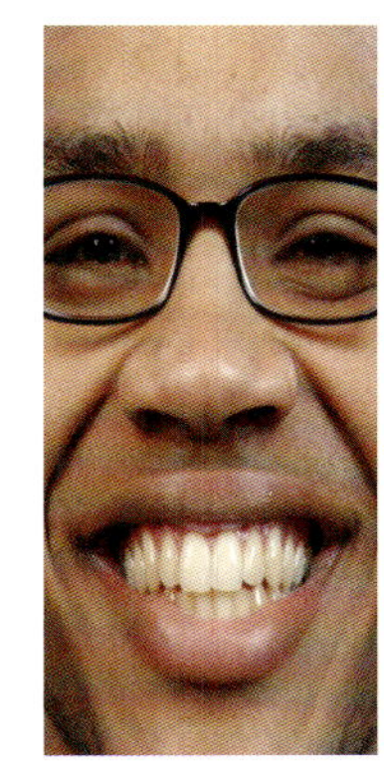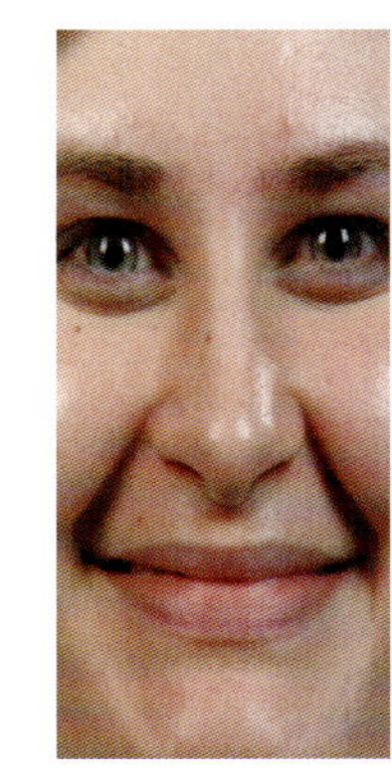
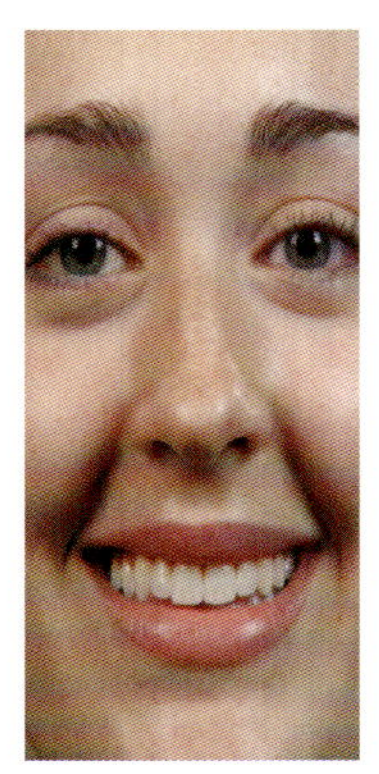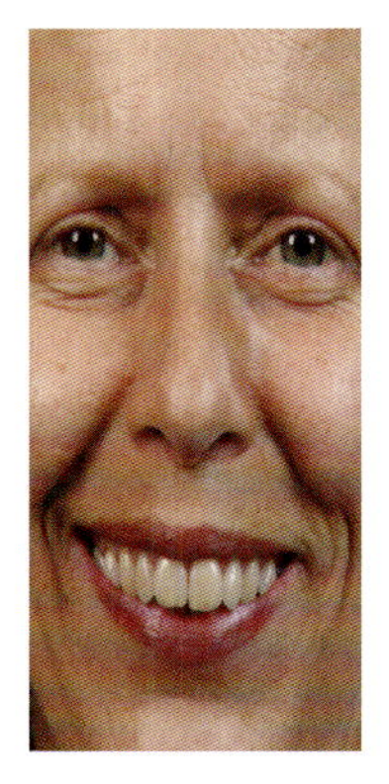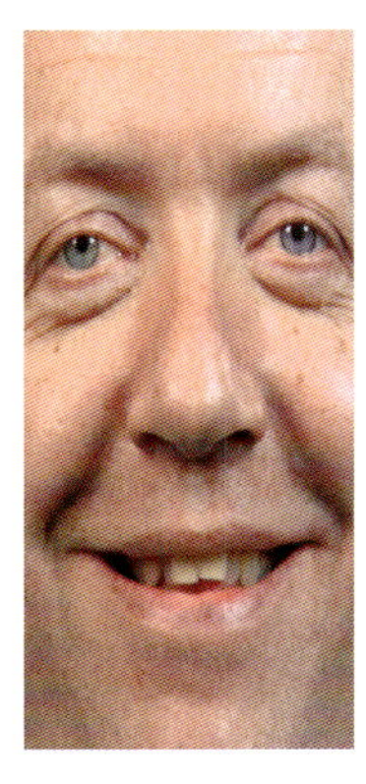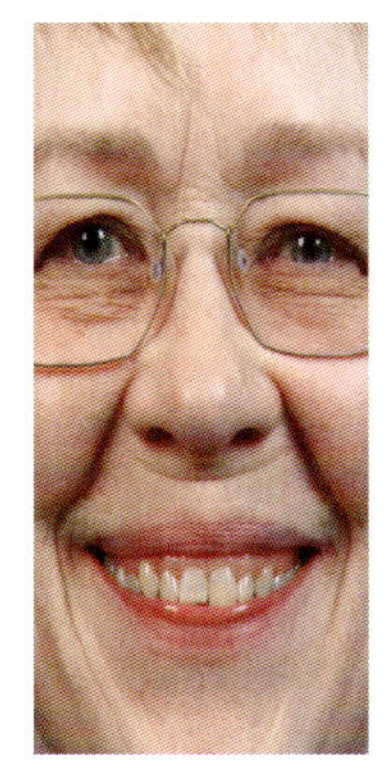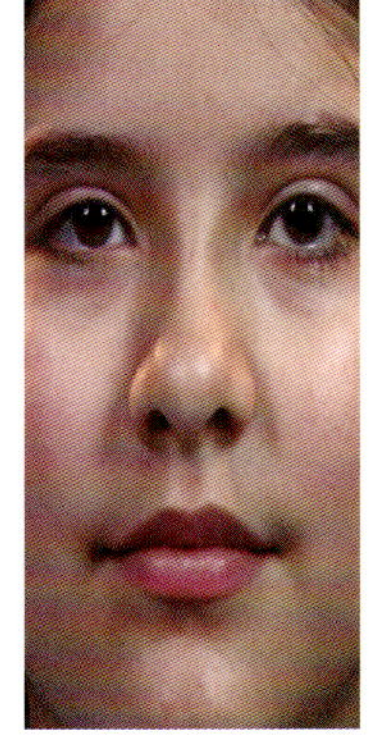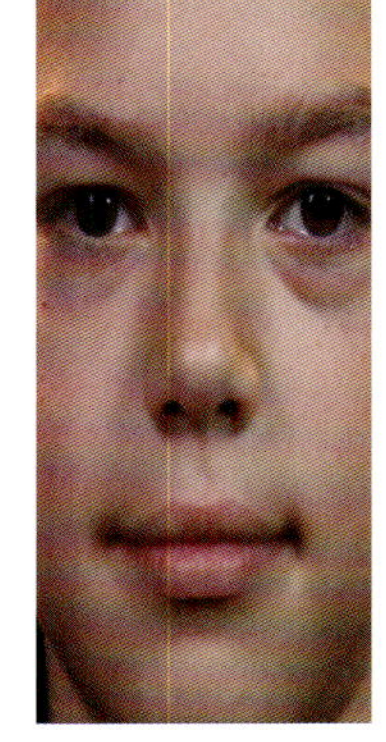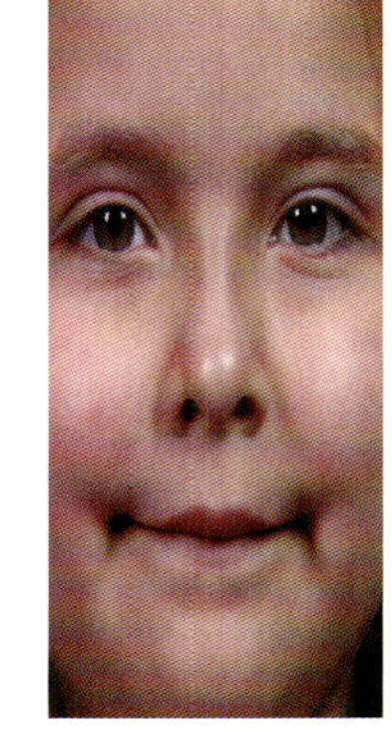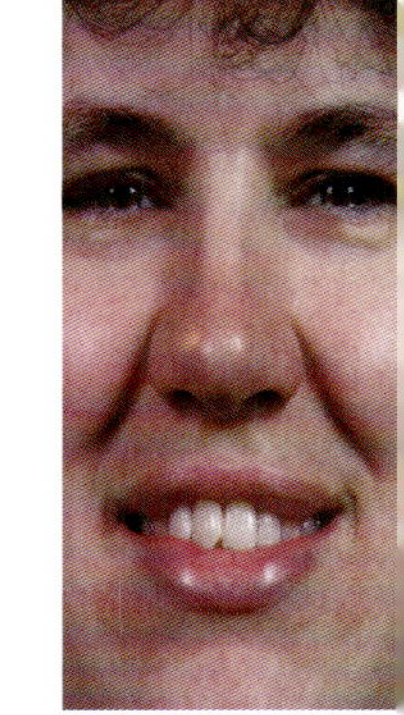
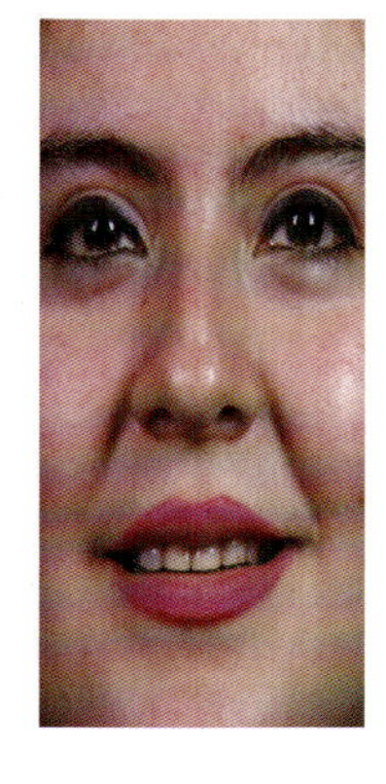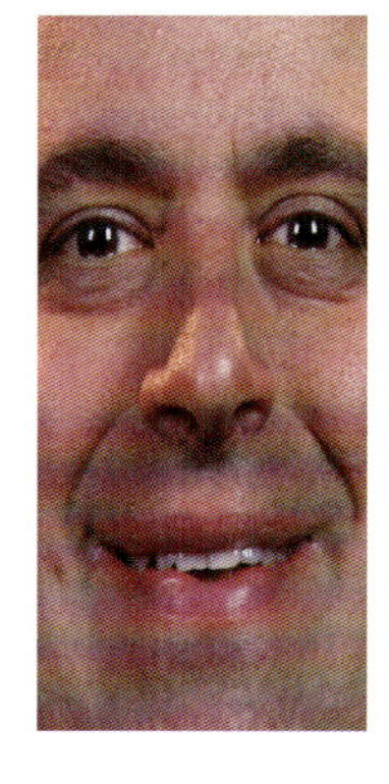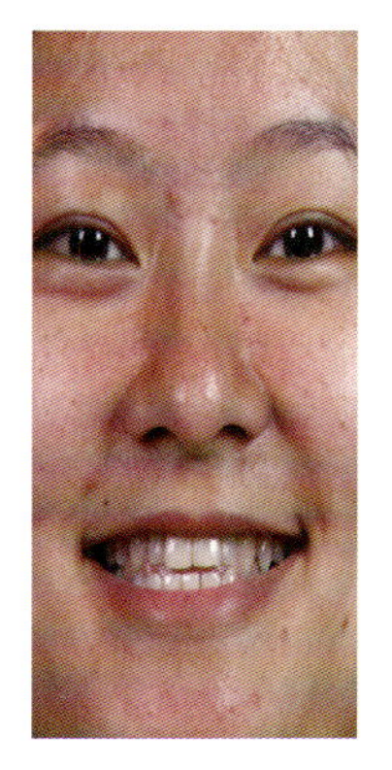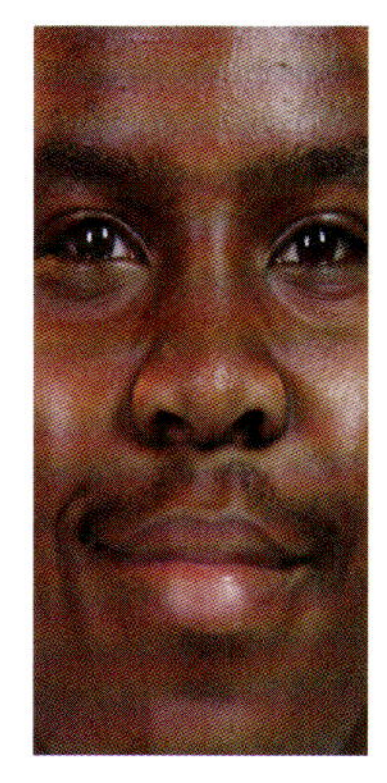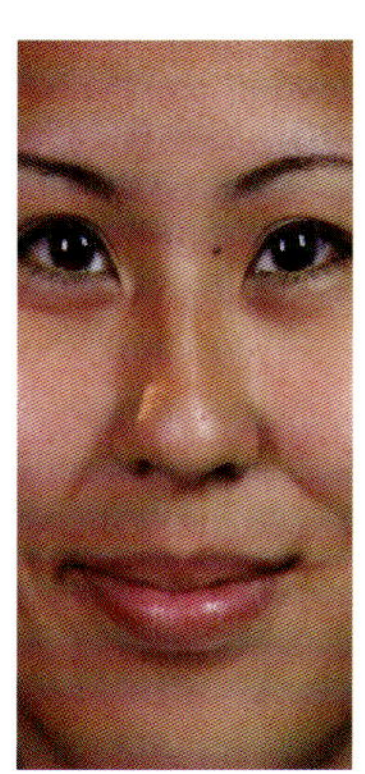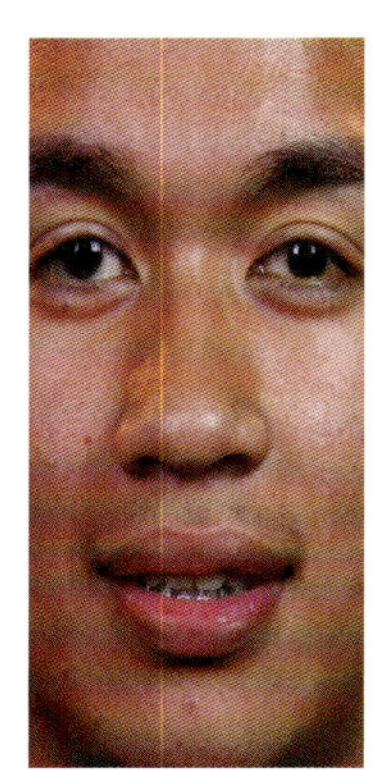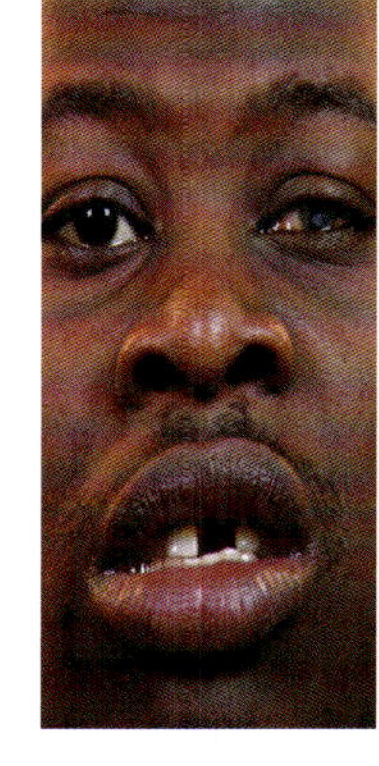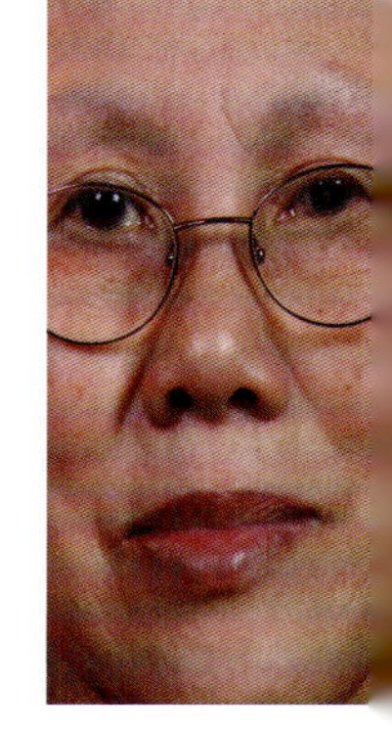
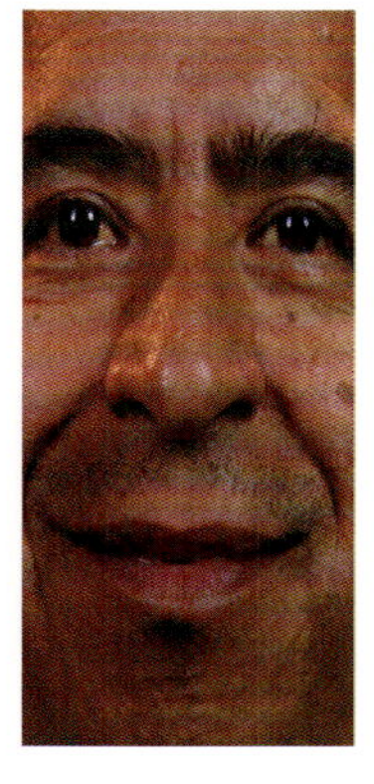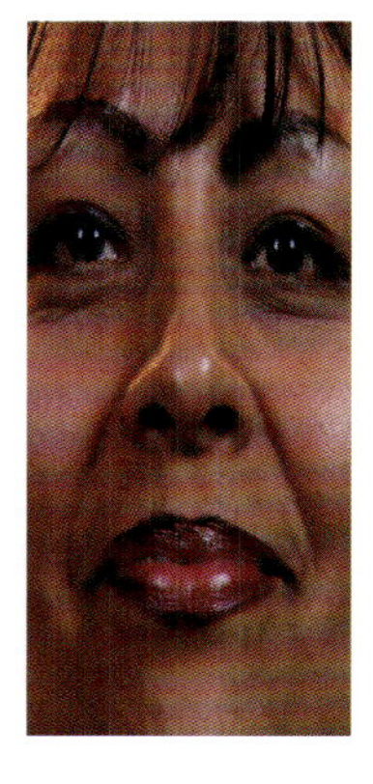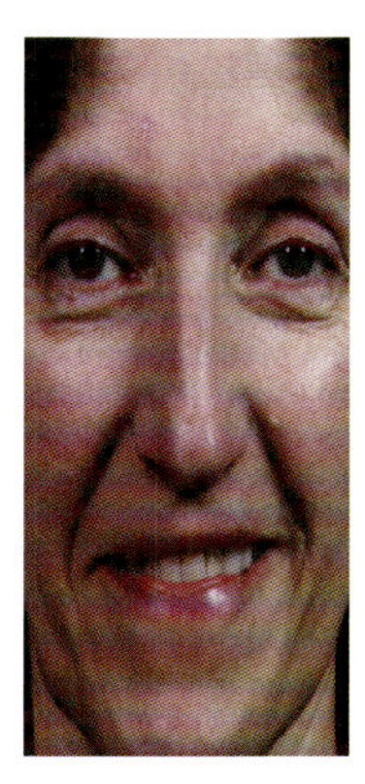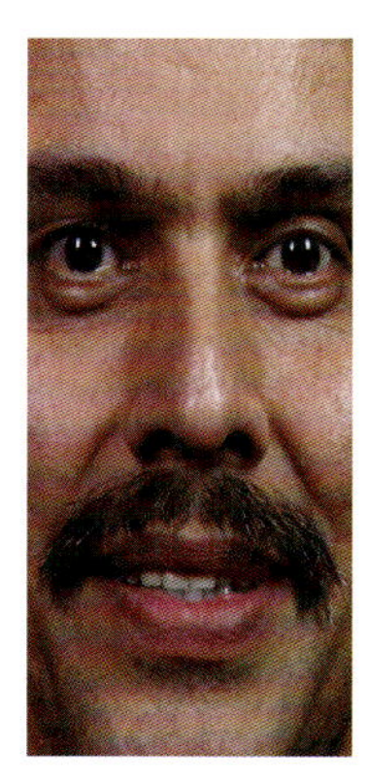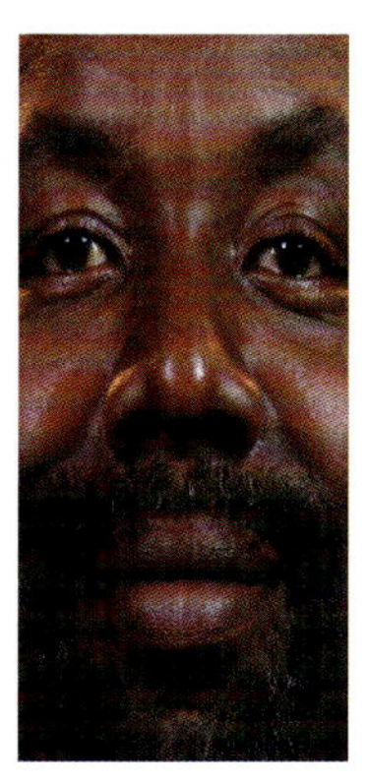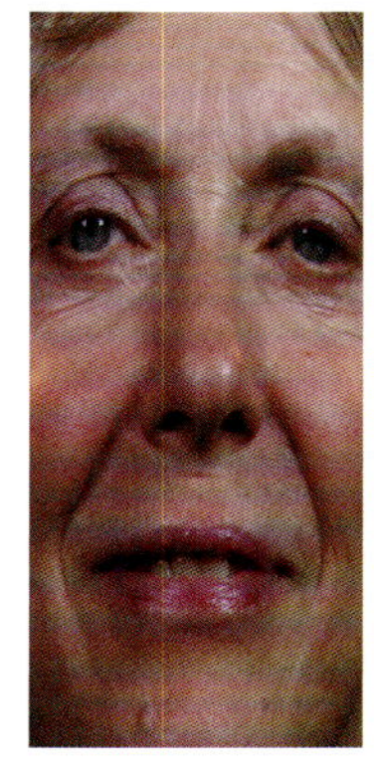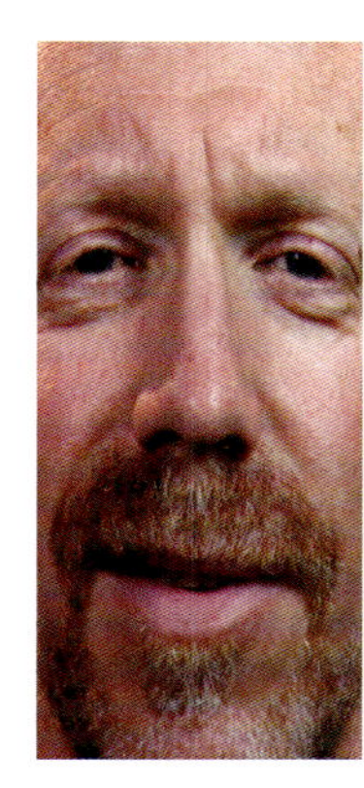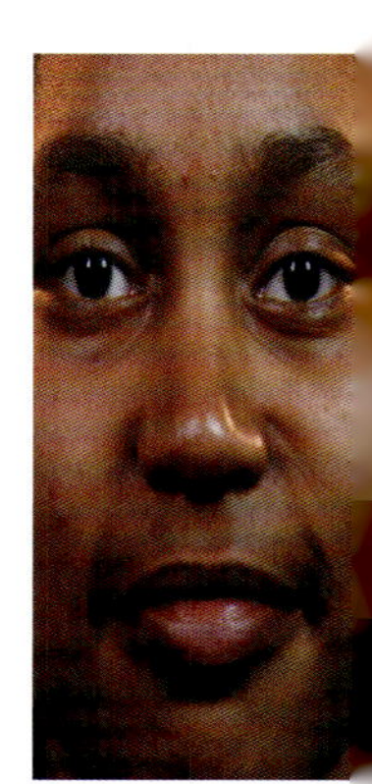

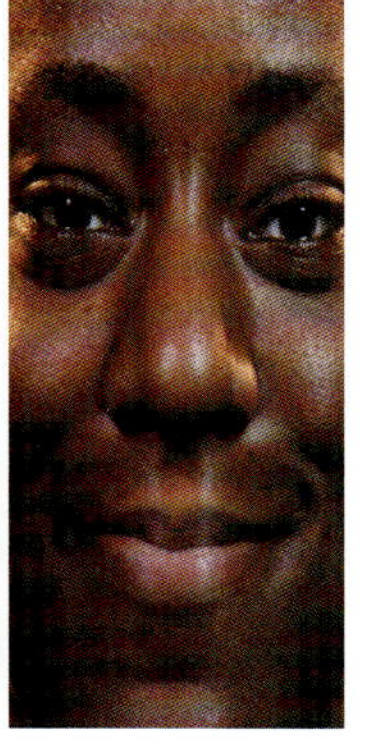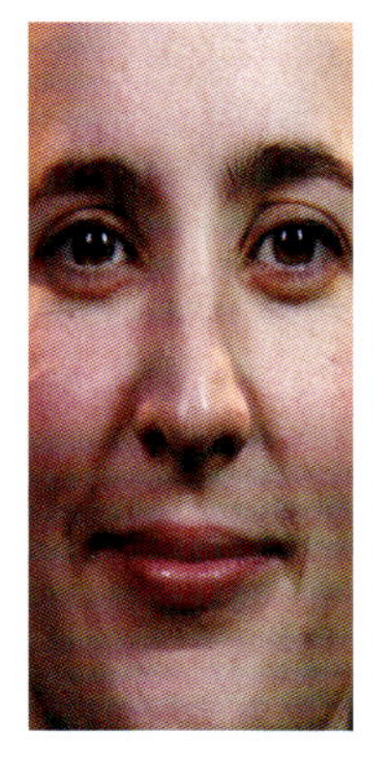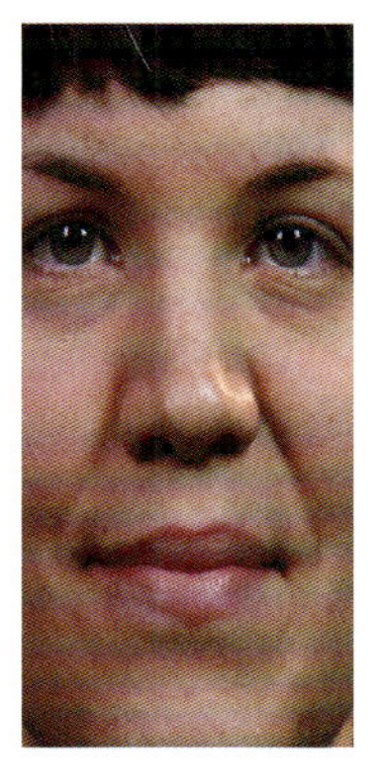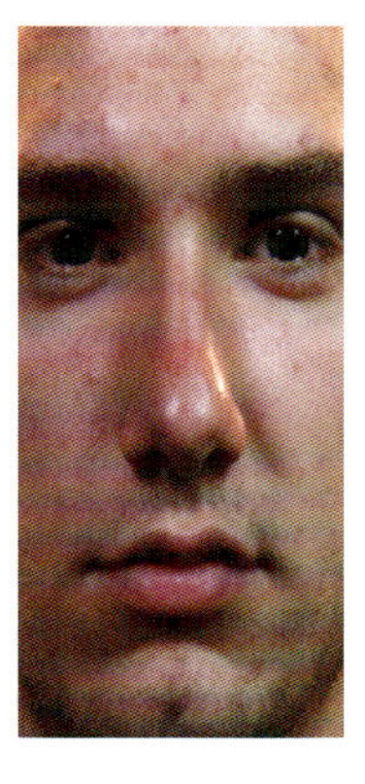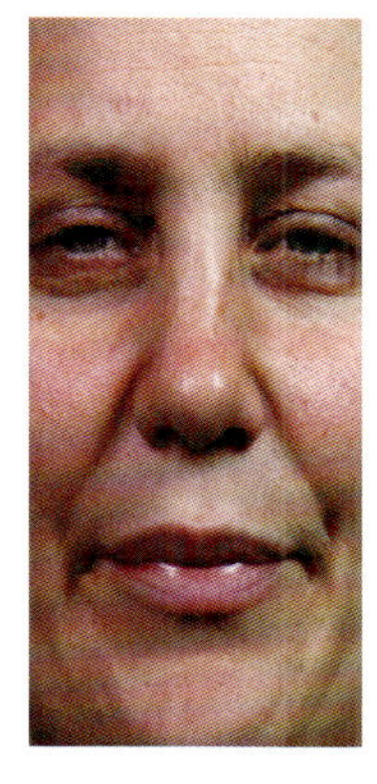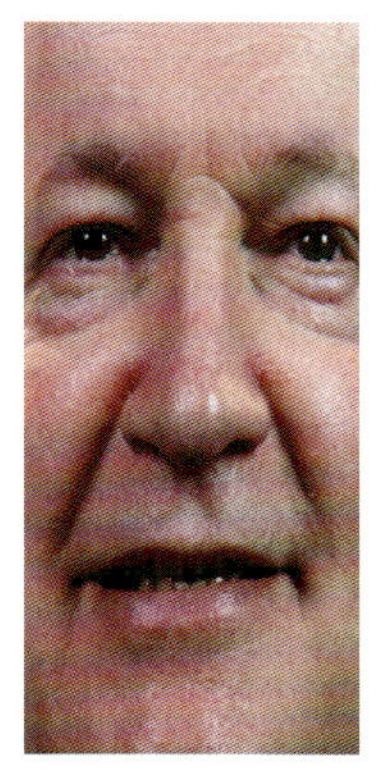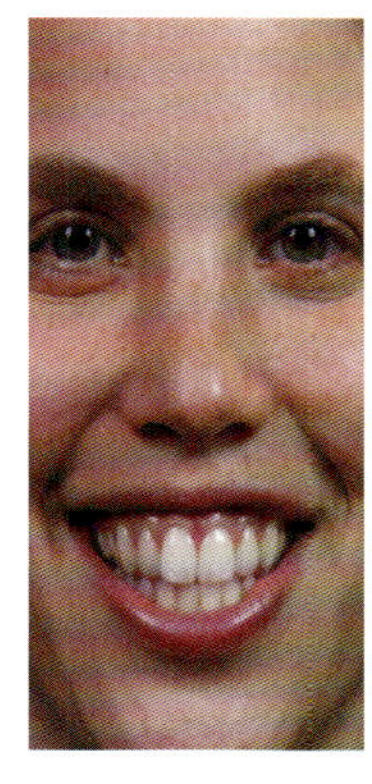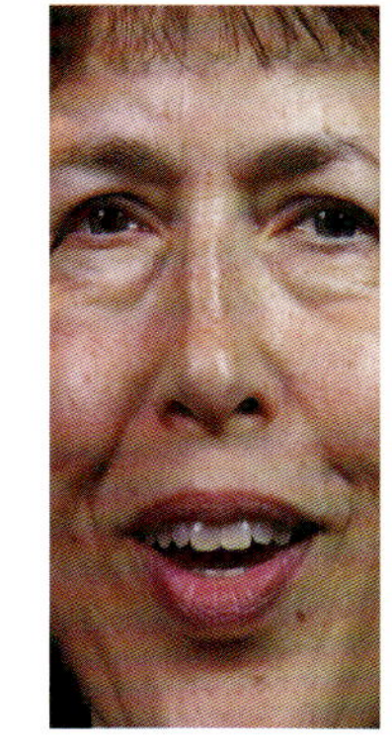
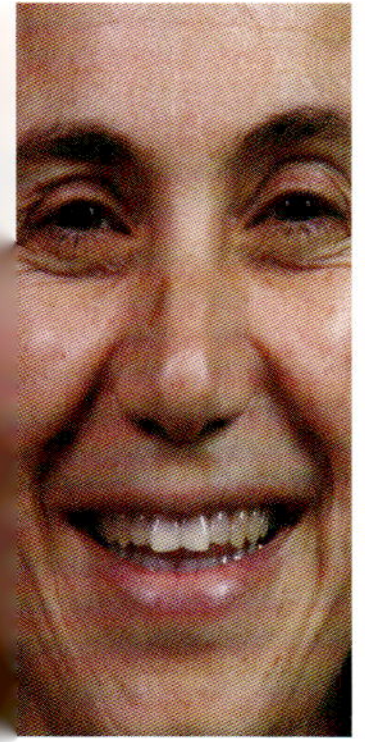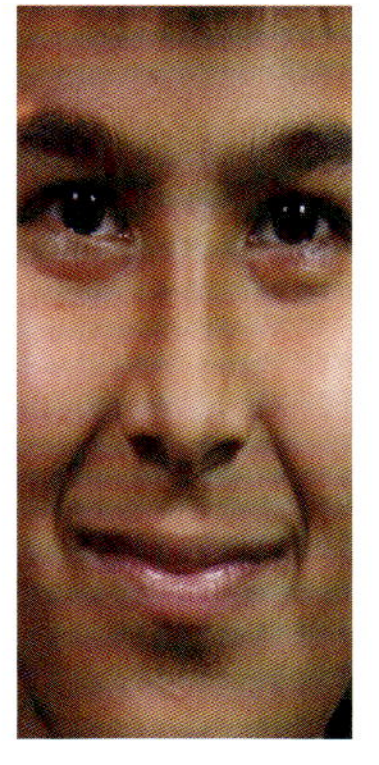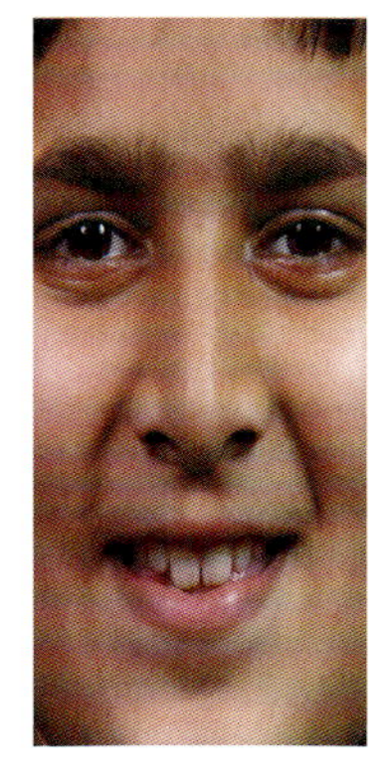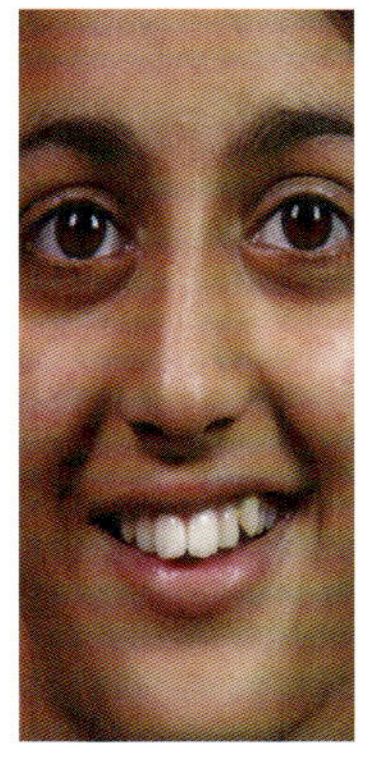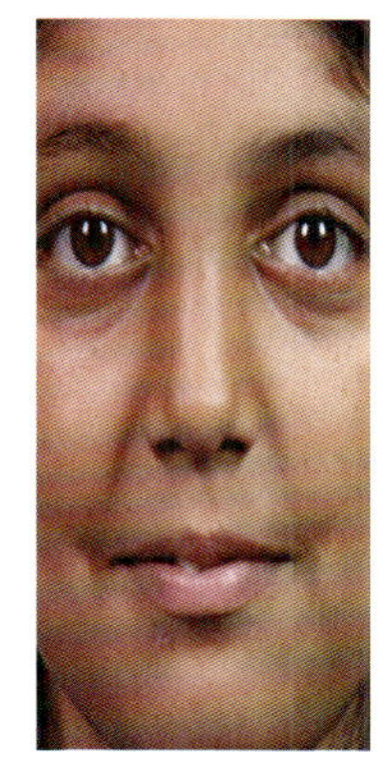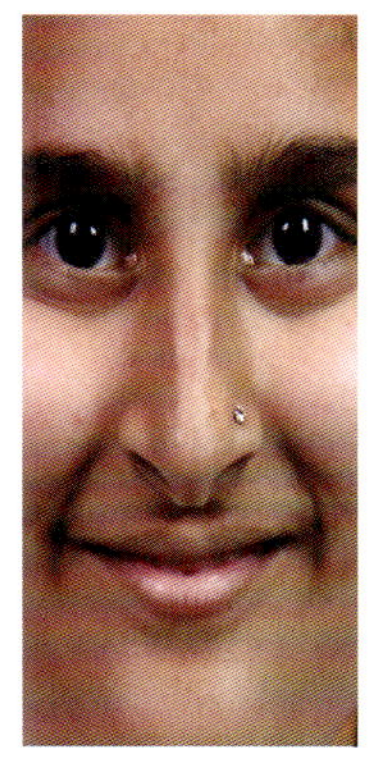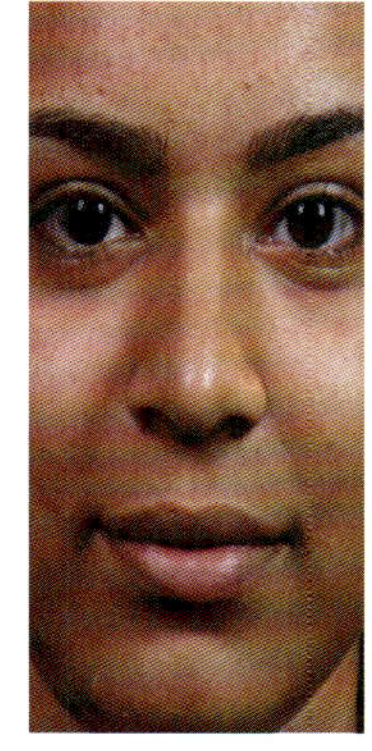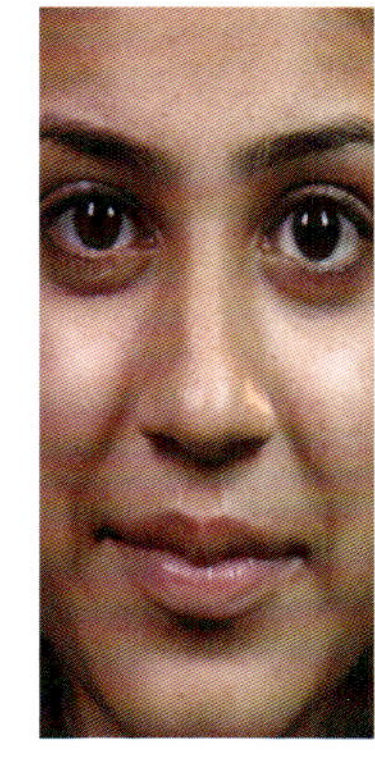
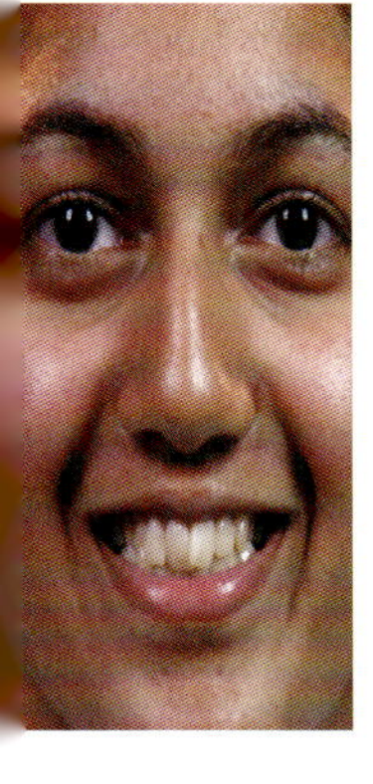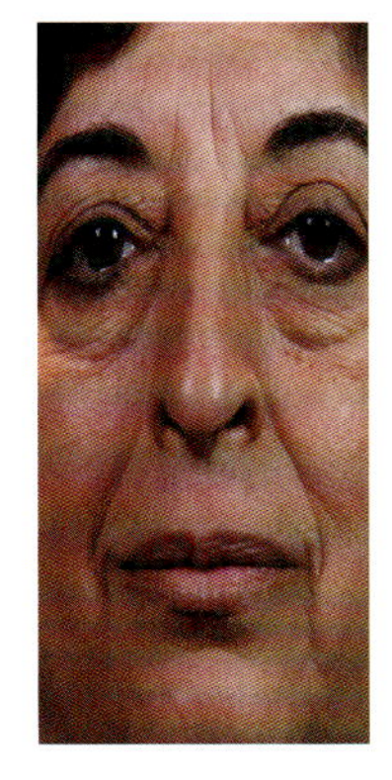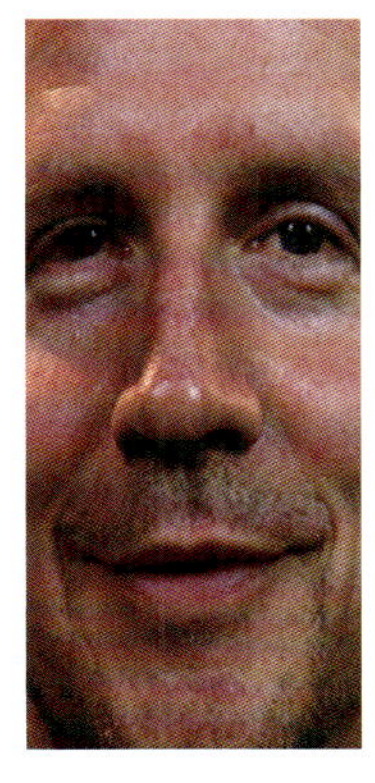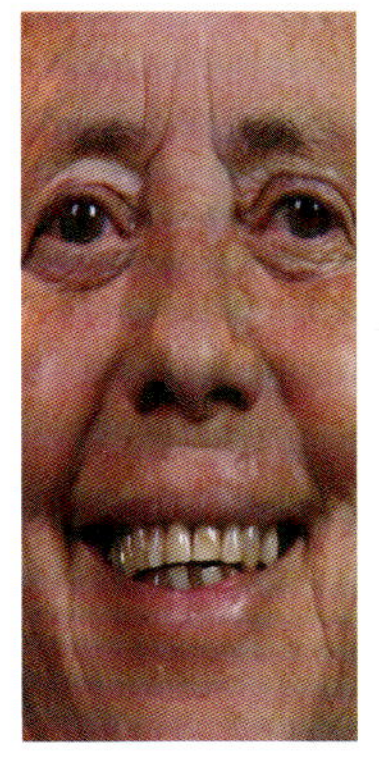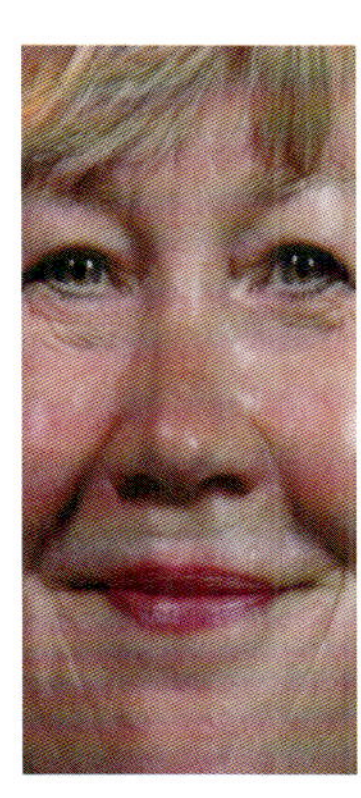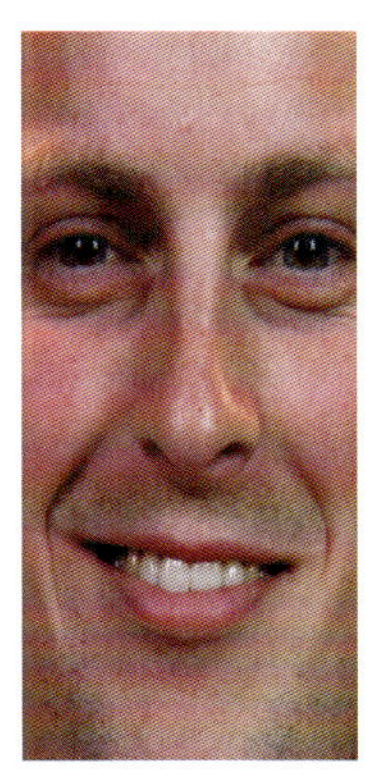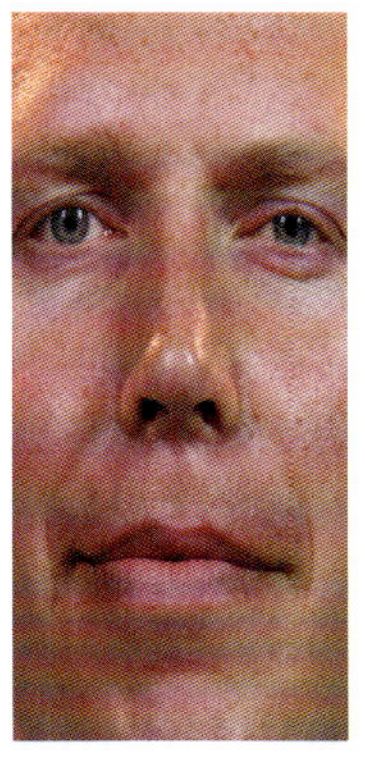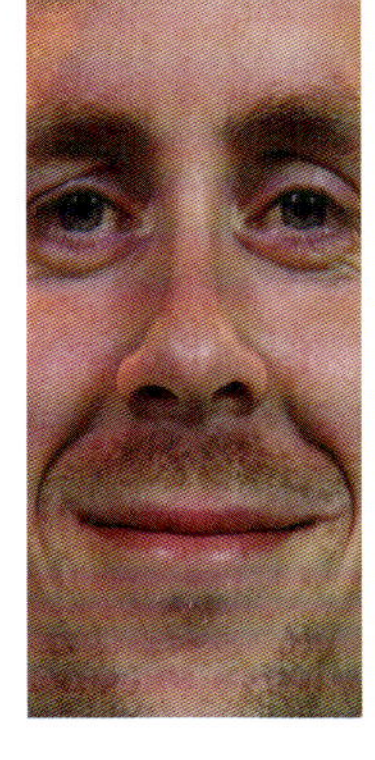
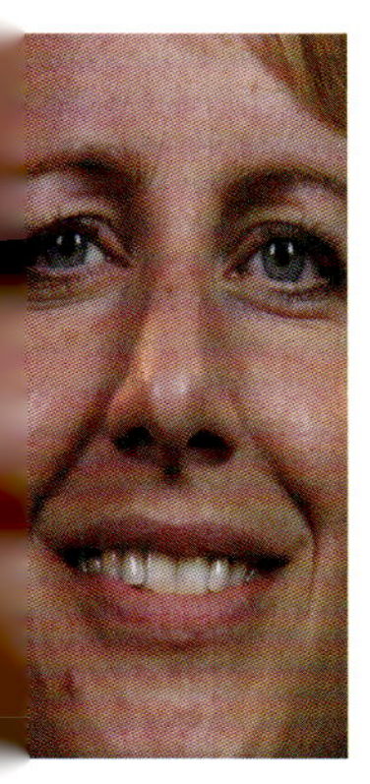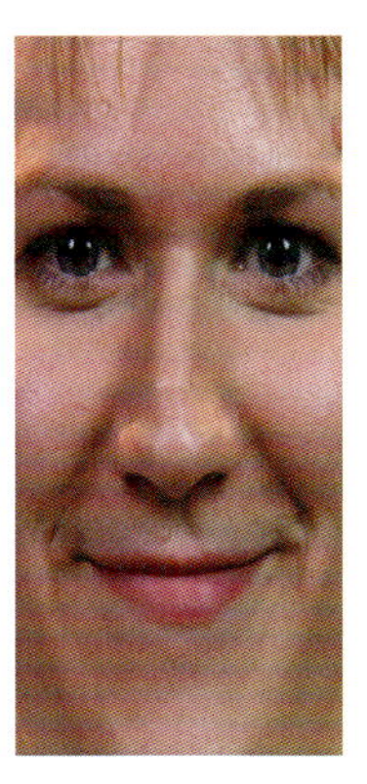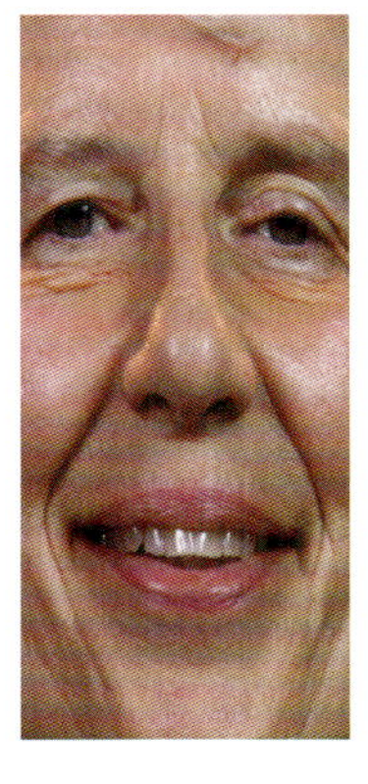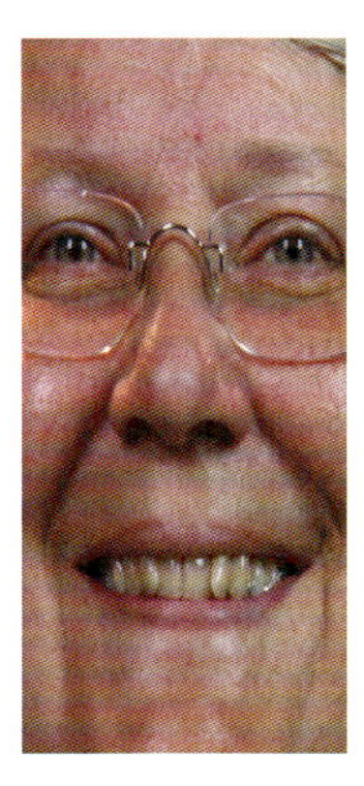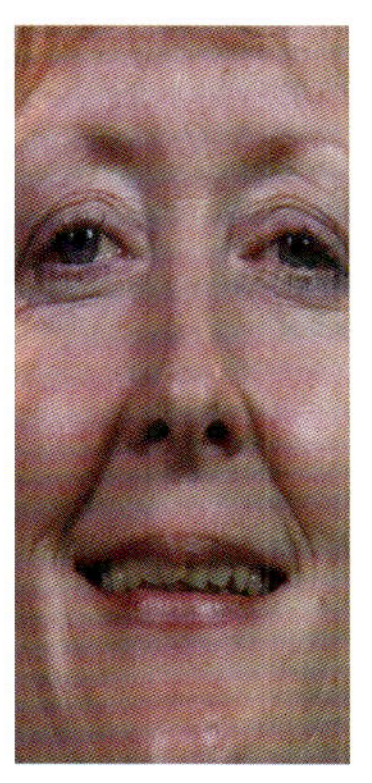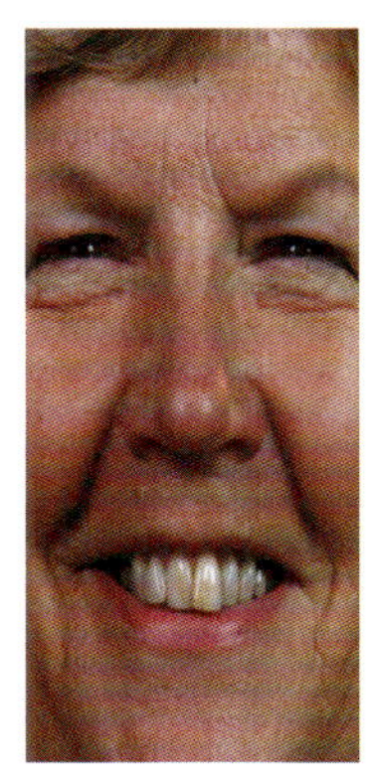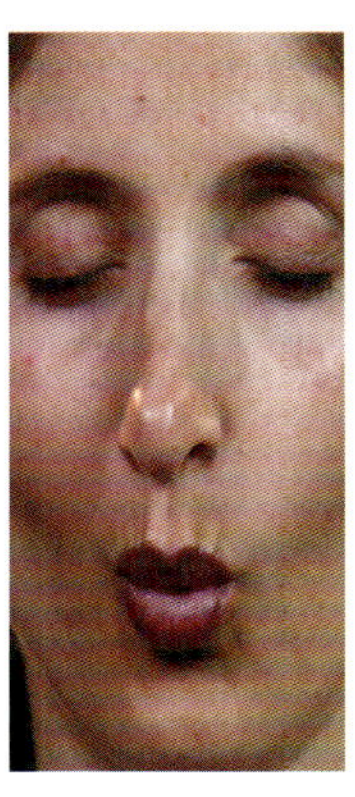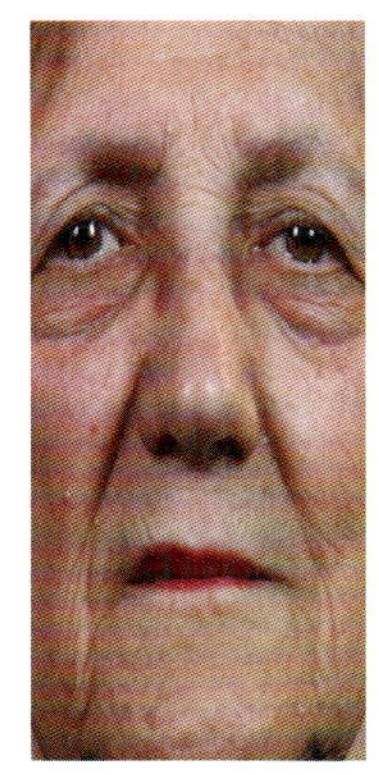

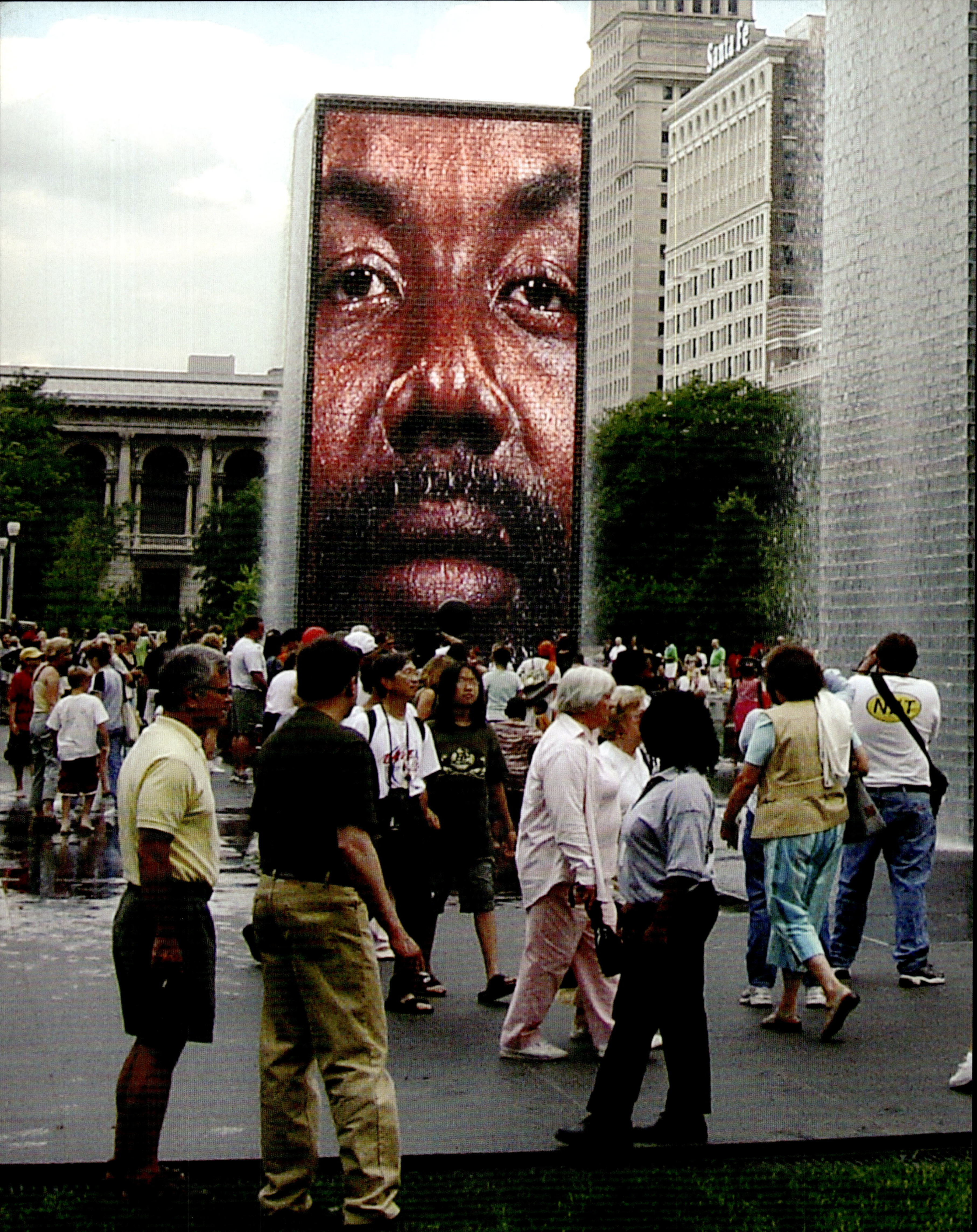

Santa Fe

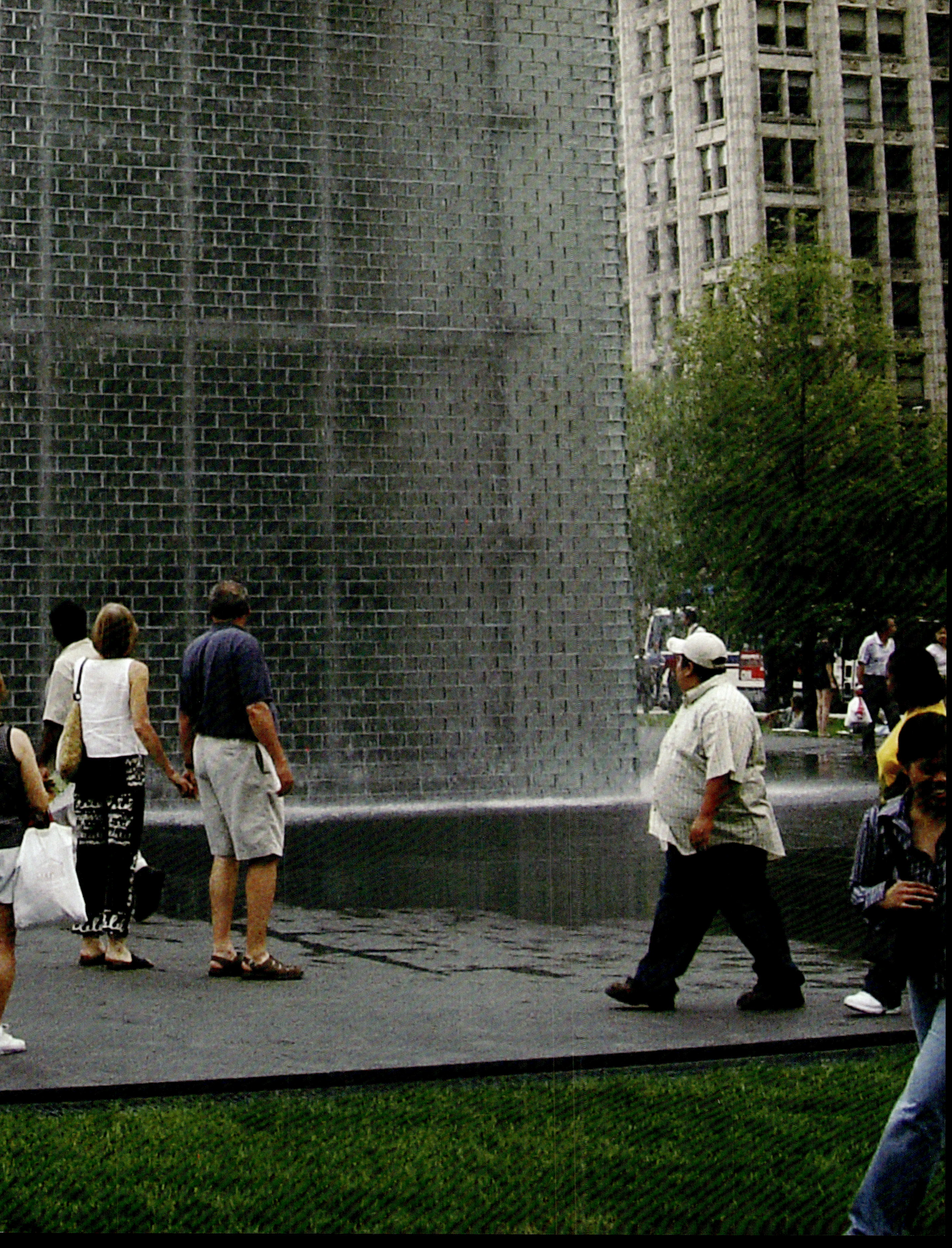

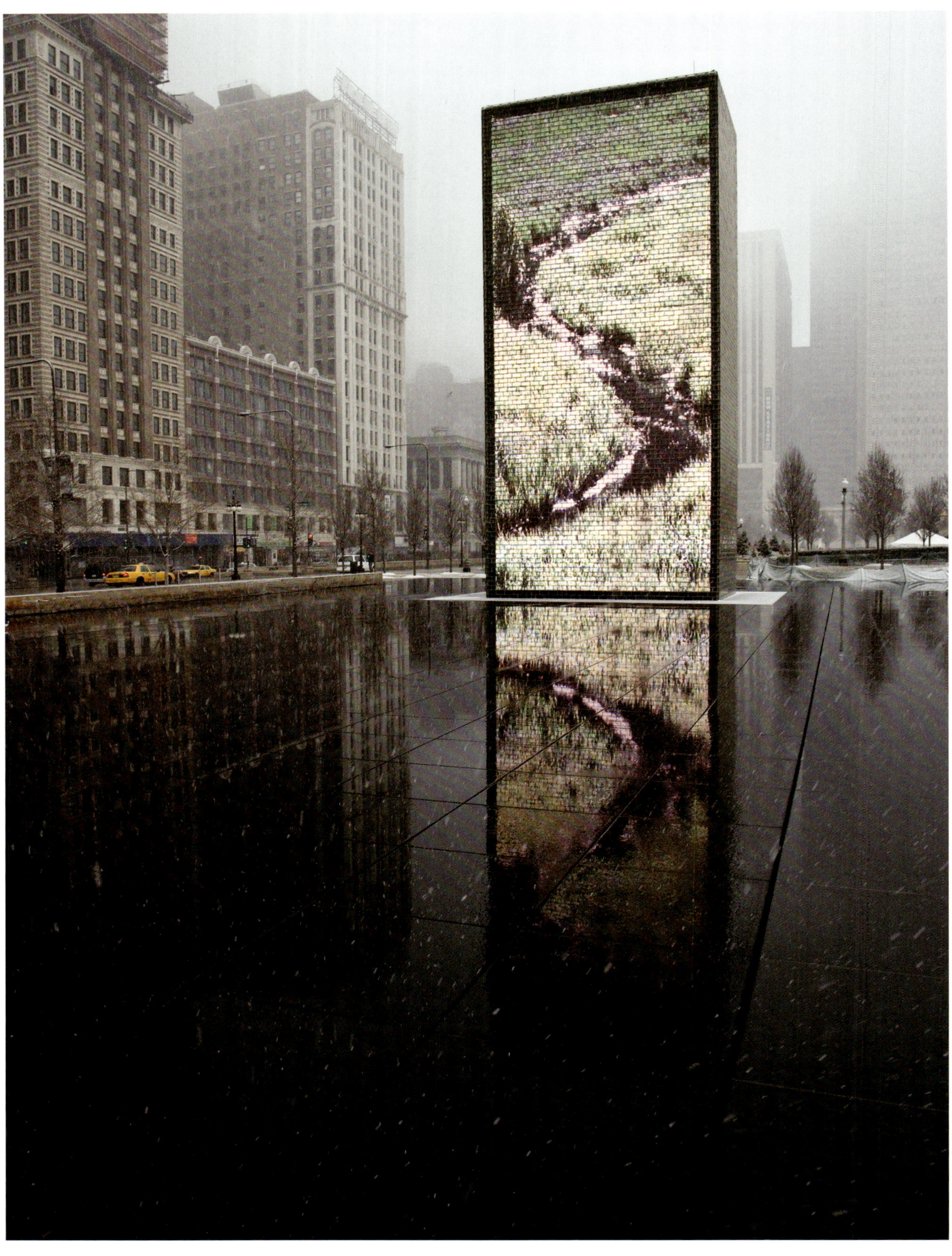

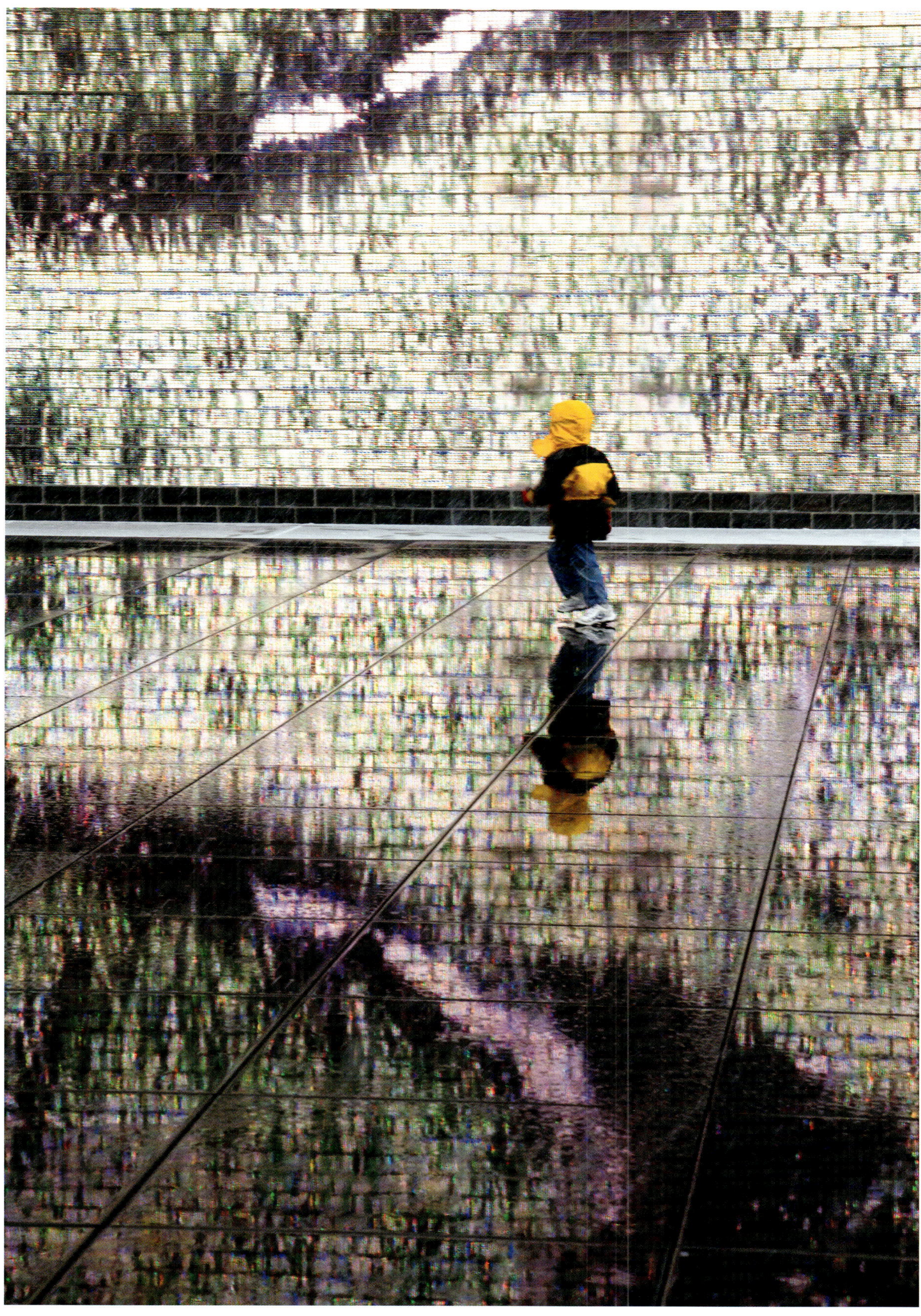

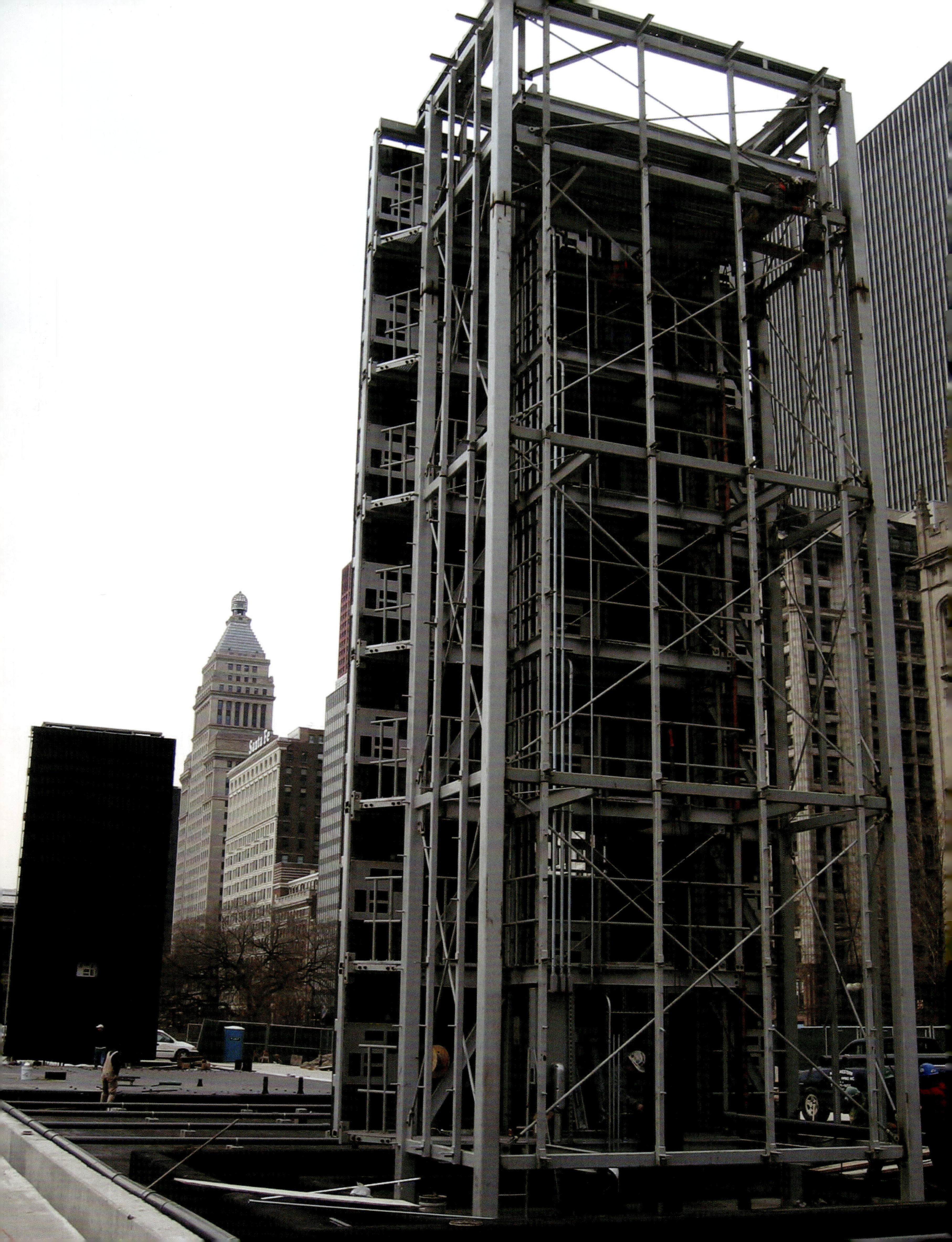

7

The Final Push

With much of the first two years lost, and with the sheer complexity of its realization, it was little short of a miracle that the project was on schedule for opening in the fall of 2004. It was also coming almost exactly within the revised seventeen-million-dollar budget that had first been calculated back in 2002.

And then word came down from Mayor Daley's office that the official inauguration of Millennium Park would be celebrated with a week of events commencing July 16. It would be a public relations disaster if the fountain were not to follow suit, with its own ceremony scheduled for July 23. As Steve Crown comments, "We just had to roll up our sleeves and get down to it."

The final weeks are fraught, with Plensa spending more and more time in Chicago as new features are installed and tested. The artist is on-site most days, largely working with technicians on the video images and the controlling computers that are housed in two dedicated rooms in the parking lot beneath.

It is a couple of weeks before the opening and everything is up and running just fine. They decide to leave it that way, nervous of the consequences of restarting a system that's been born three months premature.

The *Crown Fountain* opens without incident on the evening of Friday July 23, 2004, the day prior to a gala opening that s accompanied by an impressive

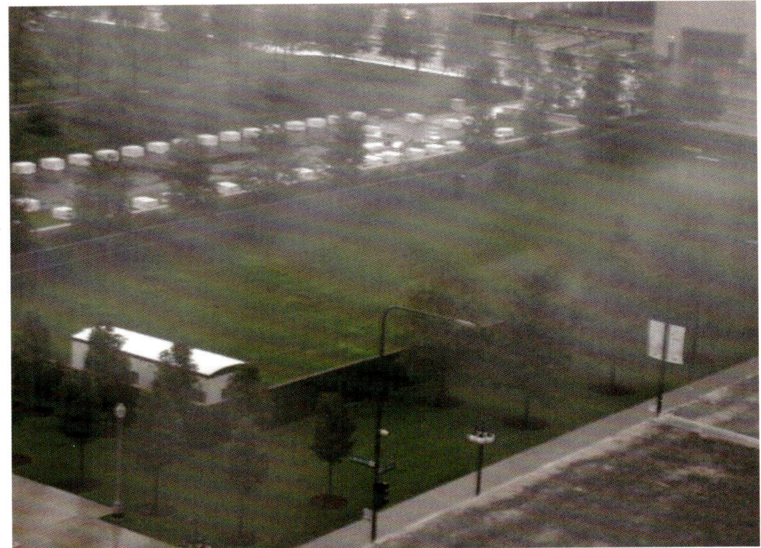
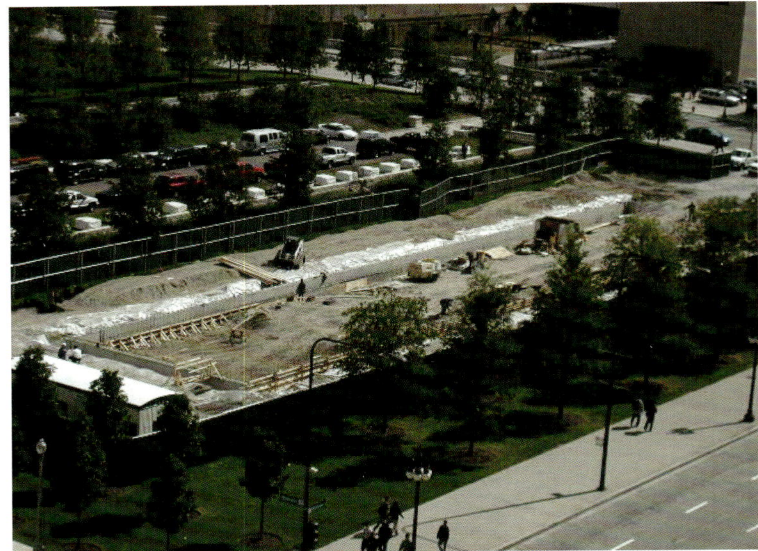
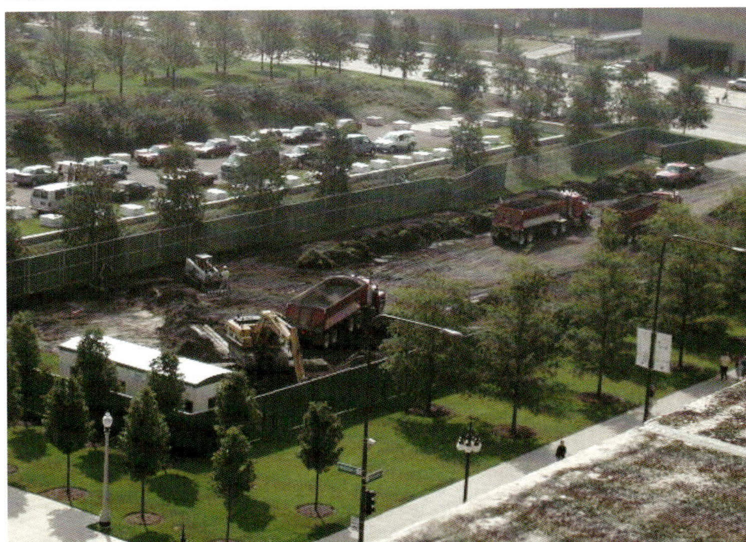
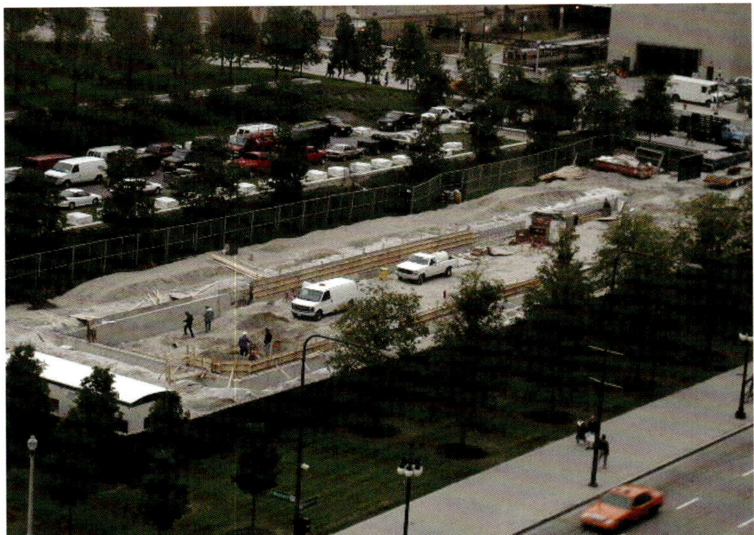
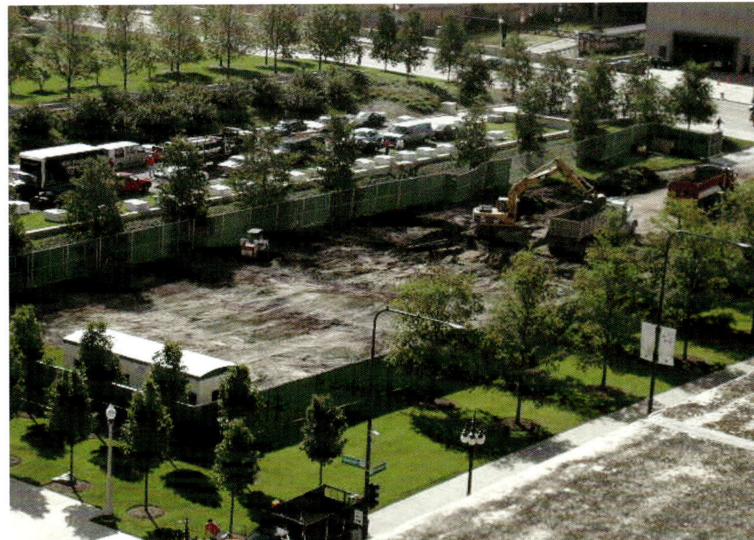
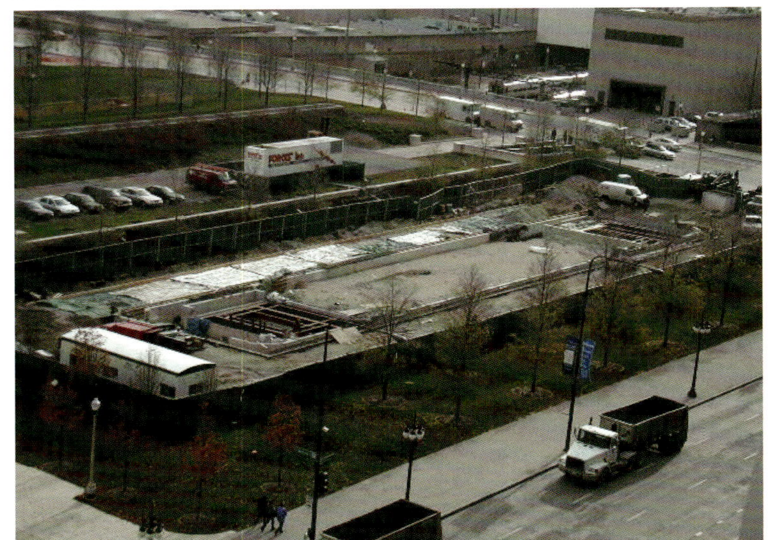
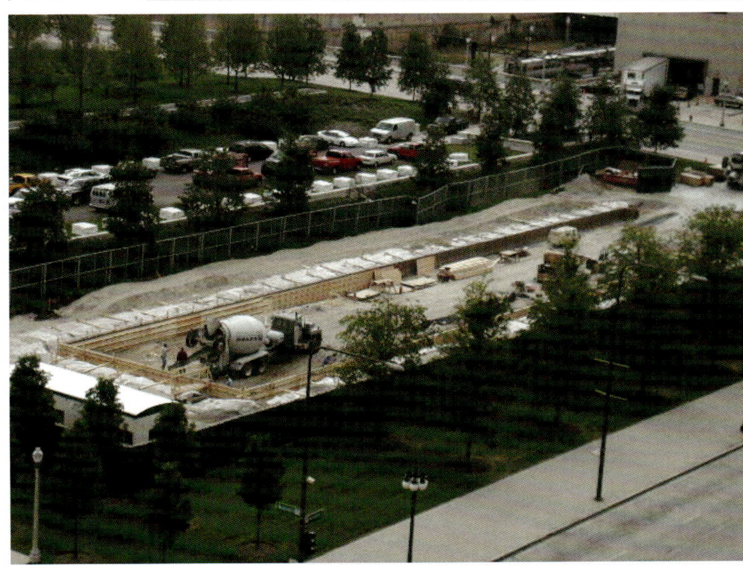
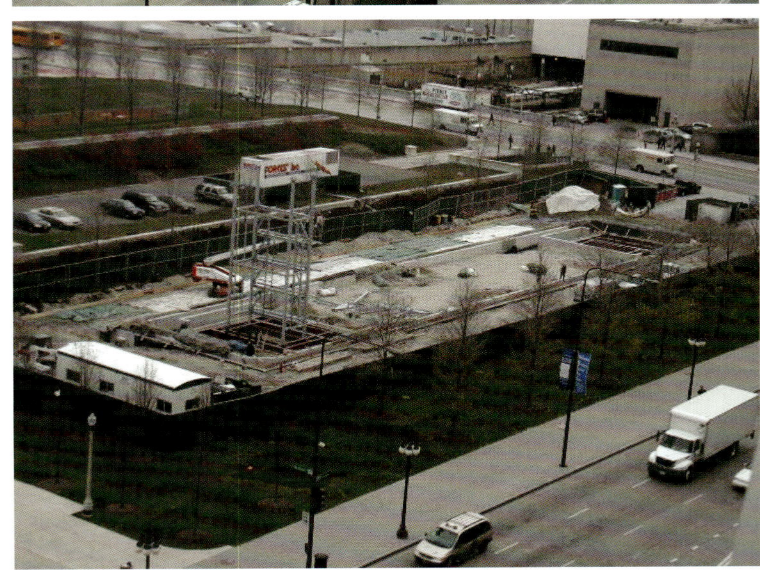

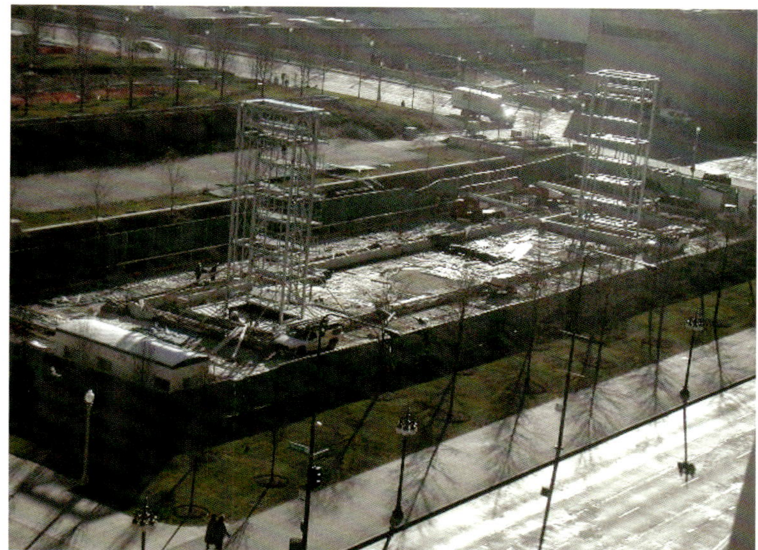
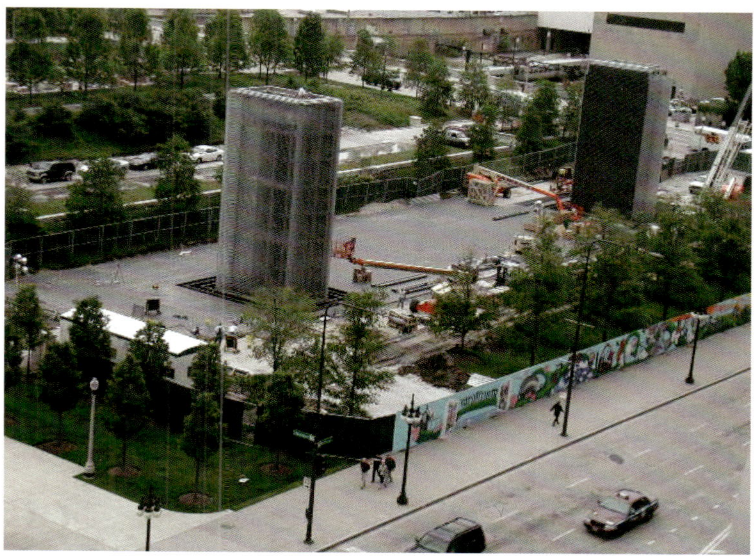
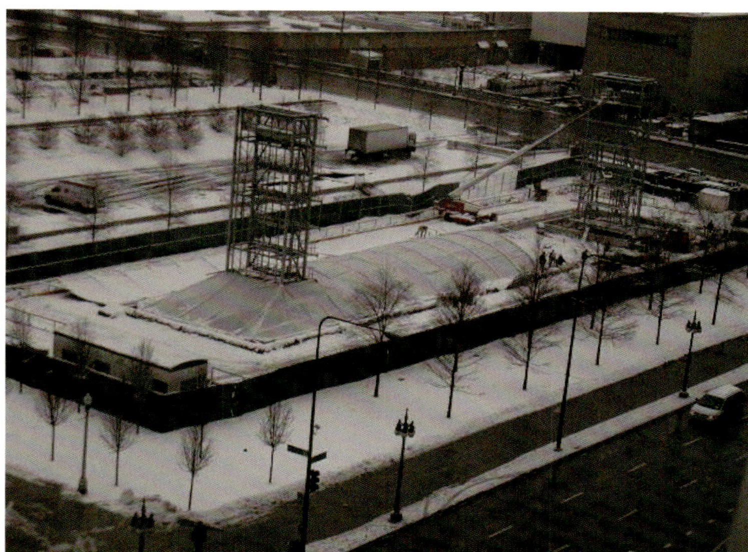
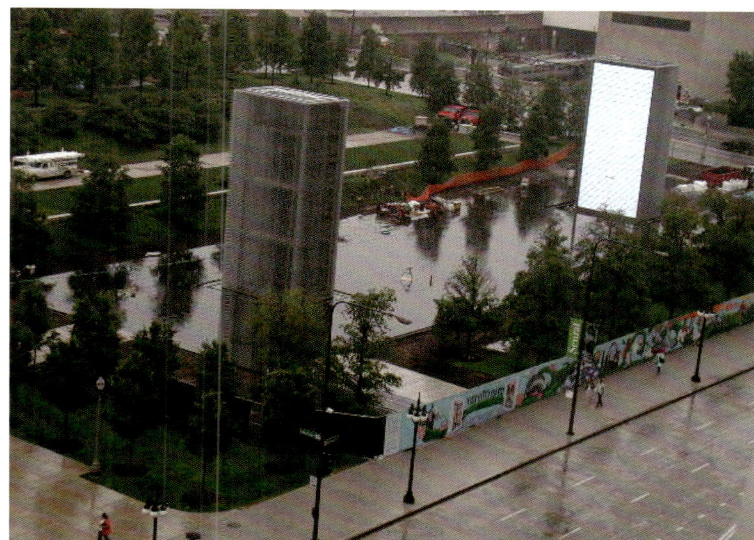
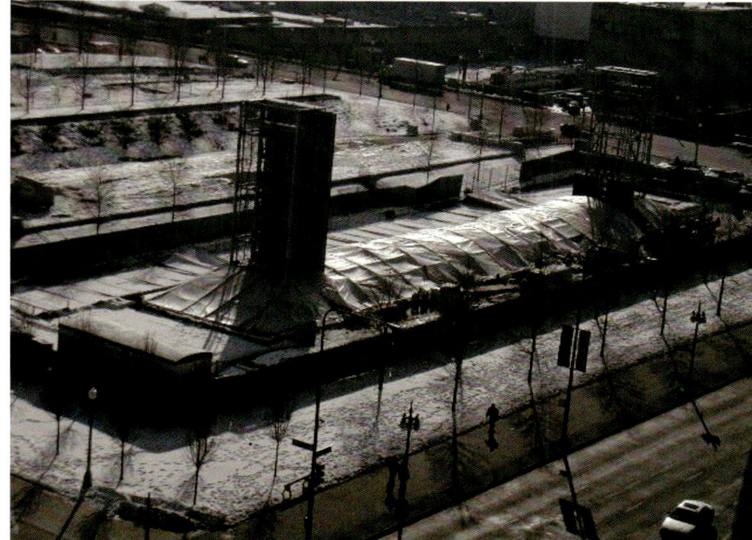
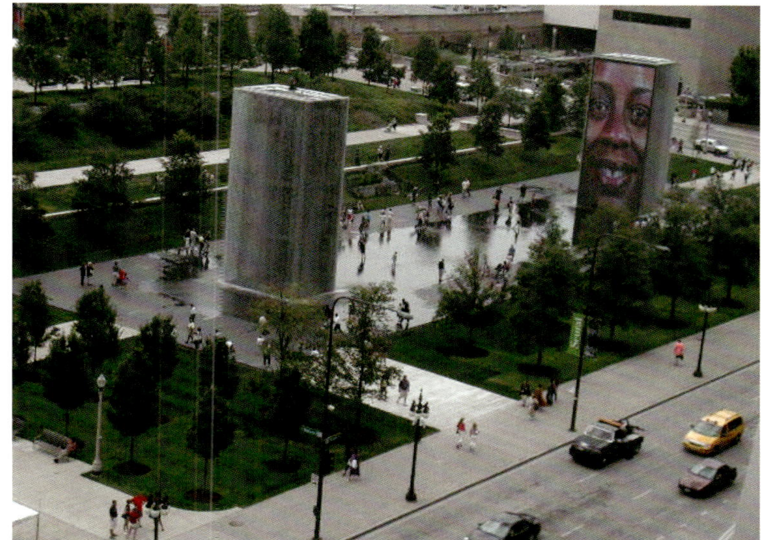
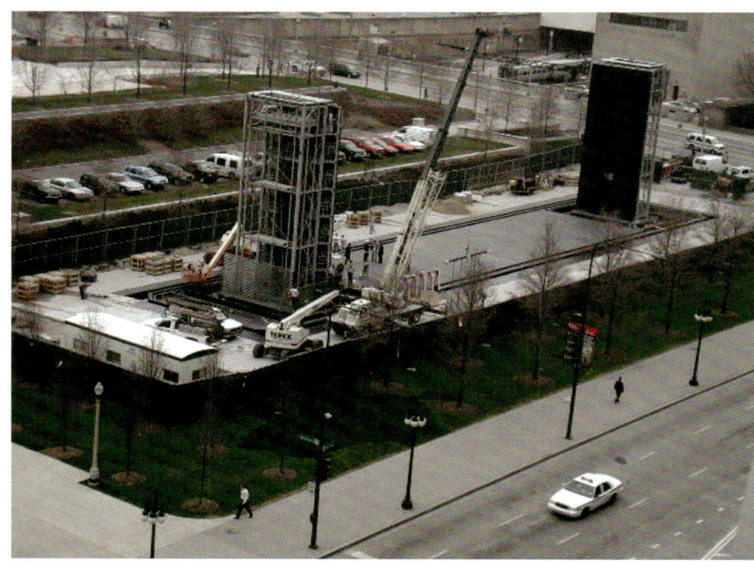
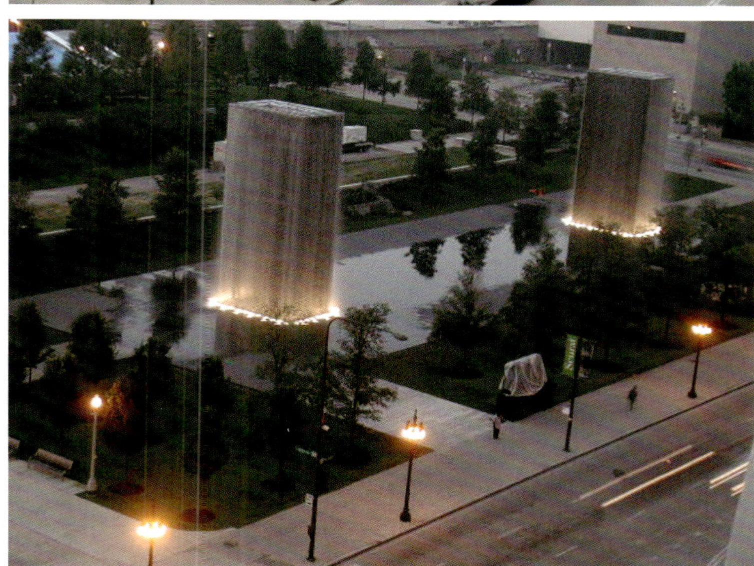

fireworks display from the rooftops of the surrounding buildings. The ceremony is attended by Mayor Daley, the entire Crown family, the artist, and many of those who have been closely engaged with the project. And thus, on an unseasonably cold night in midsummer, the central players in this production finally stand before their audience with the limpid water of the skin pool lapping around their shoes and naked feet. Thousands of Chicagoans turn out to watch, and Lester leaves the ceremony to talk with the crowds lining Michigan Avenue. "Although it was long past eleven in the evening, there were entire families with children, and everyone was entranced by the fountain."

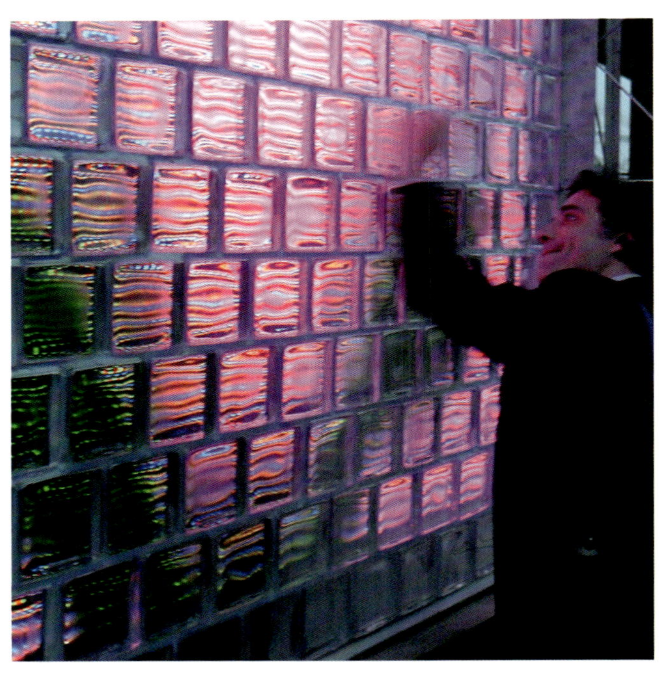

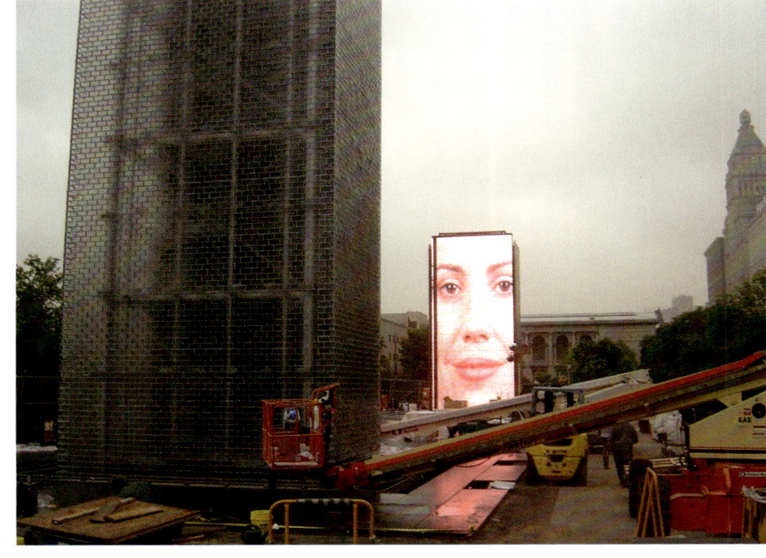

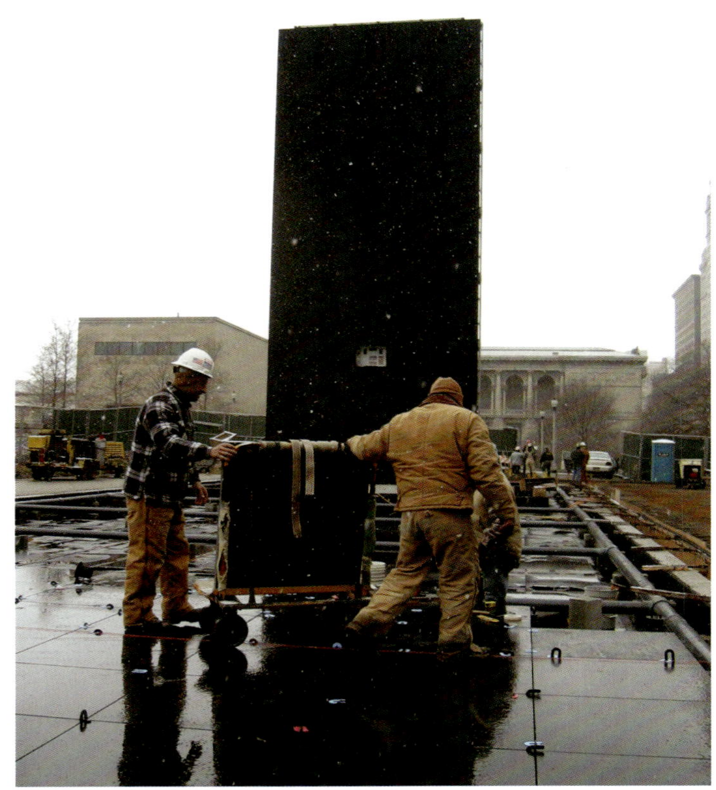

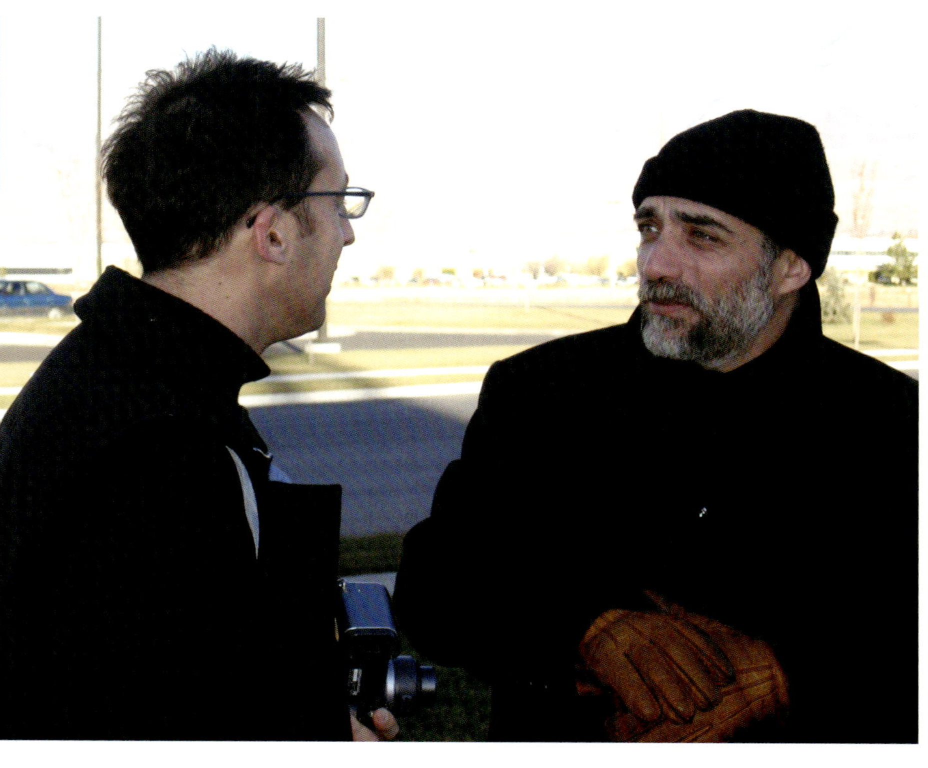

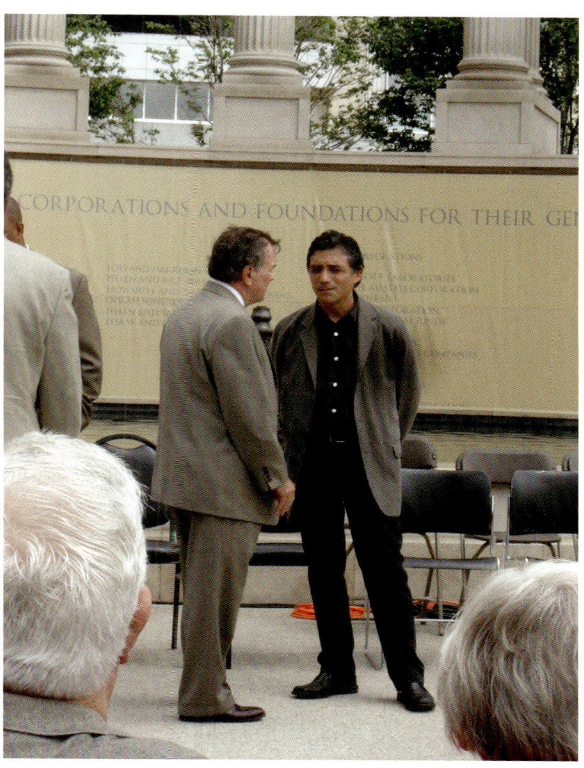

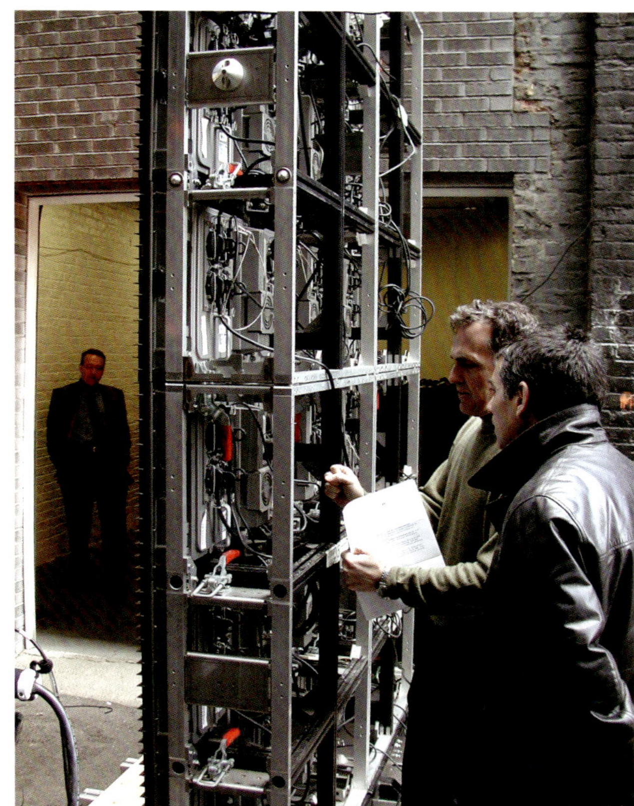

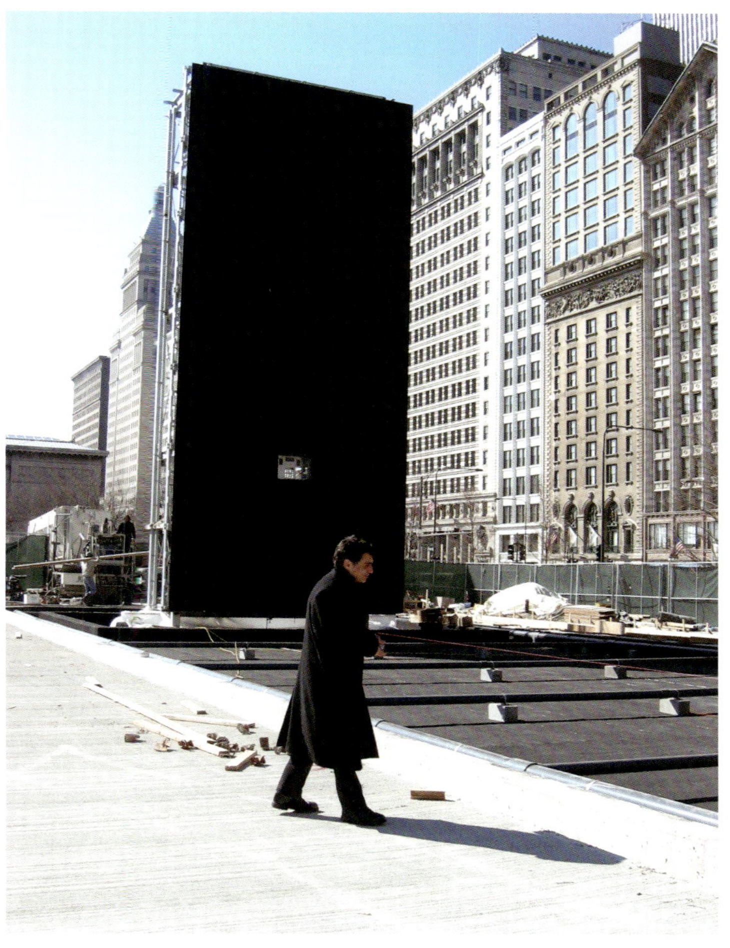

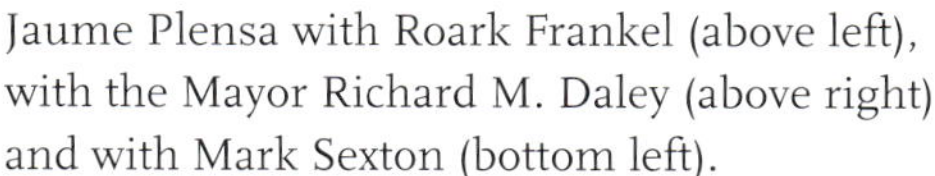
Jaume Plensa with Roark Frankel (above left),
with the Mayor Richard M. Daley (above right)
and with Mark Sexton (bottom left).

It has been a long journey, but as the fountain is formally handed over to the City of Chicago, now is not the moment to reflect on the numerous setbacks that have befallen the project in its fifty-five-month evolution. As the champagne flows, all thoughts turn to the dream that has finally become a reality.

> "I'd followed the development of the piece from the outset. But when it finally opened, I was amazed. I knew what Plensa had *hoped* to do, but he'd actually done it. It was an incredible achievement."
>
> Jack Guthman, collector

Earlier in the day Jim Crown had taken Plensa aside and over a beer confessed that, until then, the family had never truly understood what the fountain was about. Their faith had been in the artist and his dream. It was the greatest compliment of all and, now that the fountain was set to take its place as part of the city's life, that faith had been fully justified.

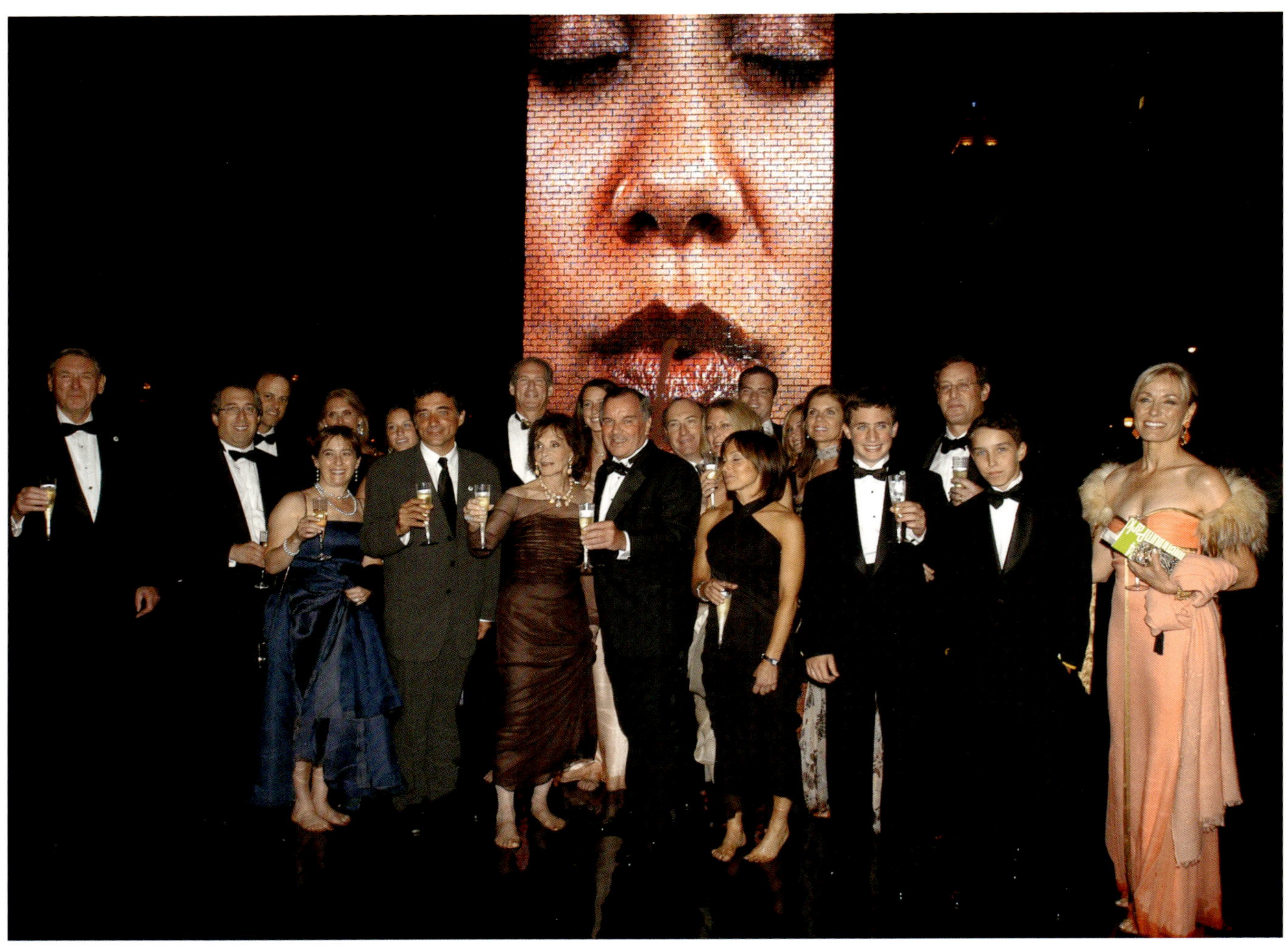

"Here I am with the Crown family and Richard M. Daley, Mayor of Chicago, the night of the project's unveiling on July 24, 2004. The Crown Fountain was launched!"

Jaume Plensa

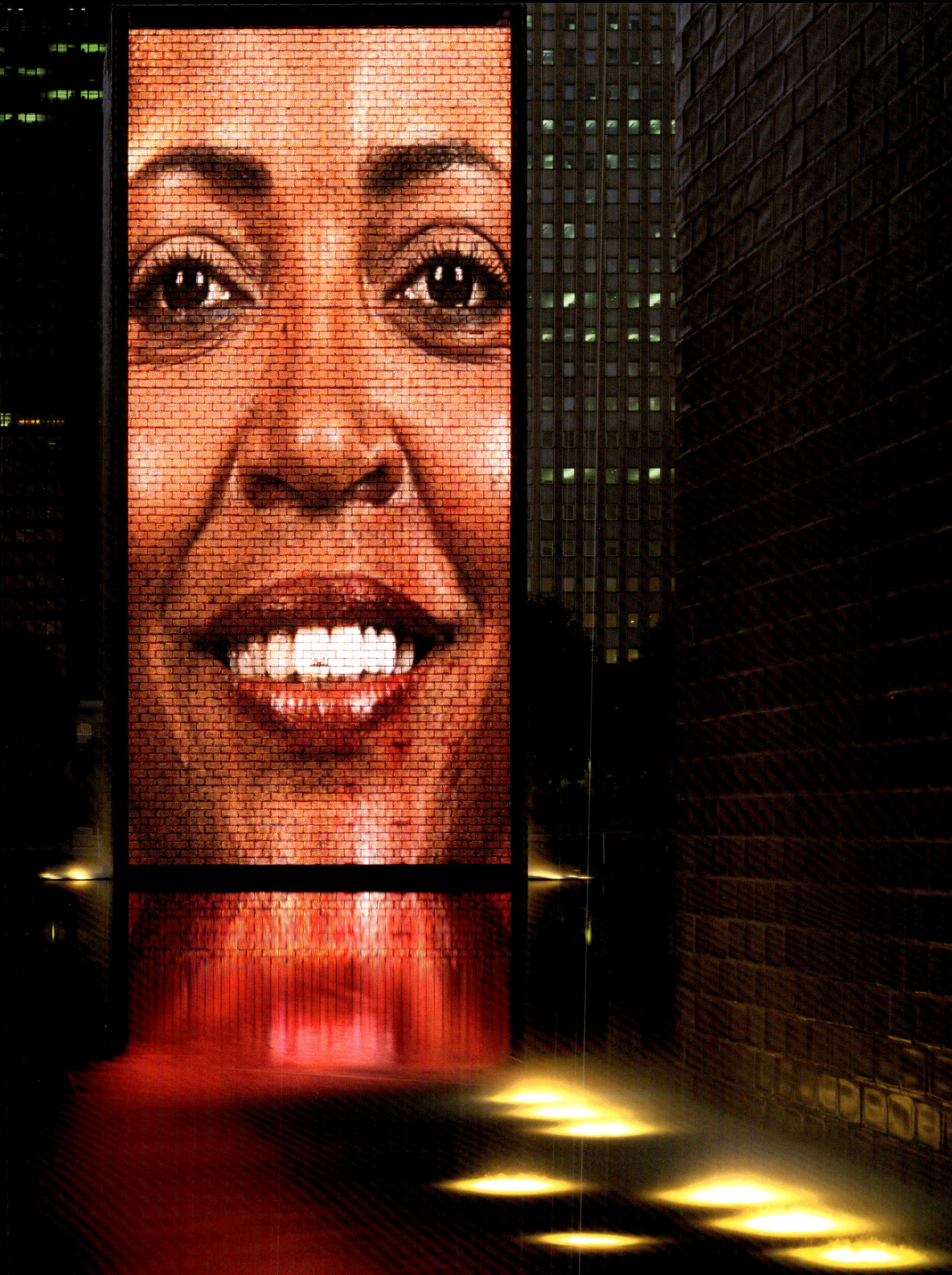

But the final word goes to Lester Crown. After all, it is to him more than to anyone else that the *Crown Fountain* owes its existence. Although all the family's members have played their part, it had ultimately been his decision that set the ball rolling and his commitment that had kept it in play. And while Lester hadn't always been hands-on, it was his background presence that gave continuity as the baton passed from Susan, Jim, and Paula to Steve. Yes, there had been doubts, and not only over costs. Jim tells me that his father's concern as to whether the gargoyle spout would demean the piece became something of a *leitmotif* in family circles. But as he sees it in action today, even Lester has to admit that Plensa was right and that this regular torrent of water appearing almost magically to issue from the mouths of the giant faces is one of the fountain's most popular features.

People speak of the Crowns as modern-day Medicis, but as I gaze over the skyline of Barcelona towards the crane-capped spires that reach skywards, it occurs to me that there is a more appropriate comparison. Lester's role has been closer to that of another visionary patron, the nineteenth-century industrialist Eusebi de Güell, whose faith in a young, Catalan architect gave birth to some of the world's finest buildings. That architect was Antoni Gaudí and today his *Sagrada Familia*—Barcelona's famous, unfinished temple, which is also said to have been inspired by a dream—plays host to an annual pilgrimage of some two million visitors.

Back in 2000, Lester's challenge to his artist was to "dream me a fountain, something unforgettable, something for Chicago." That dream has now become an icon for the city, acknowledged by architects, artists, and designers the world over, setting a new benchmark for art in the public space and redefining the role of the fountain in the twenty-first century. In creating a space that is primarily for and about people, the *Crown Fountain* presents a challenge to all future public commissions. But above all, the fountain that is so much more than a fountain is a gift to Chicago, a landmark and an amenity that will be enjoyed by Chicagoans for many years to come.

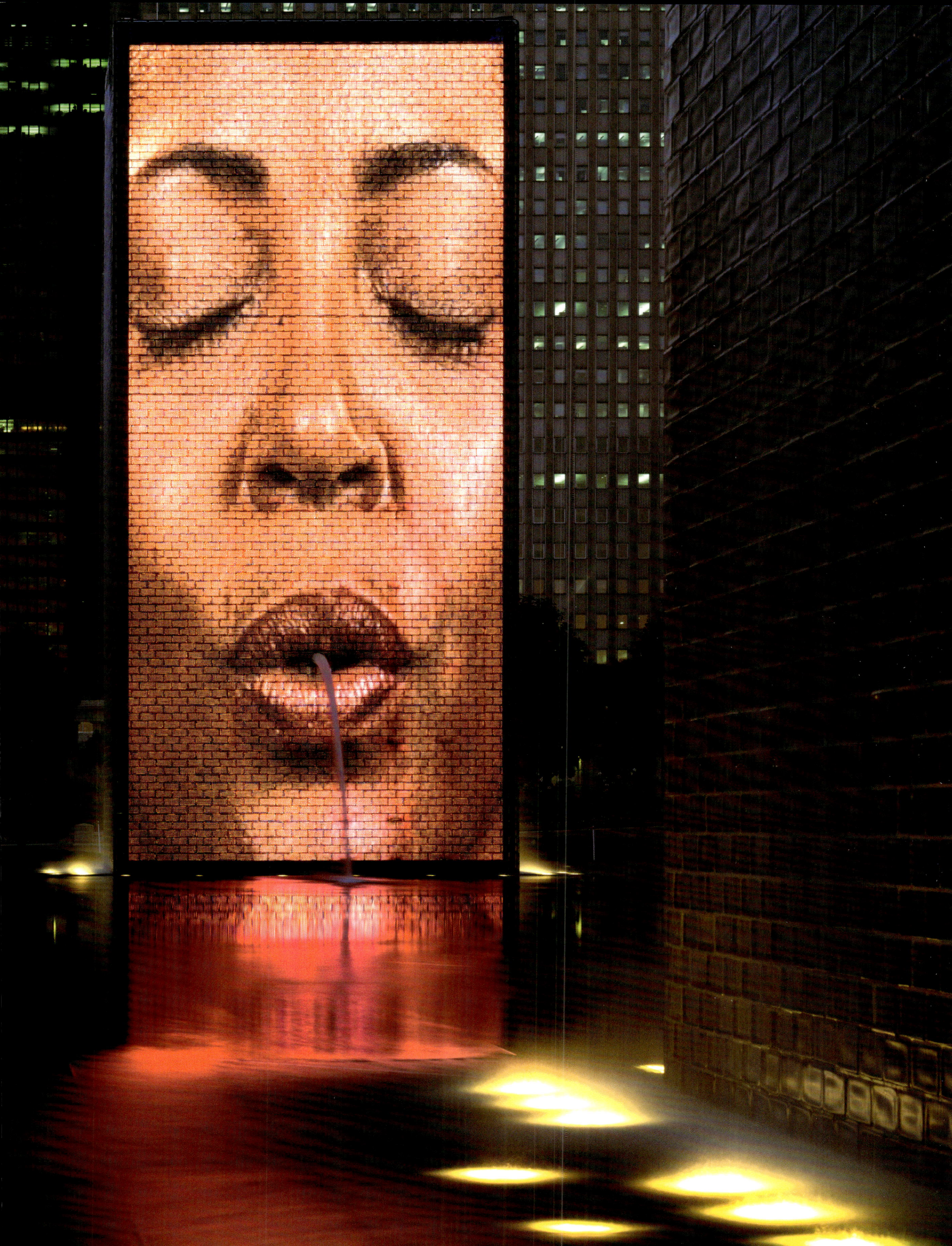

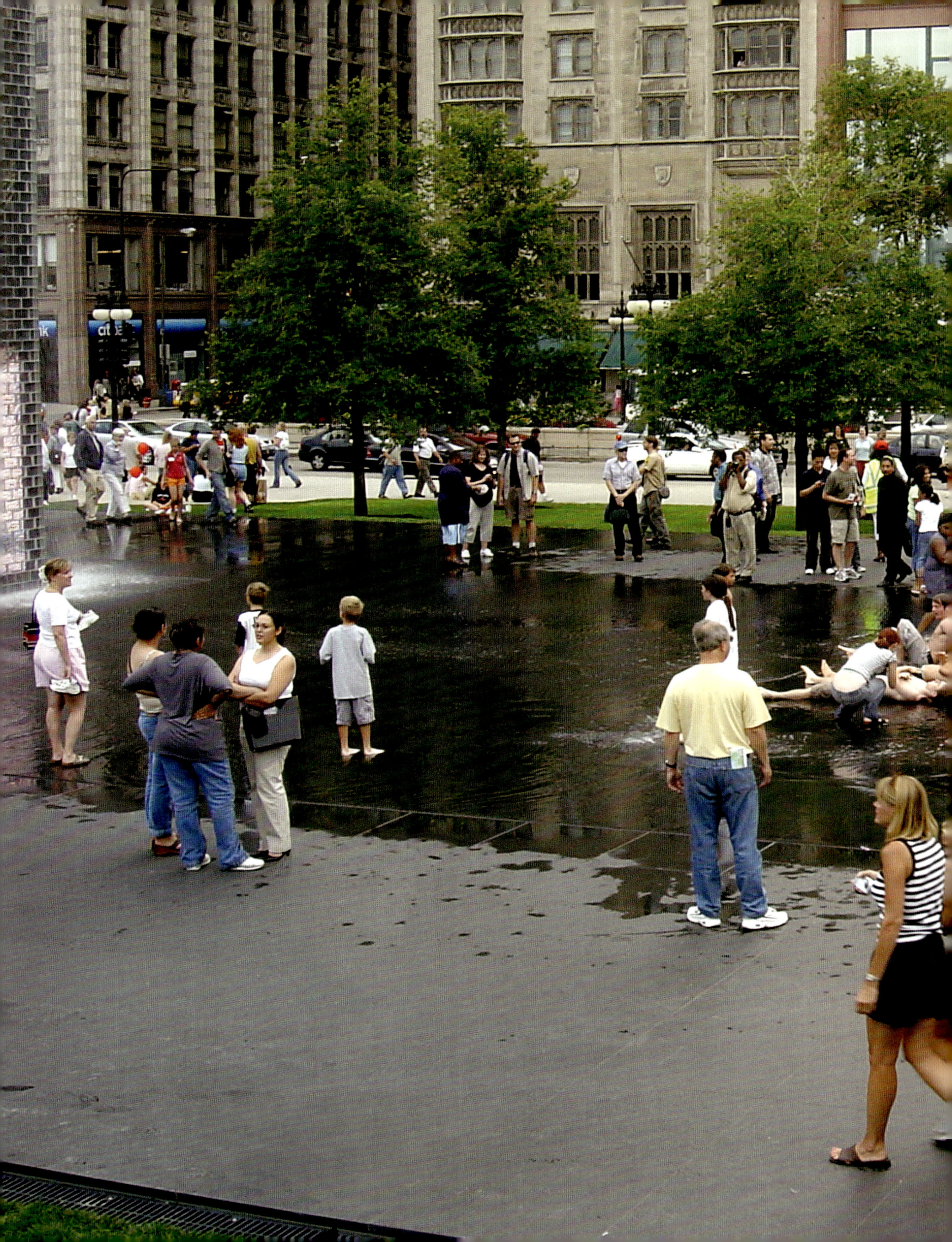

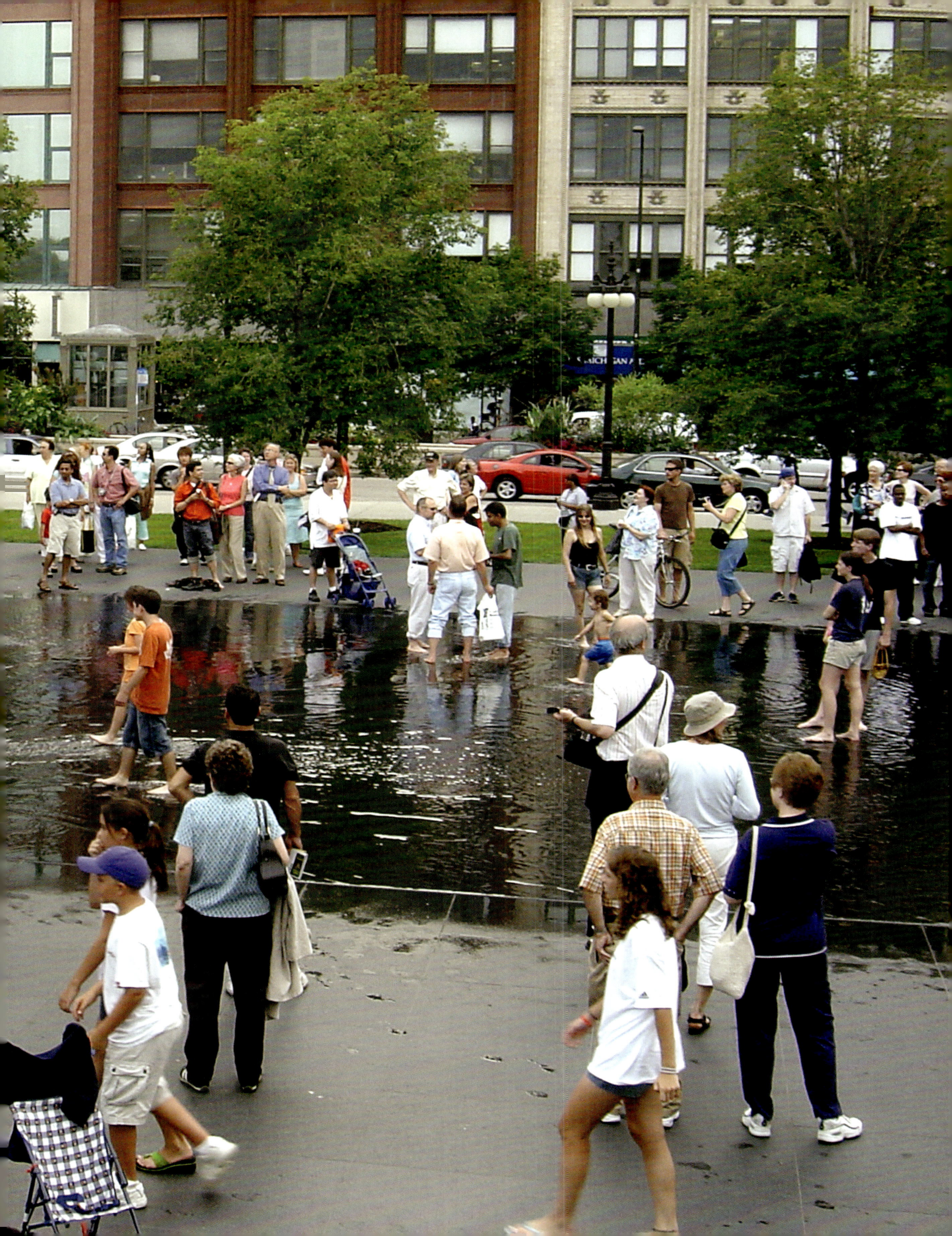

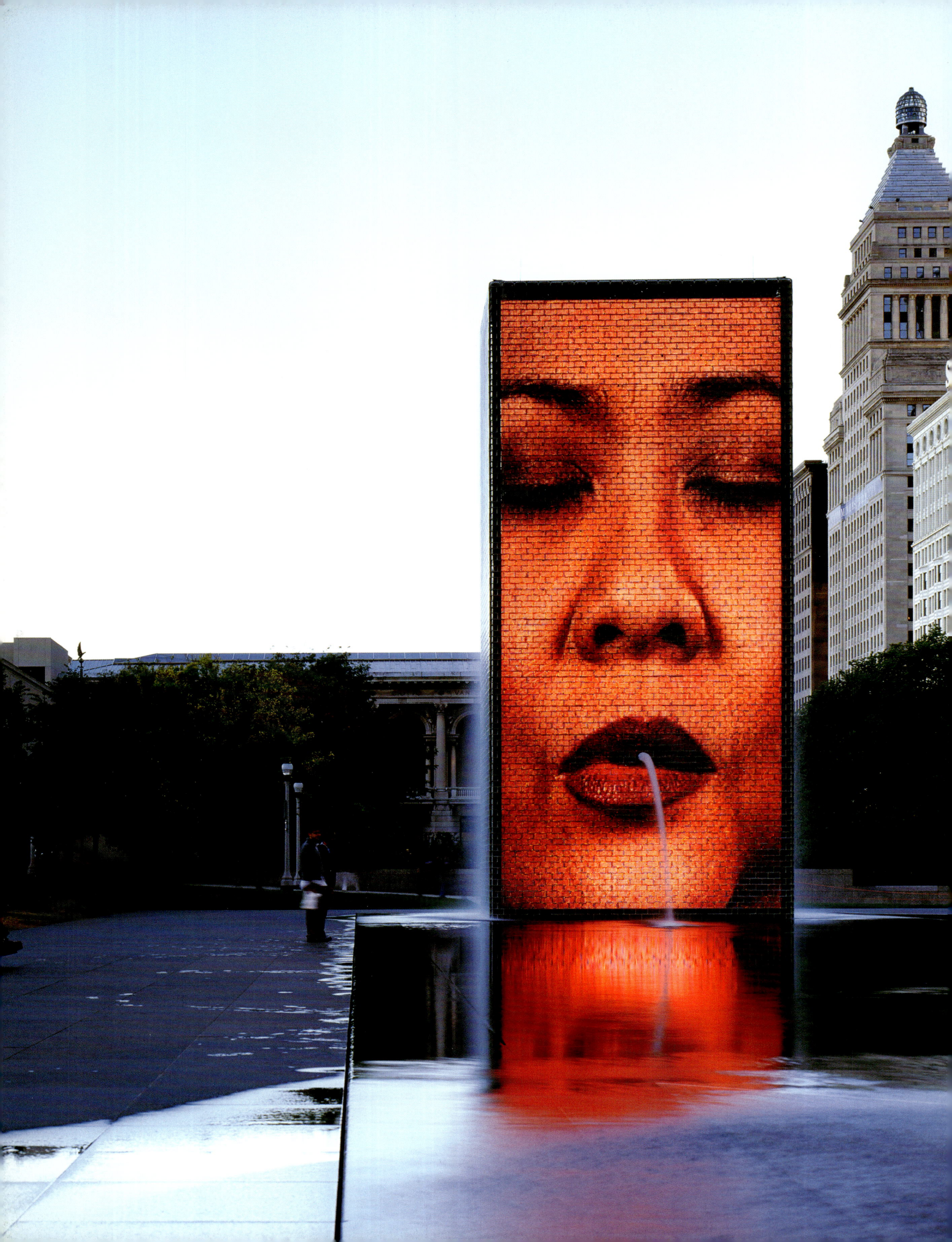

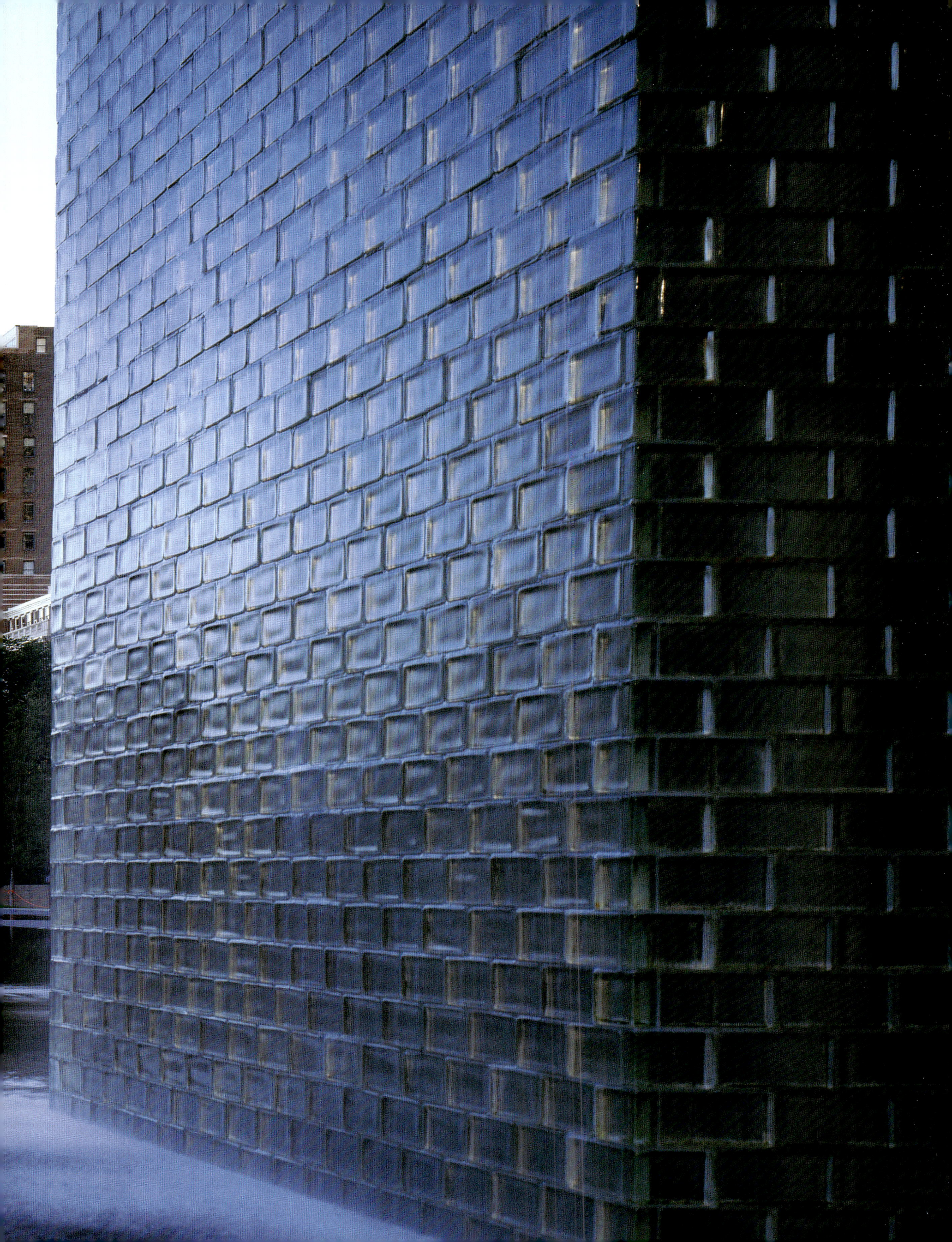

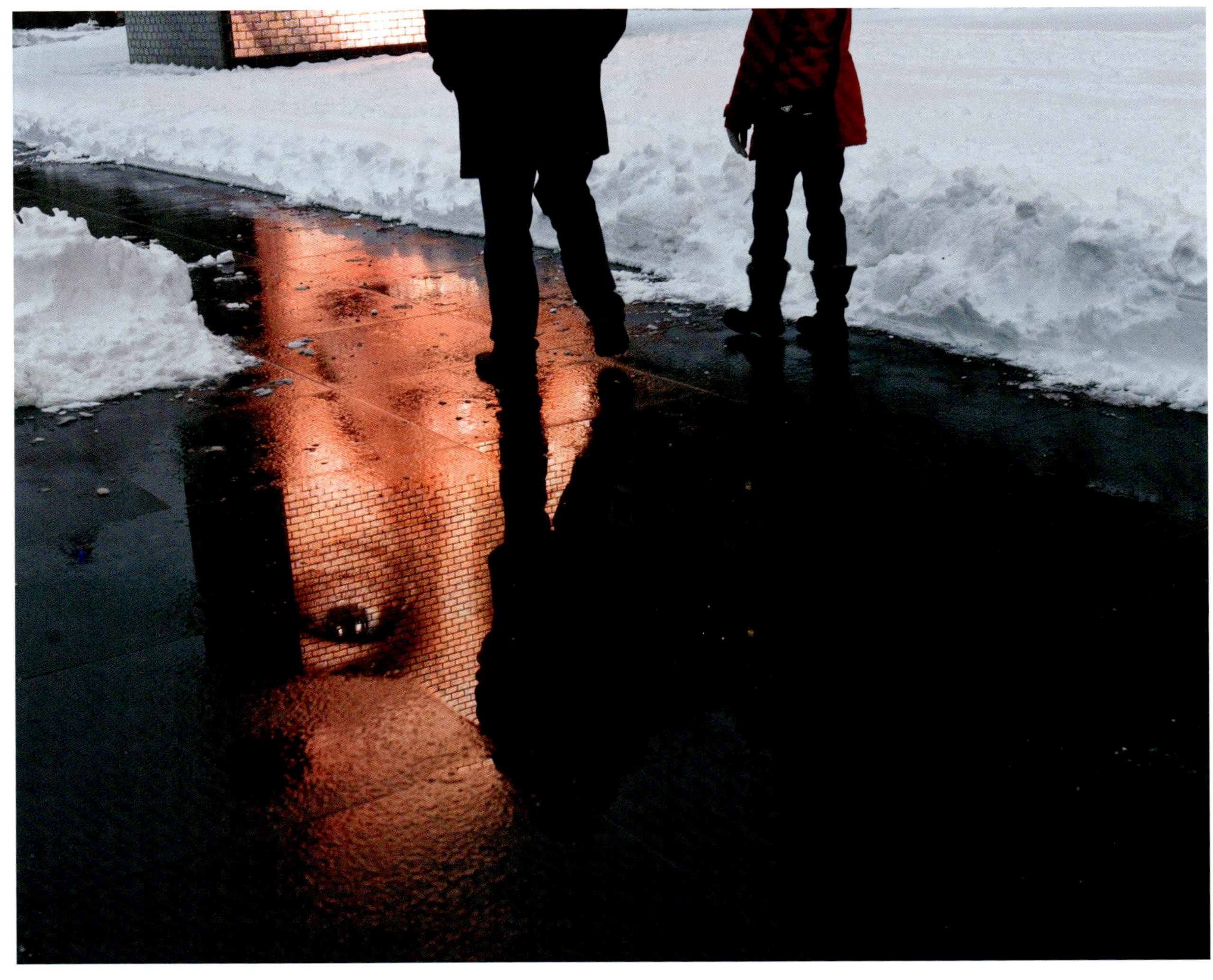

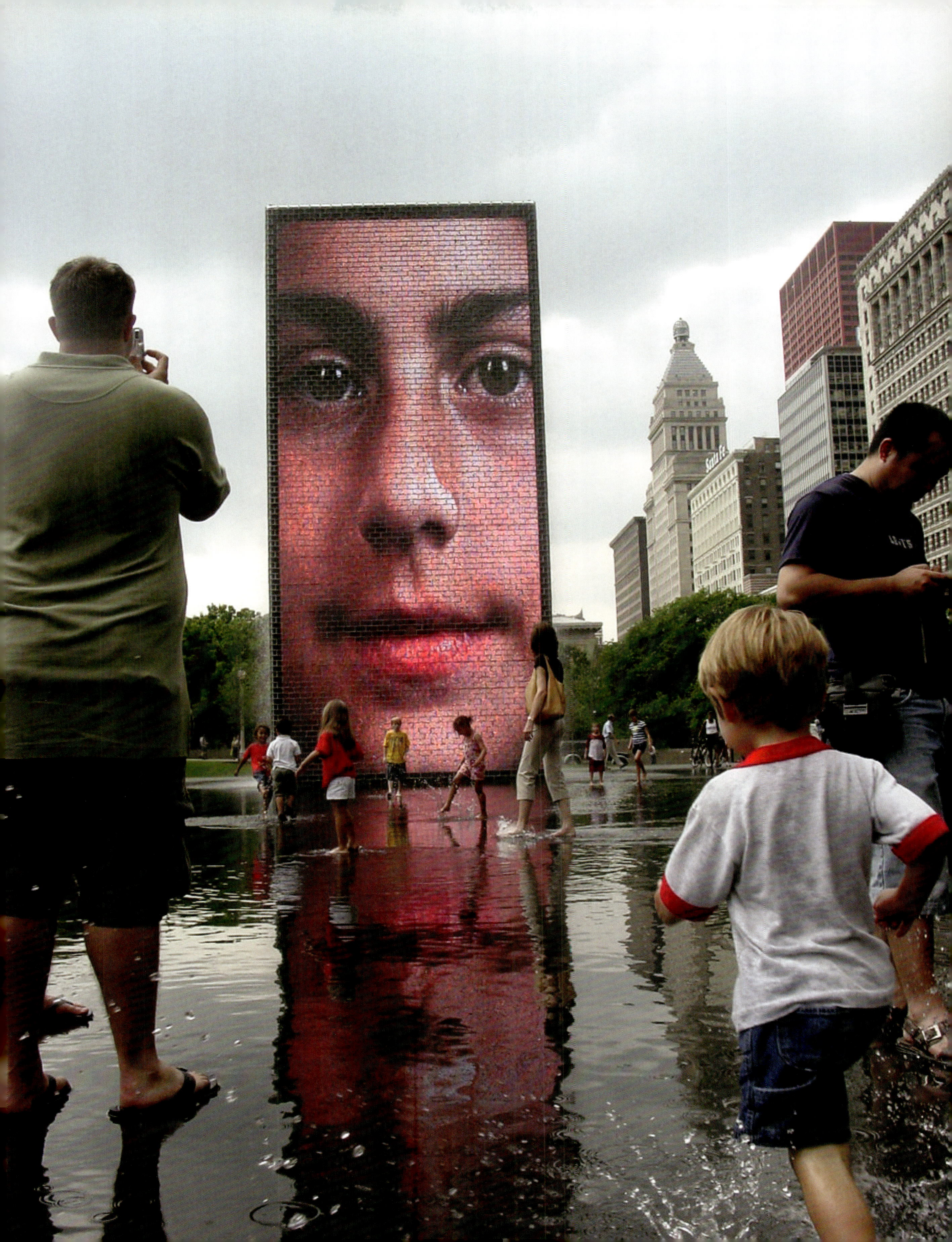

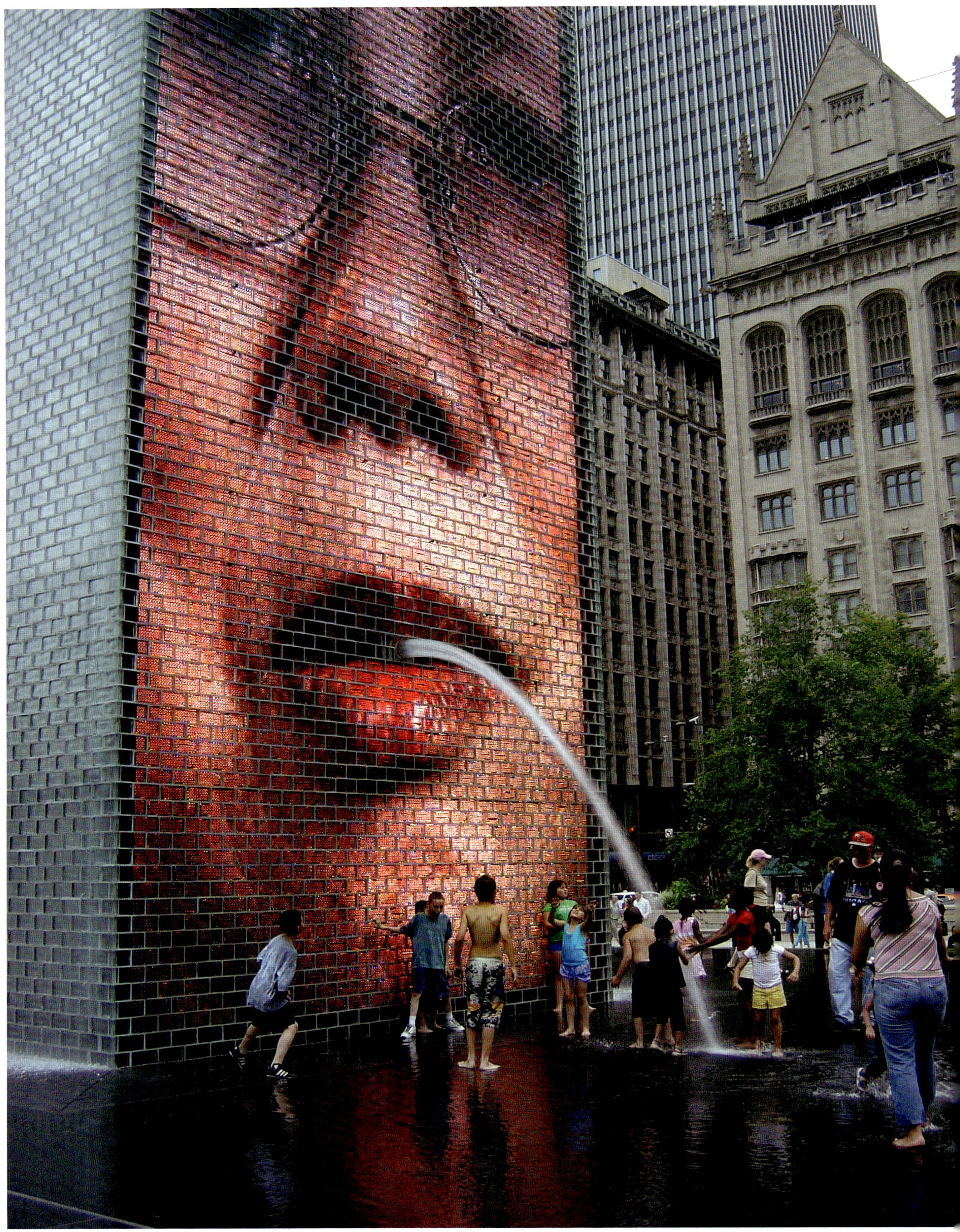

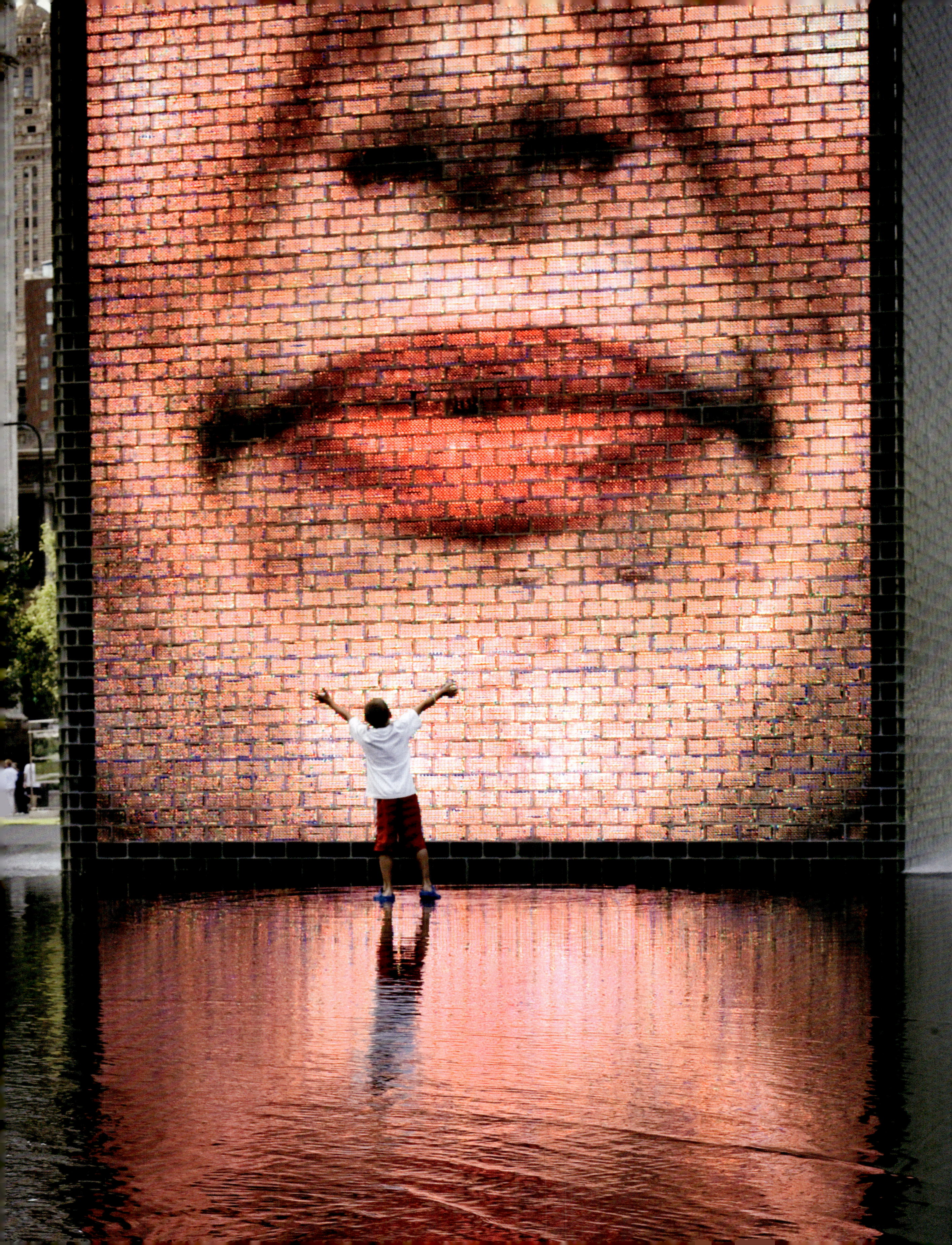

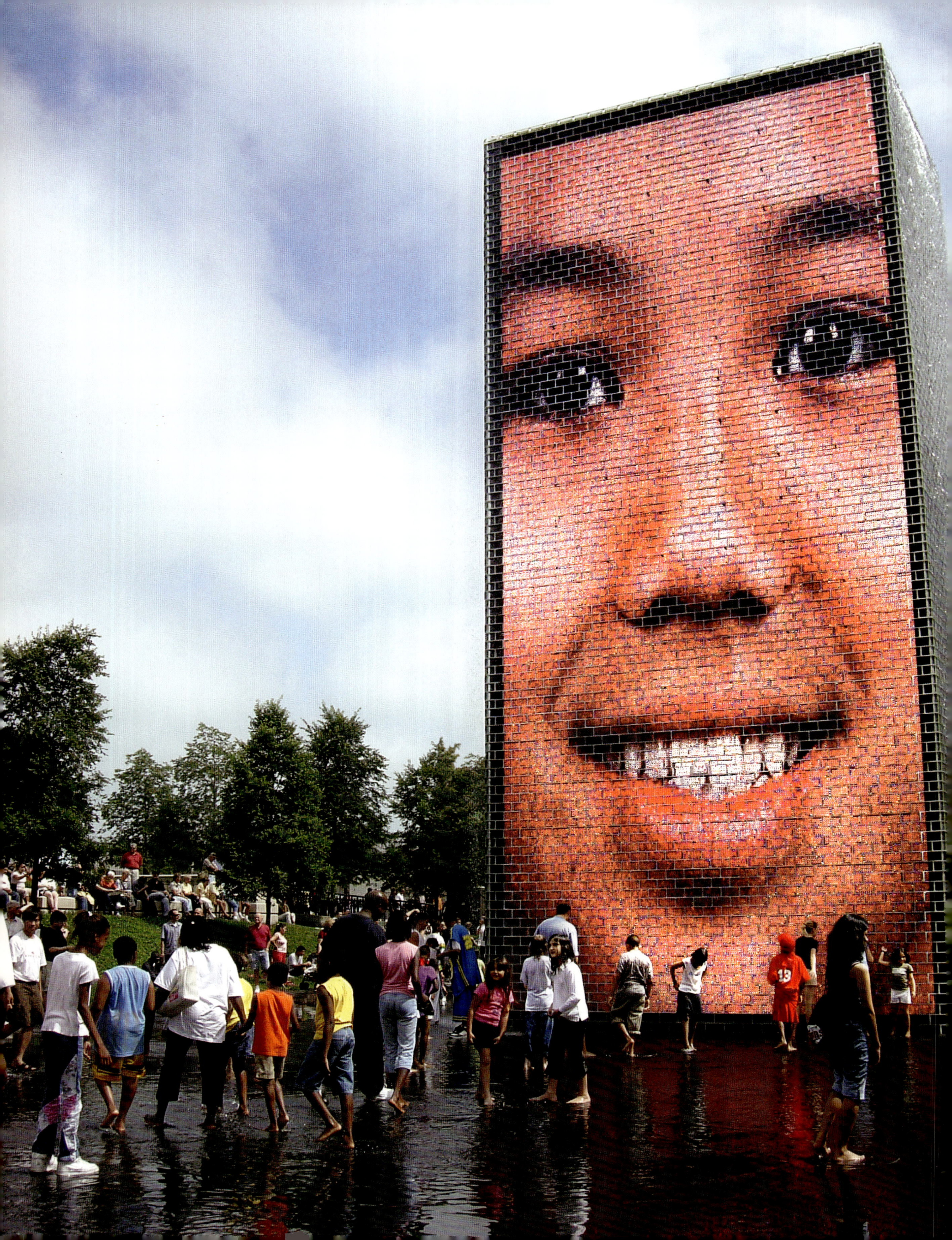

8

No Instructions Needed

However, the accolades still lie in the future. With the euphoria of the opening ceremony behind it, the fountain must now face its ultimate challenge. It's the middle of summer and the days are at their hottest. Will people visit the park and will they know how to use the fountain when they get there? From the first day, something remarkable happens. Families arrive and the children instinctively know what to do. Hundreds of children, and adults too, take off their shoes and socks and walk on the water. They quickly work out the rhythm of the gargoyle effect, surging in shrieking waves from the waterspouts to the falling curtains of water in a cycle that's repeated every few minutes. No one had quite predicted the human element that animates the fountain, the exuberance of people's reaction, the sheer uninhibited joy of the children. Still others stand around the perimeter or sit on the cedarwood benches entranced by the screens, while a pervasive spray permeates and cools the air.

> "On one of the nights when the fountain was undergoing its final tests, an event had just ended in Grant Park and streams of people who were heading home stopped by the perimeter fence to see what was happening. Jaume suggested we let them in and give the fountain its first unofficial trial. They just ran at the piece, mostly young kids and threw themselves at the water. And I think that's the moment when I knew the fountain was going to work."
>
> Roark Frankel, Project Manager

More remarkable still, the element of fun does not diminish the piece. It is not simply a water feature for children, but a place for relaxation, meditation, and contemplation. Older people and young, black and white, flood to the fountain just to sit and pass the time. It's everybody's front porch, everybody's backyard. And when night falls and the LED screens come into their own, the tempo dies down and it becomes everybody's drive-in, the shimmering images glowing against the city skyline, the illumination turning the towers into cathedrals of colored light.

Even in the coldest months, when snow blankets the black granite and the water is shut down because subzero winds are sweeping in off the lake, the warmth of the slowly smiling faces, fifty feet tall, beams out a welcome in the wintry bleakness of the downtown park.

None of which I know until I complete my journey and visit the fountain for myself.

Journey's End

My own journey began in the garden of Jaume Plensa's house in Barcelona, the tape turning, the bottle between us slowly emptying. But it also began long ago, for I've needed to draw on a lifetime's experience to truly make sense of what the artist is telling me. How can I understand his talk of city squares if hadn't lived them for myself, his talk of the importance of springs and streams if I hadn't hiked in the high Pyrenees, his references to the old gods if I hadn't visited the temples and cities that perished long before our time began? It's a complex web and I make sense of it the only way I can. But there's one place I haven't yet visited and that's the *Crown Fountain* itself.

And so I go, at the end of my story, to pay homage at this last shrine. I'm worried, because I know too much and so expect too much. I arrive at the end of a late summer's afternoon, directly from the airport, to begin an affair that doesn't start off well. It's been a long flight and I'm tired, and on first sight the fountain looks just like its photographs. Nothing more, nothing less.

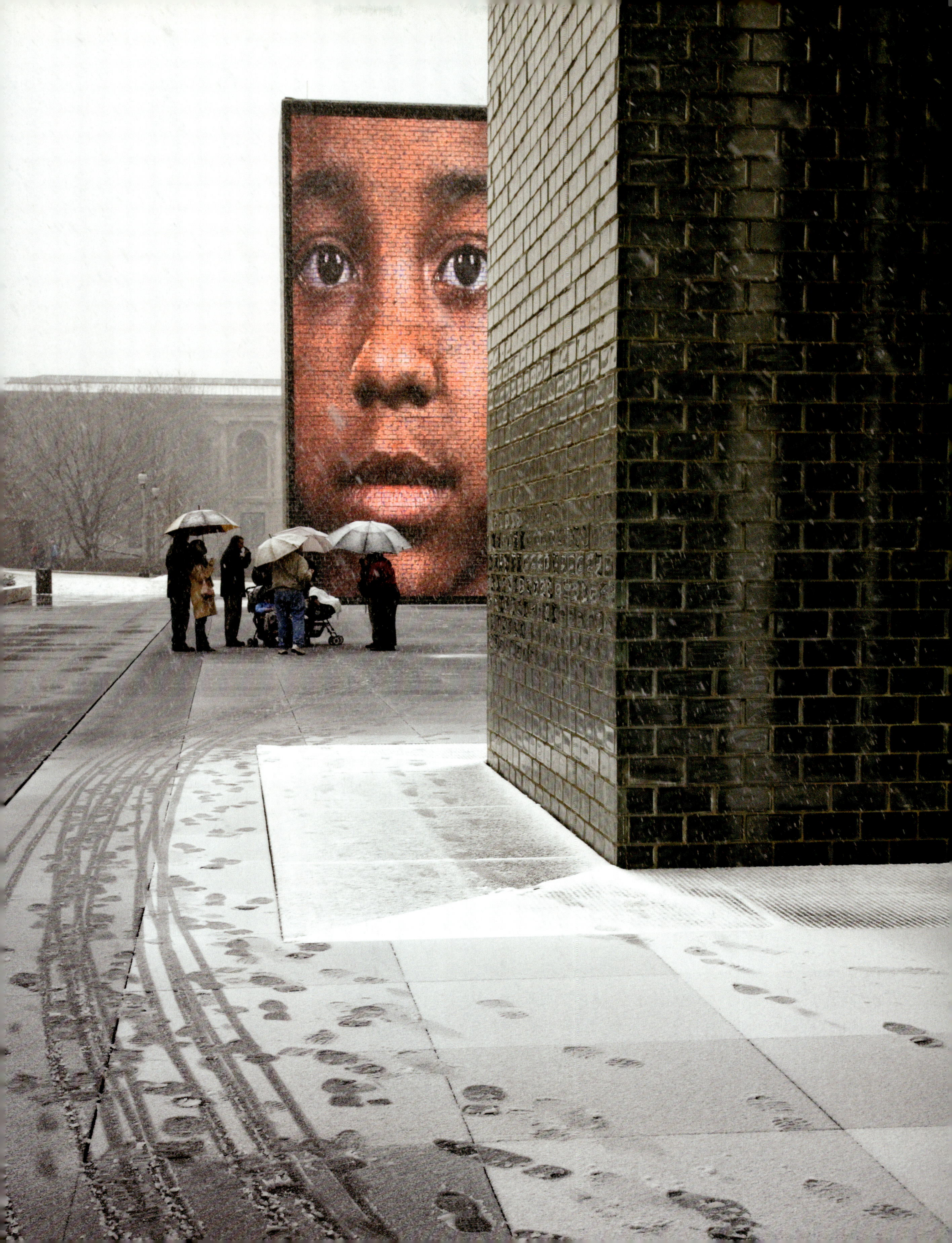

There is no immediate revelation, no epiphany, no great awakening. Then I notice a curious sight, a dozen or so perfectly groomed teenagers piling out of a stretch limo. The *quinceañeras* line up in front of the fountain for a photo-shoot, then just as energetically pile back into their white status symbol and are away up Michigan Avenue. The whole event lasts no more than two minutes, but a stopover at Chicago's newest icon has clearly become as much a part of the *quinceañera* ritual as bespoke dresses and the rented limo.

The next day is Sunday and I wake early. The water in the pool is just filling up and the irregular rivulets of water offer partial reflections of the towers framed against a clear blue sky. I go in search of breakfast and by the time I return the kids are already there, wheeling around the fountain like gulls. Their parents sit more sedately on the solid, cedarwood benches that come all the way from British Columbia and strike an organic note in this sea of granite and glass. I join them, or at least attempt to, but I'm intercepted by a couple from out of state who want their picture taken. "Be sure to get the tower in," I'm instructed. They're nice people and I find I want to spend time talking with them, picking up on their enthusiasm for the fountain. "It's become one of the must-see places in Chicago," they tell me.

I walk over and start talking to one of the park guards. She's worked here since it opened and loves it. "There are never any problems," she assures me. "People are too busy enjoying themselves."

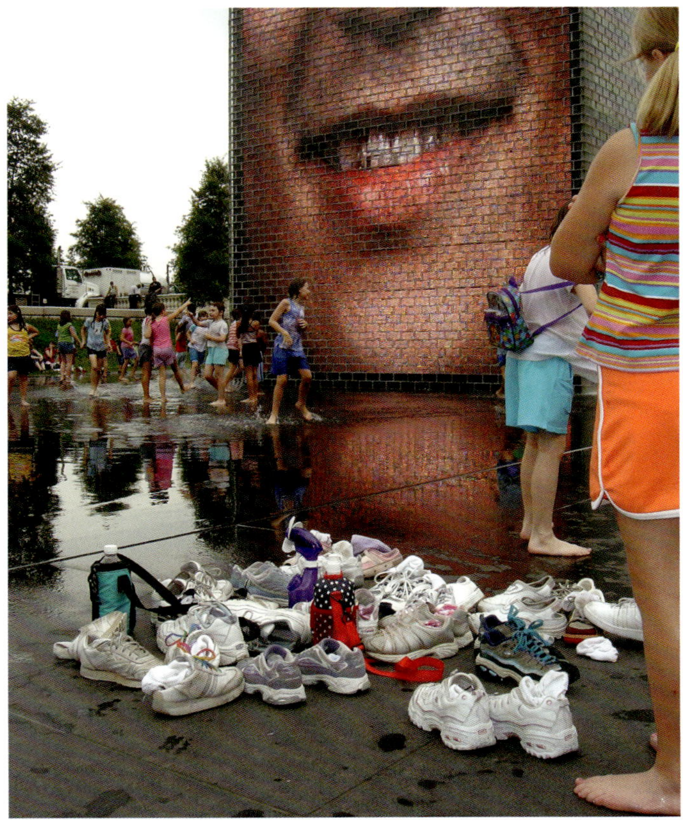
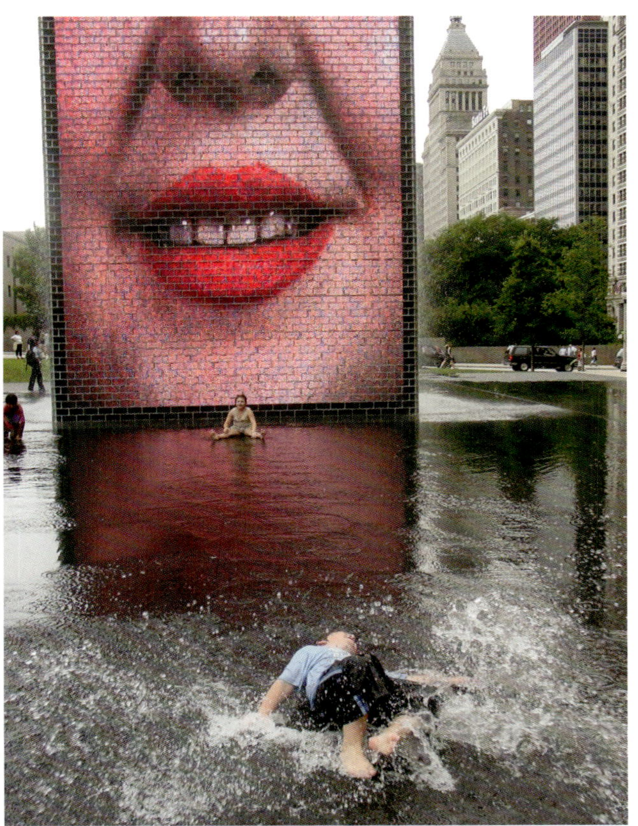

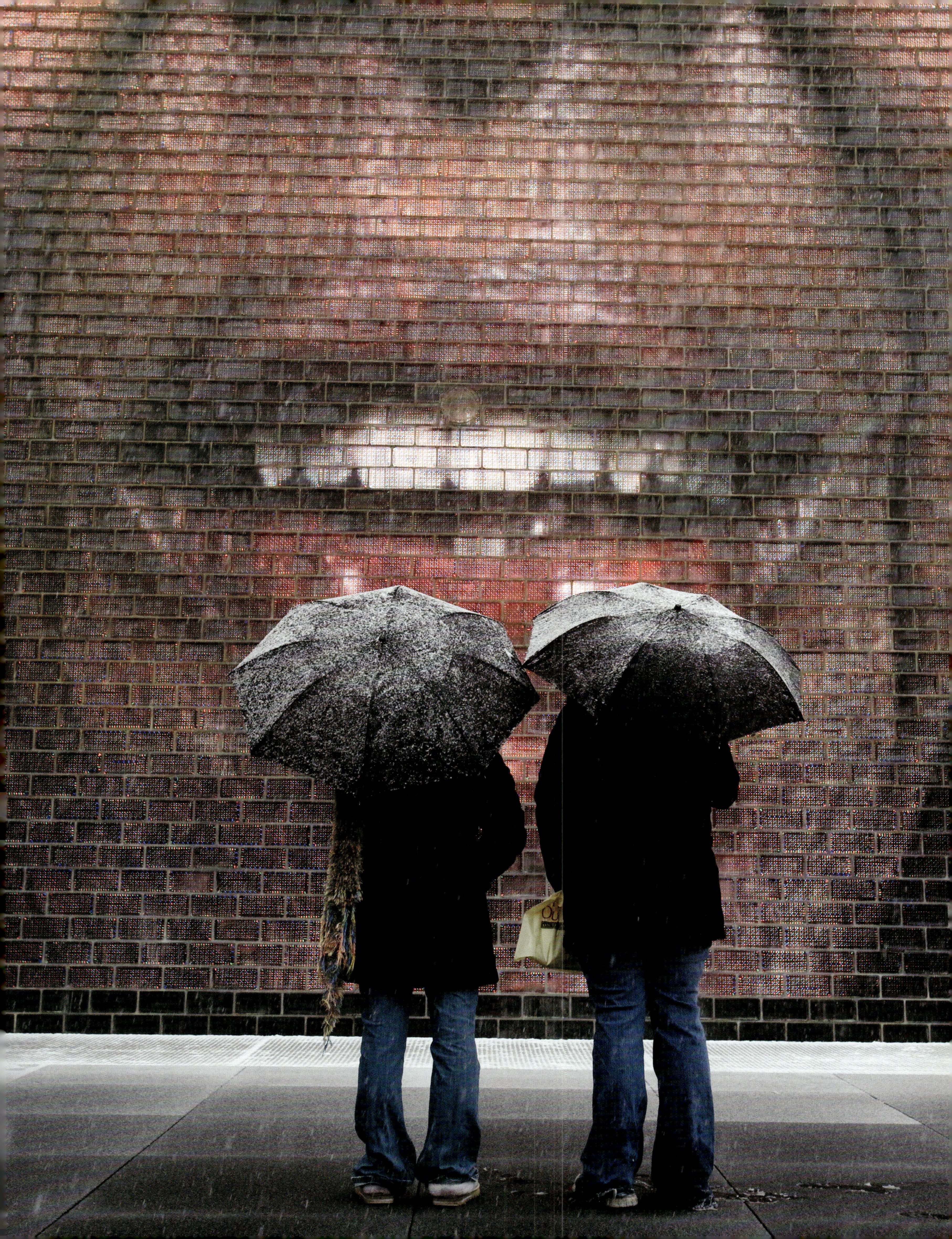

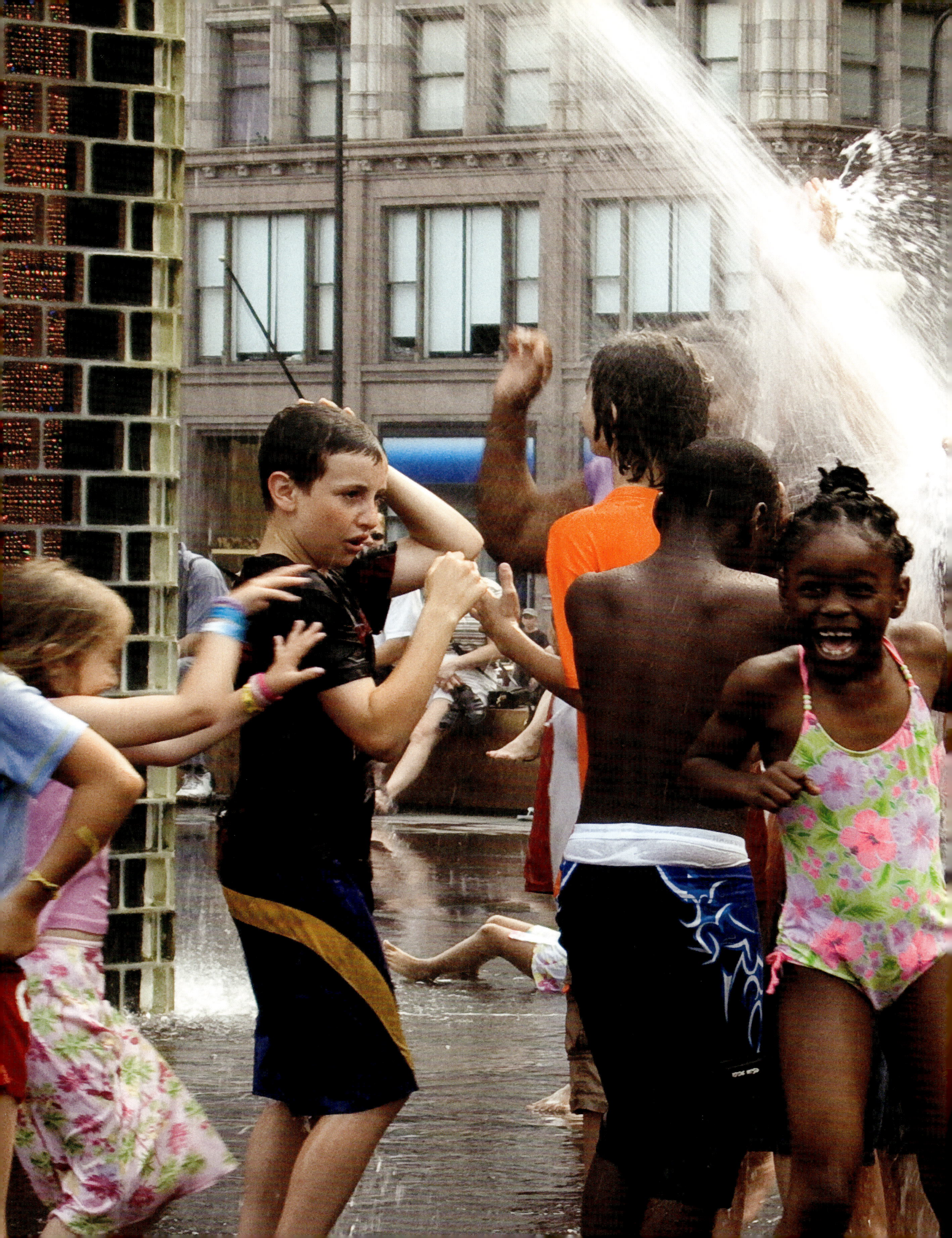

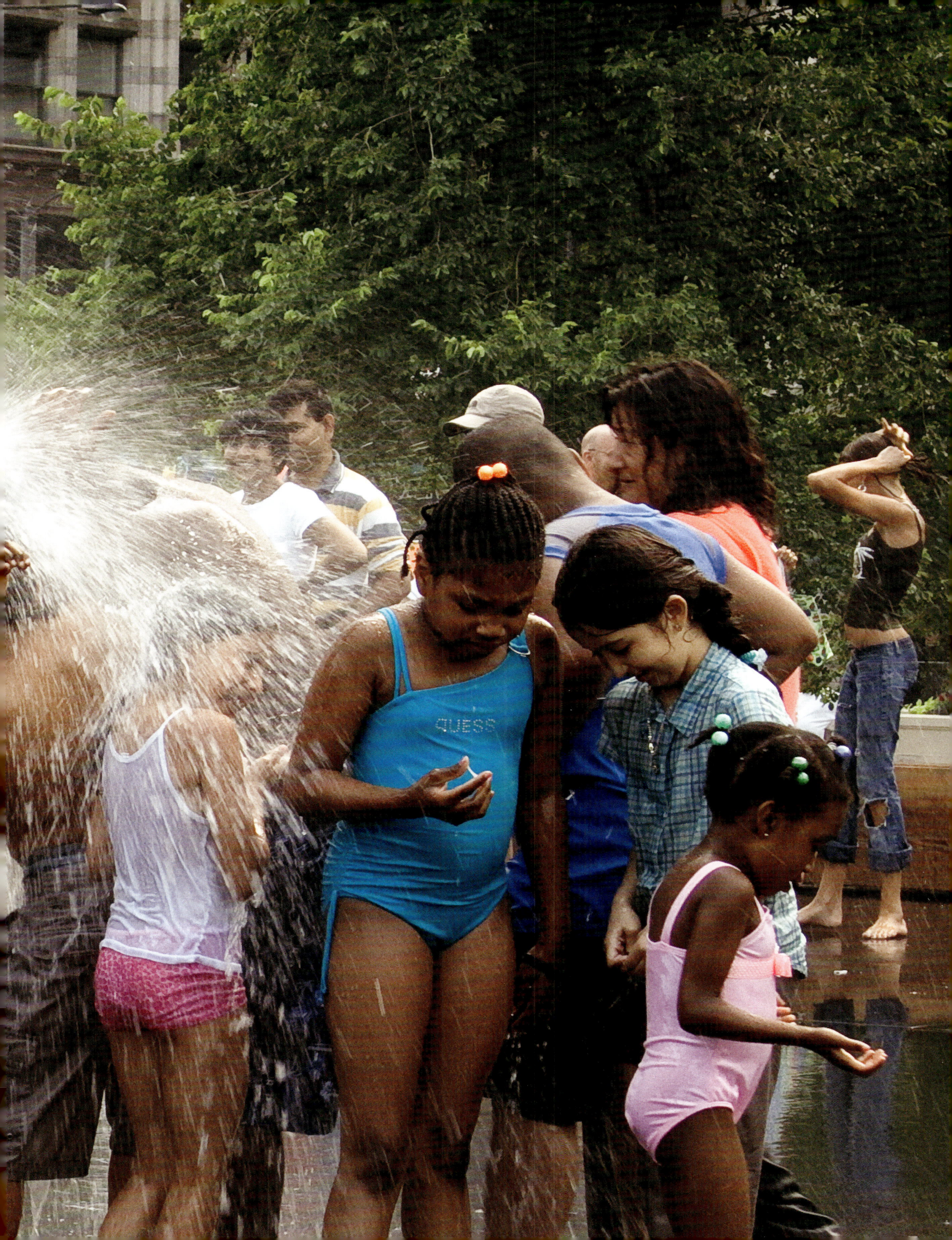

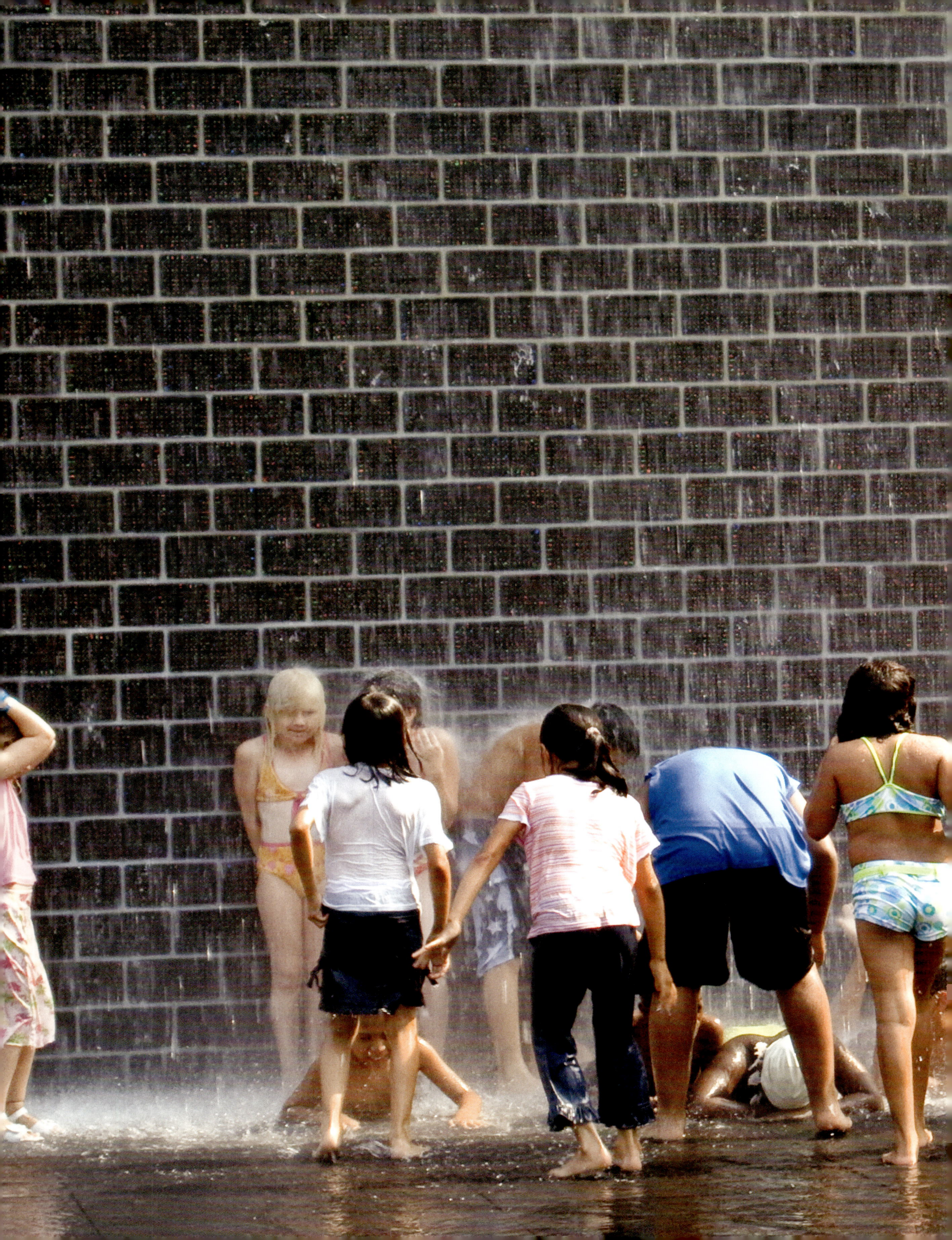

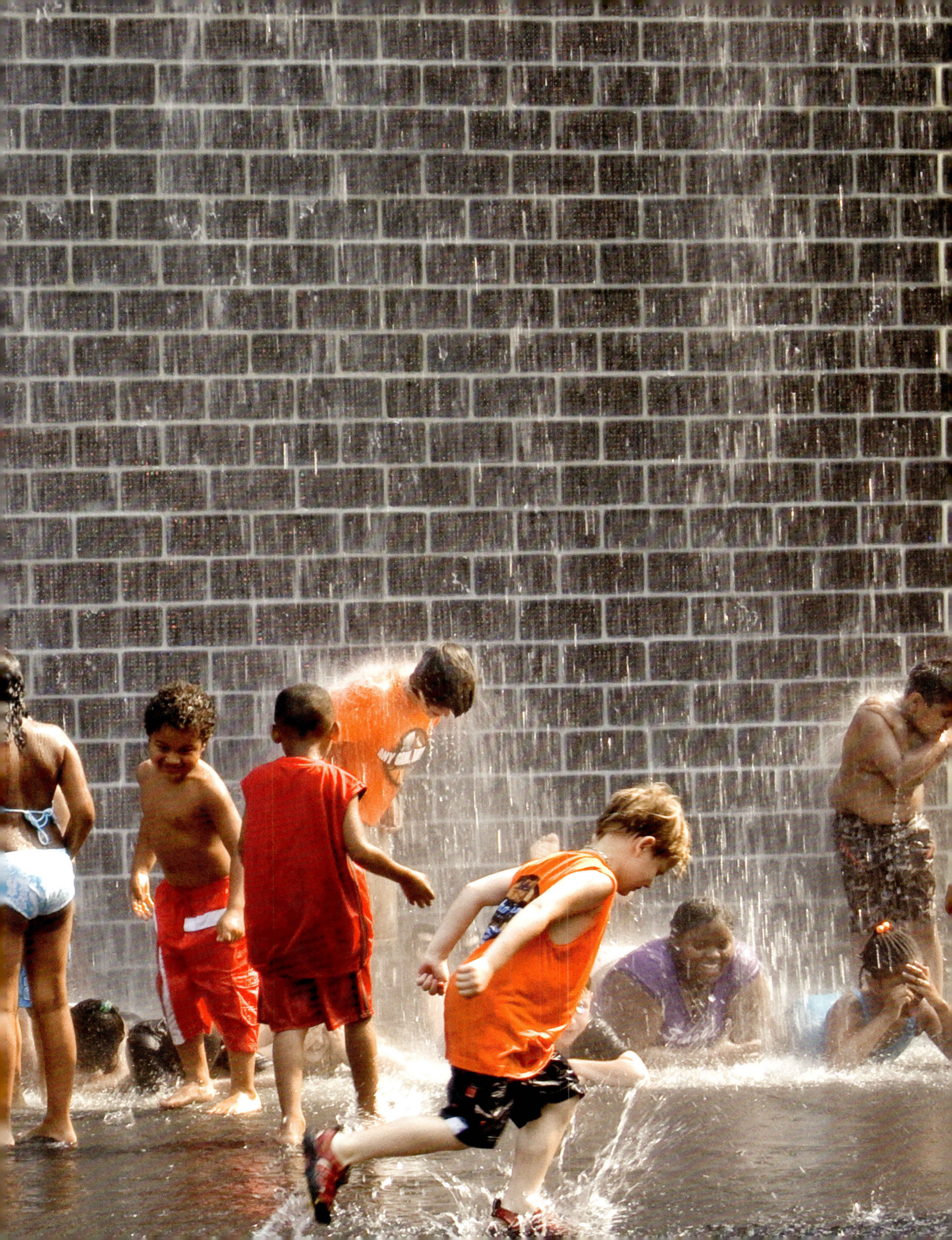

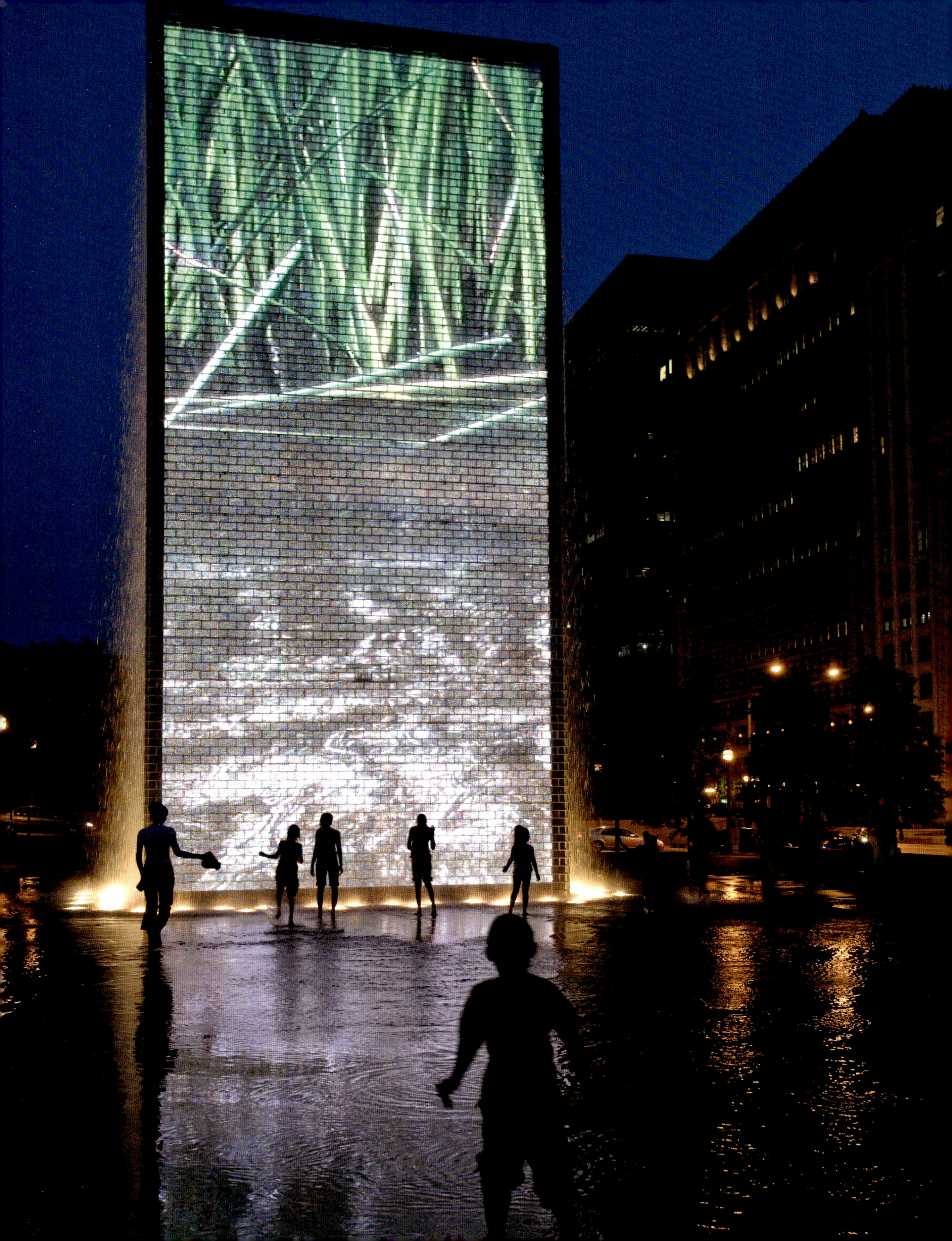

It's true. Out on the water, there's a couple dancing. They're sharing headphones, so I can't hear the music, but it's obviously a slow waltz and they're
doing well. *Dancing in Peckham* is an artist's video in which a girl called
Gillian dances in a place called Peckham. You don't hear the music here
either, because it's all in her head. These guys aren't making a video—they
are just doing it because it feels right. Even the kids give them space and
they continue to glide over the water for several more minutes.

When the artist David Hockney first visited New York back in the early sixties,
all the kids were wearing earphones. Never having seen a transistor radio, he
assumed there had been a plague of deafness. It's a virus that's continued
to evolve: first the Walkman and now the iPod. But apart from the couple
dancing, I don't see anyone wearing headphones at the fountain and that's
when I know that sound is a vital element. The falling water, the splashing
of bare feet on the wet granite, the cries and laughter. It's a communal thing
and people just want to be part of it.

I sit down, but before I can open my notebook I find myself in conversation
with the woman next to me. She's speaking Spanish, so it's a little one-sided,
but she's telling me about her grandchildren, how they love it here and how
they've made friends with other kids who come on Sunday mornings. She
points them out from the scores of other kids frolicking in the shallow pool.
All three of them are having a great time and getting soaked to the skin in
the process.

I spend a long time just people-watching before I realize that the mood of the
place is infectious. I've wandered into an enchanted forest and, like everyone
else, have fallen under its spell. People are smiling, laughing, enjoying the
moment, but in a way that feels inclusive, that draws you in, that beguiles you
with its innocence. It's the people themselves who make this happen, but it's
the space that gives them permission. I really can't say how or why, but these
complex and technical elements combine in some wonderful alchemy to
create a space that embraces people. Perhaps, as Sexton says, the secret was
to make it all look effortless, as if, like the squares in Rome and Marrakech,
it has always been here, melting effortlessly into its urban landscape.

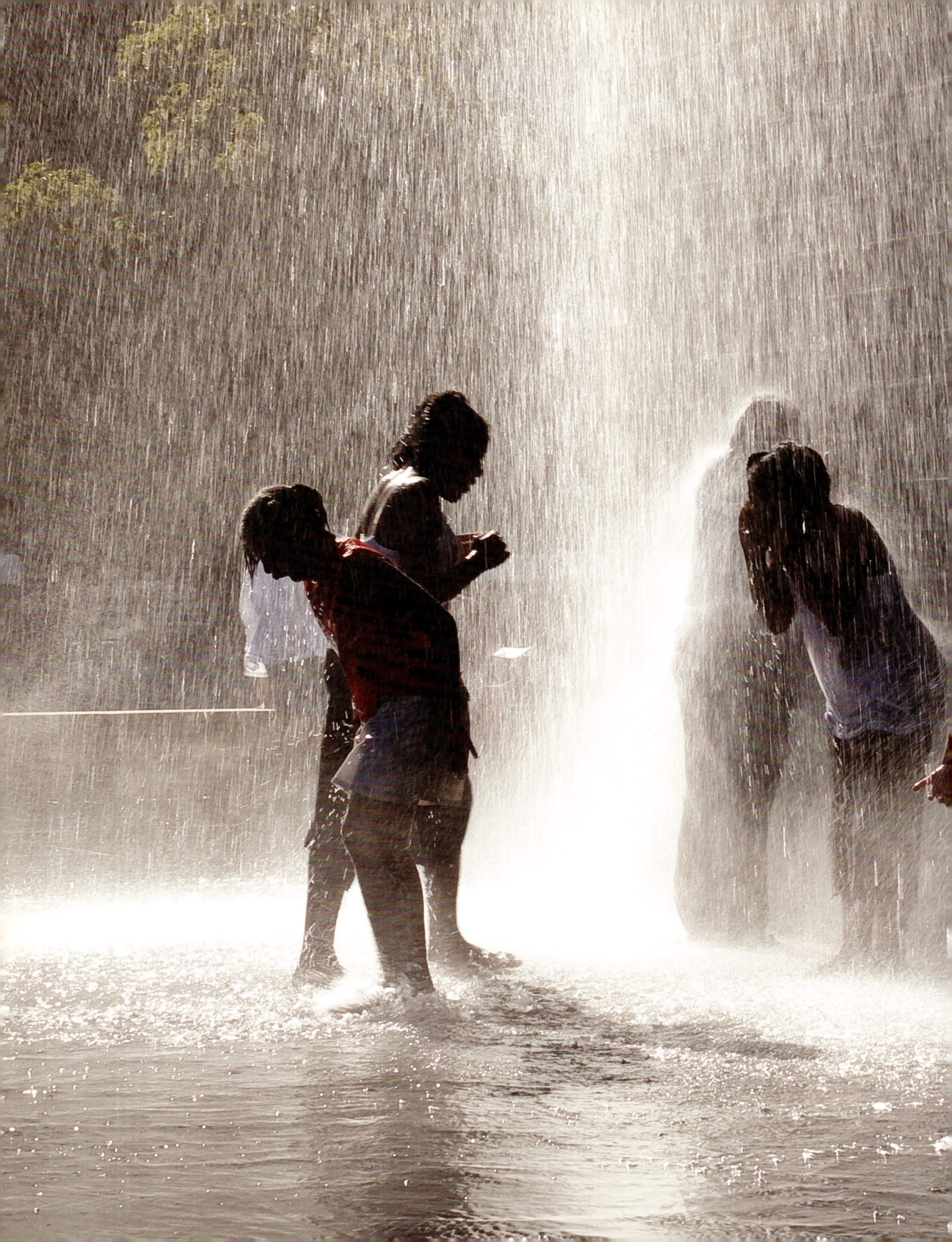

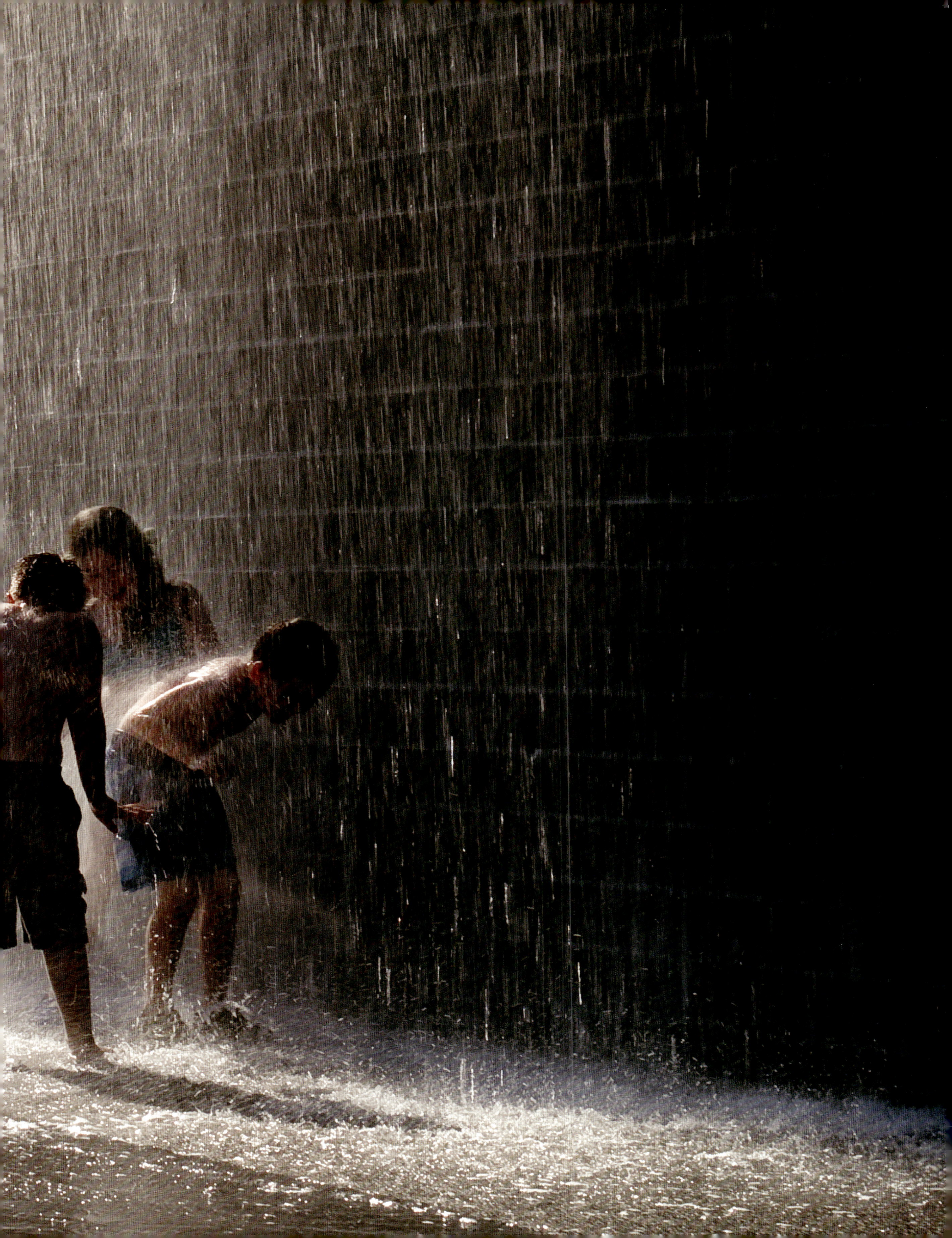

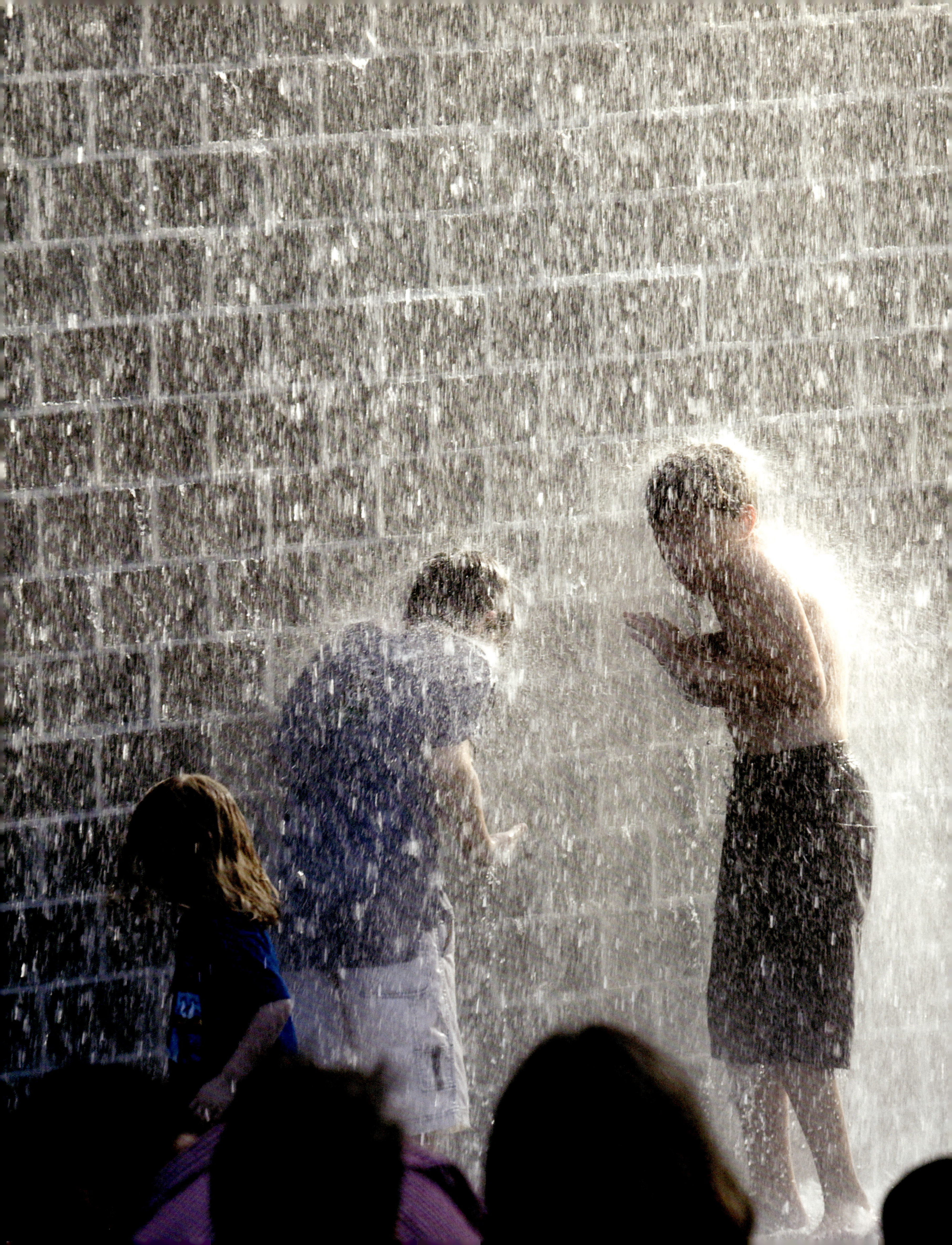

A small group of students arrives with placards proclaiming "FREE HUGS." They don't meet any resistance, but there's something superfluous to their display, for they are preaching to the converted. In a sense, people have been hugging each other all morning. Perhaps not physically (well, try telling that to the kids under the water-spout!), but emotionally. The Free Huggers give up after just a few minutes and surrender to the magic of the space.

The Art Student's Tale

The first thing I notice are her black tights with the white skull-and-crossbones motif. She's sitting on one of the cedarwood benches, attempting to draw the south tower with a fine, fiber-tipped pen. She's chosen the spot because it's in the shade, but the sun transforms the tower into a massive silhouette ominously reminiscent of Kubrick's *2001*. We start talking and I suggest charcoal might be a better medium to capture the sheer bulk of the object before us. When I mention that I know Plensa, that I'm writing a book, she looks up from her drawing and asks, "Is he a conceptual artist?"

She doesn't know it, but she's gone straight for the jugular. Is Plensa a conceptual artist? Well, all artists are insofar as any artwork needs some kind of conceptual framework. But conceptual artists tend to see that frame as the beginning and end of the work. Plensa is committed to making sculpture, but through the material object is always trying to nail down a whole universe full of ideas. As in some insane Hegelian dialectic, wherever Plensa starts his train of associations, ultimately he strives to embrace everything. Like Einstein and his elusive unified field theory. It occurs to me that Plensa is actually a mystic, but one with iron in the soul, one who is committed to the material. But I think that's all a bit too conceptual for the art student in the black tights with the white skull-and-crossbones motif.

Gods for a New Age

I come back another evening, shortly after the sun has set. It's cooler now and the children have long gone. People are still walking on the water, but more sedately, entranced by the twin towers that emerge from an all-pervading dusk. It's my farewell to the fountain; an emotional parting.

My thoughts stray to Edward Hopper's *Night Hawks,* that quintessentially
American painting of nocturnal ennui and existential isolation. With its window
of light and insular figures, it's close to the spirit of Plensa's original graphics,
but if I'm honest, it's not what is actually in front of me. So I try again to
penetrate the fountain's elusive mystery, hoping for one last revelation.

Around us a constellation of lights from the downtown offices tries in vain
to compete with the fifty-foot faces that dissolve into cascades of colored,
translucent water. I give in to the rhythm of the changing images, feeling the
coolness of the pool on my feet. At random, the computer selects one of
the images of nature: the tumbling water of a mountain spring. Then, as the
face of one young African-American woman breaks into a prolonged, slow-
motion smile, I am suddenly half a world away, back in Korea on the journey
I made some years before. I am seeing again the giant Buddha carved from
a rock as large as a three-story building and approached by a steep path that
crosses streams and cataracts. The Buddha's smile is fixed in an expression
of benevolence, of benign well-being. My newfound guide and companion,
who doesn't wear the saffron robes but who has accompanied me from the
temple below, has the same expression on his face: as transfixed as the
shimmering waters of the sea beyond.

It's a momentary vision, and it could as well have been any one of our outsized
gods, from the giant heads protecting the shores of Easter Island to the
enigmatic Sphinx at Giza. Is Plensa playing these ancient guardians at their
own game? Not quite, I feel, but especially in the female faces there is a
benevolent maternalism with all its caring and protective associations. The
slow smile that falls so benignly upon us. The water issuing from the mouth,
a traditional symbol of the giving of life. What are so many of those deities if
not a personification of the mother figure that echoes in our own psyches?
So perhaps, after all, these *are* benevolent gods for a largely secular age,
recast in pixels, glass, and steel. Or simply Niagara Falls on Michigan Avenue.

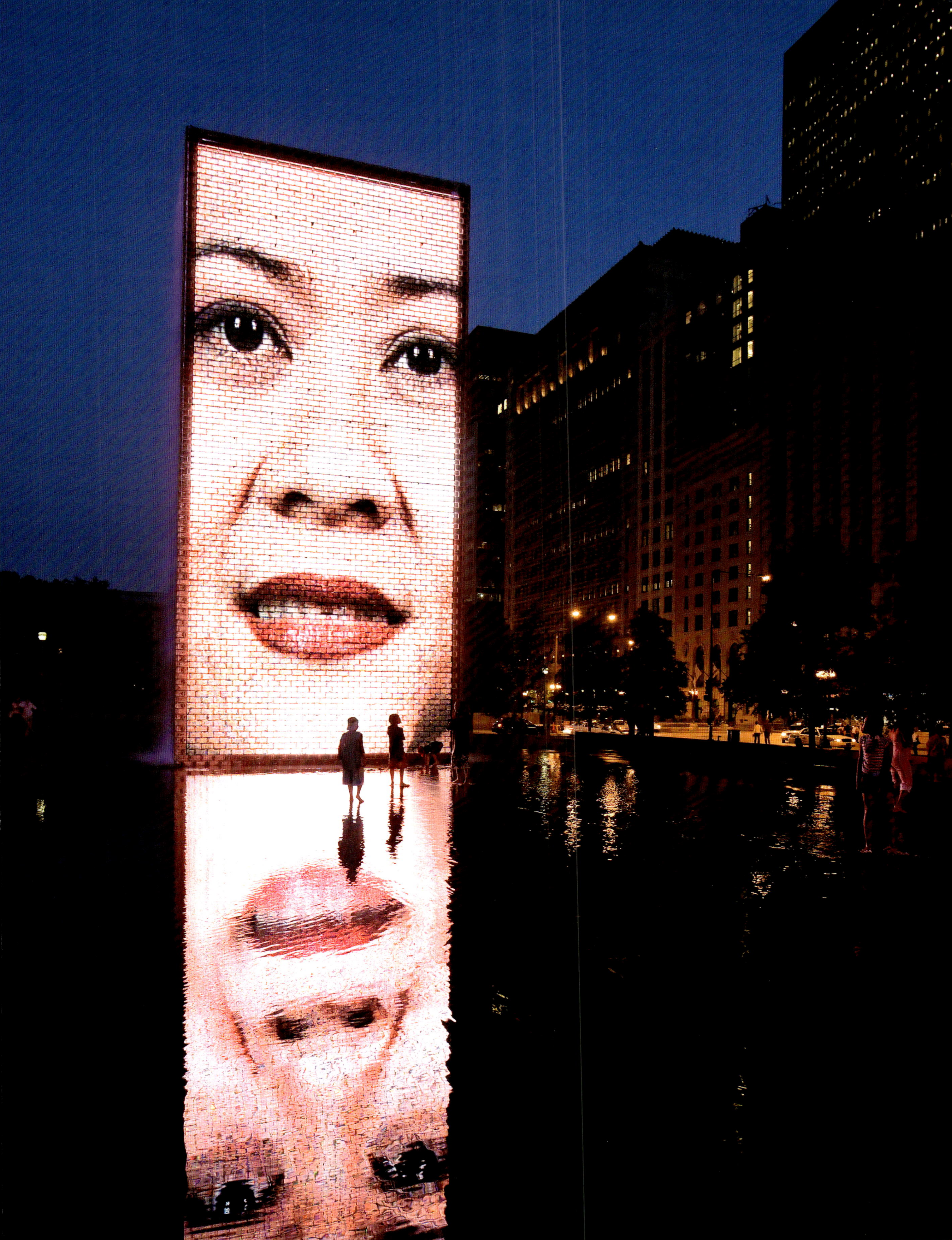

With Thanks

While every effort has been made to verify the facts, this remains a personal account based largely on individual memories of events that happened several years previously and on my own memories of places that have blurred and merged over decades, but have never dulled. I am grateful to Jaume Plensa for being so generous with his time and for inviting me to contribute this narrative to what is unquestionably *his* book, and also to his wife, Laura, for her patience in answering my many queries, however pedantic. My thanks to all those who made the time, often at short notice, to talk with me, including Lester, Jim, Paula, Susan, and Steve Crown, and Mark Sexton, Roark Frankel, Alan Labb, John Manning, Ed Uhlir, Randall Mehrberg, and Jack Guthman. Also a big thank-you goes to Paul Gray and Erin Fowler at the Richard Gray Gallery, and to the Chicago History Museum for allowing me access to certain of its archives. Thanks also to the many people in the City of Chicago who shared their own thoughts on the *Crown Fountain,* and also to Jason Neises of the Architecture Foundation for his inspiring tour of the city's public artworks. I am especially grateful to Bob Wislow for his insights and for sending me his published account of the building of Millennium Park, *Better than Perfect*. Finally, I must acknowledge Timothy J. Gilfoyle, whose research for his incisive and erudite book *Millennium Park: Creating a Chicago Landmark* answered many of my questions on the park and its history.

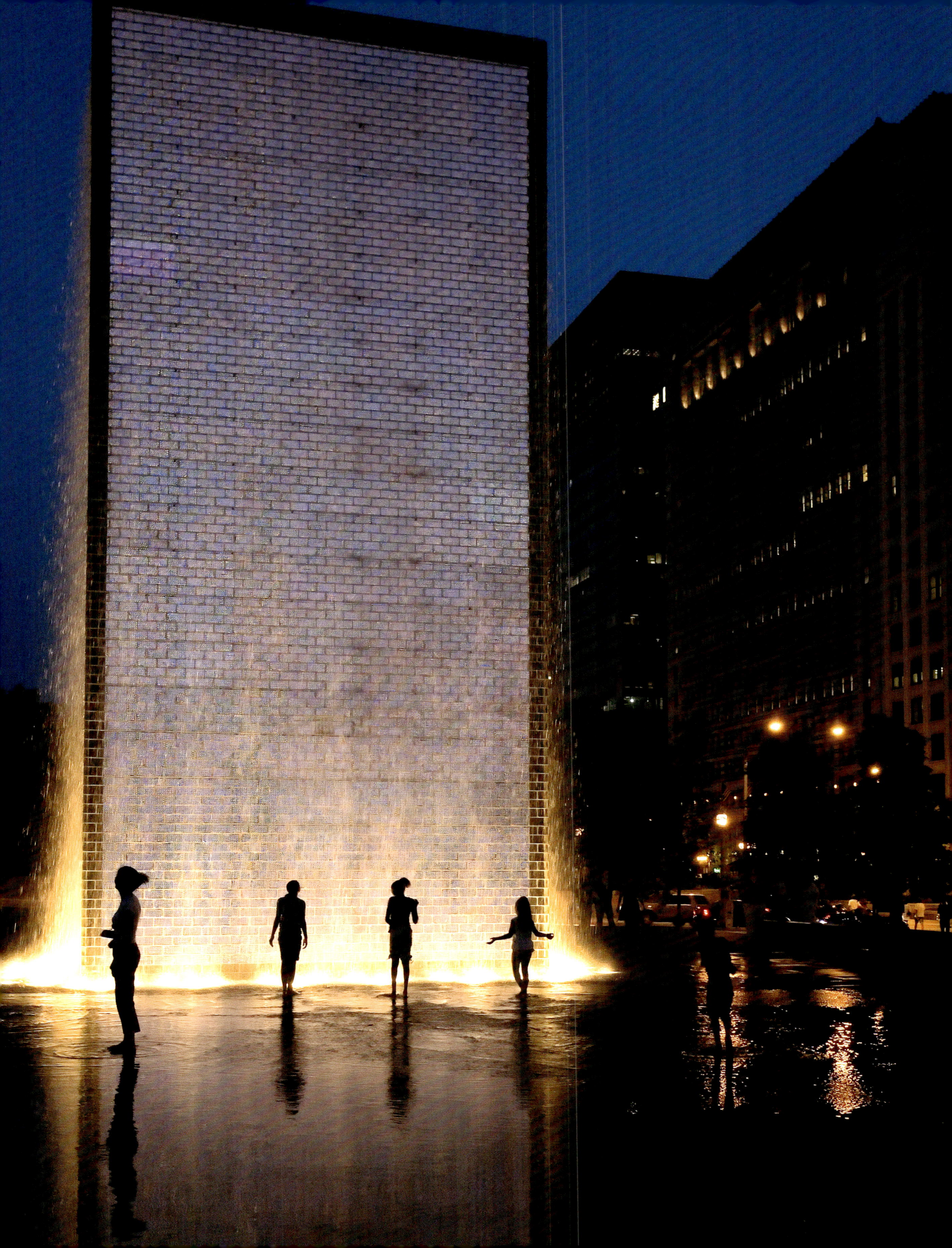

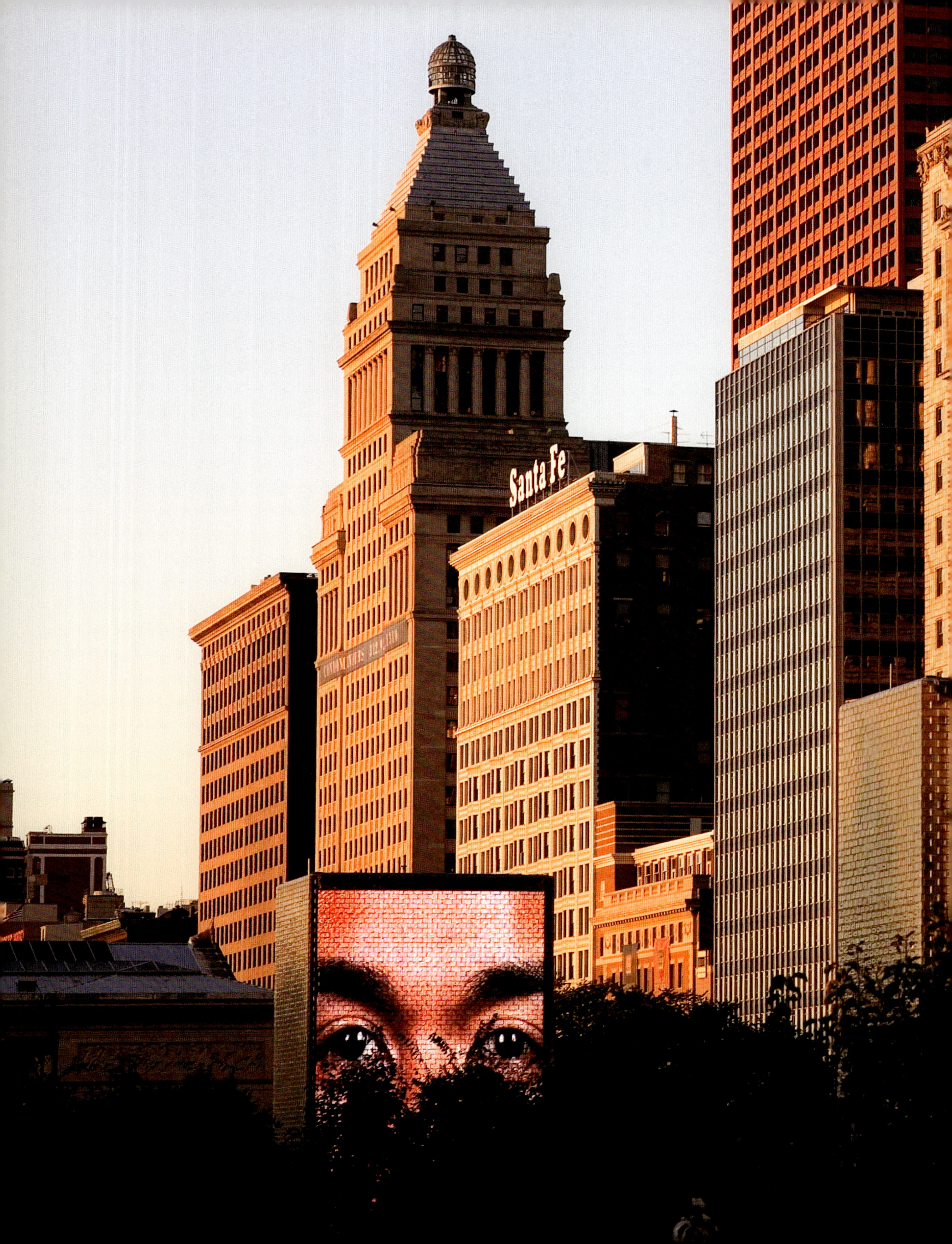

Santa Fe

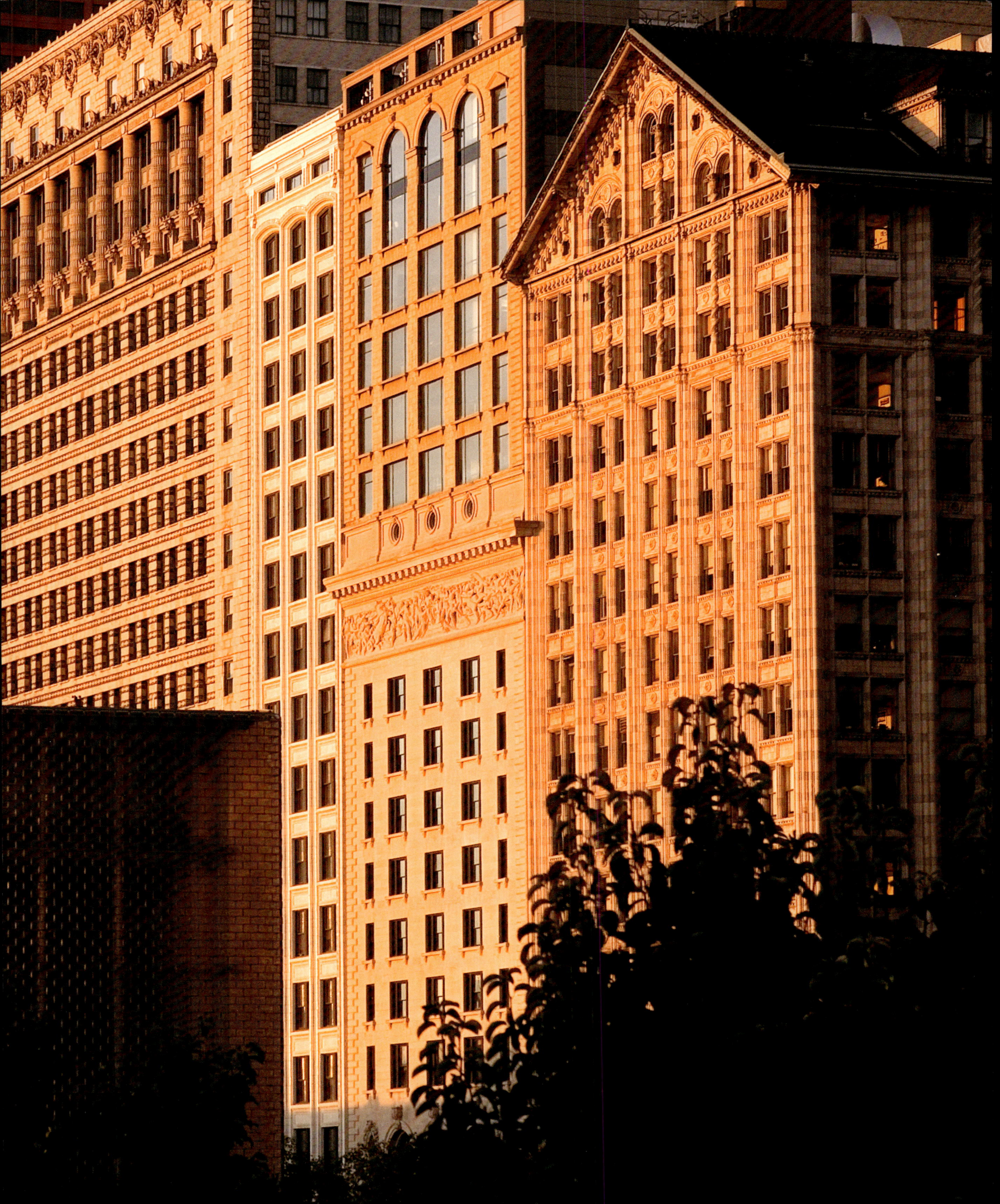

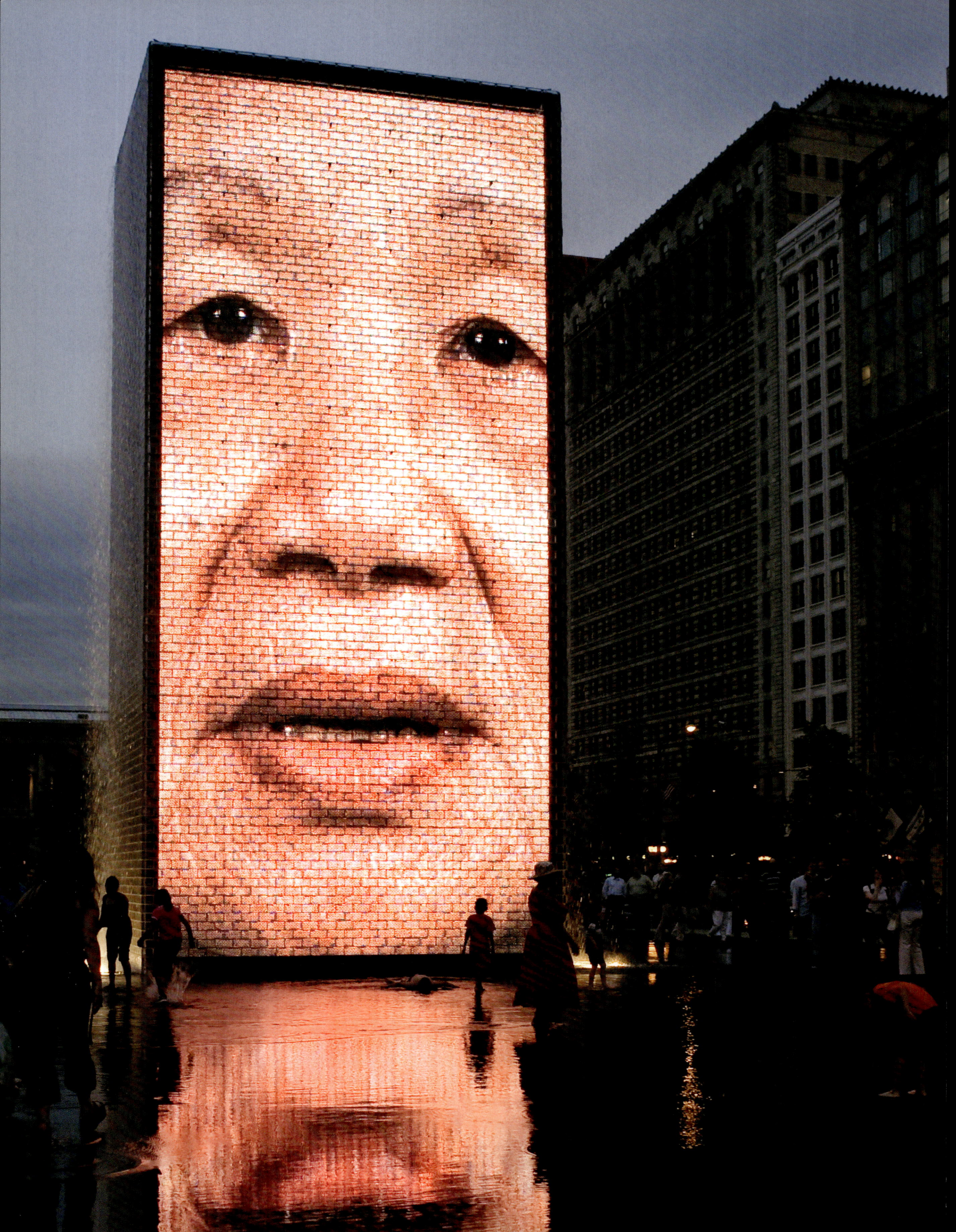

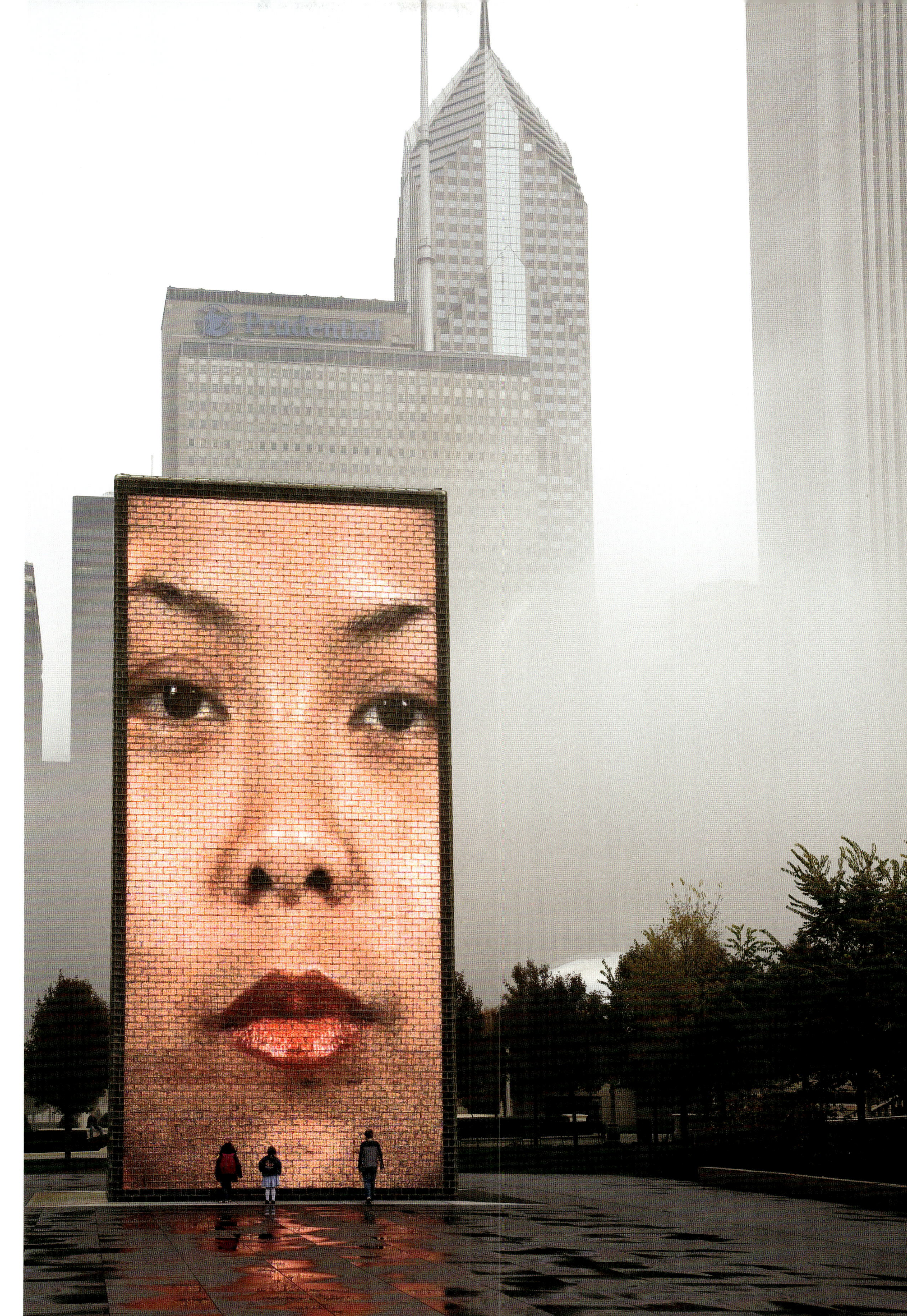

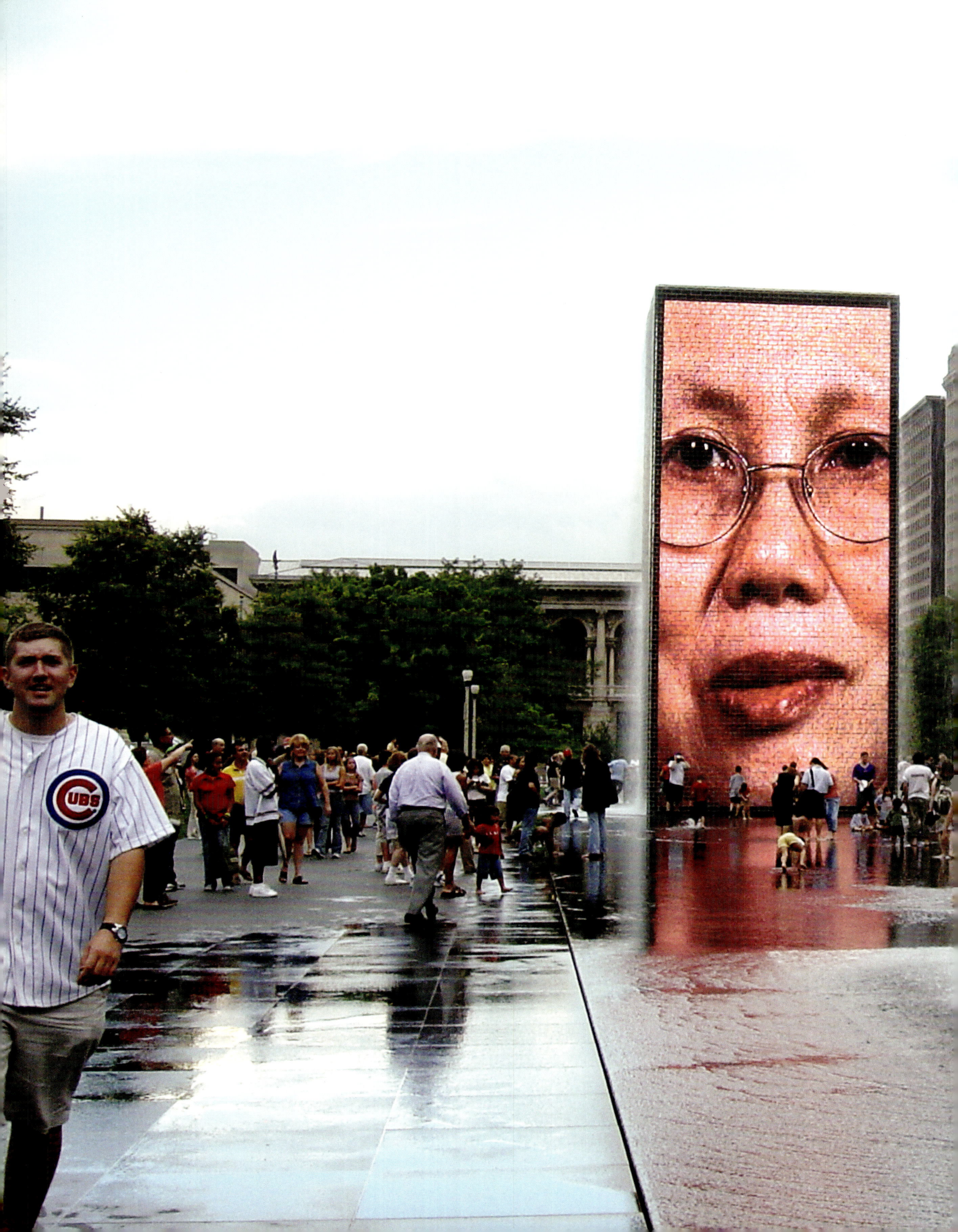

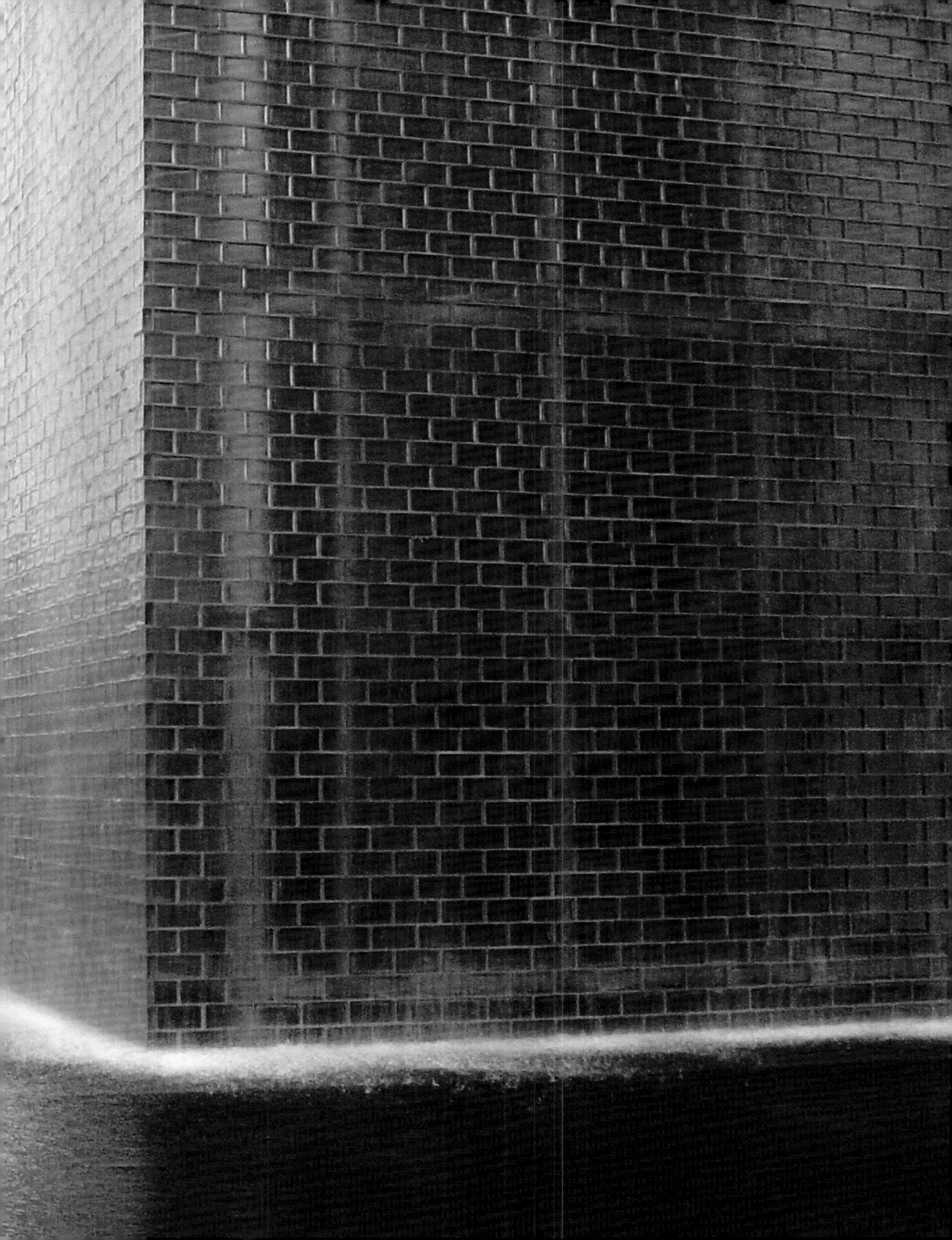

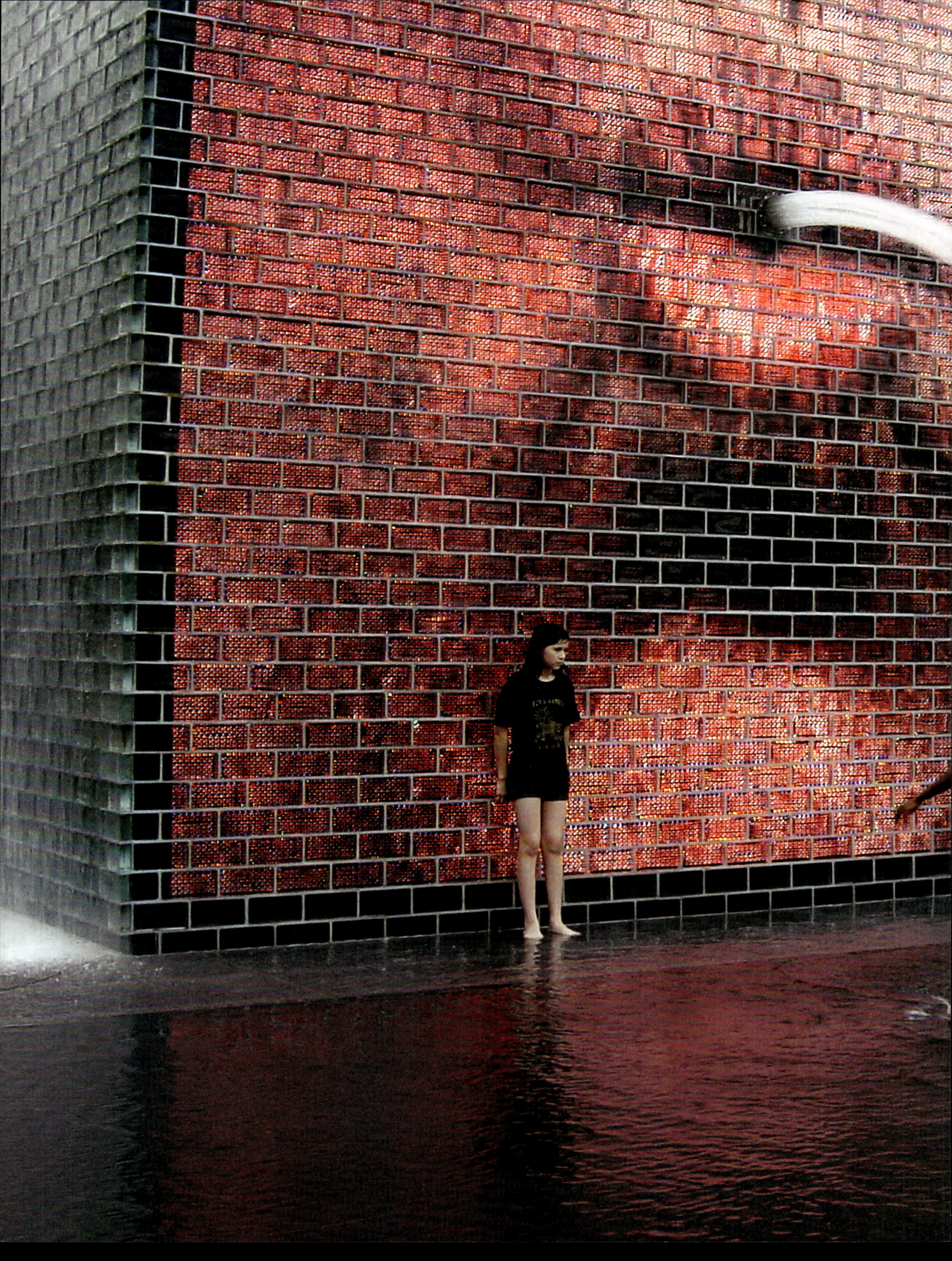

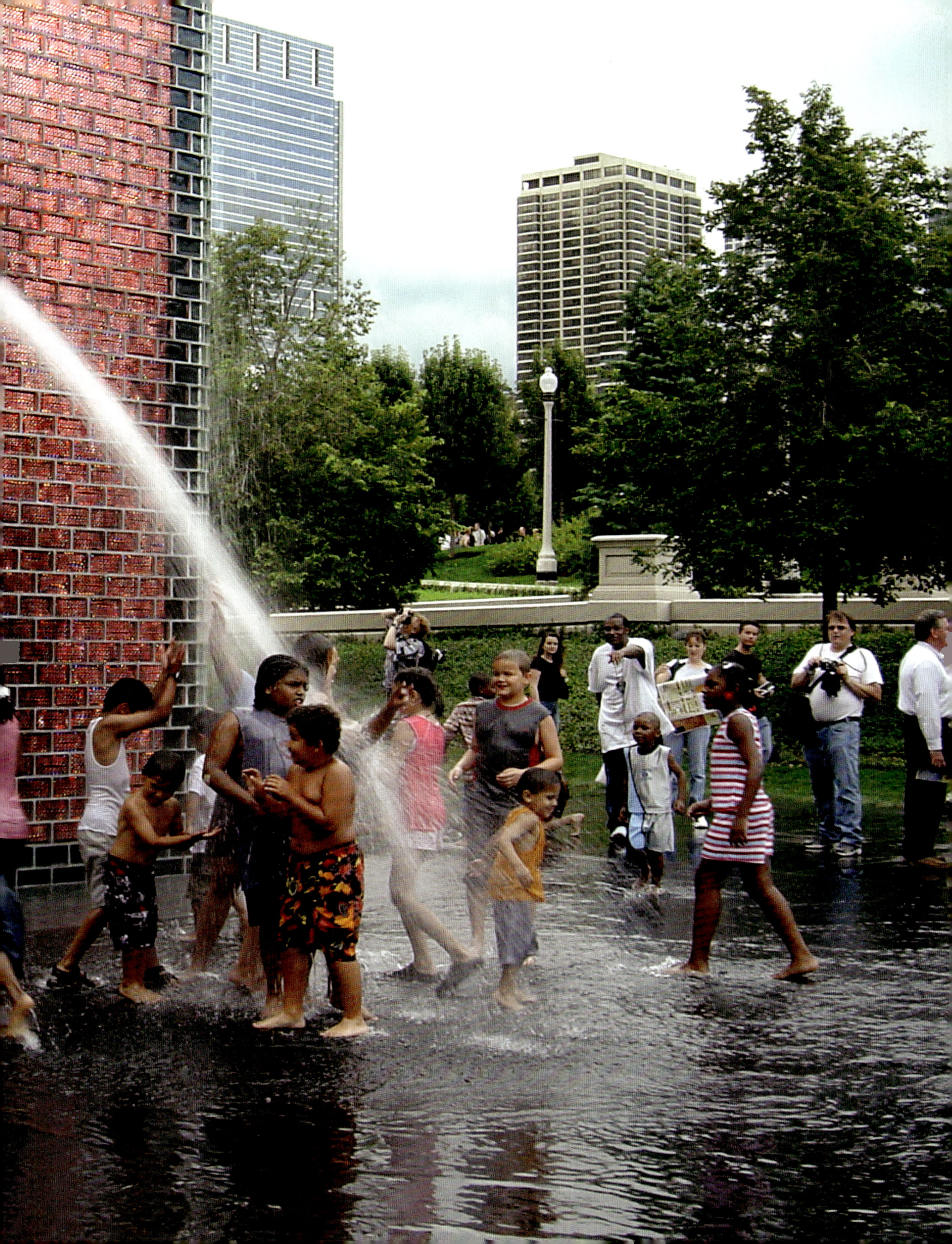

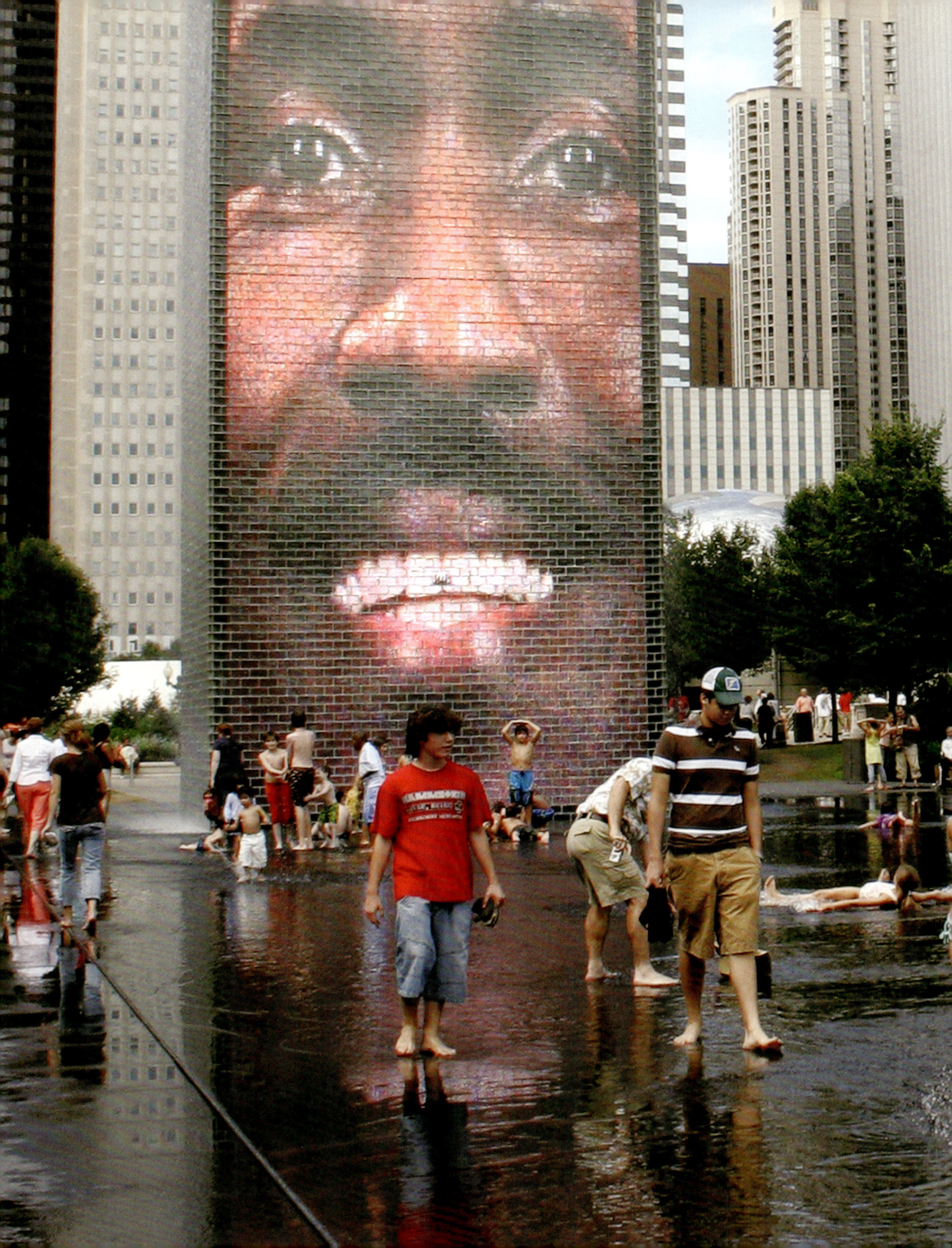

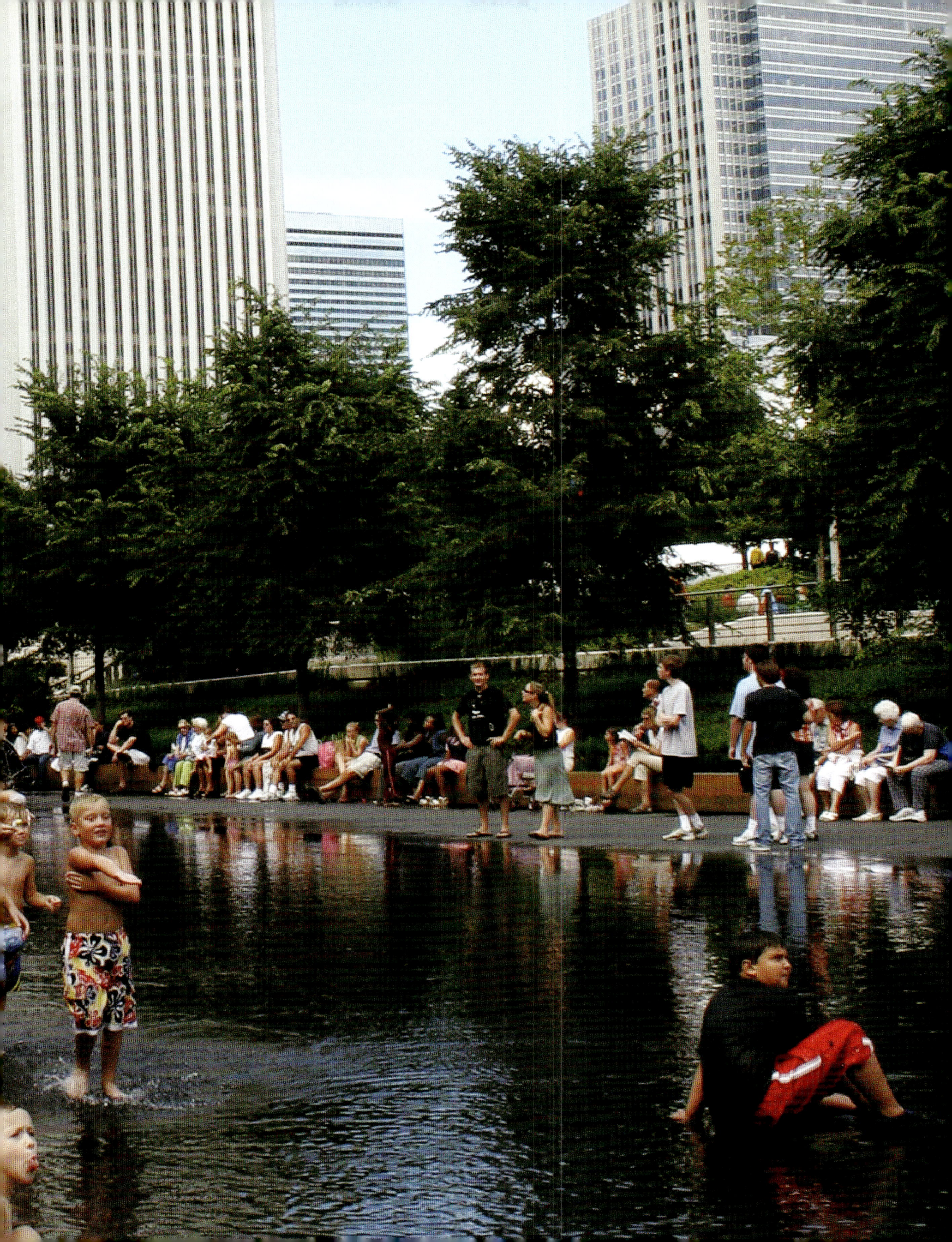

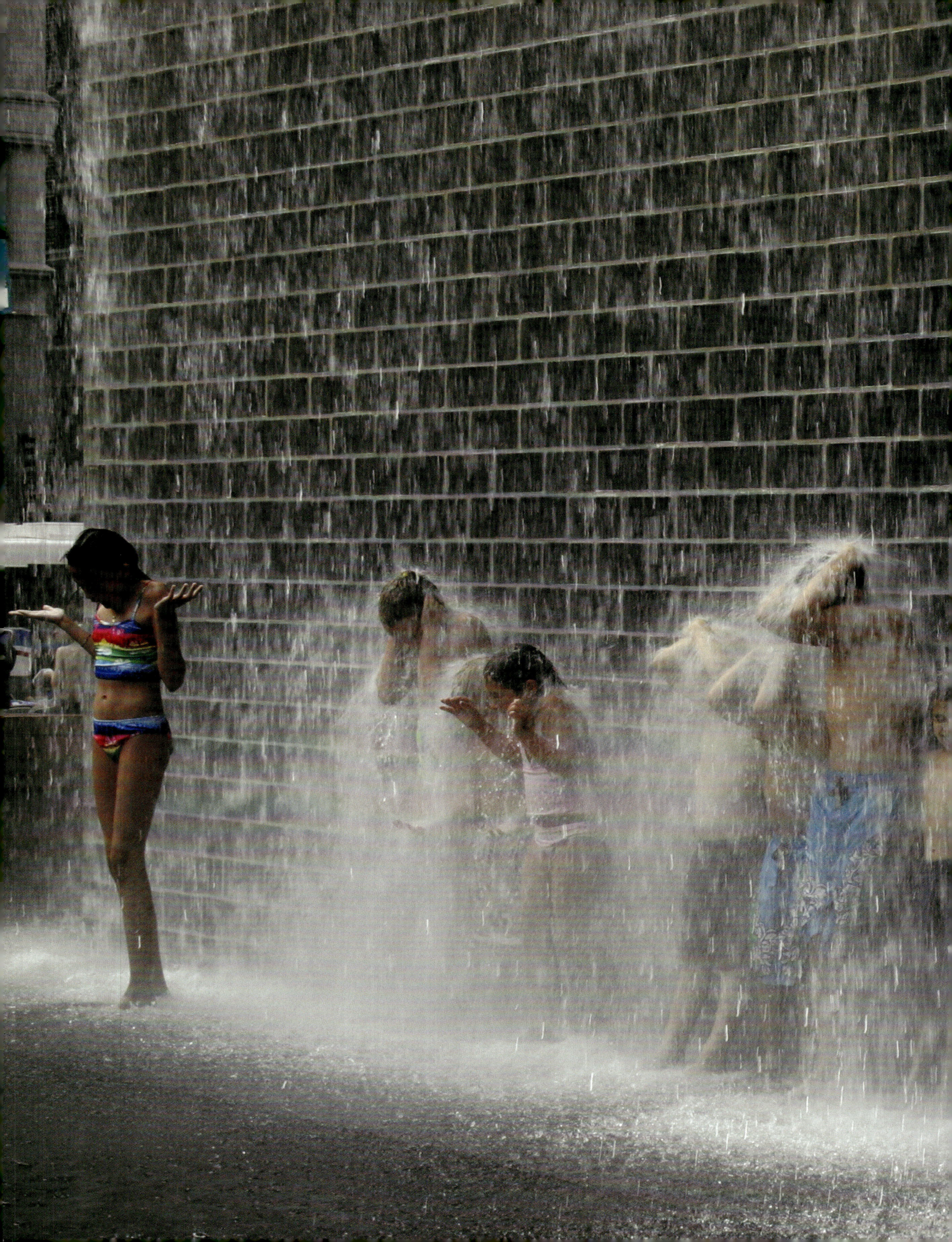

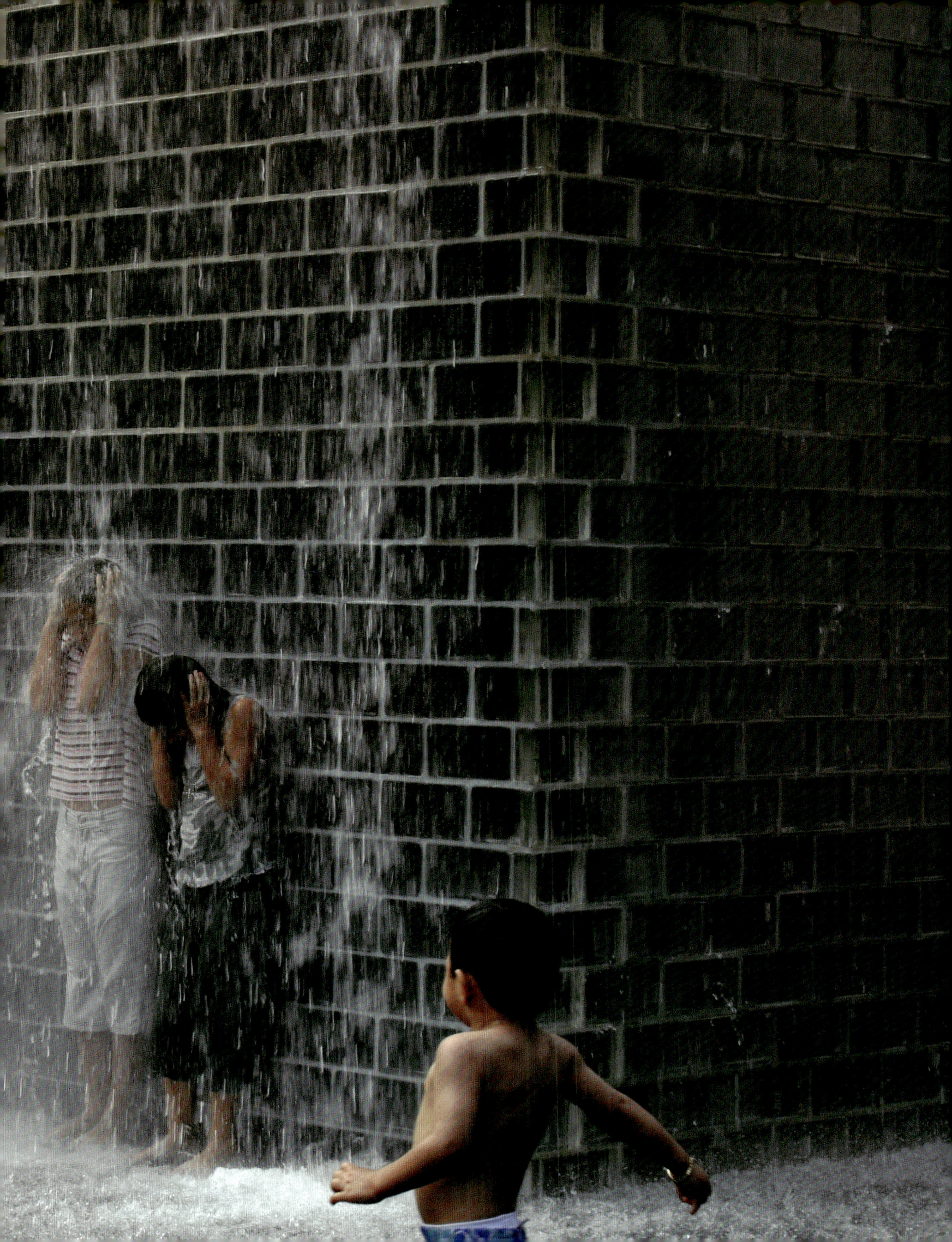

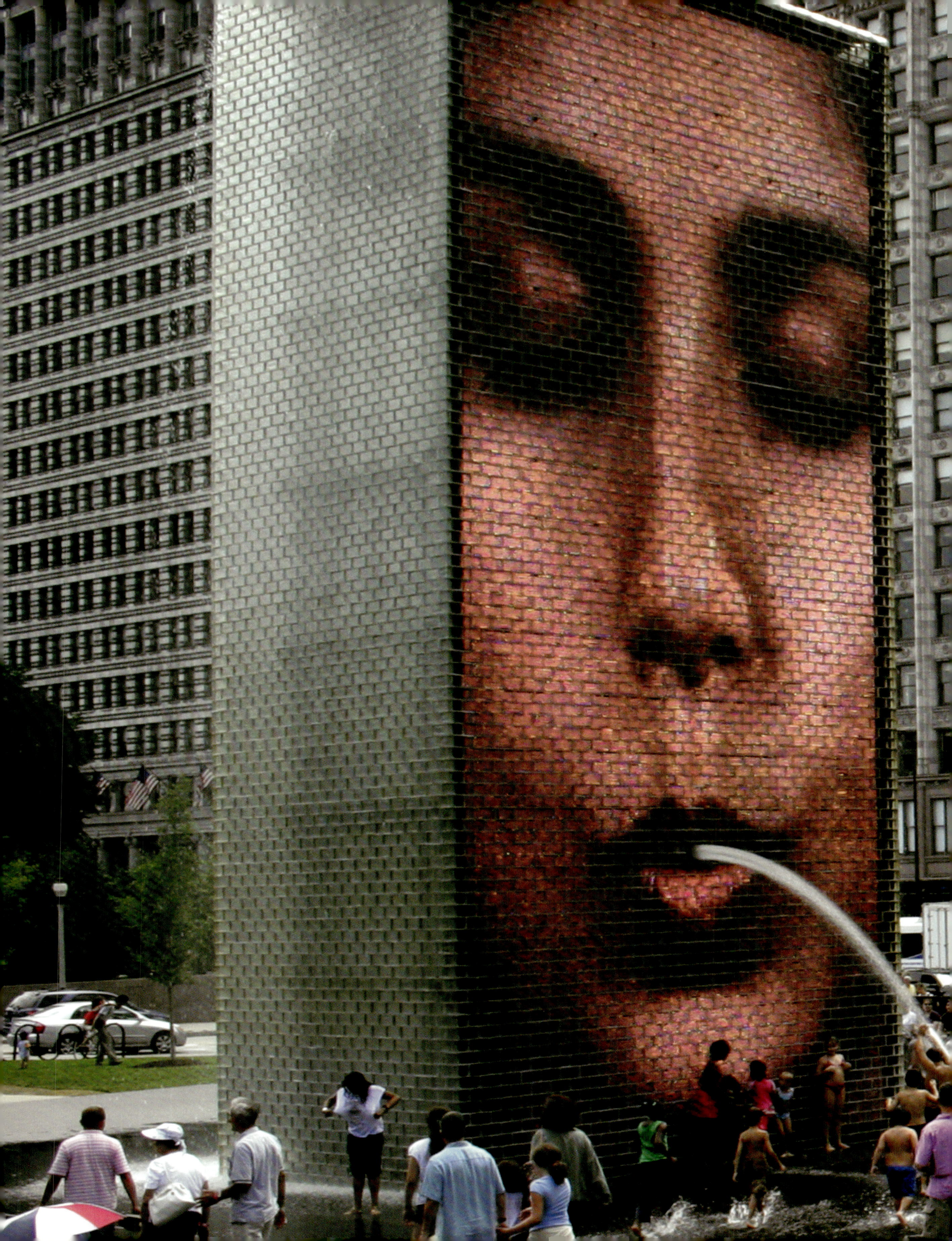

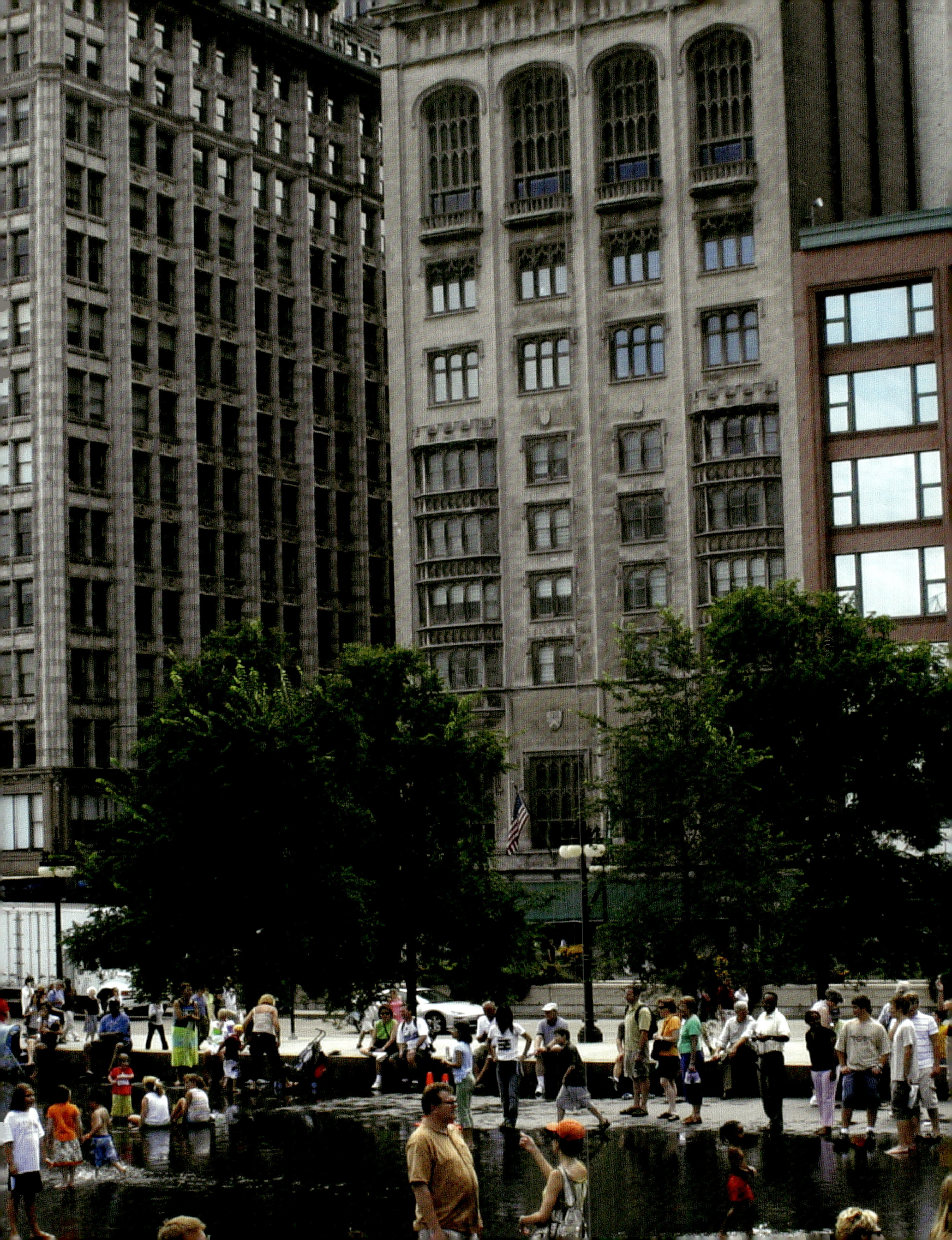

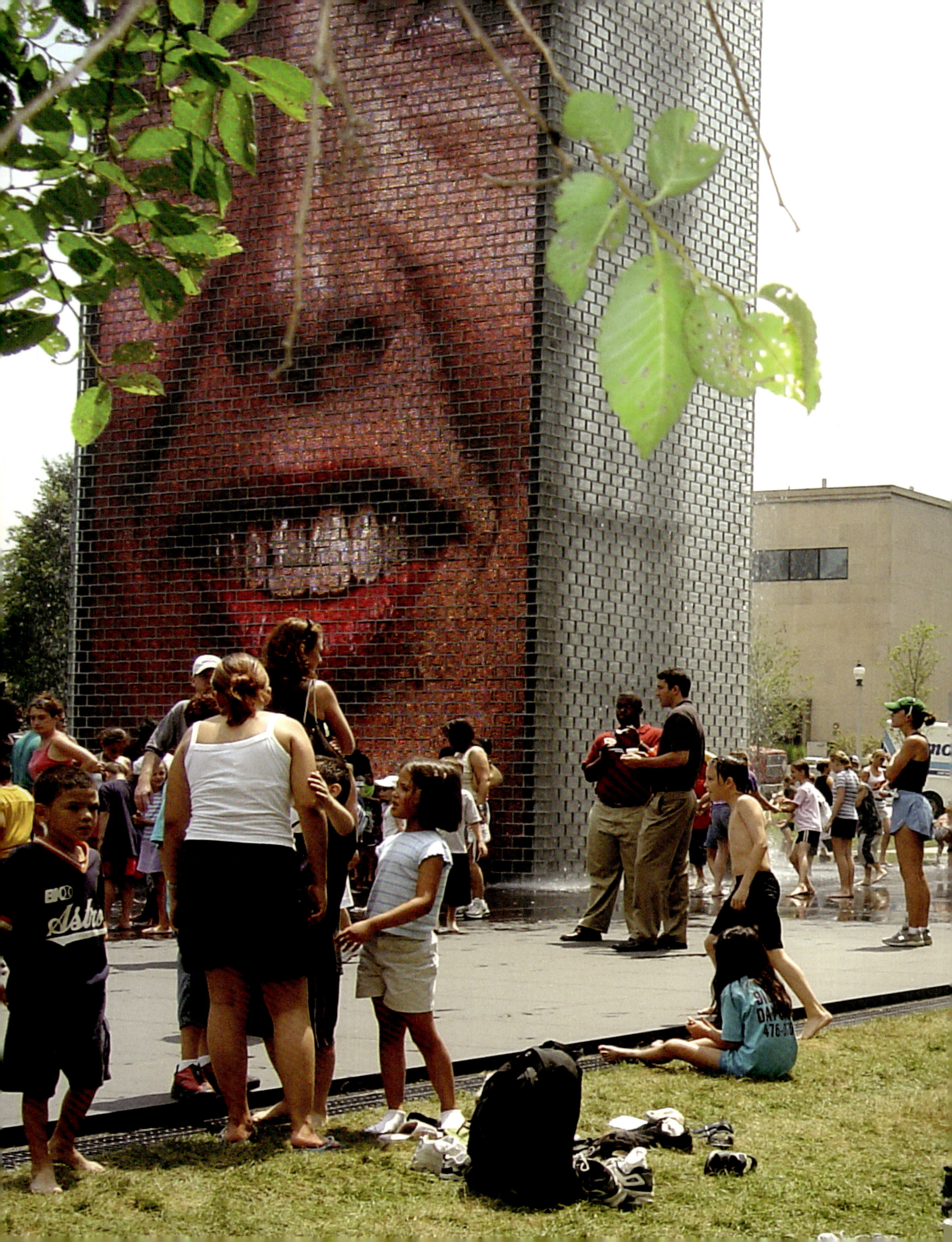

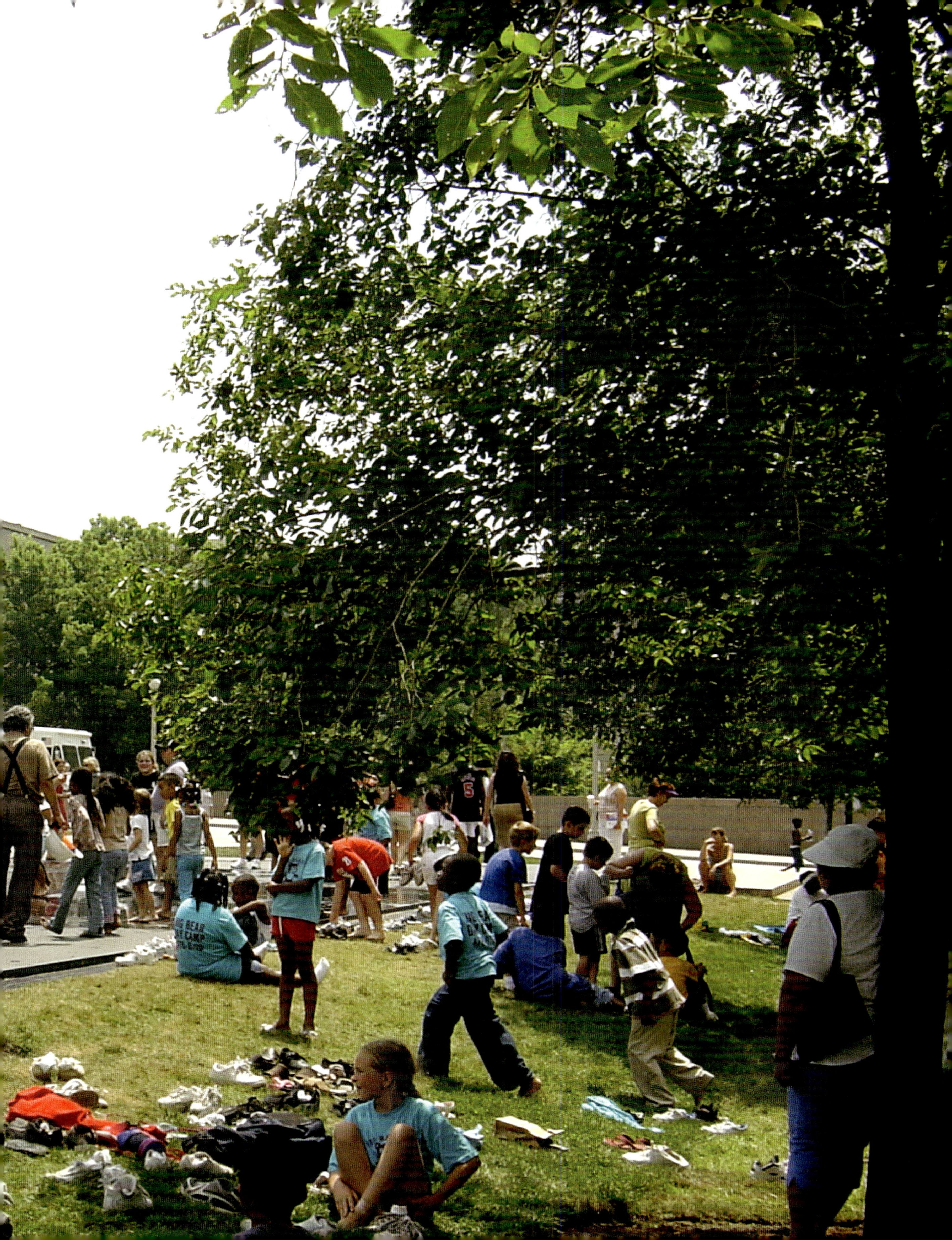

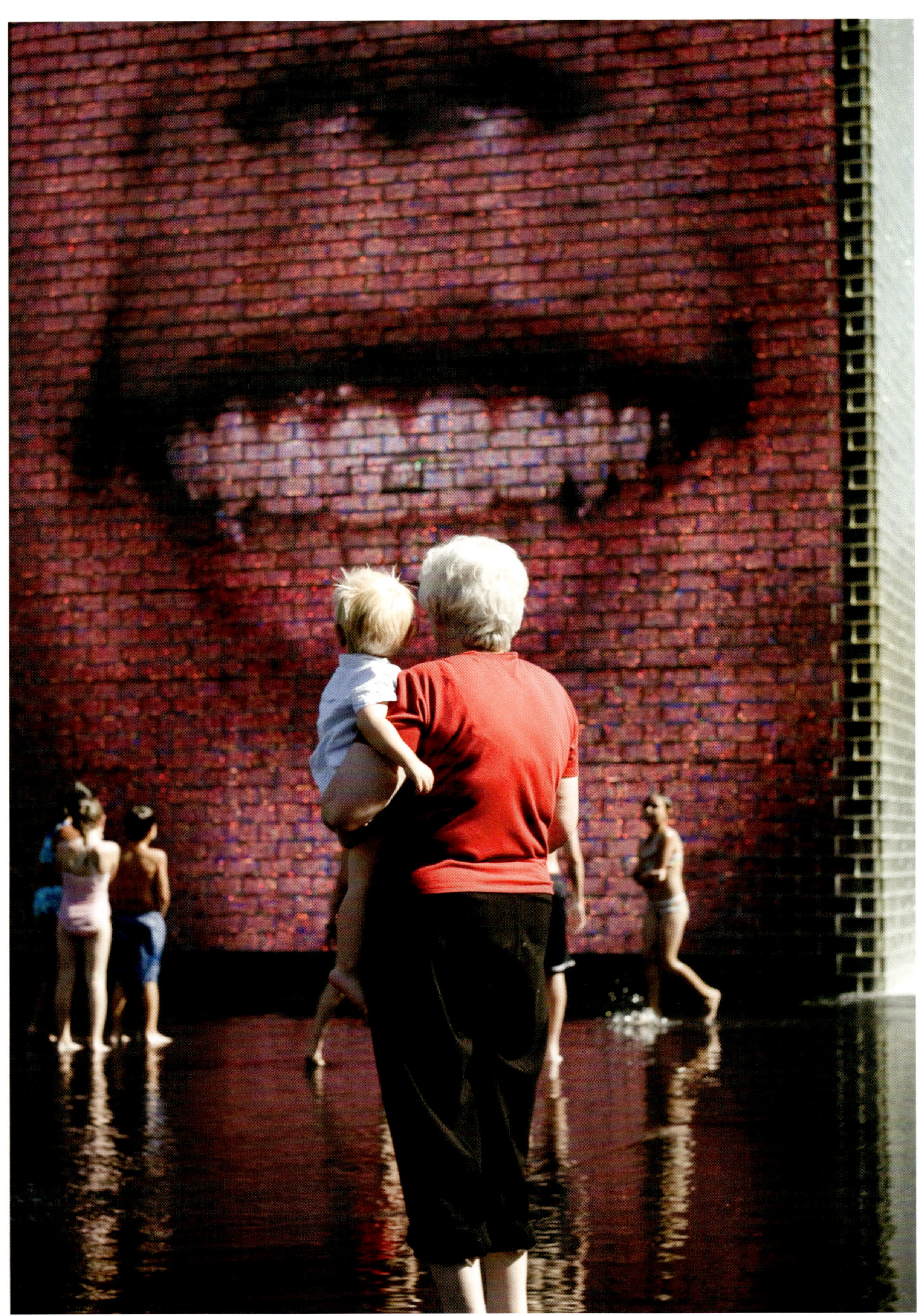

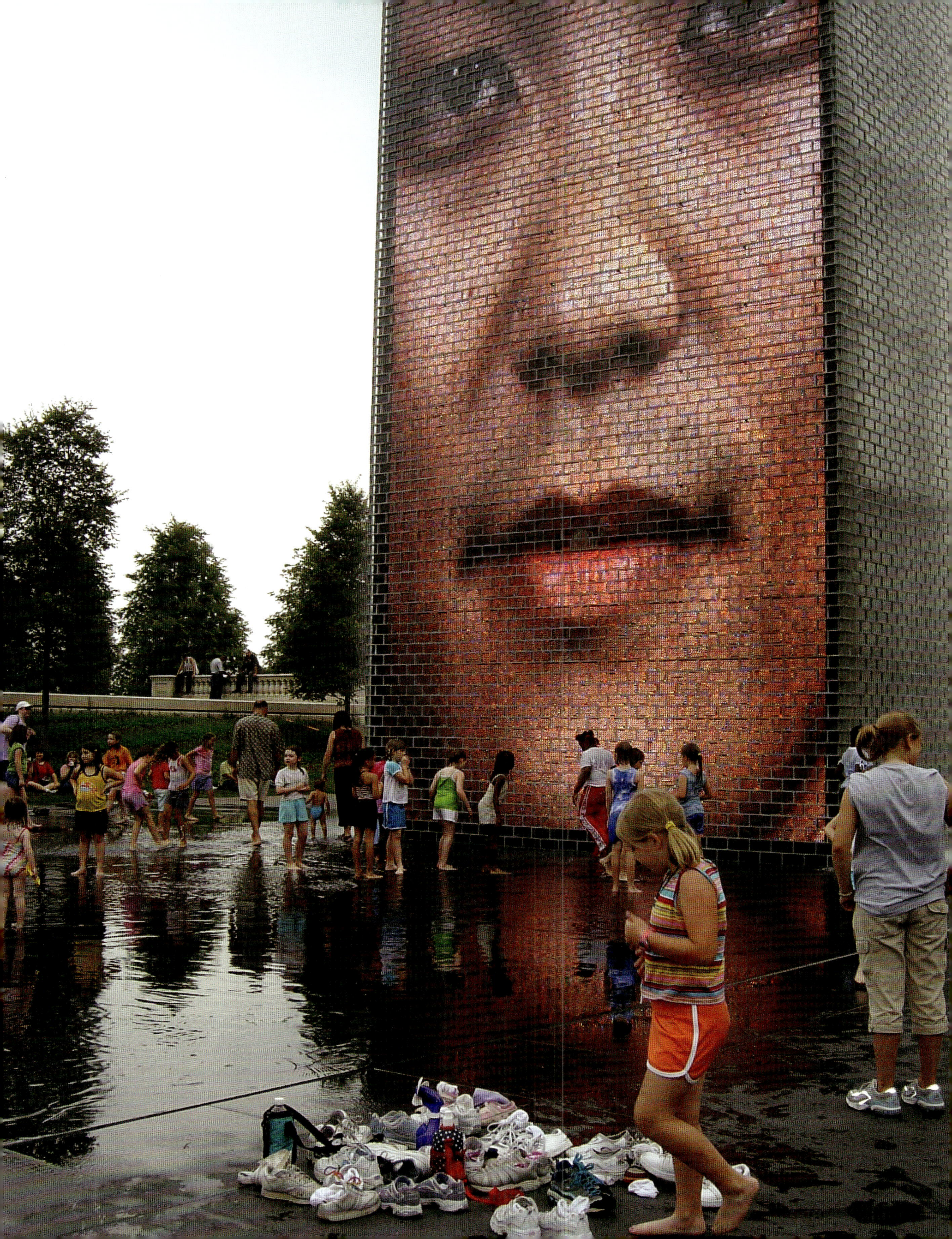

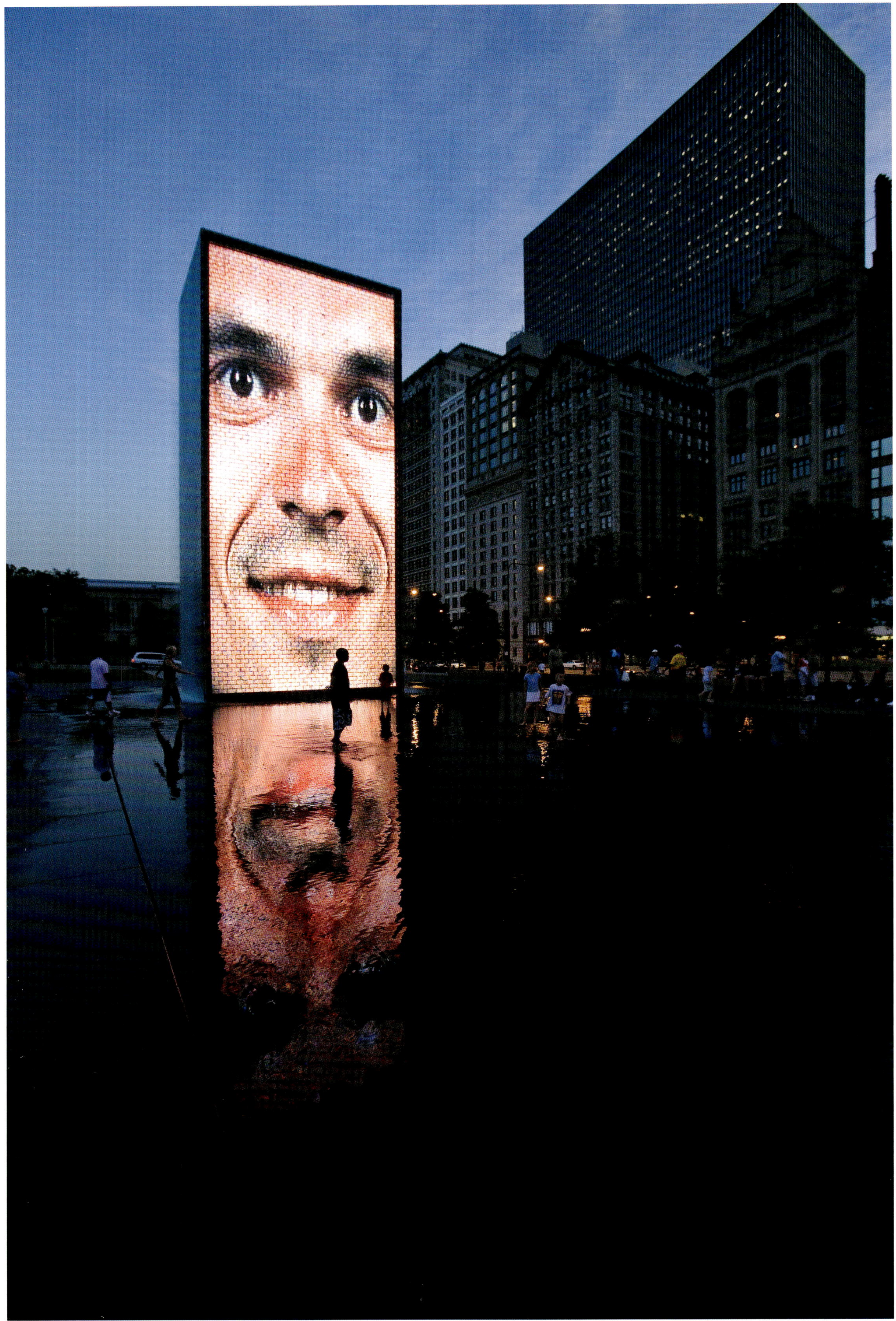

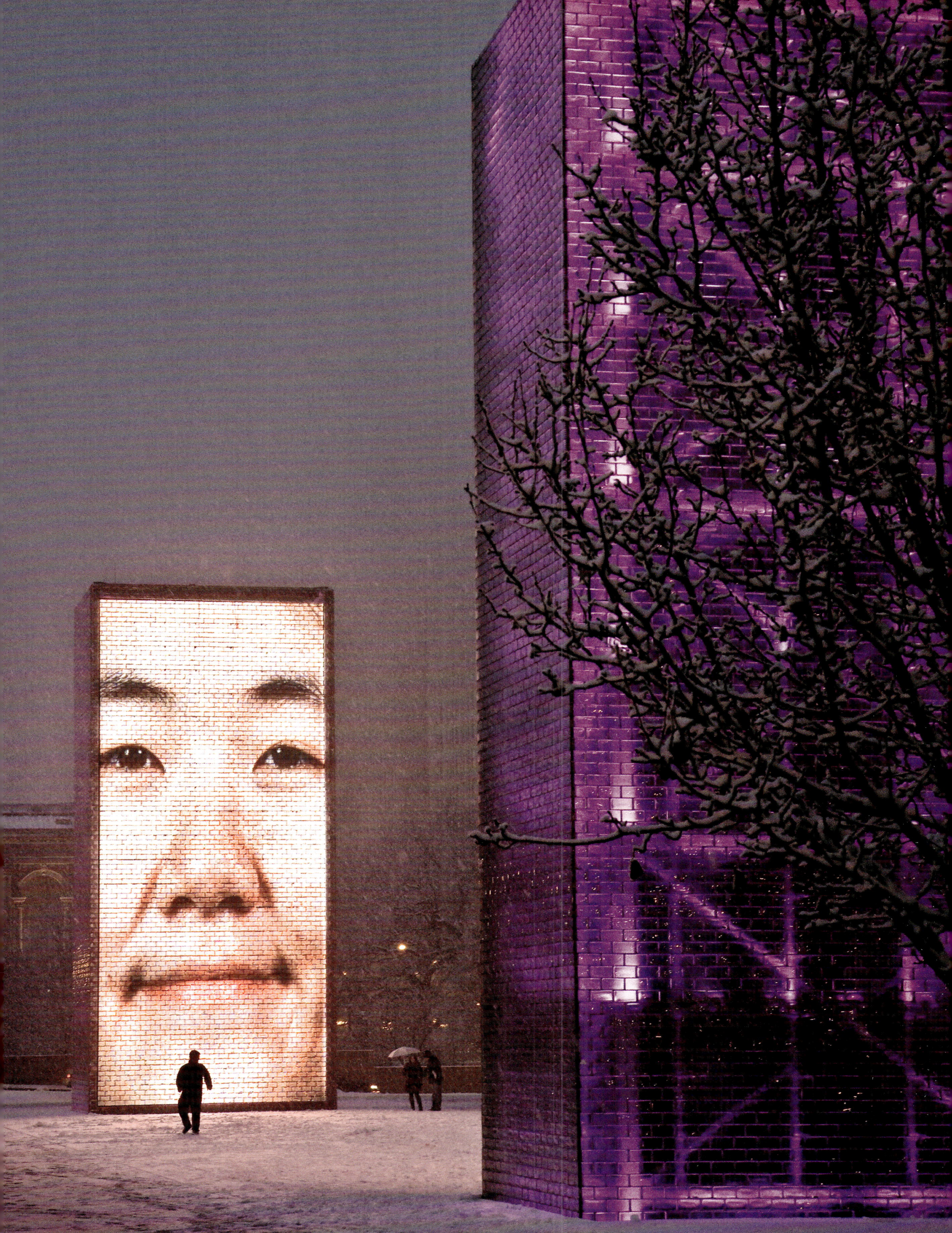

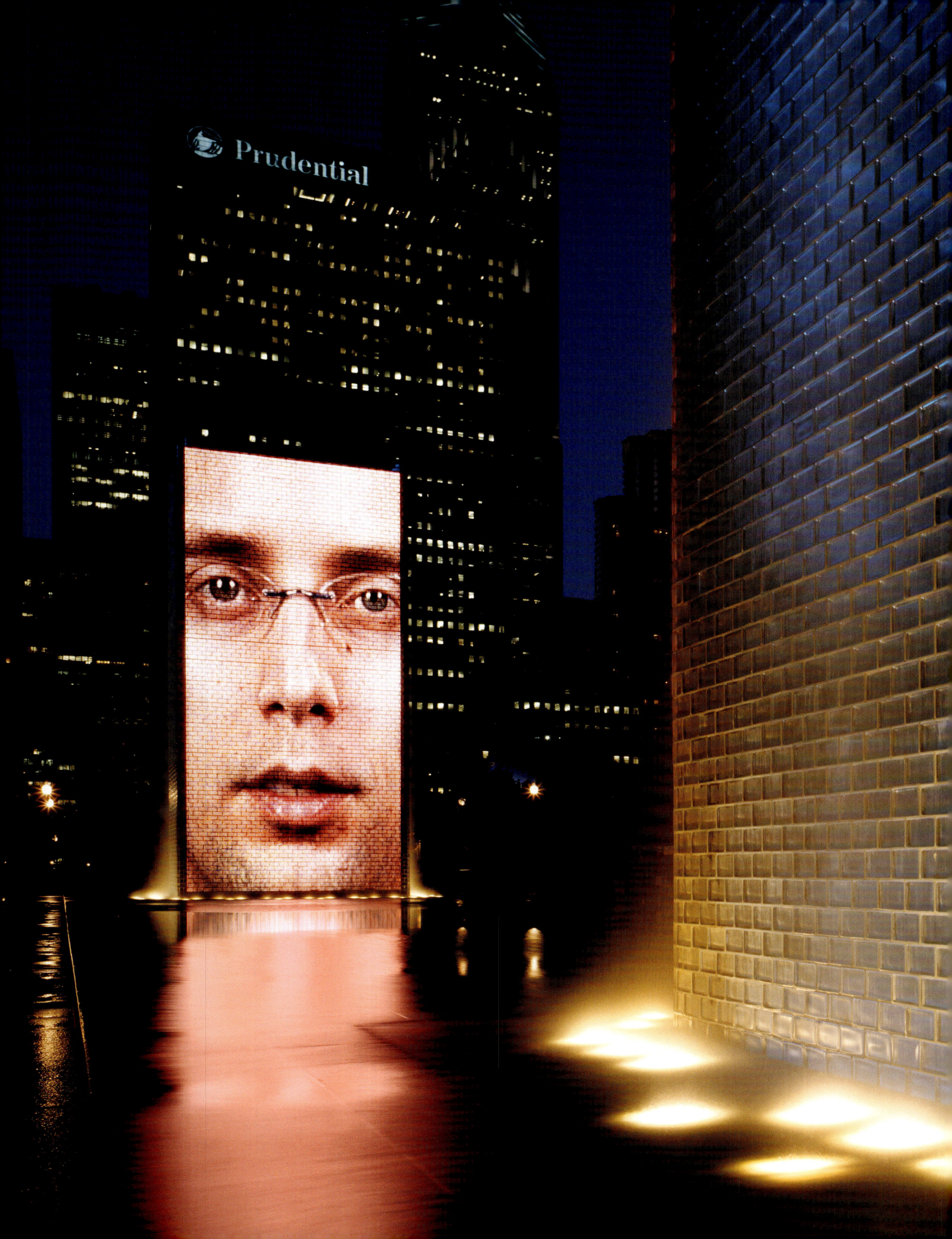
Prudential

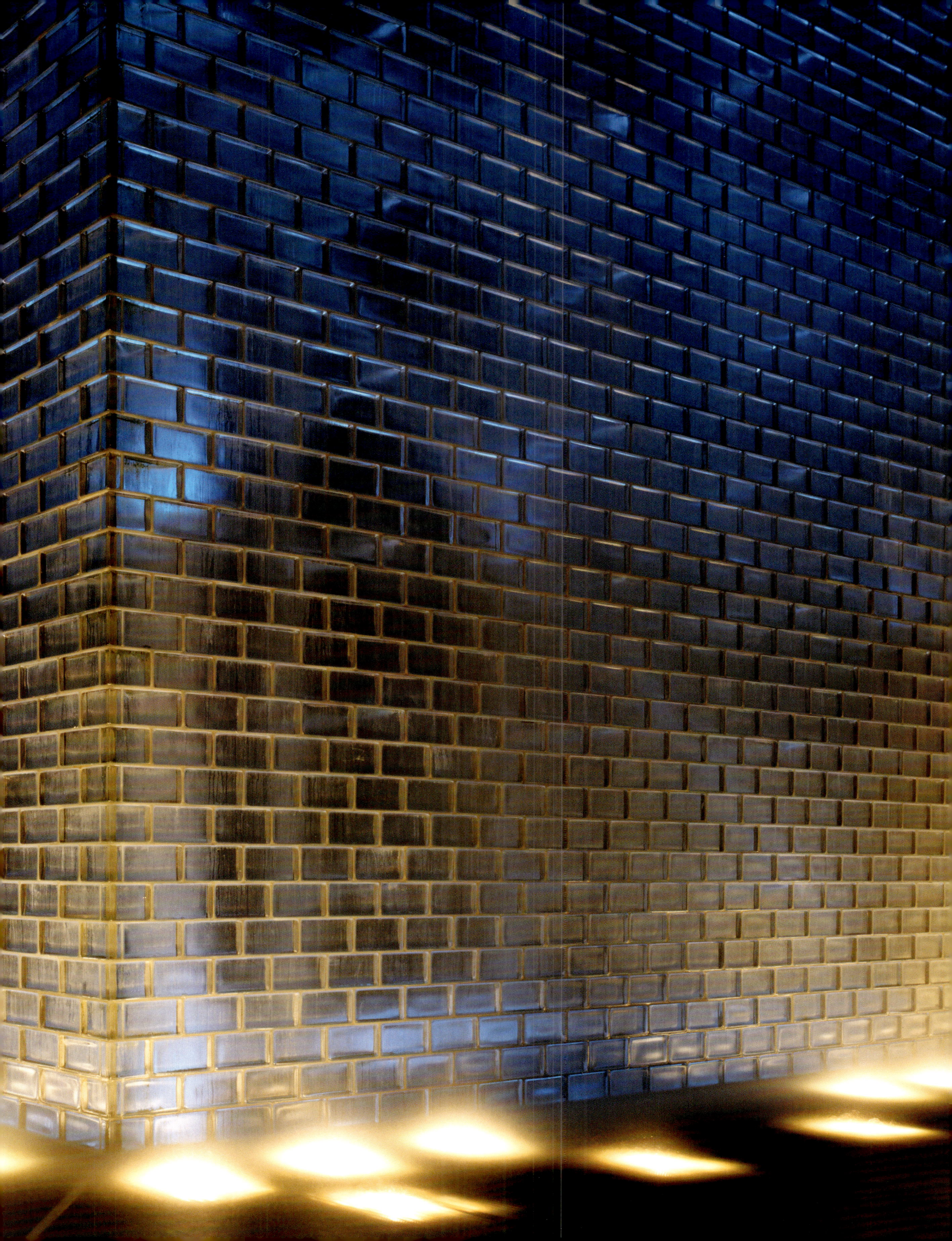

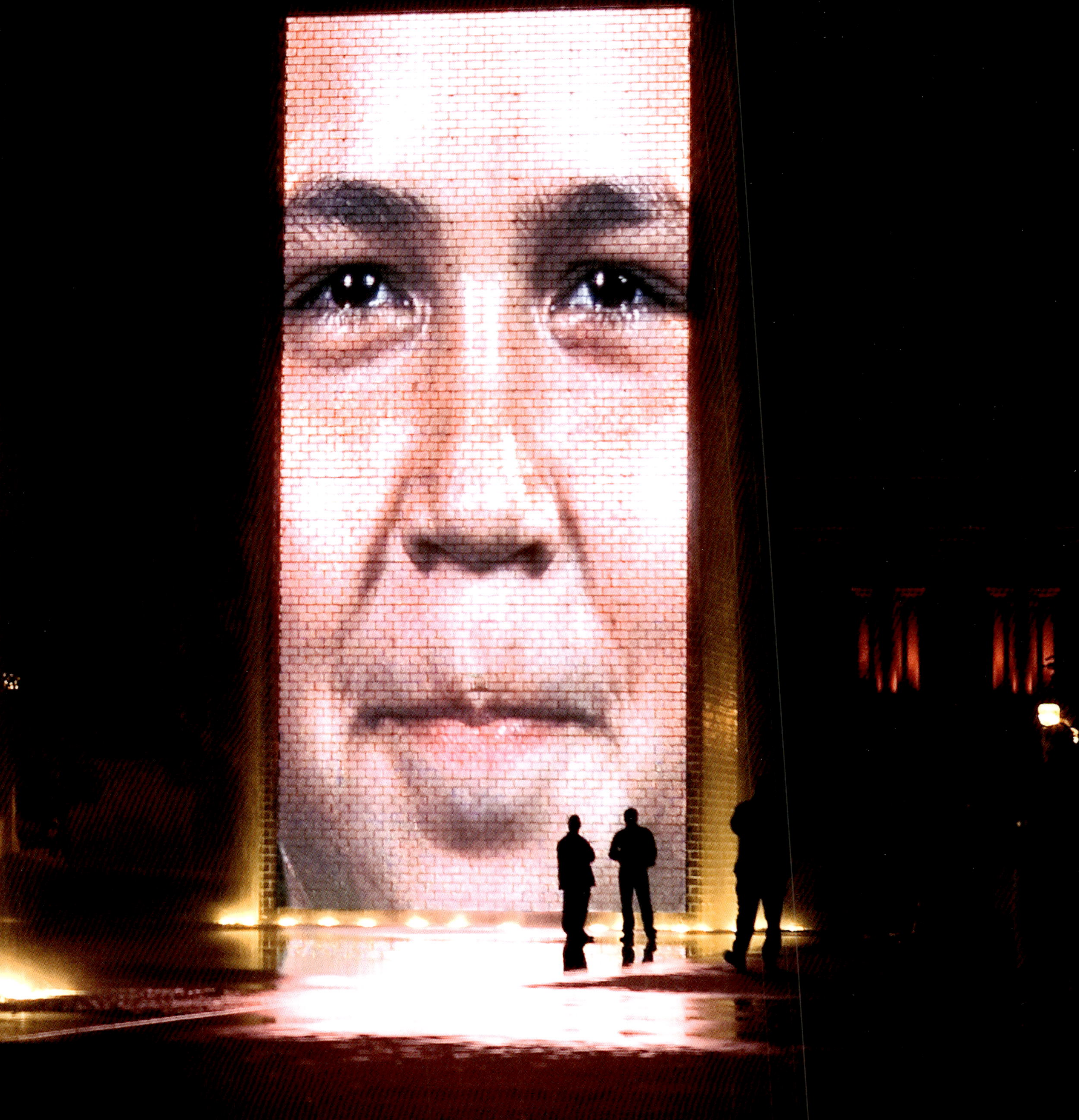

Biography

Selected Solo Exhibitions

2008

Jaume Plensa, Frederik Meijer Gardens and Sculpture Park, Grand Rapids, Michigan
La Riva di Acheronte, Im Dialog IX, Stadtkirche Darmstadt, Darmstadt
Jaume Plensa, Save our Souls, Albion Gallery, London

2007

Jaume Plensa, MAMAC (Musée d'Art Moderne et d'Art Contemporain), Nice
Jaume Plensa, IVAM (Institut Valencià d'Art Modern), Valencia
Nomade, Bastion Saint-Jaume, Quai Rambaud, organized by The Musée Picasso, Antibes / Ocean Drive, Art Basel Miami Beach, organized by Richard Gray Gallery, Chicago, and Galerie Lelong, New York
Silent Voices, Museum at Tamada Projects, Tokyo
Jaume Plensa / Shakespeare, Fundación Círculo de Lectores, Barcelona
Sinónimos, Círculo de Bellas Artes, Madrid

2006

I in his eyes as one that found peace, Richard Gray Gallery, Chicago and New York
Une âme, deux corps… trois ombres, Galerie Lelong, Paris
Jerusalem, Fundació Es Baluard Museu d'Art Modern i Contemporani, L'Aljub, Palma de Mallorca
Canetti's Dream, Mario Mauroner Contemporary Art, Vienna
Songs and Shadows, Galerie Lelong, New York
Jaume Plensa: Livres, estampes et multiples sur papier 1978–2006, Centre de la Gravure La Louvière, La Louvière / Fundació Pilar i Joan Miró, Palma de Mallorca

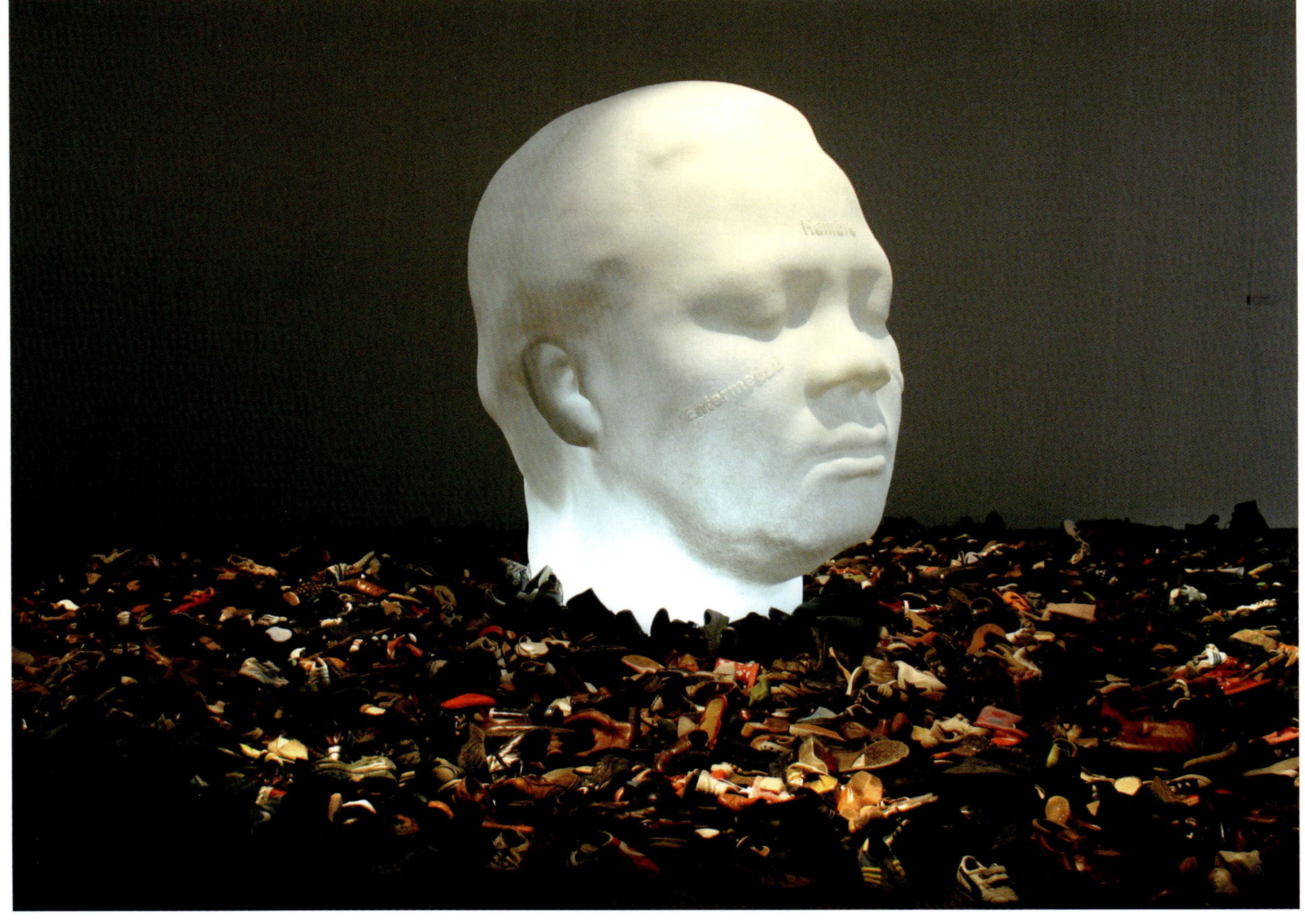

In the Midst of Dreams, 2008. El País – ARCO Art Fair 2008, Madrid.

2005

Jaume Plensa, CAC Málaga, (Centro de Arte Contemporaneo), Málaga
Is art something in between?, Kunsthalle Mannheim, Mannheim
Song of Songs, Albion Gallery, London
Glückauf?, Wilhelm Lehmbruck Museum, Duisburg
Jaume Plensa, ópera, teatro y amigos, Museo Colecciones ICO, Madrid

2004

Anònim, Galeria Toni Tàpies, Barcelona
Jaume Plensa, Galleria Gentili–Villa il Tasso, Montecatini
Jaume Plensa: Livres, estampes et multiples sur papier 1978–2003, Musée des Beaux Arts, Caen / Fundación César Manrique, Lanzarote
Il suono del sangue parla la stessa lingua, VOLUME!, Rome
Fiumi e cenere, Palazzo delle Papesse, Siena

Silent Noise, The Arts Club of Chicago, Chicago / Contemporary Arts Center, New Orleans / Fine Arts Center, University of Massachusetts at Amherst

2003

Crystal Rain, Galerie Lelong, Paris
Jaume Plensa. Galerie Academia, Salzburg
Who? Why?, Galerie Lelong, New York
Hot? Sex?, Universidad de Sevilla, Seville

2002

Rumor, Centro Cultural de España, Mexico D.F.
Wispern, Església de Sant Domingo, Pollença, Mallorca
B.OPEN, Jaume Plensa, The Baltic Centre for Contemporary Art, Gateshead
Jaume Plensa, Fondation Européenne pour la Sculpture, Parc Tournay-Sclvay, Brussels
Primary Thoughts, Galería Helga de Alvear, Madrid

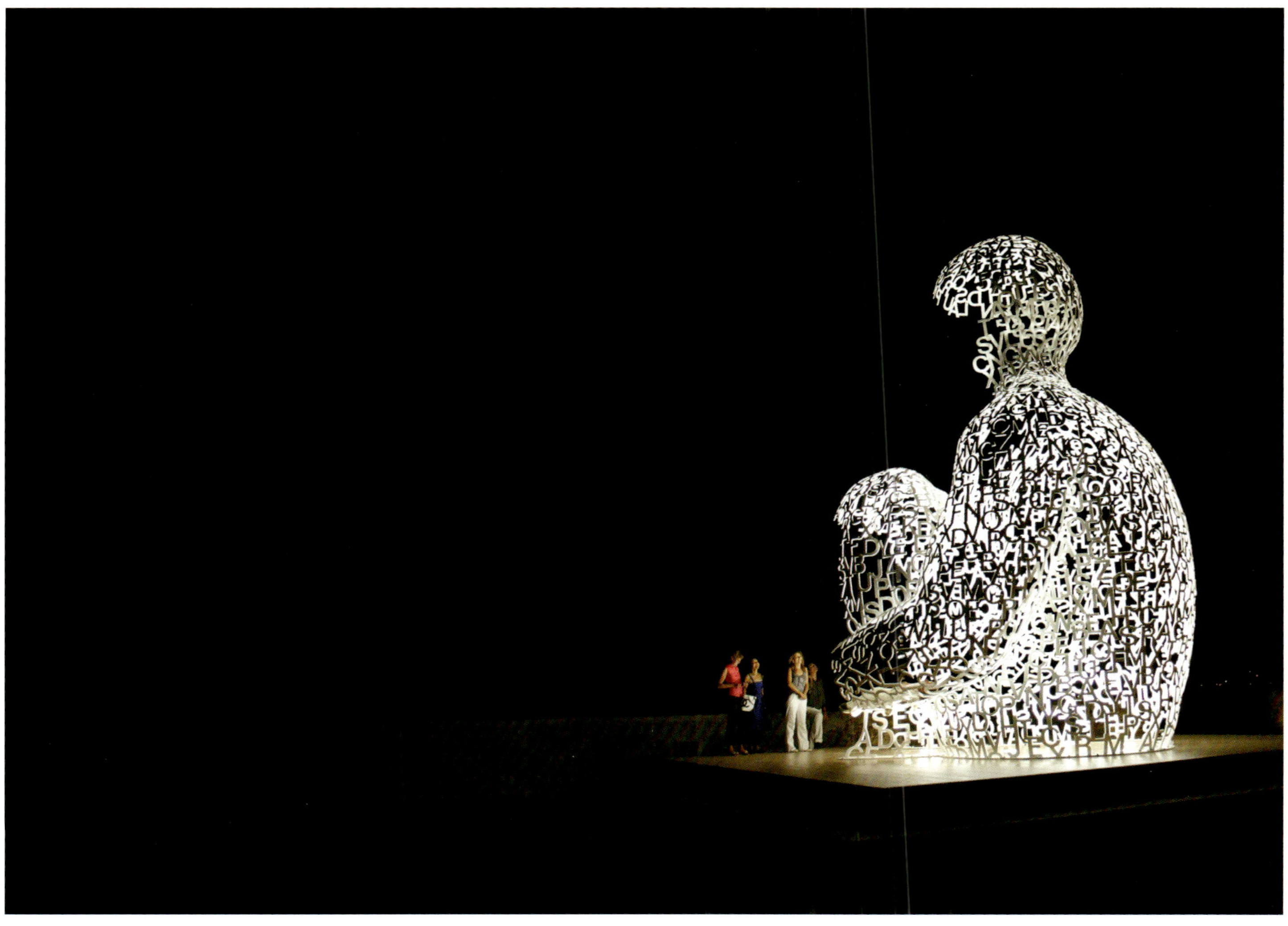

Nomade, 2007. Bastion Saint-Jaume, Musée Picasso, Antibes, France, 2007. John Pappajohn Collection, Des Moines, Iowa.

2001

Close Up, Mestna Galerija, Ljubljana
Logbook, Galerie Diehl-Vorderwuelbecke, Berlin
Europa, Galeria Toni Tàpies, Barcelona

2000

Twin Shadows, Galerie Lelong, New York / Richard
Gray Gallery, New York
Jaume Plensa: Proverbs of Hell, Mario Mauroner
Contemporary Art, Salzburg
Jaume Plensa 360º, Museo Municipal de Málaga,
Málaga
Chaos–Saliva, Palacio de Velázquez, Museo Nacional
Centro de Arte Reina Sofía, Madrid

1999

Etwas von mir, Kunsthalle zu Kiel, Kiel
Tamada Projects Corporation, Tokyo
Bruit, Galerie Daniel Templon, Paris
Komm mit, komm mit!, Rupertinum Museum, Salzburg
Whisper, Richard Gray Gallery, Chicago
Galeria Toni Tàpies, Barcelona / Edicions T, Barcelona

Wanderers Nachtlied, Museum Moderner Kunst
Stiftung Ludwig, Palais Liechtenstein, Vienna
Love Sounds, Kestner Gesellschaft, Hanover

1998

Galleria d'Arte Moderna e Contemporanea Palazzo
Forti, Verona
Dallas?... Caracas?, Fundación Museo Jacobo Borges,
Caracas / The MAC (The McKinney Avenue Contempo-
rary), Dallas
Golden Sigh, Galerie Alice Pauli, Lausanne
Galerie Pièce Unique, Paris
Water, Fonds Régional d'Art Contemporain de Picardie,
Amiens

1997

Wie ein Hauch, Galerie Volker Diehl, Berlin
Städtische Kunsthalle Mannheim, Mannheim
Malmö Konsthall, Malmö
Rumore, Fattoria di Celle, Santomato di Pistoia
Galerie Nationale du Jeu de Paume, Paris

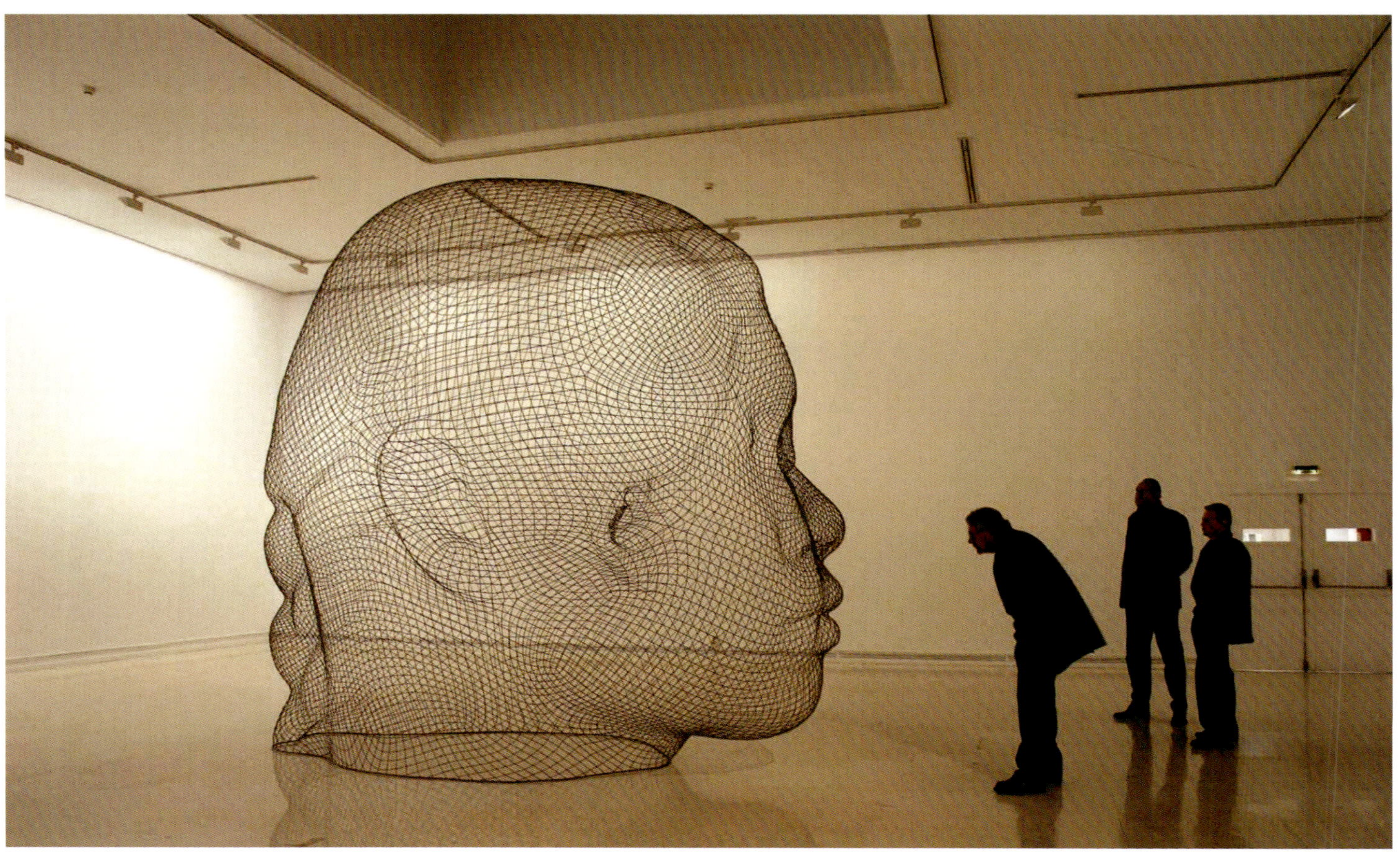

SHO, 2007. IVAM, Insitut Valencià d'Art Modern, Valencia, 2007. Richard Gray Gallery, Chicago.

1996

Fundació Joan Miró, Barcelona
Blake in Gateshead, BALTIC Centre for Contemporary
Art, Gateshead
Close Up, Office in Tel Aviv, Tel Aviv
Islands, Richard Gray Gallery, Chicago
Centre de Cultura Sa Nostra, Palma de Mallorca

1995

Wonderland, Galerie Daniel Templon, Paris
One thought fills immensity, Städtische Galerie,
Göppingen

1994

Cal.ligrafies, Edicions T Galeria d'Art, Barcelona
Jaume Plensa. Un Sculpteur, une Ville, Valence
Galleria Civica di Modena, Modena
The Personal Miraculous Fountain, The Henry Moore
Studio at Dean Clough, Halifax

1993

Galerie Volker Diehl, Berlin
Mémoires Jumelles, Galerie Alice Pauli, Lausanne /
Galerie de France, Paris

1992

The Royal Scottish Academy, Edinburgh
Galería Carles Taché, Barcelona
Galleria Gentili, Florence

1991

P. S. Gallery, Tokyo
Monocroms, Galería B.A.T., Madrid
Galerie Eric Franck, Geneva

1990

Dibuixos, Galeria Carles Taché, Barcelona
Église de Courmerlois Silo Art Contemporain, Reims
Val-de-Vesle
Galerie de France, Paris

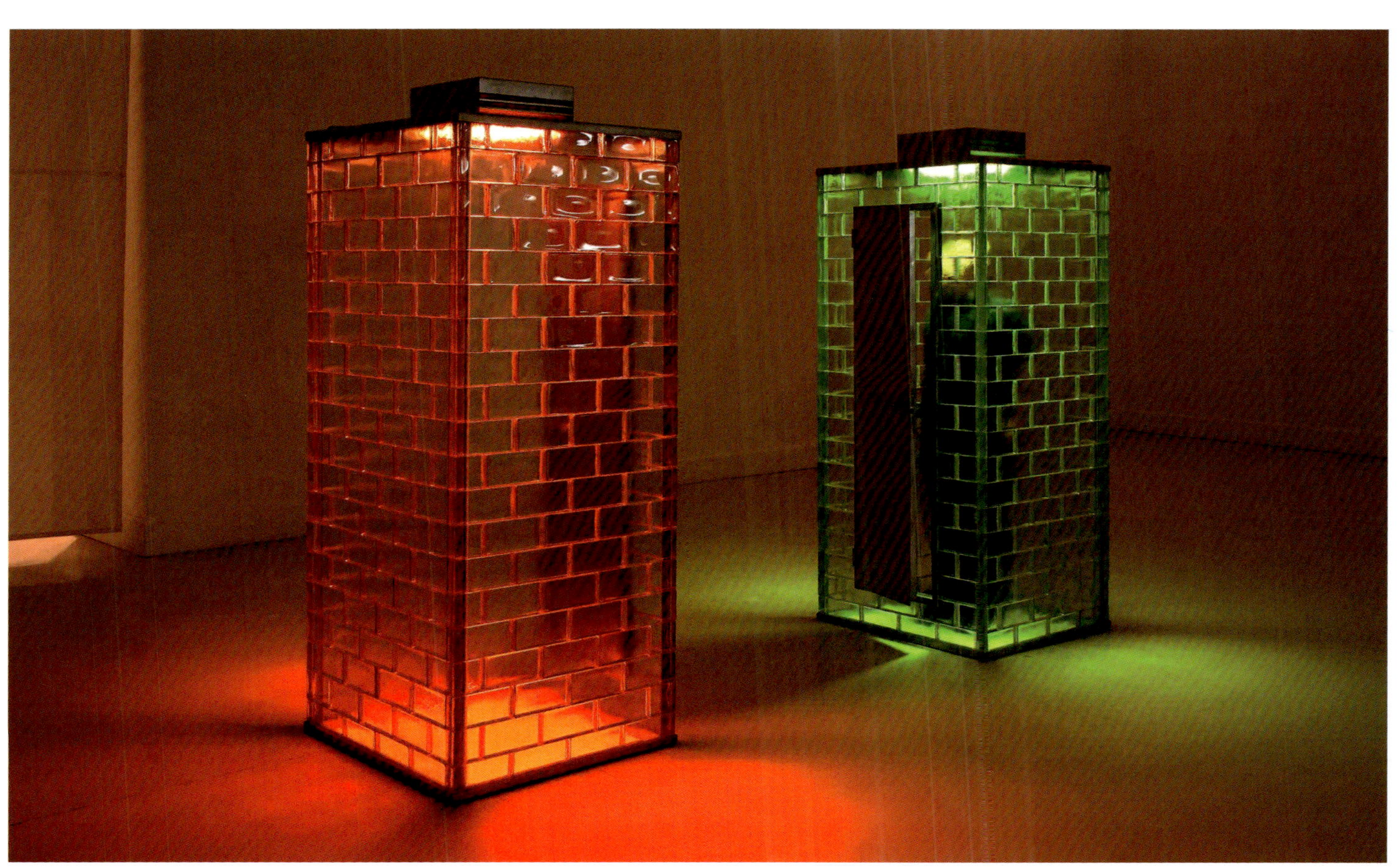

Song of Songs III–IV, 2004. Centro de Arte Contemporaneo, Málaga, 2005. Nasher Sculpture Center Collection, Dallas.

1989

The Sharpe Gallery, New York

Galerie Philippe Guimiot, Brussels

Galería Carles Taché, Barcelona

1988

The Sharpe Gallery, New York

Galerie Folker Skulima, Berlin

Musée d'Art Contemporain, Lyon

Galería Rita García, Valencia

1987

Galerie Philippe Guimiot, Brussels

Halle Sud, Geneva

1986

Galería Maeght, Barcelona

1985

Galería Juana de Aizpuru, Madrid

Galerie Lola Gassin, Nice

1984

Galerie Axe Actuel, Toulouse

Galerie Folker Skulima, Berlin

1983

Galería Ignacio de Lassaletta, Barcelona

1982

Llibre de vidre, Galería Eude, Barcelona

1981

Tres noms nous, Galería 13, Barcelona

1980

Fundació Joan Miró, Barcelona

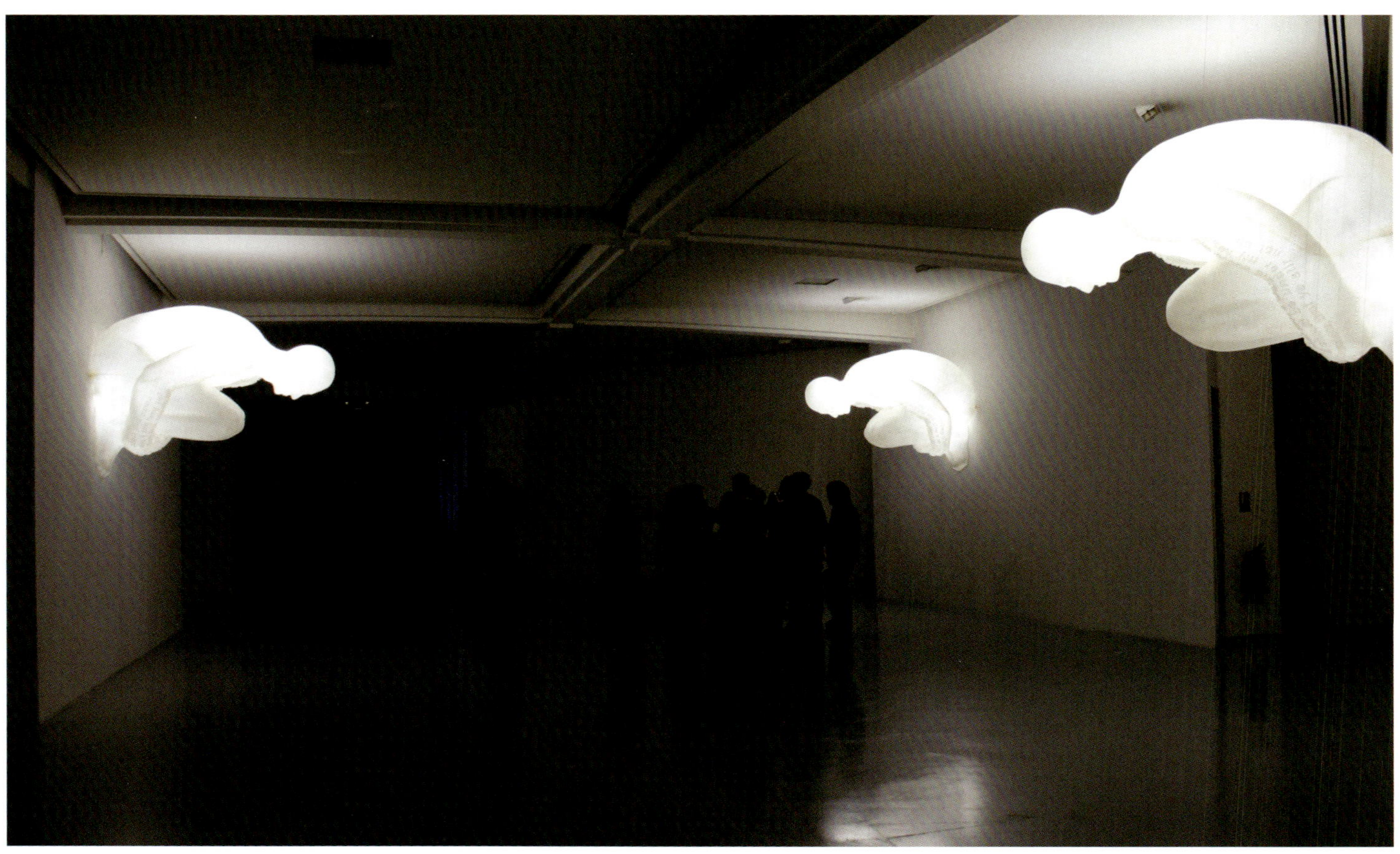

Doors of Jerusalem, 2006. MAMAC, Musée d'Art Moderne et d'Art Contemporain, Nice, 2007. North Carolina Museum of Art, Raleigh.

Selected Group Exhibitions

2008

A Year in Drawing, Galerie Lelong, New York
Shaping a Space II, Galeria Mario Sequeira, Braga
World of Glass, Museum Kunst Palast, Düsseldorf
Digital Raumkunst / Digital Artspace, Wilhelm
Lehmbruck Museum, Duisburg

2007

*Figura humana y abstracción. Esculturas de los siglos
XX y XXI. Colección Würth Alemania y España*, Museo
Würth La Rioja, Logroño
Dialogues Méditerranéens, La Citadelle, Saint Tropez
Barcelone 1947–2007, Fondation Marguerite et Aimé
Maeght, Saint-Paul-de-Vence
*Sculpture Biennale Kijkduin 2007, International Glass
& Sculpture Exposition,* Kijkduin, The Hague
La Palabra Imaginada, Museo de Arte Contemporáneo
Esteban Vicente, Segovia
Entre la palavra e a imagem, Museu da Cidade,
Lisbon / Centro Cultural Vila Flor, Guimarães
Monumental: Sotheby's at Isleworth, Windermere, Florida

2006

*Eye in Europe: Prints, Books & Multiples / 1960 to
Now,* MoMA New York
Beyond Limits: Sotheby's at Chatsworth, Chatsworth
House, Derbyshire
Femmes d'Europe, La Citadelle, Saint Tropez
Picasso to Plensa, Salvador Dalí Museum, Saint
Petersburg, Florida
Homenaje a Chillida, Guggenheim de Bilbao, Bilbao
Full House: Faces of a Collection, Kunsthalle
Mannheim, Mannheim
Snow Show, Sestriere, Turin
Dormir, rêver… et autres nuits, Musée d'art contemporain,
Bordeaux

2005

Picasso to Plensa, The Albuquerque Museum,
Albuquerque
Broken Glass, Glaspaleis, Stadsgalerij Heerlen, Harlem
81st Exhibition of Artist Members, The Arts Club of
Chicago, Chicago
*Dual, Transitos y entrecruzamientos para la Historia
del Arte,* Centre d'Art la Panera, Lleida

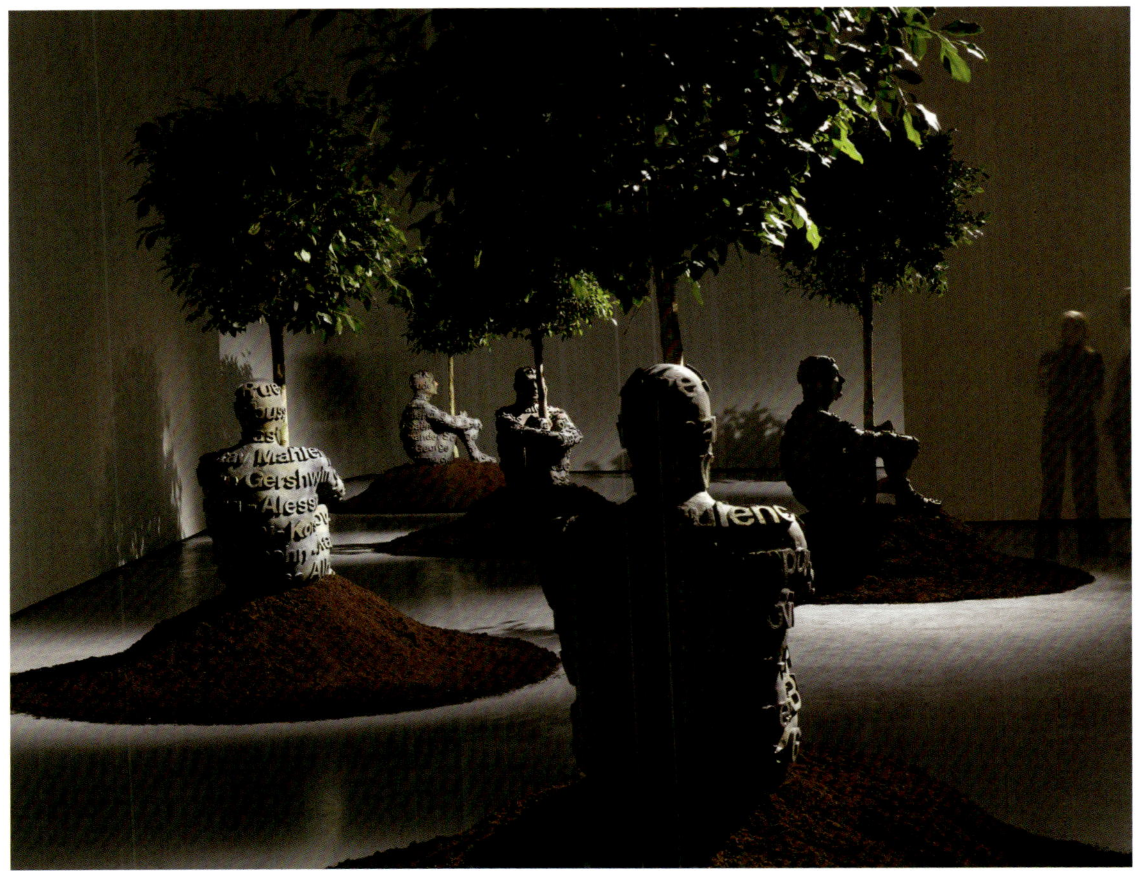

The Heart of Trees, 2007.
Albion, London, 2008.

Modern Times, Mönchehaus Museum, Goslar
Lenguajes y Sentidos, Colección Caja de Burgos, Sala
de Exposiciones del Museo de Pasión, Valladolid

2004

*Diversité des langues de l'Europe: Hommage aux vingt
langues de l'Europe sur 8 novembre,* Ministère de
la Culture et de la Communication, Façades du Palais
Royal, Paris
Festival arbres & lumières, Association Festival Arbres
& Lumières, Geneva
Outside In: Sculpture in the Natural World, Frederik
Meijer Gardens and Sculpture Park, Grand Rapids,
Michigan
A Light Crescendo: Art illuminating York St Mary's,
York Museum, York
*La création contemporaine à la Manufacture nationale
de Sèvres,* Maison René Char–Hôtel Donadeï de
Campredon, L'Isle-sur-la-Sorgue

2003

Indisciplinados, Museo de Arte Contemporánea, Vigo
Punto de encuentro. La Colección (1), Centro de Arte
Caja de Burgos, Burgos
Pintar Palabras..., Instituto Cervantes, Berlin / New York
Memoria de un recorrido, Colección Caja de Burgos,
Círculo de Bellas Artes, Madrid
Territoires nomades, Rurart Espace d'Arts, Rouillé

2002

Jaume Plensa–Fabrizio Corneli, Villa Carducci-
Pandolfini, Chiostro di Villa Vogel, Centro per l'arte
contemporanea Luigi Pecci, Florence
Avesta Art 2002, Avesta, Sweden
DAK'ART 2002, Biennale de Dakar, Senegal
*Leuchtspur, Koordinationsstelle für kulturelle
Sonderprojekte,* Kulturmeile Frankfurt, Frankfurt
Conceptes de l'espai, Fundació Joan Miró, Barcelona

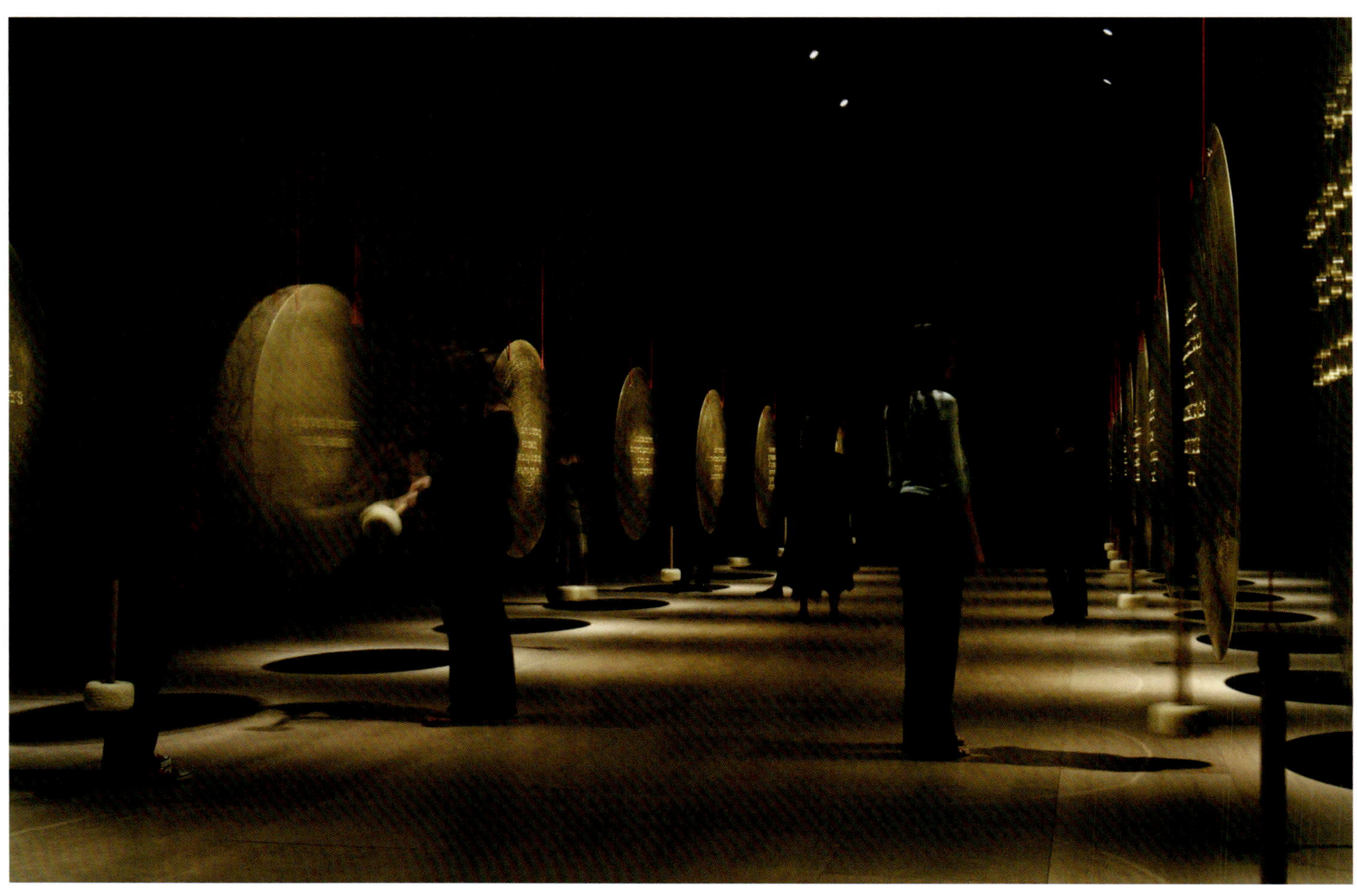

Jerusalem, 2006. Es Baluard Museu d'Art Modern i Contemporani, Palma de Mallorca, 2006.

2001

50 ans de Sculpture Espagnole, Jardins du Palais
Royal, Paris / Parque del Retiro, Madrid
Bienal de Valencia, Cuerpo y Pecado, Convento del
Carmen, Valencia
Milano Europa 2000. Fine secolo, I semi del Futuro,
Palazzo della Triennale, Milan

2000

Seven Hills: Images and Signs of the 21st Century,
Martin Gropius Bau, Berlin
Echigo–Tsumari Art Triennial 2000, Echigo–Tsumari
Faith, The Aldrich Museum of Contemporary Art,
Ridgefield

1999

La casa, il corpo, il cuore, Museum Moderner Kunst
Stiftung Ludwig, Vienna
*Museum of Contemporary Art Sarajevo–Collection
1994–1997,* Skenderija Center, Sarajevo

1998

10. Intensity in Europe, Centro per l'arte contemporanea
Luigi Pecci, Prato
Artranspennine98, Yorkshire Sculpture Park, The
Henry Moore Sculpture Trust, Leeds and Tate Gallery,
Liverpool

1997

Descoberta de la Col.lecció, MACBA (Museu d'Art
Contemporani de Barcelona), Barcelona
Areopagitica, 28 freie Seiten, G.A.M.E.S. of Art,
Mönchengladbach

1996

Abstrakt / Real, Museum Moderner Kunst Stiftung
Ludwig, Vienna
Ars Aevi 2000, Centro per l'arte contemporanea Luigi
Pecci, Prato
*Chimériques polymères, le plastique dans l'art du XXème
siècle,* Musée d'Art Moderne et Contemporain, Nice
Happy End, Kunsthalle, Düsseldorf

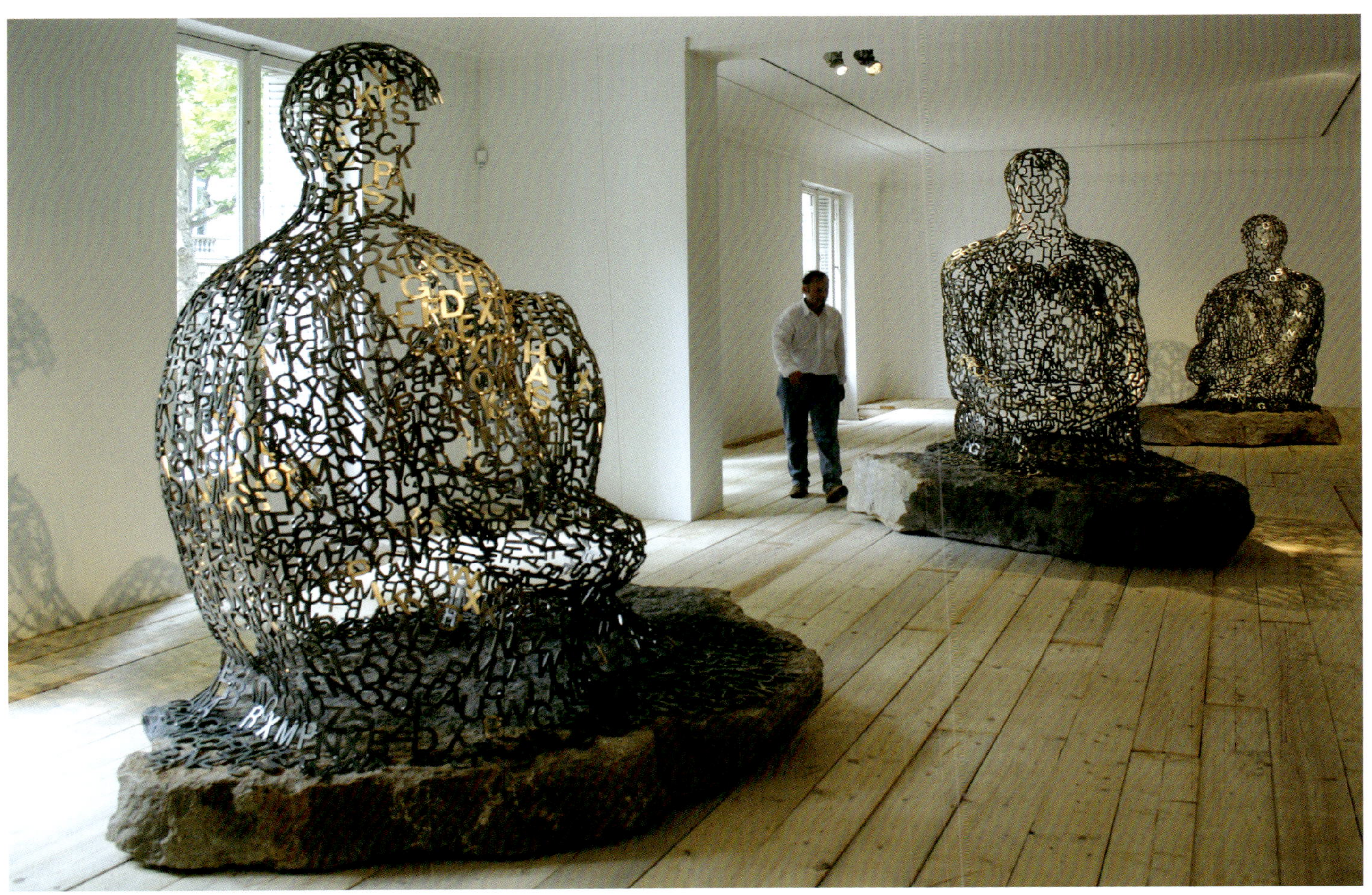

Shadows I–III, 2006. Galerie Lelong, Paris, 2006.

1995

Metàfores del real, MACBA (Museu d'Art Contemporani de Barcelona), Barcelona
Wild at Heart, Tramway Centre, Glasgow

1994

Six Voices from Spain, Atlantis Gallery, London / Arnolfini Gallery, Bristol / Wrexham Library Arts Centre, Wales / Oriel 31, Powys / Tuille House Art Gallery, Carlisle
Kommentar zu Europa, Museum Moderner Kunst Stiftung Ludwig, Vienna

1993

Gröbenwahn Kunstprojekte für Europa, Lindenger & Schmid, Regensburg
Cell-Cella-Celda, The Henry Moore Institute, Leeds
Katalanische Skulptur im 20 Jahrhundert, Wilhelm Lehmbruck Museum, Duisburg

1992

5 Triennale Fellbach 1992, Wilhelm Lehmbruck Museum, Duisburg
Configuracions Urbanes, Olimpiada Cultural Barcelona '92, Barcelona

1991

XI Salón de los 16, Palacio de Velázquez, Madrid
Histories d'Oeil, Musée d'Art Contemporain, Lyon

1990

Barcelona Avant-Garde Part 2, Barcelona and Yokohama City Creation, Yokohama
Eisenskulptur aus Spanien, Städtische Kunsthalle, Mannheim / Museum Bochum, Bochum / Haus am Waldsee, Berlin

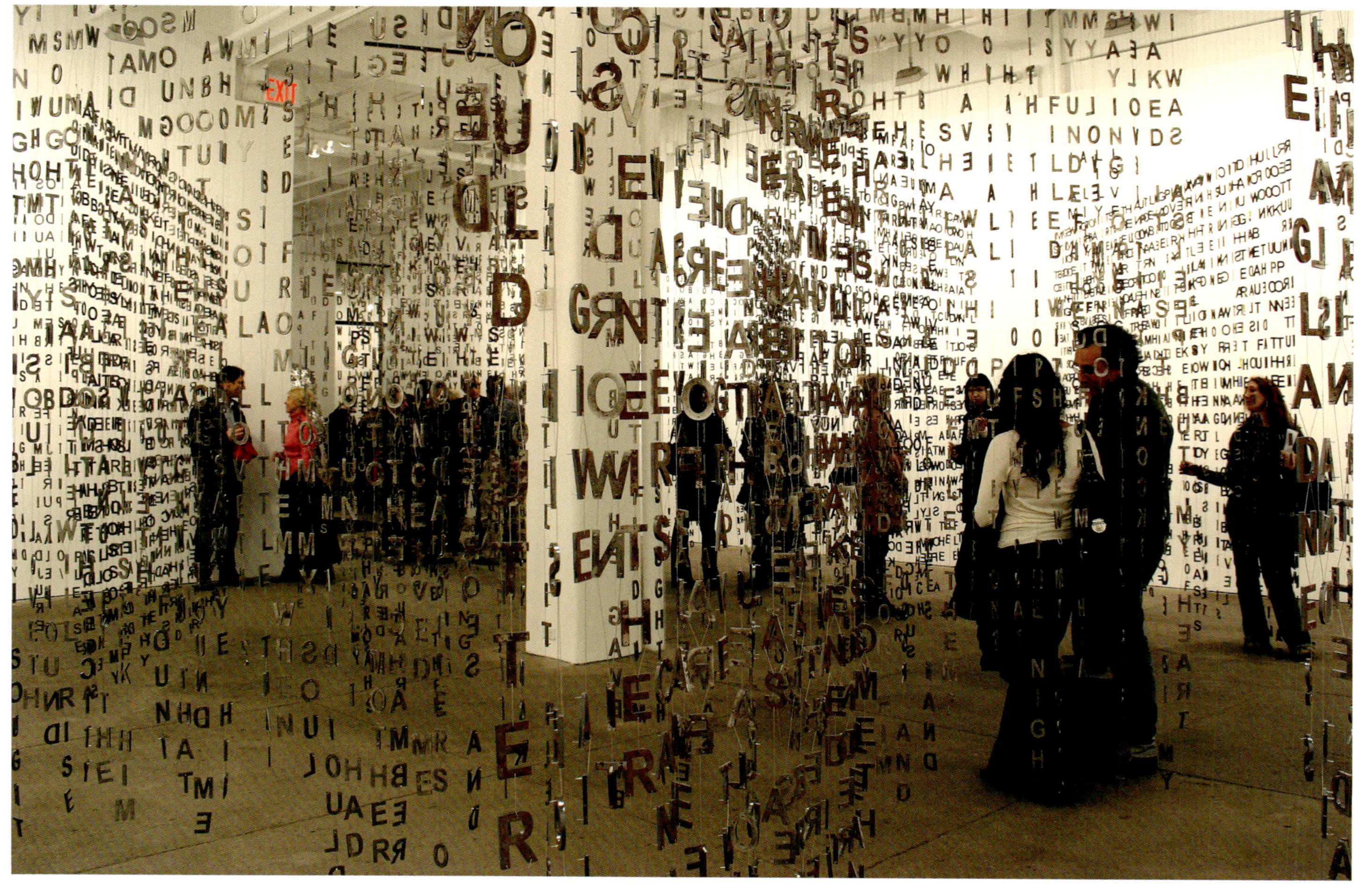

Song of Songs, 2005. Galerie Lelong, New York, 2006.

Selected Public Projects

Conversation à Nice 2007
Site: Place Masséna, Nice (France)
Commissioned by Communauté d'Agglomération Nice
Côte d'Azur, Nice, France, 2005

Breathing 2005
Site: BBC Broadcasting House, London (UK)
Commissioned by BBC Broadcasting House, 2003
Curated by Vivien Lovell

The Crown Fountain 2004
Site: Millennium Park, Chicago (USA)
Commissioned by The Public Art Program, Department
of Cultural Affairs, City of Chicago, 2000

As One 2003
Site: Lester B. Pearson International Airport, Baggage
Claim Area, Toronto (Canada)
Commissioned by The Greater Toronto Airport Authority,
2001. Curated by Elsa Cameron

Talking Continents 2003
Site: Jacksonville Arena Plaza, Jacksonville, Florida
(USA)
Commissioned by Art in Public Places Commission,
City of Jacksonville, Florida, 2003

Bridge of Light 2002
Site: Mishkenot Sha'ananim, Jerusalem (Israel)
Commissioned by The Jerusalem Foundation, 1998

Seele? 2002
Site: Neandertnal Park, Düsseldorf (Germany)
Commissioned by the Neanderthal Museum, 2000
Curated by Volker Friedrich Marten

Mi Casa en Torrelavega 2001
Site: Paseo de Julio Hauzeur, Torrelavega (Spain)
Commissioned by the Ayuntamiento de Torrelavega, 2000
Curated by Fernando Francés

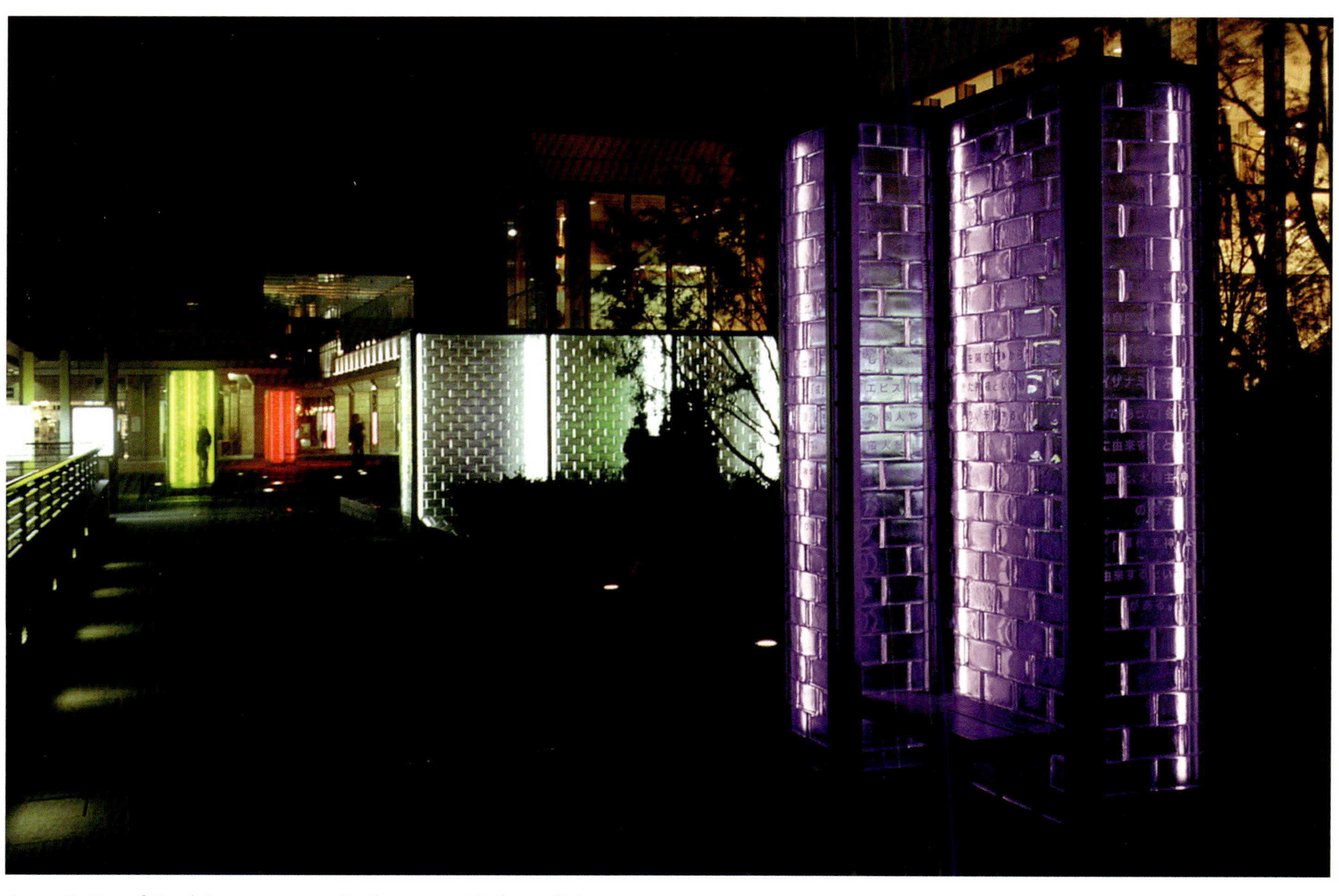

Seven Deities of Good Fortune, 2000. Daikanyama, Shibuya, Tokyo.

Magritte's Dream 2001
Site: Aino Station, Fukuroi City (Japan)
Commissioned by Fukuroi City, 2000
Project: Public Art: Japan + Practice
Curated by Fram Kitagawa

El Corazón de las Palabras 2000
Site: USA Today Headquarters, McLean, Virginia (USA)
Commissioned by Gannett / USA Today, 2000
Curated by Lisa Austin

Gläserner Seele, or Mr. Net in Brandenburg 2000
Site: Postdam, Land Brandenburg (Germany)
Commissioned by Ministerium für Wirtschaft des
Landes Brandenburg, 1999
Project: Europa, EXPO 2000 Hanover
Curated by Stefan von Senger

Seven Deities of Good Fortune 2000
Site: Daikanyama, Shibuya, Tokyo (Japan)
Commissioned by Daikanyama Project, 1999
Curated by Fram Kitagawa

Transparent Doubts 2000
Site: University of Shizuoka for Culture and Art,
Hamamatsu (Japan)
Commissioned by the University of Shizuoka for
Culture and Art, Hamamatsu, 1999
Curated by Fumio Nanjo

The House of Birds 1999
Site: Mion Nakasato (Japan)
Commissioned by the Echigo–Tsumari Art Festival
2000, 1998
Project: Tsumari-go Art Necklace Project
Curated by Fram Kitagawa

Capsa de Llum 1998
Site: Gran Via de Jaume I–Av. Ramon Folch, Girona
(Spain)
Commissioned by the City of Girona, 1997
Curated by Joan Casanovas

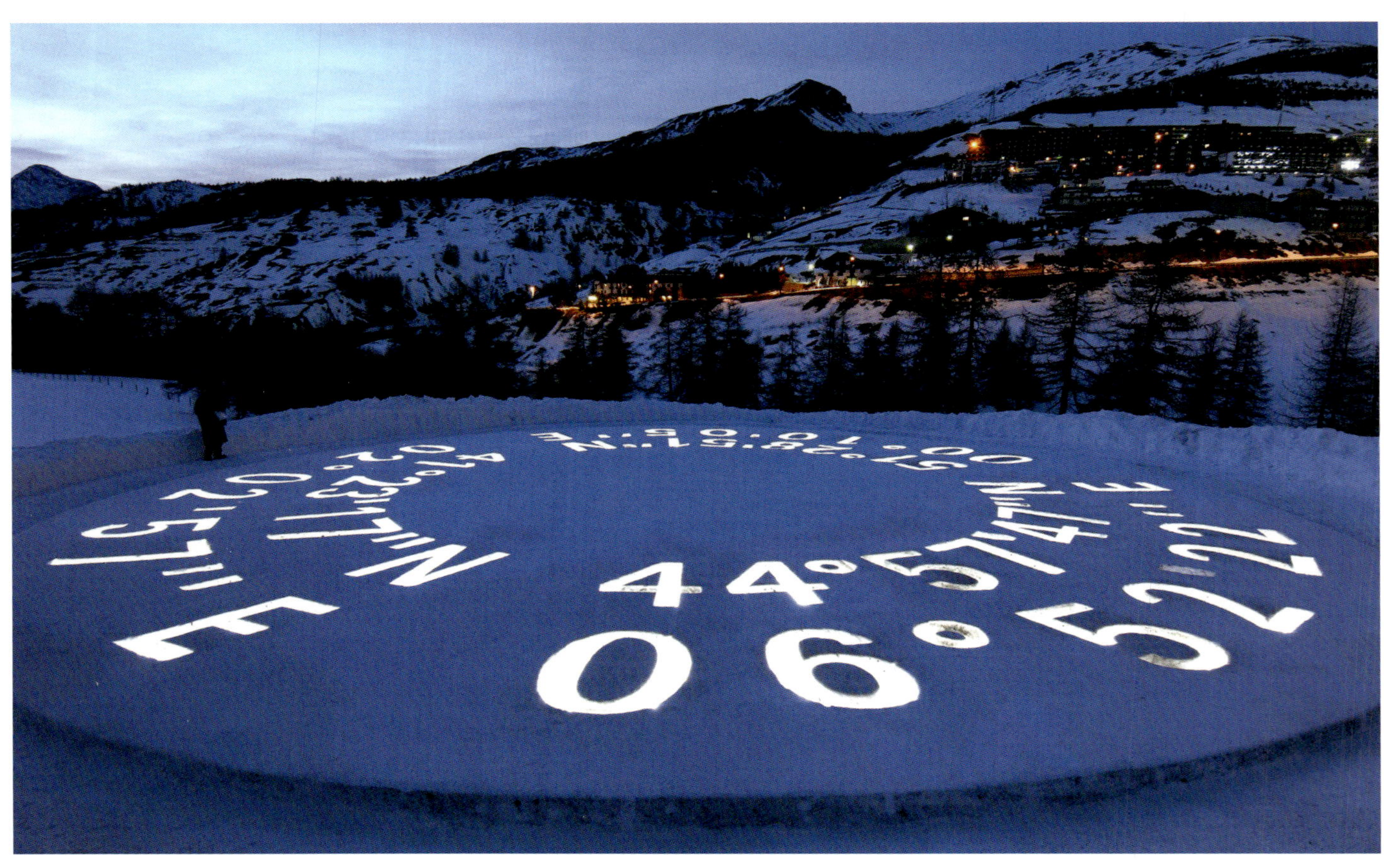

Where Are You?, 2006. Snow Show, Sestriere, Turin, Italy, 2006.

Twins II 1998
Site: Kimpo Sculpture Park, Kimpo, Seoul (Korea)
Commissioned by KBS CPE Office and Kimpo City, 1998
Project: Kimpo International Sculpture Project, Kimpo
Curated by Sounjou Seo

Blake in Gateshead 1996
Site: Baltic Centre of Contemporary Art, Gateshead
(U.K.)
Commissioned by the Metropolitan Borough Council
Libraries and Arts, Gateshead, 1996
Project: Temporary Contemporary Visual Arts Year in
the United Kingdom
Curated by Sune Nordgren

Islas 1995
Site: Avenida General Franco, Santa Cruz de Tenerife
(Spain)
Commissioned by the Colegio de Arquitectos de
Canarias, 1994
Curated by Vicente Saavedra

Faret Tachikawa 1994
Site: Tachikawa City (Japan)
Commissioned by The Housing and Urban Development
Corporation and Tachikawa City, 1993
Curated by Fram Kitagawa

Born 1992
Site: Passeig del Born, Barcelona (Spain)
Commissioned by The Cultural Olympic Games of
Barcelona and the City of Barcelona, 1992
Project: Configuracions Urbanes, Barcelona
Curated by Gloria Moure

Auch 1990–91
Site: Escalier Monumentale / Place Barbés, Auch
(France)
Commissioned by the City of Auch and the Ministère
de l'Education Nationale et de la Culture, Délégation
aux Arts Plastiques, 1990
Curated by François Barré, Béatrice Salmon, Patrice
Béghain, and Norbert Duffort

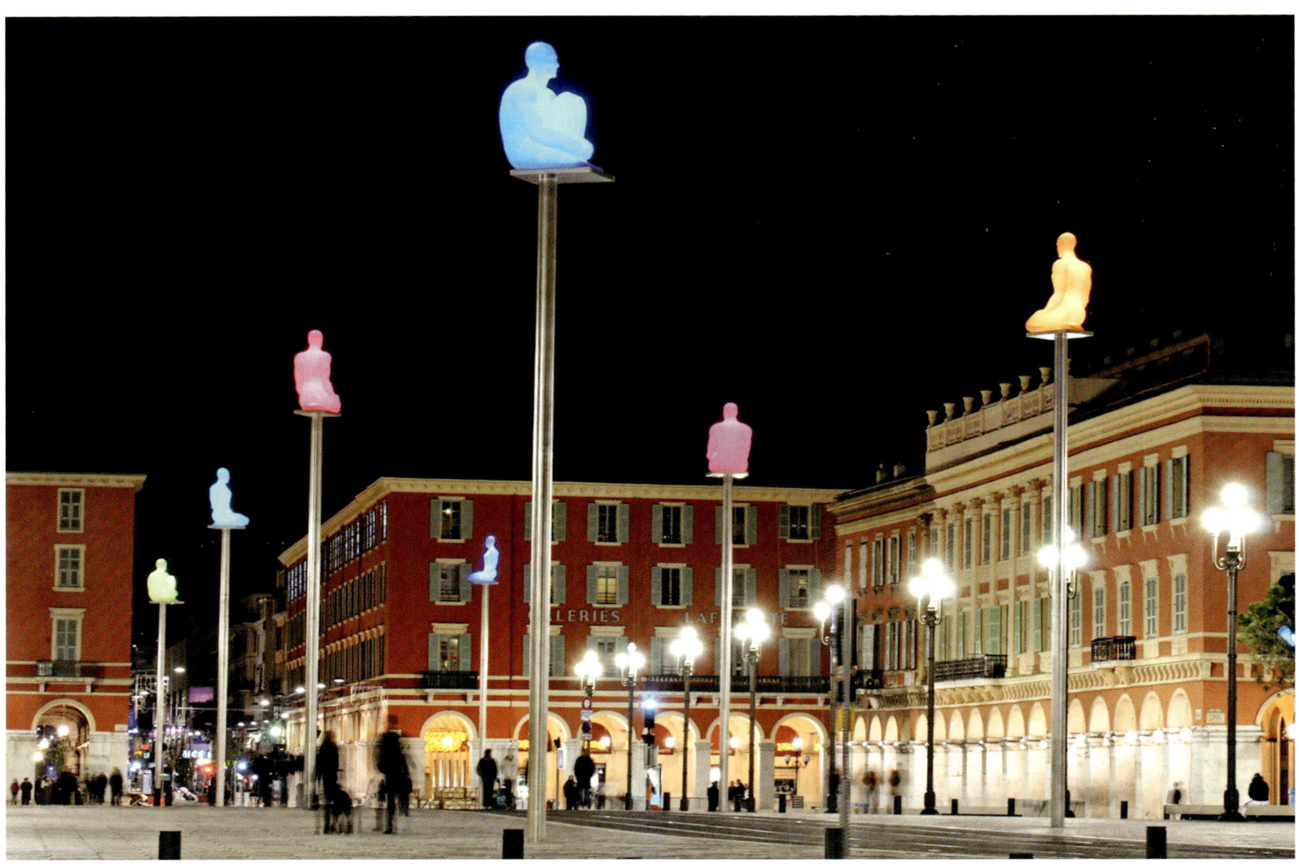

Conversation à Nice,
2007.
Place Masséna, Nice,
France.

Works in Progress

El Alma del Ebreo
Commissioned by EXPO ZARAGOZA 2008, Zaragoza
(Spain), 2006
Opening 2008

Dream
Site: Sutton Manors, St Helens, Liverpool (U.K.)
Commissioned by St Helens Council / Liverpool Biennial
for Contemporary Art U. K., 2007
Curated by Laurie Peake
Opening 2008

Wishing Well
Commissioned by EnCana Leasehold, Calgary
(Canada), 2007
Curated by Susan Halas and Emily Blumenfeld
Opening 2010

We
Commissioned by Wachovia Bank, Charlotte, North
Carolina (USA), 2007
Curated by Jennifer Murphy
Opening 2009

Opera Projects

2007
Bluebeard's Castle by Béla Bartók and **Diary of One
Who Disappeared** by Leos Janácek
Opera Garnier, Paris, France
Gran Teatre del Liceu, Barcelona, Spain
Opera House, Kobe / Tokyo, Japan

2003
The Magic Flute by Wolfgang Amadeus Mozart
Ruhr Triennale, Bochum, Germany
Opéra Bastille, Paris, France
Teatro Real, Madrid, Spain

1999
The Damnation of Faust by Hector Berlioz
Salzburg Summer Opera Festival, Salzburg, Austria
Ruhr Triennale, Bochum, Germany

1997
The Martyrdom of Saint Sebastian by Claude Debussy
Teatro dell'Opera, Rome, Italy

1996
La Atlántida by Manuel de Falla
Granada Summer Festival, Granada, Spain

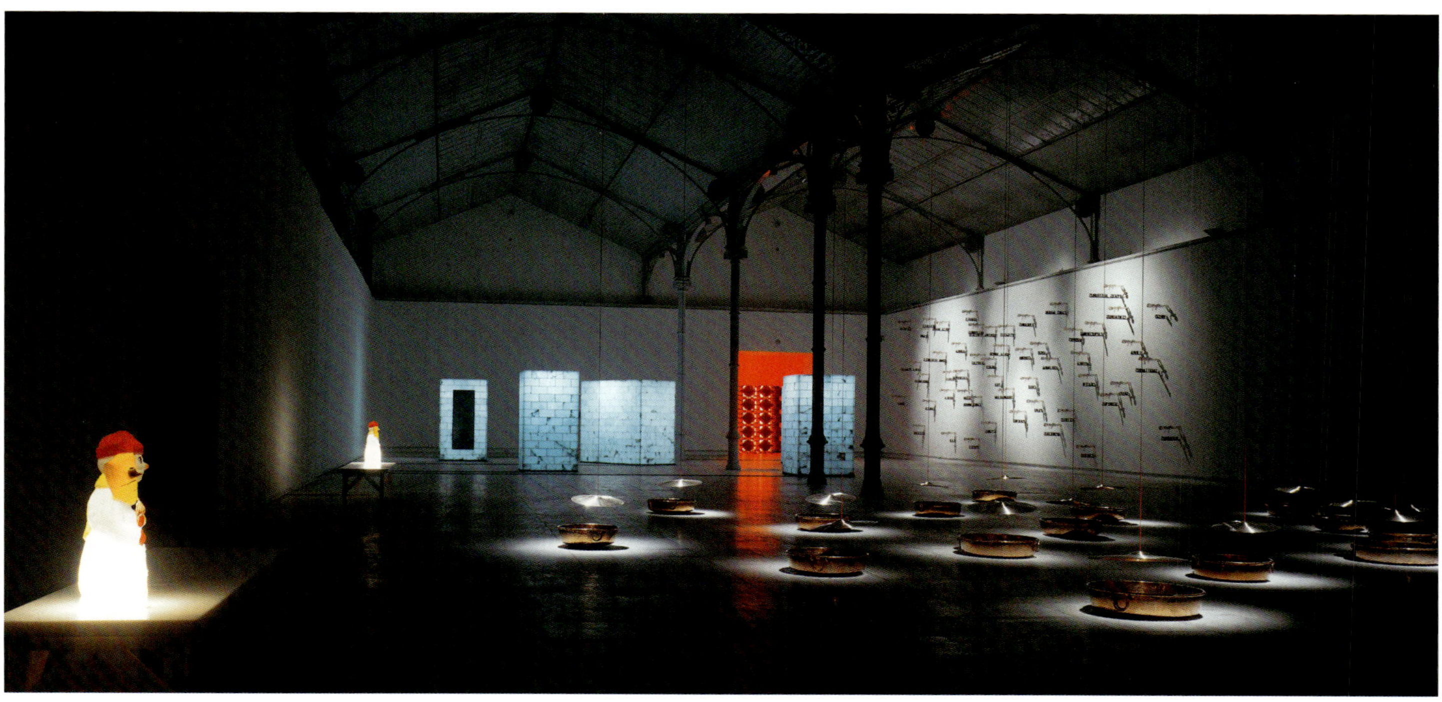

View of the exhibition *Chaos-Saliva,* 2000. Palacio de Velázquez, Museo Nacional Centro de Arte Reina Sofía, Madrid, 2000.

Selected Awards

2007
Heitland Foundation Prize
Celle, Germany

2006
The Bombay Sapphire Prize / Annual International Award for Glass Work
The Bombay Sapphire Foundation, London, U. K.

Villa de Madrid Print Award
Madrid, Spain

2005
Awarded Honorary Doctorate of the School of the Art Institute of Chicago
Chicago, USA

2003
Villa de Madrid Sculpture Award
Madrid, Spain

1999
Gold Medal of Prague Quadrennial for Stage Design and Theater Architecture
Prague, Czech Republic

1998
Koiné Award
Milan / Honorific exhibition at the Palazzo Forti, Verona, Italy
Prize of the Spanish Association of Art Critics
Madrid, Spain

1997
National Art Award of Catalonia
Barcelona, Spain

1996
Alexander Calder Foundation
Sache, France

1993
Awarded Chevalier des Arts et Lettres
Ministry of Culture, Paris, France

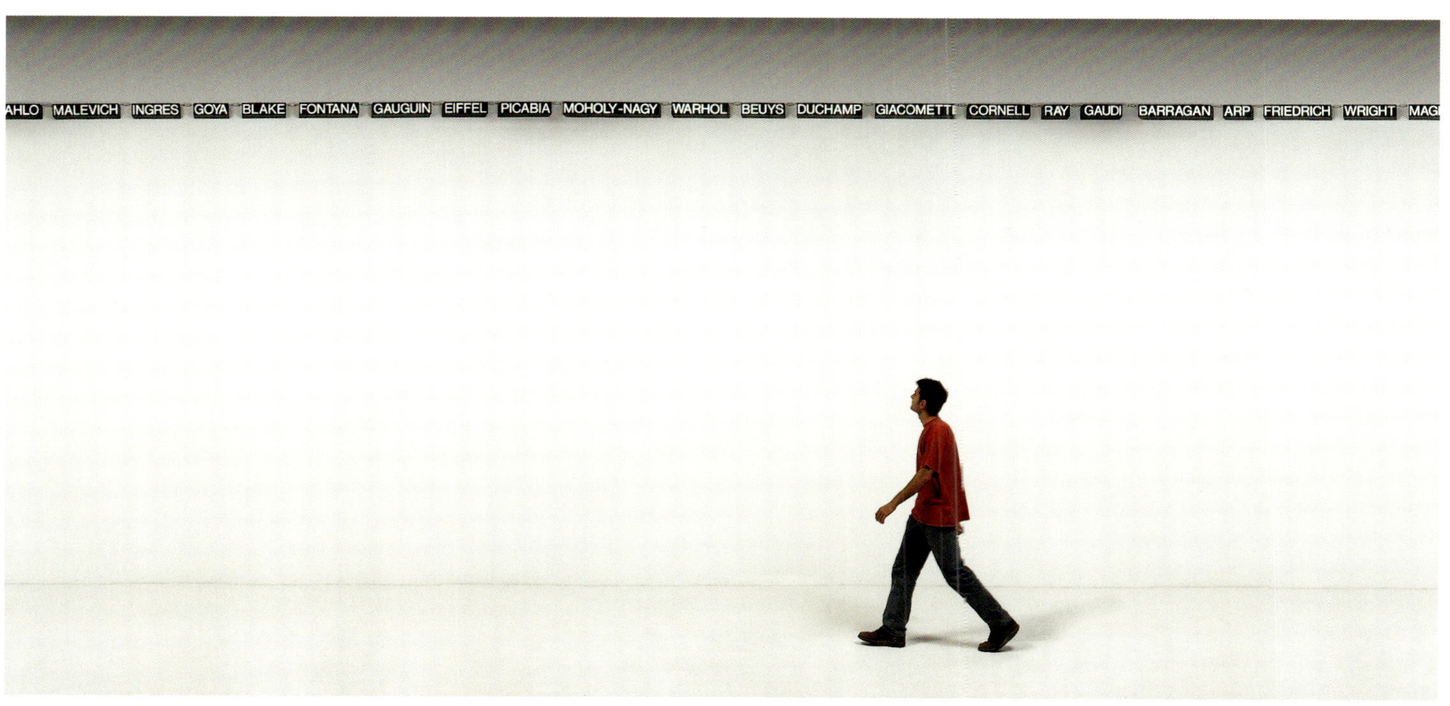

Islands II, 1996. Galerie Nationale du Jeu de Paume, Paris, 2007. Kunsthalle Mannheim Collection, Mannheim.

Photo Credits

Kenneth Tanaka:
front cover and back cover, 1, 20, 36, 37, 38–39, 49, 51, 54, 71, 75, 77,
78–79, 80–81, 82, 89, 91, 98–99, 100–101, 102, 104, 105, 114, 115,
122, 128–129, 152–153, 160, 161, 176, 179, 183, 185, 186–187,
188–189, 190, 192–193, 194, 197, 199, 200–201, 202, 203, 216, 218,
219, 222–223

Laura Medina:
8–9, 18–19, 34–35, 53, 62–63, 64–65, 158–159, 167, 172–173, 178,
184, 204–205, 206–207, 208–209, 210–211, 212–213, 214–215, 217,
224, 225, 226, 228, 231, 232, 237

Krueck & Sexton:
12, 120, 121, 126, 127, 130,131, 132, 133, 135, 136, 137, 162, 166,
167

Roark Frankel:
33, 66, 95, 97, 111, 124, 125, 130, 134, 167, 177, 184

Hedrich Blessing:
2–3, 40, 60–61, 112–113, 116, 169, 171, 174–175, 180, 220–221

Jaume Plensa:
140–141,142,148–149

School of the Art Institute Chicago:
144, 145, 146, 147

Cesar Russ:
front endpaper and back endpaper

Gunter Lepkowski:
230, 236

José Luis Gutierrez:
227

Nigel Young Foster&Partners:
234

CANCA/Èric Boizet:
235

Ed Reeve:
229

Anzai:
233

Acknowledgments

Jaume Plensa wishes to express his thanks to the following people and organizations for their support and collaboration during the creation of the Chicago *Crown Fountain* project and during the conception of this book, which acts as its record:

To Lester, Steve, Susan, Paula, and Jim Crown, and the rest of the Crown family, for their generosity, trust, and passion.

To Richard M. Daley, Mayor of Chicago, for his great capacity to unite past and future at the heart of the city.

To John H. Bryan for his total commitment to the running of Millennium Park, and to Edward Uhlir for his dedication.

To Sandy and Jack Guthman, and to Susan and Bob Wislow, always near at every stage of the project.

To Roark Frankel, who, together with Alan Schachtman and the whole team at U.S. Equities, controlled and supervised the development of this project with love and devotion.

To Mark Sexton for his meticulous work and great capacity to transform a dream into reality, and to the whole team at Krueck & Sexton for their unconditional support during this complex task.

To the School of the Art Institute of Chicago, and especially to Tony Jones, for sharing their knowledge with enthusiasm, and to Alan Labb and John Manning who, together with their students, filmed and articulated the soul of this project with rigor and poetry.

To all the companies that participated in the construction of the work, be it engineering, glass, water systems, image, or technology, for the quality and rigor of their work.

To Paul Gray and the whole team at the Richard Gray Gallery for their invaluable support and collaboration throughout the project.

To the people of Chicago, who, with their generosity, have given meaning and life to the *Crown Fountain*.

To Laura Medina and the whole team at Plensa Studio Barcelona.

To Keith Patrick, who, thanks to his imagination, experience, and curiosity, has succeeded in reuniting the various voices and stories that form the memory of this project.

To Ken Tanaka for his intimate and passionate gaze, to Herman Lelie and Stefania Bonelli for their inspiration, and to Markus Hartmann and Hatje Cantz for their support in the publication of this book.

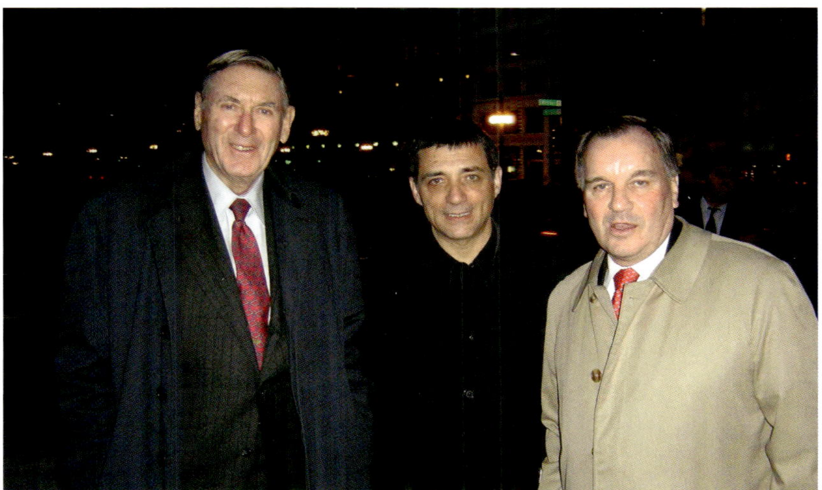

Lester Crown, Jaume Plensa, and Richard Daley.

Copyediting: Krystina Stermole

Design by Herman Lelie and Stefania Bonelli

Typeface: Trade Gothic Bold and Light
Repro by Dexter
Paper: Galaxi Supermat, 170 g/m^2
Printed by Dr. Cantz'sche Druckerei, Ostfildern
Binding: Verlagsbuchbinderei Dieringer, Gerlingen

Published by
Hatje Cantz Verlag
Zeppelinstrasse 32
73760 Ostfildern
Germany
Tel. +49 711 4405-200
Fax +49 711 4405-220
www.hatjecantz.com

Hatje Cantz books are available internationally at selected bookstores. For
more information about our distribution partners, please visit our homepage
at www.hatjecantz.com.

ISBN 978-3-7757-2080-9

Printed in Germany

Cover illustrations: Crown Fountain, Millennium Park, Chicago

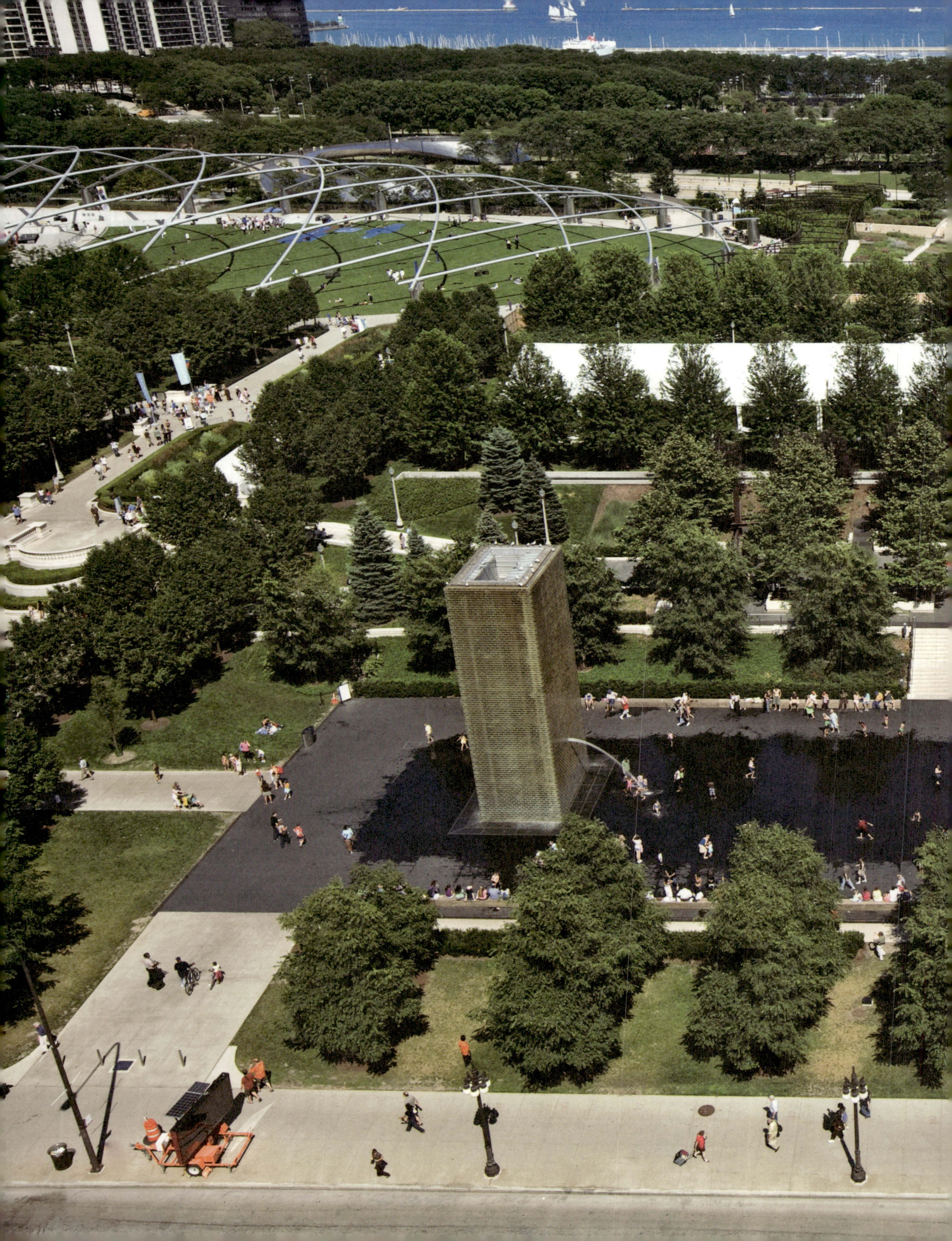